# COMMERCIAL ISSUES IN PRIVATE INTERNATIONAL LAW

As people, business, and information cross borders, so too do legal disputes. Globalisation means that courts need to apply principles of private international law with increasing frequency. Thus, as the Law Society of New South Wales recognised in its 2017 report *The Future of Law and Innovation in the Profession*, knowledge of private international law is increasingly important to legal practice. In particular, it is essential to the modern practice of commercial law.

This book considers key issues at the intersection of commercial law and private international law. The authors include judges, academics and practising lawyers, from Australia, New Zealand, Singapore and the United Kingdom. They bring a common law perspective to contemporary problems concerning the key issues in private international law: jurisdiction, choice of law, and recognition and enforcement of foreign judgments. The book also addresses issues of evidence and procedure in cross-border litigation, and the impact of recent developments at the Hague Conference on Private International Law, including the Convention on Choice of Court Agreements on common law principles of private international law.

**Volume 22 in the series Studies in Private International Law**

**Studies in Private International Law**

Recent titles in the series

The Governing Law of Companies in EU Law
Justin Borg-Barthet

Intellectual Property and Private International Law: Comparative Perspectives
Edited by Toshiyuki Kono

Child Abduction within the European Union
Katarina Trimmings

International Surrogacy Arrangements: Legal Regulation at the International Level
Edited by Katarina Trimmings and Paul Beaumont

The Hague Child Abduction Convention: A Critical Analysis
Rhona Schuz

Interregional Recognition and Enforcement of Civil and Commercial Judgments: Lessons for China from the US and EU Law
Jie Huang

The Recovery of Maintenance in the EU and Worldwide
Paul Beaumont, Burkhard Hess, Lara Walker and Stefanie Spancken

Australian Private International Law for the 21st Century: Facing Outwards
Edited by Andrew Dickinson, Thomas John and Mary Keyes

Maintenance and Child Support in Private International Law
Lara Walker

The Choice of Law Contract
Maria Hook

The Nature and Enforcement of Choice of Court Agreements: A Comparative Study
Mukarrum Ahmed

Cross-Border Litigation in Europe
Edited by Paul Beaumont, Mihail Danov, Katarina Trimmings and Burcu Yuksel

Forum (Non) Conveniens in England: Past, Present, and Future
Ardavan Arzandeh

# Commercial Issues in Private International Law

## *A Common Law Perspective*

Edited by
Michael Douglas
Vivienne Bath
Mary Keyes
and
Andrew Dickinson

•HART•
OXFORD • LONDON • NEW YORK • NEW DELHI • SYDNEY

HART PUBLISHING

Bloomsbury Publishing Plc

Kemp House, Chawley Park, Cumnor Hill, Oxford, OX2 9PH, UK

HART PUBLISHING, the Hart/Stag logo, BLOOMSBURY and the Diana logo are trademarks of Bloomsbury Publishing Plc

First published in Great Britain 2019



A catalogue record for this book is available from the British Library.

Library of Congress Cataloging-in-Publication data

Names: Commercial Issues in Private International Law (Conference) (2018 : Sydney Law School). | Douglas, Michael C., editor. | Bath, Vivienne, editor. | Dickinson, Andrew, editor. | Keyes, Mary, editor. | Sydney Law School, host institution.

Title: Commercial issues in private international law : a common law perspective / edited by Vivienne Bath, Andrew Dickinson, Michael Douglas and Mary Keyes.

Description: Oxford, UK ; Chicago, Illinois : Hart Publishing, 2019. | Series: Studies in private international law ; volume 22 | Includes papers presented at a conference titled "Commercial Issues in Private International Law" held 16 February 2018, and hosted by the University of Sydney Law School.— ECIP editor's preface. | Includes bibliographical references and index.

Identifiers: LCCN 2019001540 (print) | LCCN 2019001821 (ebook) | ISBN 9781509922888 (EPub) | ISBN 9781509922871 (hardback)

Subjects: LCSH: Conflict of laws—Commercial law—English-speaking countries—Congresses. | BISAC: LAW / International. | LAW / Commercial / General.

Classification: LCC K7340.A6 (ebook) | LCC K7340.A6 .C66 2019 (print) | DDC 340.9—dc23

LC record available at https://lccn.loc.gov/2019001540

ISBN: HB: 978-1-50992-287-1
ePDF: 978-1-50992-289-5
ePub: 978-1-50992-288-8

Typeset by Compuscript Ltd, Shannon

# FOREWORD

## THE HON WILLIAM GUMMOW AC*

Professor Adrian Briggs has adverted to the view that the 'pedagogic convenience' which segregates the study of private international law from the study of the remaining body of the law 'now does more harm than good'.[1]

That observation stimulates further consideration of the basic issues reflected in the chapters in this book. First, the study of private international law, in particular choice of law, encourages the student (and subsequent practitioners) to appreciate that the legal system operates with some concepts the interaction between which might be described as vertical rather than horizontal. Other instances appear in the study of federalism in countries such as Australia, Canada, India and the United States. In Australia, in particular, the interplay between principles of law and equity, with the latter predominating in the event of conflict, provides another example, closer perhaps to everyday legal practice.

Are the issues presented by the facts of a dispute to be characterised as attracting the law of contract, or of tort, or breach of fiduciary duty, or perhaps all three? Where the facts have connections beyond the forum, the result of characterisation by the forum may lead to choice of a foreign law which differs from that of the forum. And, as Professor Yeo Tiong Min notes under the heading 'Choice of Law for Fiduciary Duties' in his chapter on The Rise of Party Autonomy, difficult issues of characterisation are presented where the forum has a particular body of legal norms which other legal systems lack.

A striking example is the holding in *Kuwait Oil Tanker Company SAK v Al Bader*[2] that the duties imposed by arts 264 and 267 of the Kuwait Civil Code were such that, although Kuwait had a civilian system, the articles were to be characterised by the English court as imposing fiduciary duties, breach of which attracted an award of compound interest.

The second consideration is that unless the modes of thought engaged by such situations are appreciated as a matter of pedagogic necessity, rather than mere convenience, the process of legal education will have miscarried. Therefore, it is a matter of regret that not only is private international law too often seen as a

* Professor of Law at the University of Sydney and the Australian National University; Non-Permanent Judge, Hong Kong Court of Final Appeal.

[1] A Briggs, *The Conflict of Laws*, 3rd edn (Oxford, Oxford University Press, 2013) 248.

[2] [2000] EWCA Civ 160, [2000] 2 All ER (Comm) 271, [187]–[193].

specialised area, segregated from the remaining body of the law, but in too many law schools either available only as an optional subject or even not at all.

This collection of papers is enhanced by the contribution of Justice Rares and Justice Brereton who are well-placed to emphasise the pervasive and enduring relevance of issues of private international law in the day-to-day work of the superior courts in Australia.

Attention is given in several of the chapters to the view that the principles of private international law have their source in the law of nations, as understood in customary international law. However that may be in other jurisdictions; it has long appeared to this writer that the source for us is in the common law of Australia. The matter has a particular importance where on its proper construction a statute of the forum prescribes a legal norm which differs from that which, left to itself, the common law would select as the *lex causae*.

Statutory regulatory regimes and consumer protection legislation may reach conduct which at common law would not be characterised in such a way as to render the law of the forum the *lex causae*. In her chapter, Professor Mary Keyes shows that Australian courts tend to apply forum legislation, if it be applicable, explicitly or by implication, rather than to apply choice of law rules. The disagreements between scholars which are in play are described by Dr Hook in her chapter as between 'statutists' and 'traditionals'. She illustrates the considerations involved by reference to the recent decision of the New Zealand Supreme Court in *Brown v New Zealand Basing Ltd*.[3] This concerned the application of local employment legislation to Cathay Pacific pilots based in New Zealand but with contracts governed by Hong Kong law.

Mr Michael Douglas writes in defence of statutory criteria and has the support of Dr FA Mann.[4] It may be noted that the writings of Dr Mann have received great weight in recent times in the High Court of Australia.[5] Mr Douglas writes with particular reference to the prohibition on misleading or deceptive conduct by s 18(1) of the Australian Consumer Law (Cth). In the *Valve Corporation* litigation in the Federal Court, both at first instance[6] and on appeal[7] the Australian statute was applied to a dispute concerning representations made to 'videogamers' who downloaded in Australia material sourced elsewhere. The defendant was incorporated in the Washington State in the USA and there were many other factors connected with that jurisdiction. The Federal Court accepted that the closest and most real connection was with Washington but applied s 67 of the Australian

[3] [2017] NZSC 139, [2018] 1 NZLR 245.

[4] 'The Doctrine of Justification in International Law' (1954) 111 *Reueil des Cours* 1, 70.

[5] *Moti v The Queen* (2011) 245 CLR 456, [2011] HCA 50, [52]. See also C McLachlin, 'The Foreign Relations Power in the Supreme Court' (2018) 134 *Law Quarterly Review* 380, 392, 398–99, 404–06. For many years Dr Mann practised (like the future Lord Collins) as a solicitor (and partner) at Herbert Smith; their scholarship thus was leavened by practical experience at first hand.

[6] [2016] FCA 196, (2016) 337 ALR 647.

[7] [2017] FCAFC 224, (2017) 351 ALR 584.

law and disregarded contractual provisions dealing with choice of law and curial jurisdiction.

Statute may be the source of property rights rather than the imposition of prohibitions. Patents and copyrights are significant examples. It may be said that the monopolies they confer are territorial in scope. But, however this may be true of real property,[8] the joint reasons of Lord Walker and Lord Collins, a formidable combination, in *Lucasfilm Ltd v Ainsworth*[9] show that the forum may entertain an action for infringement of copyright conferred by the law of another jurisdiction, in this case, that of the United States.

Proof of foreign law, under the orthodox rule of the common law, is a matter requiring the party who wishes to rely on it to plead that law and support it by expert evidence.[10] In their chapter on proof of foreign law Justin and Dominique Hogan-Doran criticise that position. The task of the court is to evaluate the evidence as a fact-finding exercise. The number of nation states with their own legal systems has greatly increased since the common law rule was propounded. Experts may be hard to find. Their evidence may appear incomplete. Justice Brereton, in his chapter, indicates that in practice where there is doubt or conflict judges prefer to look at the foreign sources, informed by the expert evidence as far as it goes, and draw their own conclusions.

The Supreme Court of Canada recently observed that 'the natural habitat of the internet is global'.[11] Further, corporate structures are increasingly multi-jurisdictional, not the least to utilise the advantages of tax havens. The upshot is seen in the growth of duplicative litigation and the responses thereto of, on the one hand, the forum declining jurisdiction on the basis that it is an 'inappropriate forum', or some other such formulation, and, on the other hand, the issue by the forum of an anti-suit injunction.

Further, as Lockhart J explained 25 years ago in *Sterling Pharmaceuticals Pty Ltd v Boots & Co (Aust) Pty Ltd*,[12] an appropriate exercise by the forum of case management may be a temporary stay to enable the other court to try a common issue, for example, of fact. The doctrine of issue estoppel applies in multinational litigation, as decided in the celebrated *Carl Zeiss* litigation.[13] But it operates in sequential not concurrent litigation. Hence the importance of the temporary stay. Professor Mortensen in the chapter 'The Case Management Stay in Private International Law' surveys the subject both in Europe (including the tangled relationship of the United Kingdom with the EU) and in the common law jurisdictions of Australia, Canada, Hong Kong SAR, Singapore and New Zealand.

[8] *British South Africa Co v Companhia de Mozambique* [1895] AC 602.

[9] [2012] 1 AC 208, [95]–[110]. See also *KK Sony Computer Entertainment v Van Veen* (2006) 71 IPR 179.

[10] *Neilson v Overseas Projects Corporation of Victoria* [2005] HCA 54, (2005) 223 CLR 331, [115]–[116], [125].

[11] *Google Inc v Equustek Solutions Inc* [2017] 1 SCR 824, [41]. See further M Douglas, 'Extraterritorial Injunctions Affecting the Internet' (2018) 12 *Journal of Equity* 34.

[12] (1992) 34 FCR 287.

[13] [1967] 1 AC 853, 918, 927, 948, 965–67.

Another aspect of modern dispute resolution is the choice by the parties of arbitration rather than curial litigation. Dr Hayward discusses no less than nine categories where choice of law clauses in arbitration agreements are inadequate or defectively drafted, leaving various issues which arise in the subsequent arbitration to be determined under substantive laws selected by the arbitrators.

In Australia, recent revisions to the Rules of Court respecting 'long-arm' jurisdiction, initiated by the Rules Committee of the Council of Chief Justices are now in operation in the Supreme Courts of several States and are likely to be adopted by the Federal Court.

Professor Dickinson raises a number of issues, jurisprudential, substantive and procedural, respecting the growth of 'long-arm' jurisdiction over defendants not present in the forum, with or without the requirement of prior leave. It should be noted, however, as Justice Brereton emphasises, that with respect to grounds outside the traditional categories the court may grant leave only if satisfied that the claim has a real and substantial connection 'with Australia' (not confined to the State in question) and 'Australia' is the appropriate forum for the trial. In her chapter, Professor Bath explores the question whether the prospective enforcement in the relevant foreign jurisdiction of a judgment obtained in the forum after the exercise by it of such 'long-arm' jurisdiction is a matter to be taken into account initially when leave is sought to serve *ex juris*. She makes the point that prospects for international enforcement of judgments should increase as parties hold assets and carry on business in more locations than their headquarters. Her research has yielded *Wilson v Adda Investments Pty Ltd*[14] where the issues in play were given canny and insightful consideration by Garling J.

The remaining chapters in this collection deal with aspects of recognition in the forum of foreign judgments. In Australia, the Foreign Judgments Act 1991 (Cth) (with its analogues in some 30 jurisdictions, excluding the United States and Mainland China but including Hong Kong SAR) displaces the common law in respect of judgments for a sum of money, other than taxes, fines or penalties. In that setting, Dr Huang deals with reciprocal recognition and enforcement of foreign judgments in Mainland China. The 2005 Hague Convention on Choice of Court Agreements seeks to achieve the uniform treatment of 'exclusive' jurisdiction agreements and of judgments rendered in the exercise of jurisdiction based on such an agreement. There are some 23 EU Member States which are parties to the Convention but in Australia do not benefit from recognition under the 1991 Act. Ms Brooke Marshall brings to her chapter on the Convention her experience at the Max Planck Institute and the University of Hamburg. She points out that the projected Free Trade Agreement between Australia and the EU is likely to increase the occasions for the engagement of the Convention if the proposed accession of Australia to the Convention comes to pass. The chapter thus provides valuable material for those Australian lawyers who look ahead.

[14] [2014] NSWSC 381.

Enough had been said above to emphasise that the editors are to be congratulated in bringing together contributions to the commercial aspects of private international law, seen from a common law perspective. Legal advisers, advocates, judges, scholars and students will find in these pages much to engage them and stimulate further thought.

William MC Gummow
*Sydney*
*November 2018*

# SERIES EDITOR'S PREFACE

This book is a testimony to the efficiency of its writers, editors and publisher in moving from a successful conference in Sydney in February 2018 to me writing this series editor's preface a year later. The collection of talent assembled in the book is an exciting mixture of academics (experienced and relatively early career), judges and legal practitioners from a variety of countries with a strong Australian core.

The book is an excellent common law perspective on some of the key issues in commercial private international law. The book fully embraces a global perspective by careful analysis of the instruments developed by the one international institution with a mission to progressively unify private international law (the Hague Conference on Private International Law). The Hague Choice of Court Convention 2005 is the subject of much discussion in the book, notably by Dr Brooke Marshall, Professor Mary Keyes and Professor Yeo Tiong Min. They rightly assert that the core scope of the Convention does not apply to asymmetric choice of court agreements despite some obiter comments from an English judge to the contrary. Marshall highlights the importance of a knowledge of public international law (in particular the law of treaties) to being a global private international lawyer in being able to make an interesting argument in her chapter on this issue. She asserts that the deliberate decision to exclude asymmetric choice of court agreements from the definition of "exclusive jurisdiction clauses" in Article 3(a) of the Convention at the Diplomatic Session concluding the Convention in 2005 could be an "agreement" among all Contracting States "in connection with the conclusion of the Convention and therefore part of the 'extrinsic context' against which the courts of Contracting States *must* interpret the Convention in good faith." As you would expect Professors Keyes and Tiong Min give a very careful assessment of the value of the Hague Choice of Court Convention to Australia and the common law world respectively. It can only be hoped that their positive assessments will lead many more common law countries to become parties to the Convention beyond the existing parties (Cyprus, Ireland, Malta, Singapore and the UK). The UK will become an independent party to the Convention from 1 April 2019 if the Withdrawal Agreement between the UK and the EU is not ratified and approved by the UK and the EU. If that Agreement is ratified and approved the UK will remain a party to the Convention.[1]

[1] This will be achieved through the EU's approval of the Convention during the transitional period of the UK's withdrawal from the EU, at least up to the end of 2020, by the EU notifying Contracting States that the UK remains a Member State of the EU for this purpose, see https://www.hcch.net/en/instruments/conventions/status-table/notifications/?csid=1318&disp=resdn.

The Hague Convention on Recognition and Enforcement of Judgments in Civil and Commercial Matters which will hopefully be concluded at the Diplomatic Session in June/July 2019 is addressed in part by the chapters in the book by Professors Bath and Tiong Min. The new Convention has the potential to create a strong regime for recognising and enforcing a very wide range of judgments in civil and commercial matters. However, as Bath carefully analyses, it is also designed to allow States to go further in recognising and enforcing foreign judgments as it is essentially a minimum harmonisation document along the road to the progressive unification of the private international law of recognition and enforcement of foreign judgments. The new Convention will probably allow for the refusal of foreign judgments that were given contrary to a choice of court agreement and thereby boost the effectiveness of the Hague Convention on Choice of Court Agreements 2005.[2] Furthermore it will likely create a comprehensive basis for the recognition and enforcement of foreign judgments where the court of origin could have exercised jurisdiction on the basis of a non-exclusive or asymmetric jurisdiction agreement (see the draft explanatory report of December 2018 by Professors Garcimartín and Saumier at paras 219–225). In doing so it may remove any utility of using the declaration system for non-exclusive jurisdiction agreements created in the 2005 Convention but not yet used by any party to that Convention. Marshall's chapter in giving a detailed analysis of the declaration system in the 2005 Convention notes the possibility that the new Convention might cover these matters and might prove to be a better route. Readers and States should carefully scrutinise what emerges from the Diplomatic Session in July 2019 before making a final assessment on this matter.

Finally in the global law aspect of the book it is worth noting that careful analysis is given to the extent to which the Hague Principles on Choice of Law in International Commercial Contracts[3] could usefully be adopted in common law countries (Tiong Min) and in Australia (Keyes). The beauty of the Hague Principles is that it is a soft law instrument that allows for flexible adoption in different States – it is the Hague's first light touch approach to the progressive unification of private international law. Dr Hayward's chapter paying attention to choice of law in international commercial arbitration also takes account of the Hague Principles. I am glad to see that both he and Mary Keyes are sceptical about the value of following the Hague Principles in permitting the choice of non-State law to govern international commercial contracts.

Of course the book has a lot to say on many commercial issues of private international law that are not yet the subject of global law. Notably, Professor Andrew Dickinson considers the history of service out of the jurisdiction rules in New South Wales and makes some forceful points about the desirability of the

[2] See the draft explanatory report of December 2018 by Professors Garcimartín and Saumier at paras 297–299 https://assets.hcch.net/docs/7d2ae3f7-e8c6-4ef3-807c-15f112aa483d.pdf.

[3] Approved on 19 March 2015 – see https://www.hcch.net/en/instruments/conventions/full-text/?cid=135.

jurisdiction rules in a legal system being determined by a legislature with proper transparency and democratic accountability. Also of particular interest to me is Professor Reid Mortensen's comprehensive and enlightening account of the development of case management stays in the common law world. It emerges that they are particularly useful in the context of court proceedings that are running concurrently with an arbitration. There is much else in this book for the reader to enjoy. I warmly commend it to you.

Paul Beaumont, University of Aberdeen

# EDITORS' PREFACE

Private international law has become increasingly important to the practice of commercial law. With that obvious truth in mind, on 16 February 2018, the University of Sydney Law School hosted a conference titled, 'Commercial Issues in Private International Law'. The conference brought together judges, government lawyers, barristers, solicitors and academics for a day of interrogation of challenging contemporary problems at the intersection of private international law and commercial practice. The presenters hailed from Germany (via Australia), New Zealand (via Germany), New South Wales (including, in one case, via China), Queensland, Singapore, the United Kingdom (via New South Wales), Victoria and Western Australia. They brought to their contributions common law perspectives coupled with wide-ranging experience of the operation of international instruments that have begun, if only tentatively, to exert a growing influence in this field. It is a sign of the interesting times in which we live and work that many of the presenters have considerable experience and expertise in non-common law legal systems.

What is unique about a common law perspective on private international law? The common law world has an unusual relationship with the discipline. The English borrowed from civilian and Roman-Dutch ideas in developing their own solutions to cross-border legal problems; the rest of the Commonwealth, in turn, borrowed from and adapted the English model for its own purposes. Australian law, for example, has acquired many of the modern traits of other legal systems, like the judicial aversion to forum shopping. In recent years, English private international law has been significantly affected by the UK's membership of the European Union, but decisions of the English courts in particular have nonetheless remained influential in the common law world, including in Australia, New Zealand and Singapore.

In certain respects, however, common law private international law is unique. Is that something for us to lament, or to be proud of? This book was edited on the precipice of a hard Brexit, in the time of Trump. The march towards globalism, and the accompanying international harmonisation of laws, is anything but guaranteed. Whatever one's view on that, there is value in taking stock of where private international law in Australia and elsewhere in the common law world sits now, and where it is headed.

The Hon William Gummow made substantial contributions to Australian private international law as a judge of the High Court of Australia and of the Federal Court of Australia. Since then, he has taught Conflict of Laws at the ANU; he is a Professor of both the ANU College of Law and the University of

Sydney Law School. We are honoured that he has surveyed the contents of this book in his foreword.

Avoiding repetition, we simply express our sincere thanks to each of the contributors. In particular, we would like to thank Justice Rares and Justice Brereton, two of Australia's leading judges in the field of private international law. Their Honours delivered speeches which bookended the Sydney conference. We are delighted they have contributed chapters to this volume.

We would also like to thank the organisations that made the Sydney conference possible: the Sydney Centre for International Law; the Ross Parsons Centre of Commercial, Corporate and Taxation Law; and the Centre for Asian and Pacific Law, each based at the University of Sydney Law School. Thanks also to Simran Singh for her wonderful work in putting the conference together, and to everyone who made the effort to attend that day.

Michael Douglas, Vivienne Bath, Mary Keyes
and Andrew Dickinson
*Cambridge, MA, Sydney, NSW, Brisbane,*
*Qld and Oxford, UK (respectively)*
*5 October 2018*

# TABLE OF CONTENTS

PART III
CHOICE OF LAW



PART IV
THE DEVELOPING LEGAL LANDSCAPE



PART V
CONCLUDING REMARKS

# LIST OF CONTRIBUTORS

**Professor Vivienne Bath**

Vivienne Bath is Professor of Chinese and International Business Law at Sydney Law School, Director of the Centre for Asian and Pacific Law and Director of Research of the China Studies Centre Research Committee at the University of Sydney. Her teaching and research interests are in international business and economic law, private international law and Chinese law. Representative publications include 'Overlapping Jurisdiction and the Resolution of Disputes before Chinese and Foreign Courts' (2015–16) 17 *Yearbook of International Private Law* 111–50.

**The Hon Justice Paul Le Gay Brereton AM RFD**

Justice Brereton was educated at the University of Sydney, admitted as a solicitor in New South Wales in 1982, called to the Bar in 1987 and appointed Senior Counsel in 1998. In 2005, he was appointed a Judge of the Supreme Court of New South Wales, primarily in the Equity Division. On 30 August 2018 he was appointed a Judge of Appeal. Since 2013 he has been a member of the Defence Force Discipline Appeals Tribunal. He was appointed a part-time Commissioner of the NSW Law Reform Commission on 1 June 2016 and Deputy Chairperson on 1 July 2016. He is also a member of the Harmonisation of Rules Committee. He is co-author of *Nygh's Conflict of Laws in Australia*, 9th edn, (LexisNexis, 2014), with Professor Martin Davies and Dr Andrew Bell SC, and the revising author of the Conflict of Laws title in *Halsbury's Laws of Australia*.

**Professor Andrew Dickinson**

Andrew Dickinson, formerly Professor of Private International Law at the University of Sydney, is a Fellow of St Catherine's College and Professor of Law at the University of Oxford. He is one of the specialist editors of *Dicey, Morris & Collins on the Conflict of Laws*, 15th edn (Oxford, Oxford University Press, 2012) and is a member of the Mance Committee, the UK Ministry of Justice's Advisory Committee on private international law.

**Mr Michael Douglas**

Michael Douglas is a Senior Lecturer in private law at UWA Law School, University of Western Australia, where he researches private international law and teaches civil procedure. Previously, he was a Lecturer at the University of Sydney Law School, where he convened the compulsory course in private international law.

In 2018, Michael attended Harvard Law School on PhD exchange from Sydney, where he is supervised by David Rolph and William Gummow. He will co-author the forthcoming 10th edition of *Nygh's Conflict of Laws in Australia* with Professor Martin Davies, the Hon Justice Andrew Bell SC and the Hon Justice Brereton AM RFD.

**Dr Ben Hayward**

Dr Benjamin Hayward is a Senior Lecturer in the Department of Business Law and Taxation, Monash Business School, Monash University. Dr Hayward holds a PhD in law from Monash University, with his doctoral research published as *Conflict of Laws and Arbitral Discretion – The Closest Connection Test* (Oxford, Oxford University Press, 2017). Dr Hayward's research addresses a range of private international law issues, particularly as they arise in international commercial arbitration. His contribution to this volume addresses identification of the governing substantive law in international commercial arbitration, via party choice of law and arbitrators' own conflicts of laws determinations.

**Ms Dominique Hogan-Doran SC**

Dominique Hogan-Doran is a Senior Counsel of the New South Wales Bar. She graduated with a Bachelor of Laws (with First Class Honours and the Convocation Medal) and Master of Laws from the University of Sydney, and the Bachelor of Civil Law (with First Class Honours) from the University of Oxford, where she was the Sir Robert Menzies Memorial Scholar. She is a Fellow of the Chartered Institute of Arbitrators and an Accredited Mediator NMAS. Dominique served as an Australian Delegate to the G20's Business Dialogue (2016–2018) as a member of the Trade & Investment, and Integrity & Compliance, Taskforces, and is an Officer of the International Bar Association's Bar Regulation Committee.

**Mr Justin Hogan-Doran**

Justin Hogan-Doran is a barrister of the New South Wales Bar. He holds the Bachelor of Laws (with First Class Honours) from the University of Sydney, and the Bachelor of Civil Law (with First Class Honours) and Master of Philosophy (with Distinction) from the University of Oxford, where he was the Sir Robert Menzies Memorial Scholar and received the John Morris Prize for Conflict of Laws. He is a Fellow of the Chartered Institute of Arbitrators and of the Australian Centre for International Commercial Arbitration. He lectures in private international law at the University of Sydney, and is a Captain in the Australian Army Legal Corps.

**Dr Maria Hook**

Maria Hook is a Senior Lecturer in the Faculty of Law at the University of Otago, New Zealand, where she teaches private international law, public international law and torts. She is author of *The Choice of Law Contract* (Hart, 2016), and is the co-author of a forthcoming text on *The Conflict of Laws in New Zealand* (LexisNexis). Her research interests range across the field of private international law and include issues relating to jurisdiction, choice of law and conflict of laws methodology.

**Dr Jie (Jeanne) Huang**

Jie (Jeanne) Huang is an Associate Professor at University of Sydney Law School. She teaches and researches in the fields of private international law, e-commerce law, international investment law, international litigation and arbitration, and underwater cultural heritage protection. She has published four books and authored more than 40 articles in law journals, such as *Journal of Private International Law* and *Journal of International Economic Law*. She is a member of the Chartered Institute of Arbitrators. She also serves as an Arbitrator at the Hong Kong International Arbitration Center, Shanghai International Arbitration Center and Xi'an Arbitration Commission.

**Professor Mary Keyes**

Mary Keyes is Professor at Griffith Law School in Brisbane, Queensland, Australia. She researches principally in the field of private international law, particularly in the areas of jurisdiction and the use of agreements; and teaches international commercial and family litigation. She is co-author of *Private International Law in Australia*, 4th edn (LexisNexis, 2019, with Reid Mortensen and Richard Garnett), and is review articles editor of the *Journal of Private International Law*. She is currently working on several projects critically considering the use of party autonomy in private international law. Professor Keyes will give a special course at the Hague Academy of International Law in the summer session of 2020.

**Ms Brooke Marshall**

Brooke Marshall is a Senior Research Fellow at the Max Planck Institute for Comparative and International Private Law, and a doctoral candidate at the University of Hamburg, in Germany. In 2016, she was awarded the Diploma of The Hague Academy of International Law in Private International Law. She is a regional editor of the forthcoming comparative commentary *Choice of Law in International Commercial Contracts* (Oxford University Press) and will join the Faculty of Law at the University of New South Wales in 2019.

**Professor Reid Mortensen**

Reid Mortensen is Professor of Law and Head of the School of Law and Justice at the University of Southern Queensland in Toowoomba, Australia. He has written extensively on private international law in Australia and the Commonwealth, and with Mary Keyes and Richard Garnett is author of *Private International Law in Australia*. Professor Mortensen is also a Fellow of the Australian Academy of Law and the Queensland Academy of Arts and Sciences, and is a member of the Centre for Public, International and Comparative Law at the University of Queensland and the Centre for Private International Law at the University of Aberdeen.

**The Hon Justice Steven Rares**

Steven Rares was appointed a judge of the Federal Court of Australia in 2006. He is also an additional judge of the Supreme Court of the Australian Capital Territory. He graduated in Arts and Law from the University of Sydney and after two years working in a solicitors' firm he was called to the New South Wales Bar in 1980. He was appointed a Senior Counsel in 1993. In 2004 and 2005 he was a member of the Judicial Commission of New South Wales. Justice Rares is currently a National co-convening judge and the New South Wales registry convening judge for the Admiralty and Maritime National Practice Area and a member of the Comité Maritime International's International Working Group on Offshore Activities. Between October 2014 and October 2016, he was President of the Judicial Conference of Australia. He is a Deputy President and a member of the Board of Management of the Australasian Institute of Judicial Administration. He is also the Chairman of the Consultative Council for Australian Law Reporting.

**Professor Tiong Min Yeo**

Yeo Tiong Min is the Yong Pung How Chair Professor of Law at the School of Law of the Singapore Management University, where he served as Dean from 2012–17, and Associate Dean (Research) from 2009–11. He is concurrently Academic Director of the Asian Business Law Institute in Singapore. His research interests are in aspects of private law, with a focus on private international law.

# TABLE OF CASES

**Australia**

**Canada**



**China**



**Dubai**

## European Union



## France



## Hong Kong



## Ireland

**New Zealand**



**Singapore**

**South Africa**



**United Kingdom**[1]



[1] Including decisions of the Privy Council.

**United States**

# TABLE OF LEGISLATION

**NATIONAL**

*Australia*[1]



[1] This section includes legislation of the United Kingdom Parliament having effect in relation to all or part of the territory of Australia (marked 'Imp').

*China*



*Denmark*



*Dubai*

*France*



*Germany*



*Hong Kong*



*Hungary*



*Japan*



*New Zealand*

*Singapore*

*South Africa*



*South Korea*



*Switzerland*



*United Kingdom*

*Vietnam*



**EUROPEAN UNION**

**INTERNATIONAL**

# 1

# Commercial Issues in Private International Law

JUSTICE STEVEN RARES*

Private international law, as a field of legal discourse, is concerned with identifying predictable legal rules that the courts of a forum must apply in resolving disputes that involve at least the laws of two nations. Many text books carry the expression 'conflict of laws' in their titles as a neat encapsulation of what is often involved. And the theme of this book, or at least its title, harkens back to what is likely to have been the origin of private international law, namely commercial disputes that arose out of trading relationships between nationals of different states in the ancient world. That means today, as Lord Sumption JSC, speaking for the Supreme Court of the United Kingdom said, 'Litigation between residents of different states is a routine incident of modern commercial life'.[1]

The panoply of distinguished persons who contribute to this volume cover an array of significant topics. I do not propose to trespass, consciously, on what any of them will say. But I did want to use this opportunity to discuss, briefly, the enduring relevance of the central theme of this book in the day-to-day work of the superior courts in Australia.

The principles of private international law affect the resolution of commercial issues in many areas of discourse. These include not only the impact of electronic communication on our daily lives but also the recognition and enforcement in the forum of rights arising under another polity's laws in relation to commercial contracts, maritime liens, the administration or reconstruction of insolvent estates, long-arm service or service out of the jurisdiction of process and, arbitration agreements and awards. In addition, the courts of the forum must consider the degree to which they should afford comity to the laws of another jurisdiction in deciding whether or not to stay or enjoin the bringing of litigation.

* A judge of the Federal Court of Australia and an additional judge of the Supreme Court of the Australian Capital Territory. The author acknowledges the assistance of his associate, Georgia Allen, in the preparation of this chapter. The errors are the author's alone. Introductory remarks presented at the University of Sydney Law School Conference on Friday 16 February 2018.

[1] *Abela v Baadarani* [2013] UKSC 44, [2013] 1 WLR 2043, 2062, [53] (Lord Sumption JSC), 2060, [45] (Lord Clarke of Stone cum Ebony JSC).

## I. The *Leges Maritima* and *Mercatoria*

Disputes arising out of breaches of contracts for the sale of goods are quintessentially commercial as well as being inevitable. Vendors want to be paid and purchasers want to be able to enforce their contractual rights to obtain that for which they paid or agreed to pay. The legal systems of the different states in which a vendor and a purchaser are located in a cross-border transaction ordinarily recognise the importance of trade to the forum and the need to give the commercial community, both domestic and foreign, confidence that will support the future willingness of traders in both their own and other jurisdictions to do business with those in the forum.

Maritime law was one of the earliest scenarios for the development of private international law principles. Ships needed to be supplied and repaired, freight needed to be paid. All of this occurred in ports both foreign and domestic for the ship's owners. Creditors needed to be able to recover debts owed by peripatetic ships' owners. The ship became a mobile security carrying a maritime lien.

English law has grappled differently over the centuries with whether and how to recognise a maritime lien that arises outside the forum. A maritime lien is a remedy traceable at least to Roman law. Such a lien is a claim or privilege on the *res* that is carried into effect by a legal process. In Anglo-Australian law, that process is now a proceeding *in rem*. However, that form of action came late to the common law as it did not previously have a procedure that allowed proceedings *in rem*. In *The Ship 'Sam Hawk' v Reiter Petroleum Inc*,[2] the five members of the Full Court of the Federal Court of Australia discussed the history of English law's treatment of maritime liens, which were creatures of the civil law administered by the civilian lawyers in Doctors' Commons who constituted the Court of Admiralty before the Judicature Acts of 1873 and 1875 (UK).

Around the late seventeenth century, Lord Holt CJ gave a number of decisions, for the Court of King's Bench, that upheld the right of maritime creditors to proceed in the Court of Admiralty to enforce maritime liens that arose out of the jurisdiction because the lien holder had no remedy at common law that enabled the ship to be sold to answer for the liability.[3] In *Johnson v Shippen*,[4] giving the judgment of the Court, Lord Holt CJ emphasised the impact that a contrary approach would have on trade. He said:

> *When an hypothecation is made either for money to buy necessaries, or for necessaries for the ship, in a voyage, the Court of Admiralty have a jurisdiction, for the party has no other remedy*; we cannot give him any remedy against the ship; and if *the suit there should not be allowed, the master will have no credit to take up necessaries for the use of the ship.*
>
> …

[2] [2016] FCAFC 26, (2016) 246 FCR 337.
[3] ibid 410–11, [306]–[309].
[4] (1703) 2 Ld Raym 982, 92 ER 154.

> *No master of a ship can have credit abroad but upon the security by hypothecation*, and shall we hinder the Court of Admiralty from giving remedy, when we can give none ourselves? *It will be the greatest prejudice to trade that can be, to grant a prohibition in this case.* Indeed if a ship be hypothecated here in England before the voyage begin, that is not a matter within the jurisdiction of the Court of Admiralty, for it is a contract made here, and the owners can give security to perform the contract.[5] (emphasis added; footnotes omitted)

In essence, much of the underlying, perhaps often silent, judicial reasoning forming the basis of rules in private international law cases is a recognition of *first*, the potential impact on trade and, *secondly*, the perceived need for comity between or among other legal systems in order, again, to support trade. Maritime law has been a rich source of rules of private international law because, as Lord Mansfield CJ said in 1759, 'the maritime law is not the law of a particular country, but the general law of nations'.[6]

Nonetheless, as the decisions in *Sam Hawk*[7] and *The Halcyon Isle*[8] show, the issues that recognition, in one legal system, of a right given by another legal system, involves several policy issues: *first*, the categorisation in the forum of the foreign right to ascertain whether it is a right that is the same as, or closely analogous to, one given by the forum, *secondly*, the assessment of whether the foreign right is substantive or procedural and, *thirdly*, the nature of the remedy that, if it were recognised and enforceable in the forum, the local court would grant.

Of course, there can be no universally agreed solution as to which system of law a domestic court will apply to resolve a dispute where the relationship of the parties has more than one legal system in its background or, by the time of litigation, foreground.

## II. Long-arm Service

Recently, the Council of Chief Justices of Australia and New Zealand agreed to adopt uniform rules for service out of the jurisdiction.[9] The new rules re-work, but do not change substantively, the legal bases on which our two nations' superior courts exercise jurisdiction over a foreigner, and compel, at least in legal theory, him, her or it to appear in the forum, if the foreigner is not already present within the jurisdiction when the action is brought.

The selection of the criteria that the now, or soon to be, uniform rules prescribe to justify service out of the forum must reflect generally accepted bases on which

[5] ibid 983 (KB) (Lord Holt CJ).

[6] *Luke v Lyde* (1759) 2 Burr 882, 887, 97 ER 614 (Lord Mansfield CJ).

[7] *Sam Hawk* (n 2).

[8] *Bankers Trust International Ltd v Todd Shipyards Corporation (The Halcyon Isle)* [1981] AC 221.

[9] As considered by Professor Dickinson in ch 2, and by Justice Brereton in ch 13.

national courts exercise jurisdiction over foreigners. That is, the principles of private international law that most national legal systems recognise must underpin the basis on which, in any particular dispute, the forum claims jurisdiction to make orders that will be enforced against a foreigner in his, her or its home jurisdiction in default of appearance in the forum.

If the foreigner is a party to a contract that has an express jurisdiction, or perhaps choice of law, clause, it is likely that the decision of the nominated forum will be recognised in the foreigner's home and so will provide a sufficient spur for the foreigner to appear. But, the long-arm rules allow service on wider grounds than that and have done so for over a century. Lord Porter recognised in *Tyne Improvement Commissioners v Armement Anverssois S/A (The Brabo) (No 2)*[10] that, 'the right to add the foreigner should be sparingly used'.

However, the Supreme Court of the United Kingdom has recently said that it is no longer realistic to characterise the exercise of long-arm jurisdiction as 'exorbitant' or as an assertion of the local court's power over the foreign defendant. In *Abela*, Lord Sumption JSC[11] said that the adoption of the doctrine of *forum non conveniens* and the United Kingdom's accession to a number of conventions that regulate the international jurisdiction of national courts:

> means that in the overwhelming majority of cases where service out is authorised there will have been either a contractual submission to the jurisdiction of the English Court or else a substantial connection between the dispute and this country … litigation between residents of different states is a routine incident of modern commercial life.[12]

He concluded saying '[t]he decision is generally a pragmatic one in the interests of the efficient conduct of litigation in an appropriate forum'.[13]

Recently in *BY Winddown Inc v Vautin*,[14] Besanko, Middleton and Griffiths JJ dismissed an application for leave to appeal the making of an order for service of proceedings in the United States on a yacht manufacturer, pursuant to the Convention on the Service Abroad of Judicial and Extrajudicial Documents in Civil or Commercial Matters done at the Hague on 15 November 1965. In that case, the purchaser of a yacht had sued the manufacturer's Australian exclusive dealer arising from alleged breaches of contract concerning the purchase of the yacht and the dealer was likely to claim that the defects in the yacht were the fault of the manufacturer. Also, the purchaser was concerned that the dealer may not have been able to pay all the damages. Item 20 in the table to r 10.42 of the Federal Court Rules 2011 provided that a person could be served outside Australia who was a proper and necessary party to a proceedings.

[10] *Tyne Improvement Commissioners v Armement Anverssois S/A (The Brabo) (No 2)* [1949] AC 326, 339.
[11] Lord Neuberger of Abbotsbury PSC, Lord Clarke, Lord Reid and Lord Carnwath JJSC agreeing.
[12] *Abela* (n 1) 2062–63, [53] (Lord Sumption JSC).
[13] ibid; *Abela* (n 1) 2060, [45] (Lord Clarke JSC).
[14] *BY Winddown Inc v Vautin* [2016] FCAFC 168, (2016) 249 FCR 262.

Importantly, the present rule was based on one of the reforms introduced in the Judicature Act 1873 (UK) being the power to grant all remedies to which any party is entitled in respect of a claim properly brought forward by that party, so far as possible, in order to avoid multiplicity of proceedings.[15] That position is reflected in the statutes governing Australia's superior courts.[16] Besanko, Middleton and Griffiths JJ said:

> the concept of comity, which the [manufacturer] contended was relevant to the task of construction, has limited relevance in construing subordinate legislation in the form of rules of Court. As Gummow and Hayne JJ observed in *Neilson v Overseas Projects Corporation of Victoria Ltd* (2005) 223 CLR 331 at [90], comity is 'either meaningless or misleading' and 'a matter for sovereigns not for judges required to decide a case according to the rights of the parties'.
>
> in any event, the issue of comity should be approached on the understanding that considerations of comity have evidently been taken into account in determining the items which have been included in the table in r 10.42.[17]

## III. Stays and Anti-suit Injunctions

A frequent feature of international commerce has become the remedy of the anti-suit, anti-anti-suit, and even more hostile injunctions, and the stay of local proceedings.[18] Judicial consideration of this species of remedy involves assessing the underlying basis of each party's legal rights and the connection of them and their dispute to the forum and questions of comity.

Of course, the court retains a power to stay proceedings that are properly served on a foreigner on the ground that Australia is a clearly inappropriate forum, as established in *Voth v Manildra Flour Mills Pty Ltd*.[19]

Sometimes issues of practice and procedure, such as the obligation of a foreigner to answer a notice to produce or to give discovery, can generate a substantive dispute based on the foreigner's conflicting obligations under the laws of his, her or its domicile and that of the forum. For example, several jurisdictions, including Australia, have dealt with the impact of the Swiss Criminal Code's prohibition in Art 271, on anyone, without authorisation from a Swiss court or governmental authority, performing, or aiding or abetting the performance of 'acts for a foreign State'. The penalty for contravention is up to three years' imprisonment. Similarly, Swiss law prohibits officers of the banks from disclosing or

[15] *Vautin v BY Winddown Inc (No 2)* [2016] FCA 1235, [29]–[30]; cp *Thomson Australia Holdings Pty Ltd v Trade Practices Commission* [1981] HCA 48, (1981) 148 CLR 150, 161 (Gibbs CJ, Stephen, Mason and Wilson JJ).

[16] Federal Court of Australia Act 1976 (Cth) s 22.

[17] *BY Winddown Inc v Vautin* (n 14) 273, [47]–[48].

[18] See, eg, *Home Ice Cream Pty Ltd v McNabb Technologies LLC* [2018] FCA 103.

[19] *Voth v Manildra Flour Mills Pty Ltd* [1990] HCA 55, (1990) 171 CLR 538.

assisting in the production of their employer banks' documents. As Lehane J said in *Australian Securities Commission v Bank Leumi Le-Israel (Switzerland)*,[20] Lockhart and ML Foster JJ agreeing, 'it is no light matter to enforce Australian laws in circumstances which infringe the legislative policies of other countries'.[21]

The House of Lords identified the following principles as applicable in such cases:[22]

- save in exceptional circumstances, an order should not be made by a court in the forum to compel a bank to produce books or records held by it in a branch or office outside the forum; and
- a state (including courts exercising its judicial power) should refrain from demanding obedience by foreigners to its sovereign authority in respect of their conduct outside the jurisdiction.

Yet common law courts have proved to be increasingly willing to demand foreigners' obedience to their authority in respect of conduct on the internet.[23]

## IV. Electronic Communication

In our lifetimes electronic communication has assumed an importance in commerce that was unimaginable, at least to the unscientific, such as myself, at the time The Beatles first sang '*When I'm Sixty-Four*' – a topic which I unfortunately find all too timely. Today, we enter into contracts electronically, do our banking online, do research, seek entertainment and even relationships on the internet.[24] No matter where we are in the world, one can see almost ubiquitously people in the streets walking, on public transport, and scarily sometimes driving, using smart phones or similar devices.

Yet, in many ways, the internet – including emanations like Twitter, the preferred means of communication of the 45th President of the United States – is a lawless place.[25] The internet houses virtual currencies, like Bitcoin, that exist without any government that does or can regulate them effectively. The world wide web, not to mention the more sinister, dark web, is a domain beyond the control of national courts or governments in liberal democracies. The People's Republic of

[20] *Australian Securities Commission v Bank Leumi Le-Israel (Switzerland)* (1996) 69 FCR 531.

[21] ibid 552 (Lehane J).

[22] *Société Eram Shipping Co Ltd v Cie Internationale de Navigation* [2003] UKHL 30, [2004] 1 AC 260, 274–75, [22]–[23] (Lord Bingham), 286–87, [67] (Hoffmann LJ), 277, [31] (Lord Nicholls), 287, [70] (Lord Hobhouse), 299, [113] (Lord Millett); see also *Suzlon Energy Ltd v Bangad* (2011) 198 FCR 1, 11–12, [35]–[39], 12–13, [41], 13, [43].

[23] See M Douglas, 'Extraterritorial Injunctions Affecting the Internet' (2018) 12 *Journal of Equity* 34.

[24] These changes are filtering through into private international law jurisprudence; see, eg, *Valve Corporation v Australian Competition and Consumer Commission* [2017] FCAFC 224, (2017) 351 ALR 584.

[25] But see *X v Twitter* [2017] NSWSC 1300, (2017) 95 NSWLR 301.

China is the location of the Great Wall, the only man-made object that allegedly can be seen from space. Its government also restricts access of persons to cyberspace within China to internet sites using the Great Firewall of China. Thus, it and the Chinese Government has banned access to Google and it also filters access to some foreign news, a feat that would be unthinkable in Western nations.

A consequence of our legal traditions, which we share with many other countries, has been that a national court may have difficulty establishing jurisdiction over whomever has created a site on the internet.[26] Often a plaintiff will seek relief because a website conveyed defamatory matter,[27] or offered an apparently comfortable place to transact business with a person, who later appeared not to be willing to honour the contract or was a plain fraudster.

How does a court in a forum like Australia make orders that are actually enforceable in respect of what appears on an internet site that is operated by persons who cannot be identified and are in a place that cannot be found? Experience has shown that an internet site can be operated by persons in one place who route their electronic communications through several disguises to servers in another jurisdiction that then present sites that appear to be local to persons browsing the internet on the other side of the world.

This is a practical and real challenge for those who believe in the rule of law. We must develop responsible governmental institutions, including effective judicial processes underpinned by private international law principles that will ensure their general acceptance among other jurisdictions, that can regulate what happens on the internet so that persons cannot operate, as they do now in what is virtually (in both senses) uncontrolled territory. What legally effective mechanisms exist now for persons who, thinking that they are making a bona fide contract, pay money over the internet to a fraudster operating through layers of anonymity in an untraceable place?

Similarly, operators of search engines or social media platforms, like Facebook, Instagram or Snapchat, provide sites on which third parties who post matter often are not present in the forum, even though the virtual site is readily accessible or downloadable there. When someone publishes a statement on his or her blog, or on Twitter, a person named in that publication can be significantly affected, yet find that there is no remedy in the forum for want of jurisdiction over the host of the site.

## V. Cross-border Insolvency

At the present time, one area in which the principles of private international law are developing is in cross-border insolvency. The *Model Law* on Cross Border

[26] See *Google Inc v Equustek Solutions Inc* [2017] SCC 34, [2017] 1 SCR 824.
[27] See, eg, *Trkulja v Google LLC* [2018] HCA 25, (2018) 356 ALR 178.

Insolvency of the United Nations Commission on International Trade Law has now been adopted by over 40 nations, including Australia,[28] and an analogue applies within the European Union.

The drafting of the Model Law, however, did not take into account the established principles of maritime law, in particular those dealing with the right, in common law jurisdictions, to bring proceedings *in rem* or, in civil law jurisdictions, maritime attachments. The unifying theory of the Model Law is that all creditors of an insolvent debtor should bring their claims in the jurisdiction in which the debtor's centre of main interests is and that that jurisdiction's laws, including of priorities, should govern the resolution of those claims.

Unless in making an order for recognition under Arts 19, 20 and 21 of the Model Law, a court modifies its effect under Art 22(3), its orders could interfere with the rights of creditors to enforce their securities or other rights, including mortgagees of land and fixed or floating charges over corporate assets. As well, sovereign governments could be prevented from enforcing a debtor's liability to pay taxation or pecuniary orders under its penal law. As a practical matter, secured creditors in foreign jurisdictions expect to be able to realise their securities where they are located without having to resort to the centre of main interests of the debtor.

Likewise, local courts should be able to recognise the special position of their forum's taxation or penal laws by a modification under Art 22(3) to ensure that the local revenue is not prejudiced. As Lord Mansfield CJ said in *Planché v Fletcher*,[29] 'one nation does not take notice of the revenue laws of another'.

The solution adopted in Australia is to modify the application of the Model Law so as to permit sufficient of the debtor's local assets to be retained in the forum that will satisfy taxation liabilities. In *Akers v Deputy Commissioner of Taxation*,[30] as Allsop CJ, with whom Robertson and Griffiths JJ agreed, held that the Model Law and the Cross Border Insolvency Act 2008 (Cth) did not contain any provision that operated to destroy the rights of the local taxation authority. The Chief Justice held that it was fair and appropriate to allow the local taxation authority to retain so much of the debtor's assets in Australia as would equate to the likely distribution it would have received, as an unsecured creditor, had the liquidation occurred here and its claim were included in the actual final distribution that the foreign liquidators would make in due course.[31]

There can be other significant injustice to creditors if a broadly framed order prohibiting the filing of new proceedings and staying existing ones is imposed

[28] Cross Border Insolvency Act 2008 (Cth) s 6.

[29] *Planché v Fletcher* (1779) 1 Doug 251, 253, 99 ER 164 (Lord Mansfield CJ) (KB). Acknowledged in *Government of India v Taylor* [1955] AC 491. See also *Tanning Research Laboratories Inc v O'Brien* [1990] HCA 8, (1990) 169 CLR 332, 339 (Brennan and Dawson JJ), 354 (Toohey J); *Akers (as joint foreign representative) v Saad Investments Company Ltd* [2013] FCA 738, [16] (Rares J).

[30] *Akers v Deputy Commissioner of Taxation* [2014] FCAFC 57, (2014) 223 FCR 8, 32, [98].

[31] ibid 42, [139]–[143] (Allsop CJ); affd *Akers v Saad Investments* [2013] FCA 738, [38]–[42] (Rares J).

under Arts 19(1), 20(1) or 21(1) of the Model Law. For example, such an order could operate to inhibit creditors seeking to enforce a maritime lien or a ship's mortgage that arose or was granted under a foreign law. Binnie J explained why, ordinarily, maritime liens have priority over ships' mortgages when giving the opinion of the Supreme Court of Canada in *Holt Cargo Systems Inc v ABC Container Line (Trustees of)*.[32] He said:

> The reason for this privileged status for maritime lien holders is entirely practical. The ship may sail under a flag of convenience. Its owners may be difficult to ascertain in a web of corporate relationships (as indeed was the case here, where initially Holt named the wrong corporation as ship owner). Merchant seamen will not work the vessel unless their wages constitute a high priority against the ship. The same is true of others whose work or supplies are essential to the continued voyage. The Master may be embarrassed for lack of funds, but the ship itself is assumed to be worth something and is readily available to provide a measure of security. Reliance on that security was and is vital to maritime commerce. Uncertainty would undermine confidence. The appellant Trustees' claim to 'international comity' in matters of bankruptcy must therefore be weighed against competing considerations of a more ancient and at least equally practical international system – the law of maritime commerce.[33]

If such a stay were imposed in respect of foreign debtor-in-possession proceedings, such as Ch 11 of the United States Bankruptcy Code or its South Korean, Japanese or Italian analogues, an unpaid ship's crew could be prevented from arresting the ship based on their maritime lien for wages that is a generally accepted remedy of the *lex maritima*. Ordinarily, the crew are not in a financial position where they are able to leave a ship and return to their homes, which often are not in the debtor's owner's centre of main interests, whether Korea or Liberia. Even if they could return home, they would then have to engage lawyers to make a claim in the debt restructuring, which could be outvoted and eliminated. Given that position, most crew are likely to be faced with a Hobson's choice. Yet, without crew, the debtor's ship would be stranded in a faraway port. The consequence would be, as I pointed out in *Hur v Samoun Logix Corporation*,[34] that the crew could be made *de facto* slaves of the defaulting shipowner until the conclusion of the foreign insolvency, and even then, they might not be paid in full or at all.

## VI. Conclusion

This volume includes some valuable contributions, from the learned and distinguished members of the legal community, to our thinking on its theme of commercial issues in private international law.

[32] [2001] SCC 90, [2001] 3 SCR 907.
[33] ibid 925, [27] (Binnie J).
[34] [2015] FCA 1154, (2015) 238 FCR 483, 489, [31]–[33].

# PART I

# Jurisdiction

# 2

# *In Absentia*

## *The Evolution and Reform of Australian Rules of Adjudicatory Jurisdiction*

ANDREW DICKINSON*

## I. Introduction

The power to adjudicate is of central importance within the constitutional order of any legal system. It is through the exercise of that power that questions concerning the life, liberty, property, rights and obligations of natural and legal persons are determined.[1] By the act of adjudication, a man may be condemned or absolved,[2] and may lose his freedom, his status, his reputation or his financial security. A judgment in civil proceedings may alter the parties' rights and obligations, generate new obligations, place the parties under certain disabilities (not least by precluding re-litigation of the same or a related subject-matter) and sanction the use of force by the state to render the determination effective.

It should follow that questions concerning the allocation and limits of the power to adjudicate, and the processes by which the rules governing those matters are settled, will be treated within a legal order as matters of considerable importance, and will be subjected to the most careful scrutiny. The rule of law

* This chapter is based on a keynote address at the conference, 'Commercial Issues in Private International Law', held on 16 February 2018 at Sydney Law School. I am grateful to the conference organisers, Michael Douglas and Professor Vivienne Bath, for inviting me to speak on that occasion.

I am also grateful to John Mathieson (Deputy Principal Registrar of the Federal Court and Secretary of the Harmonisation of Rules Committee), Rebel Kenna (Secretary of the NSW Rules Committee) and Daniel McGivern (Judge's clerk, Auckland High Court) for their helpful replies to my enquiries regarding the legal developments described in section III of this chapter, and to Professor Mary Keyes who provided valuable comments on an earlier draft. Any errors or omissions are my own.

Work on this chapter was completed during an enjoyable and productive visit to the Max Planck Institute for Comparative and International Private Law in Hamburg.

[1] Bl Comm 55–56, 137–38; *R (UNISON) v Lord Chancellor* [2017] UKSC 51, [2017] 3 WLR 409, [71] (Lord Reed).

[2] Digest 42.1.3 (Paul, *Edict*, Book 17).

demands not only transparency in the law, but also transparency and accountability in the processes by which the law is made.[3] The act of adjudication must itself also be transparent and fair, in conformity with the principles of open and natural justice.[4]

The concerns just expressed are heightened insofar as the existence and exercise of judicial authority concerns those who are in a vulnerable position. One such class of persons is 'absent defendants', ie those not formally present or represented in court at the point of adjudication. It may be noted at the outset that the common law in England, Australia and elsewhere took the position that no judgment in a personal action could be entered against a defendant not formally present in court.[5] From the early eighteenth century onwards, that immunity was qualified by legislation in the face of concerns that the due administration of justice was being impaired through the evasion of judicial processes.[6] The legislator was nevertheless careful to strike a balance, such that a defendant could not be condemned in a civil action without being given an adequate opportunity to understand the nature of the case against him and to appear and to defend himself.[7]

Within the class of 'absent defendants', foreign absent defendants (ie those outside the territory of the legal system in question) constitute a particular subgroup. Here, the case for protection of their interests is strengthened on three fronts. First, by the fact that their ability to appreciate and exercise their procedural rights of defence may be impaired by distance, language and other factors. Although modern methods of communication and other technologies (such as automatic translation tools) no doubt ease the burden to a degree,[8] it must also be borne in mind that technology has at the same time served to increase those burdens, through an exponential increase in human capability to create and access information. Secondly, by the necessary introduction of other (in many cases, stronger) claims to exercise adjudicatory power over that defendant, made by the

[3] J Waldron, 'Representative Lawmaking' (2009) 29 *Boston University Law Review* 335, 336–40.

[4] *Al-Rawi v The Security Service* [2011] UKSC 34, [2012] AC 531, [10]–[12] (Lord Neuberger); Australian Law Reform Commission, *Traditional Rights and Freedoms – Encroachments by Commonwealth Laws* (No 129) chs 8 and 14.

[5] *Williams v Lord Bagot* (1825) 3 B & C 772, 787, 107 ER 920, 925 (Holroyd J, Bayley J); *Picquet v Swan* (1828) 5 Mason 35, 44, 19 F Cas 609, 612–13 (Story J, Circuit Ct, Massachusetts); A Stephen, *Introduction to the Practice of the Supreme Court of New South Wales* (Sydney, D L Welch, 1843), 103; A Dickinson, 'Keeping Up Appearances: The Development of Adjudicatory Jurisdiction in the English Courts' (2016) 86 *British Yearbook of International Law* 6, 10–16.

Formal presence could be secured by compulsion, through the arrest and imprisonment of the defendant, or through a voluntary appearance. Even in the latter case, the defendant might enter that appearance only to secure his release from custody or in response to the seizure or threatened seizure of his assets.

[6] See Section II.C below. As to the development of the law in England, see Dickinson, 'Keeping Up Appearances' (n 5) 16–44.

[7] See eg Dickinson (n 5) 20.

[8] *Agar v Hyde* [2000] HCA 41, (2000) 201 CLR 552, [42] (Gaudron, McHugh, Gummow and Hayne JJ); *Abela v Baadarani* [2013] UKSC 44, [2013] 1 WLR 2043, [43] (Lord Sumption).

judicial institutions of the legal system(s) within whose territory the defendant resides, carries on business or acts. The existence of those competing claims may offer a reason for the exercise of restraint (often expressed in common law systems using the language of 'comity'). Thirdly, by principles of public international law which regulate the outer limits of the exercise of a state's regulatory jurisdiction, which require 'a substantial and bona fide connection between the subject matter of a dispute and the source of jurisdiction of a national court over its resolution',[9] and which are much more likely to be engaged in such a case.

Common law jurisdictions outside Australia have recognised the constitutional significance of the rules regulating the exercise of adjudicatory authority over foreign absent defendants. In the United States, the exercise by state and federal courts of 'long-arm' jurisdiction over foreign defendants has long been controlled through the 'due process' clause in the Fourteenth Amendment, requiring that the exercise of adjudicatory jurisdiction 'does not offend "traditional notions of fair play and substantial justice"'.[10] In Canada, the courts have been inspired by the 'constitutional underpinnings of private international law',[11] as well as considerations of comity, to formulate a central principle that adjudicatory jurisdiction must 'be established primarily on the basis of objective factors that connect the legal situation or the subject matter of the litigation with the forum'.[12] One does not need to endorse these particular approaches,[13] or to accept as correct every instance of their application,[14] to recognise the importance of adjudicatory jurisdiction within the constitutional framework.

By contrast, in Australia, as in England and Wales, the rules governing adjudicatory jurisdiction[15] lack this explicit constitutional dimension. In substantial part, those rules consist of delegated legislation in the form of rules of court regulating the service of process and the court's authority to issue judgments in

[9] *Dow Jones & Co Inc v Gutnick* [2002] HCA 56, (2002) 210 CLR 575, [101] (Kirby J).

[10] *International Shoe Co v Washington* (1945) 326 US 310, 316. As to the later case law, see RA Brand and C Mariottini, 'Note on the Concept of "Purposeful and Substantial Connection" in Article 5(1)(g) and 5(1)(n)(ii) of the February 2017 Draft Convention', Hague Conference Preliminary Document No 6 of September 2017, [8]–[13].

[11] *Club Resorts Ltd v Van Breda*, 2012 SCC 17, [2012] 1 SCR 572, [21] (Le Bel J). For discussion of the relationship between constitutional law and private international law in Canada, see J Blom, 'Constitutionalizing Canadian Private International Law – 25 Years after *Morguard*' (2017) 13 *Journal of Private International Law* 259.

[12] ibid [82].

[13] Critics suggest that the courts have overused the constitutional framework as a tool for developing specific rules (see Blom, 'Constitutionalizing Canadian Private International Law' (n 11); F Juenger, 'A *Shoe* Unfit for Globetrotting' in *Selected Essays on the Conflict of Laws* (New York, Brill, 2001), 71ff).

[14] In its decisions to date, the Supreme Court has interpreted the 'real and substantial connection' requirement liberally (see *Van Breda* (n 11); *Chevron Corp v Yaiguaje* [2015] 3 SCR 69, 2015 SCC 42; *Lapointe Rosenstein Marchand Melançon LLP v Cassels Brock & Blackwell LLP* [2016] 1 SCR 851, 2016 SCC 30). The US courts on the other hand have presently settled upon a narrower approach in defining both 'general' and 'specific' jurisdiction (*J McIntyre Machinery Ltd v Nicastro* (2011) 564 US 873; *Bristol Myers Squibb Co v Superior Court of California* (2017) 582 US _).

[15] ie the set of rules which provide the foundation of the court's power to give a decision upon a particular subject-matter so as to bind the parties.

default of appearance.[16] Delegated legislation seems, at first sight, a potentially unsuitable vehicle for the adoption of rules of this kind, which by their nature 'have a significant impact on individual rights and liberties', 'confer enforceable rights on citizens or organisations', and/or involve 'procedural matters that go to the essence of a legislative scheme'.[17] Moreover, the use of rules of court as instruments for the creation or removal of adjudicatory authority gives rise to heightened concern, insofar as the holders of that authority, the judiciary, frequently exercise an influential, if not dominant, role within the mechanisms for promulgating such rules.[18] To be clear, within Australia's strongly embedded constitutional order, the concern being expressed here is not that the authority to make or influence legal rules governing adjudicatory authority will be abused, but rather that the separation of powers and the need to instil public trust and confidence in adjudicatory processes demand that those who hold judicial authority within a legal system should not also hold the reins in the legislative settlement of the most important of judicial powers, that of adjudication.

Against this background, this chapter looks at the historical development of the rules governing adjudicatory jurisdiction over absent defendants in the New South Wales Supreme Court as a prelude to an assessment of the recently introduced (but little heralded[19]) reforms contained within the Uniform Civil Procedure (Amendment No 83) Rule (NSW) 2016.[20] As these reforms seek to implement 'harmonised rules approved by the Council of Chief Justices with respect to service of an originating process and other documents outside of Australia',[21] and as identical or similar reforms have been adopted in South Australia,[22] Victoria[23] and Tasmania[24]

[16] *Agar v Hyde* (n 8) [44]–[46].

[17] Department of Prime Minister and Cabinet (Cth), *Legislation Handbook* (1999) 3, quoted in the Report of the Australian Law Reform Commission, *Traditional Rights and Freedoms* (n 4) [17.49]. See now the 2017 edition of the *Handbook*, available at www.pmc.gov.au/resource-centre/government/legislation-handbook, [1.10].

[18] See sections II.C(ii) and III.A below; also E Campbell, *Rules of Court* (Sydney, Law Book Co, 1985), esp at 34–36, 236–41; H P Lee and E Campbell, *The Australian Judiciary*, 2nd edn (Cambridge, Cambridge University Press, 2013) 272–74. In England and Wales, Civil Procedure Rules are made by the Civil Procedure Committee, consisting of eight judicial and eight non-judicial members (Civil Procedure Act 1997, s 2). Practice Directions, which play an important role in this area (see n 84 below) are made by a judge designated by the Lord Chief Justice with the agreement of the Lord Chancellor (Civil Procedure Act 1997, s 5; Constitutional Reform Act 1997, sch 2, pt 1).

[19] M Douglas and V Bath, 'A New Approach to Service Outside the Jurisdiction and Outside Australia under the Uniform Civil Procedure Rules' (2017) 44 *Australian Bar Review* 160.

[20] 2016 No 755, made under s 9 of the Civil Procedure Act 2005 (NSW), inserting a new div 1A within pt 11 and a new sch 6 into the Uniform Civil Procedure Rules (NSW) (UCPR).

[21] ibid, explanatory note.

[22] Supreme Court Civil Rules 2006 (SA) pt 4, introduced by the Supreme Court Rules 2006 (Amendment No 32 (SA)).

[23] Supreme Court (General Civil Procedure) Rules 2015 (Vic) ord 7, introduced by the Supreme Court (Service Out of Australia Amendment) Rules 2016 (Vic).

[24] Supreme Court Rules 2000 (Tas) div 10, introduced by the Supreme Court Amendment Rules 2017 (Tas).

The Australian Capital Territory has also adopted rules inspired by the Council's harmonised rules (Court Procedures Rules 2006 (ACT) div 6.8.9, introduced by Court Procedures Amendment Rules 2017 (No 3) (ACT)), but differing in one important respect (see text to n 183 below).

with respect to proceedings before the Supreme Courts there, this survey and assessment prompt a wider critical examination of the regulatory approach in Australia and in other common law jurisdictions to matters of adjudicatory jurisdiction.

## II. The Development of Adjudicatory Jurisdiction in New South Wales

### A. Origins of the Administration of Justice in New South Wales

The Supreme Court of New South Wales was established by Royal Charter issued under the provisions of the New South Wales Act[25] on 13 October 1823 and proclaimed in Sydney on 17 May 1824.[26] The Court opened three days later. By s 2 of the Act, the Court was designated as a court of record with cognisance in New South Wales of all pleas – civil, criminal or mixed – as the King's courts of King's Bench, Common Pleas and Exchequer at Westminster lawfully exercised in England. The judges of the Court were vested with the same jurisdictions, power and authorities as their English counterparts. By s 9 of the Act, the Court was also designated as a court of equity with the same power and authority as was exercised by the Lord High Chancellor in England.[27]

By s 17 of the Act, provision was made for the making of Rules and Orders concerning matters of procedure, pleading and practice, either directly by Order in Council or indirectly by an authority conferred by Order in Council upon the judges. Such authority was granted to the (then) single judge of the New South Wales Court[28] by Order in Council dated 19 October 1824, with the injunction that the Rules and Orders so made 'shall be consistent with and similar to the law and practice of His Majesty's Supreme Courts at Westminster, so far as the condition and circumstances of the said Colony will admit' and 'shall be so framed, as to promote as far as possible, economy and expedition in the dispatch

[25] 4 Geo IV c 96 (Imp), enacted in 1823. As to the judicial infrastructure before this time, see the *Report of the Commissioner of Inquiry on the Judicial Establishments of New South Wales and Van Diemen's Land* (House of Commons, 21 February 1823).

[26] In addition to the primary materials cited, the following sources have been consulted in the preparation of this account: A Stephen, *Introduction to the Practice of the Supreme Court of New South Wales* (Sydney, 1843); NSW Government, State Archives and Records website, 'Supreme Court of New South Wales', www.records.nsw.gov.au/agency/23?page=61&title=; M Gleeson, speech on the occasion of the 175th Anniversary of the Supreme Court of New South Wales, 17 May 1999, www.hcourt.gov.au/assets/publications/speeches/former-justices/gleesoncj/cj_175anni.htm.

[27] The Act also vested the Court with admiralty, ecclesiastical and other jurisdiction. These areas will not be considered further in this chapter, which focuses on civil jurisdiction in personal actions.

[28] The Chief Justice, Francis Forbes.

of the [Court's] business ... avoiding all unnecessary, dilatory or vexatious forms of proceeding'.[29] The rule-making power was exercised by the Chief Justice for the first time in January 1825, adopting the rules and orders, forms and manner of proceeding in the principal courts at Westminster, subject to certain, limited modifications.[30] Under these rules, a party seeking to compel the appearance of any person in an action was required to file a document setting forth the nature of the action and the writ or other process required.[31] The rules also provided for the fixing of a return date, depending on the defendant's place of residence within the colony.[32]

The New South Wales Act of 1823 was only temporary, being expressed to continue until the end of the session of Parliament following 1 July 1827.[33] In 1828, after a brief continuation,[34] it was repealed and replaced by the Australian Courts Act, which additionally vested in the Supreme Court common law jurisdiction corresponding to that exercised by the Lord High Chancellor in England.[35] Also temporary in its original effect,[36] the Australian Courts Act was given perpetual effect in 1842.[37]

By s 16 of the Australian Courts Act, the judges of the Court, now up to three in number,[38] were directly authorised to make Rules and Orders concerning matters of procedure, pleading and practice with statutory force, subject to the possibility of being overridden by the King. Section 24 of the Act also extended to New South Wales all laws and statutes in force in England with respect to the administration of justice, insofar as consistent with the Act or any provision made thereunder and capable of being applied to the colony.[39] The Governor, acting on the advice of the Legislative Council (itself established in accordance with the provisions of the same Act[40]) was empowered to declare whether such laws and statutes should

[29] Order of His Majesty in Council, empowering the judges of the Supreme Courts of New South Wales and Van Diemen's Land, to make and alter Rules and Orders relating to their respective Courts, 19 October 1824.

[30] Rules and Orders of the Supreme Court of New South Wales (as published in the Sydney Gazette and New South Wales Advertiser, 13 January 1825) r I. This represented the general rule of practice also in the Rules and Orders of Court adopted in 1834 and in 1840 (see Stephen, *Introduction to the Practice of the Supreme Court of New South Wales* (n 5) 55–56).

[31] ibid, r VI.

[32] ibid, r VII.

[33] 4 Geo IV c 96 (Imp) s 45.

[34] 7 & 8 Geo 4 c 73 (Imp).

[35] 9 Geo IV c 83 (Imp).

[36] ibid, s 41, as continued by 6 & 7 Will IV, c 46, by 7 Will IV and 1 Vict c 42, by 1 & 2 Vict c 50, by 2 & 3 Vict c 70, by 3 & 4 Vict c 62, by 4 & 5 Vict c 44.

[37] 5 & 6 Vict c 76 (Imp) s 53.

[38] 9 Geo IV c 83 (Imp) s 1.

[39] For trenchant criticism of the terms and limitations of this Act, see Stephen (n 5) 80–82, professing the view 'that the clause has introduced more evils, if not more difficulties, than any which it was meant to remedy'.

See also the Imperial Acts Adoption Act 1969 (NSW).

[40] 9 Geo IV c 83, s 20 (see also 4 Geo IV c 96, s 24). The Legislative Council was granted power and authority to make laws and ordinances for the peace, welfare and good government of the colony, subject to certain conditions.

be deemed to extend to the colonies, and to make such limitations and modifications as appeared expedient. In 1839, the New South Wales legislature was given a broader legislative authority, including the power to repeal and replace the legislation extended under the earlier Act.[41] In an early exercise of this authority, the local legislature dealt with a number of matters pertaining to the administration of justice, including a provision enabling the Governor to nominate a single judge to exercise the Court's equity jurisdiction.[42]

## B. The Supreme Court Today

The constitution and jurisdiction of the Supreme Court, as established under the Australian Courts Act, is today continued and extended under the Supreme Court Act 1970.[43] By s 23 of the Act, the Court is vested with all jurisdiction which may be necessary for the administration of justice in New South Wales.

The rule-making powers formerly exercised by the judiciary in relation to proceedings before the Supreme Court are now vested in the Uniform Rules Committee in accordance with the provisions of the Civil Procedure Act 2005.[44] The Committee comprises 11 members, including 9 representatives of the judiciary at various levels and 2 representatives of the legal profession.[45]

## C. Adjudicatory Authority over Absent Persons

### *i. From 1824 to 1970*

The history of the colony, and its geography, made it inevitable that absent defendants would present a significant practical problem for the administration of justice. Such defendants would include not only local residents who, for whatever reason, could not be located by the sheriff but also those who were no longer present or resident within the territorial limits of New South Wales.

From the outset, the Supreme Court inherited and applied the same foundational rule of adjudicatory jurisdiction as the superior courts of common law and equity in England: that no judgment could be validly granted against a defendant who was not formally present before the Court, such formal presence being secured by means of the entry of an appearance.[46] At common law, that act

[41] New South Wales and Van Diemen's Land Act, 2 & 3 Vict c 70 (Imp) s 2.
[42] Act for Administration of Justice, 4 Vict No 22 (NSW) s 20.
[43] Act 52 of 1970, s 22 (NSW).
[44] Civil Procedure Act 2005 (NSW) ss 9, 19 and sch 2–3.

Rules made by the Uniform Rules Committee are statutory rules, subject to disallowance by a motion of either House of Parliament in accordance with the procedure laid down in s 41 of the Interpretation Act 1987 (NSW) (*cf* Civil Procedure Act 2005, s 15(3)).

[45] ibid, s 8(1).
[46] Stephen (n 5) 103. See text to n 5.

could be performed only by the defendant personally, although the 2nd Statute of Westminster (1285) enabled the defendant's duly authorised attorney to do so on his behalf.[47] From the eighteenth century onwards, various statutory devices had enabled the English courts, subject to strict conditions, to treat defaulting defendants as if they had entered an appearance or to authorise the plaintiff or his attorney to enter an appearance on the defendant's behalf or to proceed to judgment on some other basis.[48] As appears below, many of those statutory provisions found their way across the globe to New South Wales. Nevertheless, the position of plaintiffs in New South Wales was, in certain respects, both more and less favourable than that of their English counterparts.

Amongst the imperial legislation extended to New South Wales under s 24 of the Australian Courts Act,[49] were the provisions of the Arrests Act of 1827[50] and those of the Chancery Contempts Act of 1830.[51] Although the application of these enactments to the administration of justice in New South Wales left much to be desired,[52] they opened up the possibility for plaintiffs, in limited circumstances, to proceed to judgment against non-appearing defendants who had either refused to appear following service or who had absconded to avoid being compelled to enter an appearance.

Prior to this, the 1823 New South Wales Act had made provision, for which no precedent existed in the King's courts in England but which followed instead the practice of the City of London mayoral courts, for the new Supreme Court to proceed against an absent defendant in certain cases (debt upon specialty, a bill or note under hand, book debts) by process of foreign attachment, ie by attachment of the defendant's assets within the jurisdiction.[53] Under that provision, the plaintiff was authorised to enter judgment and levy execution against the attached assets, upon swearing by affidavit that the debt was due and providing security for double the debt with treble damages, if it should subsequently be disproved.[54]

Subsequently, more detailed provision for foreign attachments was made by a local statute, adopted in 1832.[55] Notably, the introductory words to this legislation recited that:

> Creditors in New South Wales frequently lose their just demands by reason of their debtors not being forthcoming.

[47] Stephen (n 5) 103.
[48] Dickinson (n 5) 16–24, 32–33.
[49] Text to n 39 above.
[50] 7 & 8 Geo IV, c 71 (Imp), as adopted by 9 Geo IV No 1 (NSW).
[51] 11 Geo IV and 1 Will IV, c 35 (Imp), as adopted by 5 Will IV No 8 (NSW).
[52] As to the 1827 Act, see Stephen (n 5) 100–02, describing the manner of adoption of the Act as 'very embarrassing' and calling for its repeal or amendment.
[53] 4 Geo IV c 96 (Imp) s 11. This provision would appear to have been inspired by the practice of the mayoral courts in the City of London (see *London Corporation v Cox* (1867) LR 2 HL 239).
[54] ibid.
[55] Foreign Attachments Act, 2 Will IV No 7 (NSW).

The 1832 legislation applied to debts and other fixed money demands contracted or arising in New South Wales against a debtor who 'is absent from the said Colony or keeps out of the way to avoid being served with the process of the said Court'. It proved, however, to be both too narrow and defective in certain other respects, leading to its replacement in 1840 by an Act 'to consolidate and amend the laws relating to Actions against Persons absent from the Colony and against Persons sued as joint Contractors'.[56] This legislation applied more broadly to actions in contract[57] in which the plaintiff could demonstrate by affidavit that the cause of action arose within the colony or its dependencies and that the defendant, a non-resident, held assets locally.[58] In such a case, the plaintiff was authorised to proceed by foreign attachment in the manner set out, including by causing an appearance to be entered for the defendant and to proceed (having given security) 'as if such defendant resided in Sydney … and had appeared to such action in person'.[59]

Rules of court adopted by the first Chief Justice, Francis Forbes during the late 1820s and 1830s, also made provision of various kinds for the consequences of a default in appearance.[60] A later rule of court, adopted in June 1850, made general provision for a plaintiff to enter an appearance for a defendant in the event of his failure to appear or put in bail following service of a writ of summons.[61] Primary legislation remained, nonetheless, the principal means of regulating the Court's adjudicatory jurisdiction over foreign absent defendants.

More significant legislative changes followed in the late 1840s and early 1850s, mirroring developments in England. Most significantly, these enactments opened up the possibility of pursuing proceedings against a defendant outside the territory of New South Wales, otherwise than by means of a foreign attachment. In 1849, the Supreme Court Process Act, applicable to proceedings in the Supreme Court's equitable jurisdiction, replicated the provision made in England by statutes of 1832 and 1834[62] to enable the Court in a limited class of cases[63] to order service of a subpoena and other process upon a defendant residing out of the jurisdiction and, upon being satisfied that service had been properly effected, to order an appearance to be entered for the defendant and to proceed upon such appearance

[56] 4 Vic No 6 (NSW), revived by 18 Vic No 7 (NSW). The foreign attachment procedure was continued under the Common Law Procedure Act, Act No 21 (1899) (NSW) ss 183–208, before being abolished by the Supreme Court Act 1970 (NSW) s 5 and sch 1.

[57] ibid, s 23, excluding actions in trespass or other action in tort (trover or detinue excepted).

[58] ibid, s 2.

[59] ibid, s 8.

[60] See the paper by John P Bryson, 'Rules of Court in the Time of Chief Justice Francis Forbes' available at www.forbessociety.org.au/wordpress/wp-content/uploads/2013/03/NSW-Rules-of-Court-1823-1839.doc.

[61] General Rule of Practice No 158, *New South Wales Government Gazette*, 2 August 1850.

[62] 2 and 3 Will IV, c 33 (Imp); 4 and 5 Will IV, c 82 (Imp).

[63] Suits concerning 'lands or hereditaments situate in the Colony or concerning any charge lien judgment or incumbrance thereon or concerning any money vested in any Government or public stock or public shares in public or joint stock companies or concerns in the said Colony or concerning the interest dividends or produce thereof'.

'as fully and effectually as if such appearance had been duly entered by a defendant residing or such service had been duly made within the jurisdiction of the said Court'.[64] On the common law side, the Common Law Procedure Act of 1853, following its English counterpart of 1852,[65] authorised the issue and service of a writ upon a British subject (or notice of a writ on a non-British subject) out of the jurisdiction, with further provision for the Court to direct that the plaintiff should be at liberty to proceed with his action to judgment, provided that (1) the Court was satisfied by affidavit evidence that (a) the proceedings were founded on a cause of action which arose within the jurisdiction or in respect of a breach of a contract made within the jurisdiction, (b) the writ was either served personally on the defendant or came to his knowledge following reasonable efforts to effect such service, and (c) the defendant had either wilfully neglected to appear to such writ or was living out of the jurisdiction in order to defeat and delay his creditors; and (2) the plaintiff, before obtaining judgment, had proved the amount of the debt or damages claimed before a jury on a writ of enquiry or before the Court prothonotary.[66] The 1852 Act also made provision, more generally, for plaintiffs to enter judgment against defendants in the event of their non-appearance.[67]

These provisions were continued, and those relating to the Court's equitable jurisdiction extended, by later legislation: on the equity side, the Service of Equitable Process Act 1897 (now providing 9 different grounds for service out of the jurisdiction[68]) and, on the common law side, the Common Law Procedure Act 1899.[69] Separately, but of more limited significance for present purposes, the Service and Execution of Process Act 1901[70] made detailed provision for the service of a writ in other parts of the Commonwealth of Australia and for the continuation of proceedings in cases where no appearance was entered by the defendant in such cases.

### ii. *From 1970 to 2016*

The Supreme Court Act 1970, already mentioned, represents a pivotal moment in the development of the Supreme Court's adjudicatory jurisdiction. Under its provisions, the position of absent defendants, both within and outside the territory of New South Wales, would be regulated not by primary legislation but by rules of

[64] 13 Vic No 31 (NSW).

[65] 16 and 17 Vic, c 76 (Imp) ss 18–19.

[66] 17 Vic No 21 (NSW) ss 16–17.

[67] ibid, ss 23–24, 31–33. See C Pilcher, *Common Law Procedure Acts* (Sydney, John Sands, 1881).

[68] Act No 11 (1897) (NSW) s 3, as consolidated in the Equity Act, Act No 24 (1901) s 30.

[69] Act No 21 (1899) (NSW) ss 18–19, subsequently repealed and replaced with provision (s 18) in substantially the same terms by the Common Law Procedure Act, Act No 13 (1957) s 13 and sch 1.

[70] Act No 11 (1901) (Cth), as subsequently amended before being repealed and replaced by the Service and Execution of Process Act 1992 (Cth). See also the Trans-Tasman Proceedings Act 2010 (Cth) pt 2, authorising the service of Australian process in New Zealand. For earlier legislation governing service within Australia, see the Australian Civil Process Act, Act No 3 (1886).

court made by a committee consisting predominantly of judicial members. Under s 122(1), the rules set out in the Fourth Schedule to the Act were to come into operation on the commencement of the Act, 'subject to and together with rules made by the Rule Committee'. Under the remaining provisions of that section, that Schedule was to be repealed after six months but was to continue to have effect as rules made by that committee, subject to any other provision made by them. Under s 123, the committee was to consist of the Chief Justice, the President of the Court of Appeal or a Court of Appeal judge nominated by the President, the Chief Judge in Equity or a judge nominated by him, three other judges (including an appellate judge) appointed by the Chief Justice, and two non-judicial members (a barrister and a solicitor), also appointed by the Chief Justice. Under s 124, the committee was vested with wide rule-making powers including (s 124(1)(o)) to make provision to regulate and prescribe any matter for which provision was made in the Fourth Schedule (see below). Under s 125, rules made by the committee were to have effect following their publication in the Gazette, subject only to the possibility of a negative resolution by either House of the State Parliament.

The Fourth Schedule to the 1970 Act made detailed provision governing the position of absent defendants. Rule 3 within Part 7 required that the originating process contain a note requiring the defendant to enter an appearance and advising of the prospect that judgment would be entered if the defendant did not appear. Part 17 provided for the entry of judgments in default of appearance. Part 10 provided for the service of originating process outside the jurisdiction, in 22 categories of case.[71] Rule 2 within Part 10 provided that such service was to be valid, and capable of laying the foundation for subsequent proceedings, only if either the Court had given prior leave (under sub-rule (2)[72]) or had subsequently confirmed service (under sub-rule (4)[73]) or if the person served 'waives objection' by entering an appearance.[74] Rule 8 within Part 11 empowered the Court, on application by a defendant (who need not enter an appearance for this purpose[75]) to set aside the service of originating process or discharge any order validating service under sub-rule (2) or sub-rule (4).

In following this course, yielding control over the future development of rules of adjudicatory jurisdiction to the judiciary, New South Wales was something of a laggard. The same transition had occurred in England following the Judicature Acts almost a century earlier,[76] and in other Australian States and Territories from the early part of the twentieth century onwards.[77]

[71] Supreme Court Act 1970, sch 4, pt 10, r 1 (see text to nn 78–84 below).

[72] Requiring that the Court be 'satisfied that the proceedings are proceedings to which rule 1 applies' and 'that the applicant has a prima facie case for the relief that he seeks'.

[73] Requiring that the Court be satisfied on the matters set out in sub-rule (2) and that there was a sufficient explanation for the failure to apply for leave.

[74] Supreme Court Act 1970, sch 4, pt 2, r 2(1).

[75] Supreme Court Act 1970, sch 4, pt 11, r 8(2).

[76] Supreme Court of Judicature Act 1875, 38 & 39 Vict c 77 (E&W) s 17, a rule-making power first exercised by the adoption of the Rules of the Supreme Court 1883.

[77] PE Nygh, *Conflict of Laws in Australia*, 2nd edn (Sydney, Butterworths, 1971) 147, fn 31–37.

Change does not, however, always represent progress. The service out provisions in the Fourth Schedule, representing what Professor Nygh described as 'an elaborated version of the English Revised Rules of the Supreme Court 1965',[78] marked a significant extension of the cases in which foreign service had formerly been allowed in proceedings at common law and in equity.[79] This appears to have been attributable, at least in substantial part, to a wish to bring the New South Wales practice more closely into line with that in England and in other Australian legal systems that had long-since left the promulgation of rules governing absent defendants to rule-making committees controlled by members of the judiciary. The evolution of the rules in those jurisdictions had shown a ratcheted expansion of the categories of case in which a plaintiff could proceed to judgment against a non-appearing defendant, placing a greater emphasis upon the role of the judge in the individual case, through discretion or evaluation of the circumstances. In England, for example, 7 grounds for service out within the Rules of the Supreme Court 1883[80] had expanded to 9 by 1932 (with significant extension of the jurisdiction over claims in contract and tort),[81] 12 in the Rules of the Supreme Court 1965,[82] 21 in the rules annexed to the Civil Procedure Rules 1998[83] and 22 today.[84]

Prior to being supplanted in 2005, the Rules Committee established under the 1970 Act made only modest changes to the circumstances in which the New South Wales courts could exercise jurisdiction over defendants outside Australia, extending the provision relating to arbitration proceedings,[85] and adding two

[78] ibid 147.

[79] As appears from the marginal notes to pt 10, r 1, in the version to be found at www.legislation.nsw.gov.au/acts/1970-52.pdf, the former common law regime was seen as supporting only 4 of the new heads and the former equitable regime only 10.

[80] Rules of the Supreme Court 1883 (E&W) ord XI, r 1(a)–(g). The original ord XI, appended in the First Schedule to the Supreme Court of Judicature Act 1875, had a single, undivided provision containing a number of general grounds for service out. These were in certain respects narrower and in other respects broader than those in r 1 of the 1883 Rules. Service out in probate proceedings was addressed separately in both sets of rules.

[81] RSC ord XI, rr 1(e), introduced in 1921, and 1(ee), introduced in 1920.

[82] Rules of the Supreme Court (Revision) 1965 (E&W) ord 11, r 1(a)–(l).

[83] Civil Procedure Rules 1998 (SI 1998/3132) (E&W) (CPR) sch 1, ord 11, r 1(a)–(u).

[84] CPR, Practice Direction 6B, para 3.1(1)–(4), (4A), (5)–(21). The rules were rationalised and a number of heads combined in 2000 (Civil Procedure (Amendment) Rules 2000 (SI 2000/221) sch 1), reducing the overall number to 18 without reducing their scope. Since then, a number of the grounds have been extended and new grounds added. See, in particular, the amendments to PD6B in the 81st Update to the Practice Directions published in 2015.

In England, the grounds for service out were regrettably relegated to a Practice Direction in 2008 (Civil Procedure (Amendment) Rules 2008 (SI 2008/2178) sch 1, r 6.36) (see A Dickinson, 'Service Out of the Jurisdiction in Contract Cases: Straightening Out The Deck Chairs?' [2010] *Lloyd's Maritime and Commercial Law Quarterly* 1, 11–12). This was 'no doubt to increase flexibility' (*Four Seasons Holdings Inc v Brownlie* [2017] UKSC 80, [2018] 1 WLR 192, [43] (Lady Hale)). In particular, it removed the irksome impediment of even negative Parliamentary scrutiny.

[85] Supreme Court Rules 1970 (2005 version) pt 10, r 1A(1)(u), corresponding to Uniform Civil Procedure Rules (2016 version) sch 6, para (t).

new grounds.[86] Its most significant intervention, in 1988, had been to replace the mechanism within Part 10 for obtaining the Court's advance permission to serve process outside Australia, with a new mechanism in r 2 of that Part requiring the plaintiff only to obtain the Court's leave to proceed in the event that the defendant, once served, did not enter an appearance.[87] Additionally, a new r 6A within Part 10 specifically contemplated that a defendant may make an application under Part 11, r 8[88] on the grounds (a) that the service of the originating process is not authorised by the rules; or (b) that the Court is an inappropriate forum for the trial of the proceedings.[89] The committee's successor, the Uniform Rules Committee,[90] had done almost nothing of note for present purposes before the 2016 reforms referred to in section I of this chapter, to be examined further in the next section.[91]

The most notable developments between 1970 and 2016 arose from a more orthodox form of judicial activity: the interpretation and application of the law governing matters of adjudicatory jurisdiction over absent defendants to cases brought before the New South Wales' courts. Two decisions in this period are of particular note for present purposes. First, the New South Wales Court of Appeal's decision in *Flaherty v Girgis*,[92] concerning the interpretation and constitutional validity of the rule authorising proceedings founded upon tortious damage suffered wholly or partly in New South Wales. Secondly, the High Court's 2000 decision in *Agar v Hyde*,[93] concerning the tests to be applied and the matters to be considered in granting the plaintiff leave to proceed under Part 10 of the (post-1988) Supreme Court Rules, and the relationship between the plaintiff's leave application and an application by a non-appearing defendant challenging jurisdiction under Part 11, r 8. Both decisions reflect an expansionist tendency. Neither can be considered to have left the law of New South Wales (or of Australia) in a particularly happy state.

In *Flaherty*, the plaintiff, a resident of New South Wales, was injured in a road traffic accident in Queensland, and was subsequently treated for her injuries in her home State. She brought proceedings in New South Wales against the defendant, a resident of Queensland, relying on the rule permitting service out of the jurisdiction 'where the proceedings are founded on, or are for the recovery of,

[86] Supreme Court Rules 1970 (2005 version) pt 10, rr 1A(1)(v) (foreign judgments) and (w) (proceedings relating to minors, corresponding to Uniform Civil Procedure Rules (2016 version) sch 6, paras (u) and (v).

Another provision within the 1970 Rules (r 1A(1)(j)) was removed in the version of the rules annexed to the Civil Procedure Act 2005 (NSW) following the repeal of the Service and Execution of Process Act 1901 (Cth), to which it referred.

[87] Supreme Court Rules (Amendment No 209) 1988, para 4(f). See now UCPR, r 11.4.

[88] Text to n 75 above. See now UCPR, r 12.11.

[89] Supreme Court Rules (Amendment No 209) 1988, para 4(i). See now UCPR, r 11.7.

[90] Established under pt 2, div 1 of the Civil Procedure Act 2005 (NSW). See text to n 45 above.

[91] A small adjustment to sch 6 was made by Uniform Civil Procedure Rules (Amendment No 1) 2005, sch 1, [66].

[92] *Flaherty v Girgis* (1985) 4 NSWLR 248.

[93] [2000] HCA 41, (2000) 201 CLR 552.

damage suffered wholly or partly in the State caused by a tortious act or omission wherever occurring'.[94] The Court of Appeal addressed three questions. First, a majority (Kirby P and Samuels JA; McHugh JA dissenting) held that there was no inconsistency between Part 10 and Commonwealth legislation in the form of the Service of Execution and Process Act 1901.[95] The ruling on this point was later affirmed by a majority of the High Court.[96] Secondly, the Court interpreted the relevant service out rule broadly as applying to a case in which some damage had occurred within the State, interpreting 'damage' as including 'all the detriment, physical, financial and social which the plaintiff suffers as a result of the tortious conduct of the defendant' and not being limited to damage directly suffered or necessary to complete the cause of action.[97] Thirdly, the Court rejected the submission that the rule, and the provision of the Supreme Court Act 1970 under which it was made, fell outside the class of 'laws for the peace, welfare and good government of New South Wales' authorised by s 5 of the Constitution Act of New South Wales[98] and that it was, in consequence, invalid. In the view of McHugh JA (with whom the other members of the Court agreed on this point) the necessary 'real connection with the State' required under s 5 was established by reason of the existence of a tortious liability arising under the law of New South Wales, including its choice of law rules, which the New South Wales courts had (subject-matter) jurisdiction to determine: in his view the service out rule 'does no more than provide machinery for permitting the Supreme Court upon proof of the cause of action to give judgment, in the absence of a defendant, in respect of a liability which has already arisen under the law of New South Wales'.[99]

This reasoning on this last point seems far from satisfactory, and may need to be revisited by the High Court in the future.[100] The service out rules, coupled with the rules empowering plaintiffs to proceed to judgment in default of appearance,

[94] Supreme Court Rules 1970, pt 10, r 1(1)(ee).

[95] *Cf* Service of Execution and Process Act 1992, s 8(4). The corresponding provisions in pt 11 and sch 6 of the UCPR now apply in terms only to service outside Australia (r 11.4(1)).

[96] (1987) 162 CLR 574 (Mason ACJ, Wilson and Dawson JJ; Brennan and Deane JJ dissenting).

[97] (1985) 4 NSWLR 248, 266 (McHugh JA), recently referred to with approval by Lady Hale (at [52]) and Lord Clarke (at [69]) in the UK Supreme Court in *Four Seasons Holdings v Brownlie* (n 84), but compare the approach of Lord Sumption, ibid, at [23]–[31]. See also the cases referred to by the editors of *Nygh's Conflict of Laws in Australia*, 9th edn (Sydney, LexisNexis, 2014) 60, fn 233–35.

[98] Act 32 of 1902. See also Australia Act 1986 (Cth) s 2.

[99] (1985) 4 NSWLR 248, 270. See also *Seymour-Smith v Electricity Trust of South Australia* (1989) 17 NSWLR 648. *Cf Gosper v Sawyer* (1985) 160 CLR 548, esp at 557–58 (Gibbs CJ, Wilson and Dawson JJ), 563–66 (Mason and Deane JJ); M Leeming, *Authority to Decide: The Law of Jurisdiction in Australia* (Sydney, The Federation Press, 2012) 2 ('the court must have *subject matter* jurisdiction and *personal* jurisdiction in order to have authority to decide any particular proceeding').

[100] See R Mortensen, R Garnett and M Keyes, *Private International Law in Australia*, 3rd edn (Sydney, LexisNexis, 2015), [2.72], reaching the same conclusion.

In *Dow Jones Inc v Gutnick* [2002] HCA 56, (2002) 10 CLR 575, [101], Kirby J (who had been a member of the NSWCA in *Flaherty*) noted a possible conflict between rules of this character and public international law, adding (fn 112) that no appeal on the point had been taken to the High Court in *Flaherty*.

extend the adjudicatory jurisdiction of the New South Wales Supreme Court over absent defendants. They are as much a component of the Court's adjudicatory jurisdiction as rules of subject-matter jurisdiction to which McHugh JA referred. Given that there are very few limits on the Court's subject-matter jurisdiction, the rules that control the Court's competence to proceed to determine the subject-matter of the dispute even if one of the parties does not appear are, in practice, much more important. Moreover, by its very nature, the Court's act of adjudication has a legal force in its own right, distinct from the alleged liability which gave rise to the proceedings. Accordingly, it is submitted, the Court of Appeal focused incorrectly on subject-matter jurisdiction and on the underlying liability recognised under New South Wales' choice of law rules, rather than upon the entire body of rules regulating adjudicatory jurisdiction and on the legal effects of adjudication. It should have asked itself whether there existed a real – even if remote and general – connection between the State of New South Wales and either the subject-matter of the asserted power to adjudicate or the defendant against whom that power would be exercised.[101]

In *Agar*, the plaintiffs, residents of New South Wales, had suffered serious spinal injuries during games of rugby union played within the State. They brought proceedings in the New South Wales Supreme Court against Australian and non-Australian members of the sport's international rule-making body, alleging that a duty of care had been owed to them in the framing of the rules relating to scrummaging. The non-Australian defendants, without entering an appearance in the proceedings, applied to set aside the originating process against them and sought declarations that the Court did not have or that it should not exercise jurisdiction. The plaintiff applied for leave to proceed against those defendants. Both applications were heard together, with fluctuating outcomes as the case proceeded: the defendants succeeded at first instance before Grove J,[102] and the plaintiffs before the Court of Appeal.[103] In the High Court, each side succeeded upon its own application, yielding overall victory for the defendants.

The central issue related to the merits of the claim in tort: none of the members of the High Court considered it to be arguable that the defendants owed the plaintiffs a duty of care.[104] The High Court, however, encountered greater difficulty in fitting that finding within the framework of the rules governing the Supreme Court's adjudicatory jurisdiction over absent defendants (contained, at that

[101] By contrast with *Flaherty* and *Seymour-Smith* (n 99), see *Cotter v Workman* (1972) 20 FLR 318; *Coppin v Tobler Bros Canberra Marine Centre Pty Ltd* (1980) 1 NSWLR 183; also E Campbell, *Rules of Court* (n 18) 70–79; *Club Resorts Ltd v Van Breda* [2012] 1 SCR 572 (Supreme Court of Canada), [75], [82], [86], [92], [95], [100] (LeBel J). See generally *Pearce v Florenca* (1976) 135 CLR 507; *Union Steamship Co of Australia Pty Ltd v King* (1988) 166 CLR 1.

[102] *Hyde v Agar* (1998) 45 NSWLR 487, 499–501.

[103] ibid 501–09.

[104] See *Agar v Hyde* (n 8) [92] (Gaudron, McHugh, Gummow and Hayne JJ).

time, principally within Part 10 of the Supreme Court Rules, following the 1988 amendments[105]).

The reasoning of the plurality on this aspect may be briefly summarised as follows:

1. It is necessary to pay close attention to the Rules, which differ in important respects from rules performing equivalent functions in other jurisdictions.[106] The starting point for enquiry should be the terms of the Rules, not any general considerations of comity and judicial restraint.[107]
2. The Rules depart from the model adopted in England, and formerly adopted in New South Wales (before 1988), in not requiring permission to be secured in advance to serve originating process outside Australia.[108] Instead, the Rules require that the plaintiff shall not proceed against a non-appearing defendant without the leave of the Court, while remaining silent about what matters can or should be taken into account in granting or refusing that leave.[109]
3. In deciding whether the Rules permit service outside Australia, attention must be directed to the way in which the plaintiff frames his claims: the reference to 'proceedings … founded on' particular matters focuses attention on the nature of the claim which is made. The question to be asked is: 'is the claim a claim in which the plaintiff *alleges* that he has a cause of action which, *according to those allegations*', fits within one of the classes of case referred to in the Rules?[110]
4. This inquiry neither requires nor permits an assessment of the strength of the plaintiff's claim. Once the claim is seen to be of the requisite kind, the proceeding falls within the class of cases in which service outside Australia is permitted and *prima facie* the plaintiff should be given leave to proceed if the defendant does not appear.[111]
5. Sometimes, the plaintiff's statement of case will not reveal all that it is necessary to know to determine whether the claim is of the requisite kind. For example, the place of making of a contract, or place of breach of a contract may not appear. In such a case, 'some evidence may be required' to establish that the case is one in which service outside Australia is permitted.[112]
6. No such evidence was, however, needed in the case before the Court: '[t]he claim … is framed in negligence and alleges that tortious acts or omissions caused the damage which the respondent suffered when injured in New South Wales'.[113]

[105] Text to nn 87–89 above.
[106] *Agar v Hyde* (n 8) [39].
[107] ibid [43].
[108] ibid [46]–[47].
[109] ibid [47].
[110] ibid [50] (emphasis in original).
[111] ibid [51]; also [54] ('[I]n the absence of some countervailing consideration, leave to proceed should then be given').
[112] ibid [52].
[113] ibid.

7. A wider range of matters may be raised upon a defendant's application to set aside originating process. Without seeking exhaustively to describe the matters that might be considered upon such an application, it will always be open to the defendant to assert (1) that the claims are not claims of a kind for which service outside Australia is permitted; (2) that the Court is an inappropriate forum for the trial of the proceedings, and (3) that the claims have insufficient prospects of success to warrant putting an overseas defendant to the time, expense and trouble of defending the claim.[114]
8. In addressing the claim's prospects of success, the same test should be applied to claims brought against Australian and non-Australian defendants and, however expressed, should require a high degree of certainty that the plaintiff would not succeed if the matter were to go to trial.[115]

The most problematic element of the reasoning in *Agar* is that concerning the evidential requirements for a plaintiff to bring his claim within the grounds for service outside Australia. Unless the defendant enters an appearance or applies successfully to set aside the originating process, that service (if valid) provides the foundation for the Court's adjudicatory jurisdiction. The plurality appears to commit to a view which treats as conclusive allegations of fact made within the plaintiff's statement of claim concerning matters relevant to the grounds for service out. Moreover, if the plaintiff's statement of claim is silent as to a particular matter of relevance, it appears that that plaintiff need only provide 'some evidence' of material facts referred to in those cases. The plurality acknowledges the possibility of a challenge to the basis for service out by the defendant, but does not suggest that it is open to the defendant to present countervailing evidence or for the Court to consider the strength of the plaintiff's allegations based on the evidence presented to it by both parties.

The apparent conclusion that the Court's adjudicatory jurisdiction may be founded upon an unchallengeable assertion by the party invoking that jurisdiction is surprising, and (if sustained) a potential cause of significant injustice to foreign defendants who will have no opportunity to contest the factual basis upon which the Court proceeds to judgment in default of appearance. It is difficult to reconcile with the High Court's reasoning in an earlier case,[116] upon which Callinan J relied in *Agar* as supporting his view that the existence of the conditions for the existence of jurisdiction should be tested by reference to the standard of a

[114] ibid [55].
[115] ibid [57], [60].
[116] *Contender 1 Ltd v Lep International Pty Ltd* (1988) 82 ALR 394, 396–97 (Wilson, Dawson, Toohey and Gaudron JJ), 399 (Brennan J). That case concerned the pre-1988 version of the Supreme Court Rules, under which the plaintiff was ordinarily expected to seek leave to serve out in advance. This procedural difference does not, it is suggested, make a difference to the point presently under discussion. Under the pre-1988 rules, the need for the Court to be satisfied that the case was one in which service out was authorised was also distinct from any examination of the merits of the claim (r 2(2)).

'strong argument for the opinion'.[117] It is, therefore, perhaps understandable that commentators and at least one judge have been reluctant to take the High Court's reasoning at face value. The learned editors of *Nygh* suggest that the High Court did not address the treatment of 'jurisdictional facts'[118] and advance what they describe as 'a respectable view' that such facts must be demonstrated at the outset and on the balance of probabilities.[119] More recently, Robb J concluded, spiritedly but unconvincingly, that the High Court in *Agar* had not disturbed the reasoning of the New South Wales Court of Appeal on this point, and that a 'good arguable case' was required.[120]

Whether one takes the statements in *Agar* at face value or not, it is surely a cause for criticism of the current Australian law that the position on so fundamental a point as the burden and standard of proof for establishing the Court's adjudicatory jurisdiction remains unsettled almost half a century after the Supreme Court Rules were adopted. That uncertainty may, however, be seen as a symptom of a disease that affects all legal systems that treat service on a foreign defendant as a gateway to establishing jurisdiction.[121]

# III. The 2016 Reforms

## A. Introduction

Against this background, it is necessary to consider the changes to Part 11 and sch 6 of the New South Wales' UCPR made by the Uniform Rules Committee through the Uniform Civil Procedure (Amendment No 83) Rule 2016 (the Amendment Rule).[122]

As noted, these changes were made to give effect to harmonised rules approved by the Council of Chief Justices of Australia and New Zealand. The Council, which has no legislative functions, traces its origins to a conference of the

[117] *Agar v Hyde* (n 8) [116]. See also ibid [8], where Gleeson CJ endorses the test of a 'good arguable case' favoured by the New South Wales Court of Appeal in *Agar*.

[118] But *cf* ibid [50]–[52], [54] (Gaudron, McHugh, Gummow and Hayne JJ).

[119] *Nygh's Conflict of Laws in Australia* (n 97) 45, fn 121. The editors of Mortensen, Garnett and Keyes, *Private International Law in Australia* (n 100) [2.42]) contrast the approach formerly taken in Victoria (*Schib Packaging Srl v Emrich Industries Pty Ltd* (2005) 12 VR 268), favouring a test of 'strongly arguable case' without expressing a view. See now *Madden International Ltd v Lew Footwear Holdings Pty Ltd* [2015] VSCA 90, in which the courts of Victoria fell into line with *Agar v Hyde*.

[120] *Benson v Rational Entertainment Expenses Ltd* [2015] NSWSC 906, [94]–[118]. His Honour appears to have taken the view (at [108], [105]) that the plurality did not address this point, and to have regarded the endorsement by Gleeson CJ of the NSWCA's position (n 117), and the similar reasoning of Callinan J (text to n 117), as of greater significance.

[121] For an account of the malady within the English legal system, see *Four Seasons Holdings Inc v Brownlie* (n 84), noted A Dickinson [2018] *Lloyd's Maritime and Commercial Law Quarterly* 190 and A Briggs [2018] *Lloyd's Maritime and Commercial Law Quarterly* 196.

[122] (n 20).

Chief Justices of the Australian States in 1962.[123] Among its activities, the Council has established a Harmonisation of Rules Committee, which 'works on harmonisation of court rules and practice in particular areas according to referrals from the [Council]'.[124]

The membership of the Council consists of the Chief Justices of the High Court, the Federal Court of Australia, the Family Court of Australia, the Supreme Court of New Zealand and the Supreme Courts of the Australian States and Territories. At the time of adoption of the recommendation under discussion, the Harmonisation of Rules Committee comprised 13 judicial members (two from New South Wales and Victoria and one from each of the Australian courts represented other than the High Court, and a representative of the New Zealand High Court), an academic member[125] and a secretary.

## B. Background to the Recommendation of the Council of Chief Justices

The possible harmonisation of Australian service out rules was first mooted by the Harmonisation of Rules Committee in 2007, as part of a wider consideration of overseas service in light of Australia's possible accession to the Hague Service Convention.[126] Although some work was carried out in the period from 2009, fresh impetus was given to the Committee's work in 2012 by Chief Justice Spiegelman, the then Chief Justice of New South Wales. He wrote to his fellow members of the Council of Chief Justices, urging them to ask the Committee to address the many divergences between Australia's legal systems.[127] That correspondence having been passed on by Chief Justice French, the Committee discussed the matter in March 2012. The member from New Zealand offered to provide information concerning the reforms undertaken relatively recently in that jurisdiction,[128] and the academic member agreed to provide an analysis of the current position in Australia's legal

[123] R French, 'The State of the Australian Judicature' (2017) 13 *The Judicial Review* 153, 154.

[124] ibid 155.

[125] Professor Gregory Reinhardt, Australian Institute of Judicial Administration and Monash University.

[126] In March 2008, the Standing Committee of Attorneys-General specifically requested the Harmonisation of Rules Committee to develop model rules of court to implement the Hague Convention (see www.nswbar.asn.au/circulars/scag.pdf, 6). In New South Wales, a new pt 11A of the UCPR was adopted in 2009, giving effect to the uniform rules developed by the Harmonisation Committee (see Uniform Civil Procedure Rules (Amendment No 27) 2009 (NSW), 2009 No 326.

[127] See also A Dickinson, 'The Future of Private International Law in Australia' (2012) 19 *Australian International Law Journal* 1, 6–10; J Allsop and D Ward, 'Incoherence in Australian Private International Laws' and A Bell, 'Rationalisation and Rationale: Approaching the Reform of Rules for the Assertion of Jurisdiction over Foreign Defendants', chs 3 and 4 in A Dickinson, M Keyes and T John, *Australian Private International Law for the 21st Century* (Oxford, Hart Publishing, 2014).

[128] Judicature Act 1908 (NZ) sch 2, pt 6, sub-pt 4, as substituted by the Judicature (High Court Rules) Amendment Act 2008 (NZ). See now High Court Rules 2016 (NZ) pt 6, sub-pt 4.

systems. Thereafter, the Committee reported to the Council in advance of the latter's August 2012 meeting that:[129]

> The Committee considered the recently revised New Zealand Rules (rules 6.27 and 6.28 of the High Court Rules 2009, 2nd Schedule to the Judicature Act 1908). Those rules are comprehensive, covering most areas designated in the rules of other jurisdictions and are drawn widely enough to provide for any absence of jurisdiction. So far there has been general consensus for accepting the proposal that the New Zealand Rules be the basis for model rules.

The Committee discussed the matter again at a meeting in November 2012. At that stage, it had before it (in addition to material from New Zealand) the academic analysis of the current Australian rules and comments from several judges, including a draft by Justice Rein (NSW Supreme Court) of possible rules based upon the New Zealand model. The Committee agreed to use Justice Rein's proposal as the starting point for its drafting efforts. It was also agreed that the Federal Court would instruct Parliamentary Counsel to draft amendments to the Federal Court Rules along the lines set out in that proposal.

The latter process, and concerns arising from the operation of the then prevailing rules, led to further delays in the Committee's work. It was not until June 2015 that the Committee agreed to establish a working group consisting of Justices Cavanough (Victoria), Brereton and Rein (NSW) and Blue (South Australia) to take the proposal forward. The working group prepared a draft for the Committee's consideration at a meeting in November 2015. At that meeting, the Committee made a number of small changes to the draft, which it agreed to recommend to the Council. The Committee reported to the Council in advance of its April 2016 meeting attaching a draft of the rules and a draft explanatory memorandum. The Council approved the rules and explanatory memorandum at that meeting. The explanatory memorandum records that:

> The Service out of Australia Harmonised Rules are modelled on the relevant provisions of the New Zealand High Court Rules[130] ... The New Zealand Rules on overseas service were chosen because they were the most recently revised of the relevant rules of the jurisdictions represented on the Harmonisation Committee.

## C. Adoption of the Rules in New South Wales

In September 2016, Justice Rein wrote to the Secretary of New South Wales' Uniform Rules Committee attaching a copy of the text of the rules approved by the Council, with the explanatory memorandum, and requesting that the rules

[129] This extract and other information in this section relating to the work of the Harmonisation of Rules Committee were kindly provided by John Mathieson, Secretary to the Committee.

[130] The memorandum refers at this point to the Rules scheduled to the Judicature Act 2008 (NZ). See now High Court Rules 2016 (NZ) pt 6, sub-pt 4.

be considered at the Committee's next meeting, to be held on 7 November 2016. The full minute on this agenda item states as follows:[131]

> The proposed change was put forth by Justice Rein to take into consideration changes made by the Harmonisation Committee that had been approved by the Council of Chief Justices and that were now ready for promulgation in each State in respect of Service Outside of Jurisdiction.
>
> No issues were raised by the committee and it was agreed that the rules should be adopted and a draft amendment should be obtained from Parliamentary Counsel.

A draft of the proposed Amendment Rule was circulated to members of the Uniform Rules Committee in advance of its next meeting, on 5 December 2016, and approved on that occasion. The Amendment Rule was published in the Gazette on 9 December 2016, and entered into force on that date.

## D. Key Features of the 2016 Reforms

For present purposes, the following features of the new Part 11 and sch 6 are to be noted:[132]

1. The introduction of a new rule (r 11.5) authorising service of originating process out of the jurisdiction with the prior leave of the Court in cases not provided for under the newly formulated sch 6 (read together with the new r 11.4), provided that the Court is 'satisfied' that (a) the claim has a real and substantial connection with Australia,[133] (b) Australia is an appropriate forum for the trial, and (c) in all the circumstances the court should assume jurisdiction.[134]
2. The new r 11.6, entitled 'Court's discretion whether to assume jurisdiction' and modelled in part on the former r 11.7, gives the Court a wide discretion to dismiss or stay the proceeding or set aside the originating process on the defendant's application, including (r 11.6(2)) on the three grounds identified by the High Court of Australia in *Agar v Hyde* (service not authorised; inappropriate forum; insufficient prospects of success).[135]
3. A continuing requirement (now r 11.8AA) in all cases to obtain leave to proceed from the Court if the defendant does not enter an appearance.

[131] This minute and other documentation referred to under this heading were kindly provided by Rebel Kenna, Secretary to the Uniform Rules Committee.

[132] For a more detailed commentary, with a valuable table of comparisons to the former Rules, see Douglas and Bath, 'A New Approach to Service Outside the Jurisdiction and Outside Australia under the Uniform Civil Procedure Rules' (n 19).

[133] Not New South Wales (see section III.E(ii)(c) below).

[134] UCPR, r 11.5(5). Under r 11.5(4), an application for leave must be supported by an affidavit 'stating any facts or matters related to the desirability of the court assuming jurisdiction, including the place or country in which the person to be served is or possibly may be found, and whether or not the person to be served is an Australian citizen'.

[135] Text to n 114 above.

4. A significant re-working of the grounds for service out in the revised sch 6, reducing the overall number of grounds from 23 to 19, but in terms which extend their overall scope significantly.[136] The most striking (or alarming) feature of this new regime is that the connecting factors in the sub-paragraphs of sch 6 (and the new r 11.5[137]) now refer to 'Australia', 'Australian law' and 'an Australian court' rather than 'New South Wales', 'New South Wales law' and 'New South Wales court'. For example, the new sub-para (b) concerning contractual matters provides that originating process may be served out of Australia:[138]

> when the claim is for the enforcement, rescission, dissolution, annulment, cancellation, rectification, interpretation or other treatment of, or for damages or other relief in respect of a breach of, a contract which:
>
> (i) was made or entered into in *Australia*, or
> (ii) was made by or through an agent trading or residing within *Australia*, or
> (iii) was to be wholly or in part performed in *Australia*, or
> (iv) was by its terms or by implication to be governed by *Australian law* or to be enforceable or cognizable in an *Australian court*

## E. Appraisal of the 2016 Reforms

### *i. Legislative Processes*

The circumstances leading to the adoption of the Amendment Rule raise a number of concerns of a procedural character. Before outlining these, however, it is important to emphasise that the following statements are not to be understood as criticisms of the individuals involved in the processes, who at all times appear to have acted in accordance with established frameworks and in the pursuit of a goal, the harmonisation of an important element of Australian rules of adjudicatory

[136] In terms of subject-matter (putting to one side the required territorial connection, discussed below), sub-para (a) (tort) in the new Sch 6 merges and extends old sub-paras (e) and (f). New sub-paras (b) and (c) (contract) merge and extend old sub-paras (b) and (c). New sub-para (d) (injunctions and interim relief) extends old sub-para (n). New sub-para (e) (land and property) merges old sub-paras (j), (k) and (m). New sub-para (f) (trusts) replaces old-sub-para (p), but now applies only to trusts of written instruments of which the person served is a trustee. New sub-para (g) (domicile etc) extends old sub-para (g). New sub-para (h) (necessary or proper party) merges and extends old sub-paras (f) and (i). New sub-para (i) (administration of estates) replaces old sub-para (o). New sub-paras (j) and (p) (statutory claims) in combination replace old sub-paras (l), (r) and (s). New sub-para (k) (submission to the jurisdiction) replaces old sub-para (h), but (in excluding reference to an agreement to submit) is arguably narrower. New sub-para (l) (restitution and constructive trusts) has no direct counterpart. New sub-para (m) (judgments) extends old sub-para (u). New sub-para (n) (causes of action generally) replaces old sub-para (a). New sub-para (o) (membership of corporate bodies) replaces old sub-para (q)). New sub-paras (q) (arbitration), (r) (proceedings relating to minors) and (s) (multiple subject-matters) replace old sub-paras (t), (v) and (w) respectively.

[137] Text to n 133.

[138] Emphasis in italics added.

jurisdiction, identified as beneficial to the legal system of New South Wales and other legal systems within Australia.

1. The opening section of this chapter identified a concern that rules of court made by committees dominated by members of the judiciary are not a suitable vehicle for the adoption of rules of adjudicatory jurisdiction. To the extent that the Amendment Rule was adopted by the Uniform Rules Committee,[139] that concern applies here. In the present case, however, a further concern arises insofar as the guiding force behind the reforms was evidently the Council of Chief Justices and its Harmonisation of Rules Committee, bodies with no statutory rule-making power in New South Wales or elsewhere in Australia.

   As the minute of the Uniform Rules Committee records,[140] the proposals were presented by Justice Rein (not a member of that Committee) and adopted by the Uniform Rules Committee without any issues being raised. Although the author does not profess expertise in Australian public law, a question at least presents itself as to whether this was a valid exercise of the rule-making power vested in the Committee under s 9 of the Civil Procedure Act 2005, ie whether it applied an independent mind to the exercise or simply 'rubber stamped' the recommendation from the Council.[141]
2. Even if the exercise of the power were technically valid, an onlooker might still entertain doubts as to whether it is appropriate for non-statutory, self-appointed bodies to wield so great an influence in the legislative process, however experienced and eminent their members might be.
3. The above concerns are heightened by the lack of information publicly available concerning the activities of the Council of Chief Justices and the Harmonisation of Rules Committee in this field. At the time of writing, more than two years after the adoption of the Council of Chief Justice's recommendation and over a year after the adoption of the Amendment Rule, the text of the Council's recommendation and the accompanying explanatory memorandum are not available on its website[142] or, so far as the present author has been able to determine, anywhere else in the public domain.[143] The Council and its Harmonisation of Rules Committee do not conduct their proceedings in public, the minutes of their meetings are not in the public domain

[139] Text to n 45.

[140] Text to n 131.

[141] *Telstra Corp v Optus Vision Pty* (2000) 105 FCR 322, [337] (Wilcox J).

[142] The website of the Council (www.ccjanz.gov.au) consists of a single, publicly accessible page with the statement that: 'Outputs, including proposed Court Rules, of the Council of Chief Justice's Harmonisation of Rules Committee will be published here shortly'.

[143] A copy was provided to the author, on request, together with other information concerning the activities of the Harmonisation of Rules Committee. That is not sufficient to put those documents in the public domain, or to render the activities of the Committee and the Council fully transparent.

(and have not been disclosed), and the membership of the Committee is not widely publicised.

4. Moreover, it does not appear that either the Harmonisation of Rules Committee or the New South Wales' Uniform Rules Committee published its proposals before their adoption, or undertook any formal process of consultation with practitioners, academics, businesses, consumer and other representative organisations, or governmental bodies (at State or Commonwealth level).
5. Finally, although the Amendment Rule was published in the NSW Government Gazette (a necessary prerequisite to its legislative force, with immediate effect[144]), its contents were not widely publicised in advance of or following that publication. The changes took many practitioners and academics working in the field by surprise.

It is instructive to compare the legislative processes followed in the reform of the Australian rules of adjudicatory jurisdiction with those adopted by the European Union at the time of its most recent review of the Union legislation (Brussels I Regulation) dealing with questions of the jurisdiction of Member State courts and recognition and enforcement of judgments between the Member States' legal systems.[145] In that case, the Commission first published (in 2009) a Green Paper setting out what it regarded as the key elements of a possible reform act, inviting 'all interested persons' to submit comments.[146] Having considered the responses to that consultation, the Commission published (in 2010) a legislative proposal.[147] Both documents appeared immediately on the Commission's website and were widely advertised. The proposal was considered concurrently by the European Parliament, advised by a number of its working groups, and by the Council of Ministers, advised by its civil justice working group, in accordance with the legislative procedures laid down in the EU Treaties. The European Parliament's working groups held a number of public meetings and events to solicit the views of practitioners, academics and other interested parties upon the proposal. The Council's working group comprised experts from the Member States. Throughout the process, key documents were released into the public domain, and available on the European Union's websites. After the adoption of the Regulation, a large volume of documentation relating to the legislative process was released in accordance with the Union's rules governing access to documentation.[148] The Regulation was published in the Union's Official Journal and entered into full effect more than two years after that publication, giving businesses and legal practitioners in

[144] Interpretation Act 1987 (NSW) s 39.

[145] Regulation (EU) No 1215/2012 of the European Parliament and of the Council of 12 December 2012 on jurisdiction and the recognition and enforcement of judgments in civil and commercial matters (recast) [2012] OJ L351/1 (Brussels I Regulation).

[146] COM (2009) 175 final.

[147] COM (2010) 748 final.

[148] Regulation (EC) No 1049/2001 regarding public access to European Parliament, Council and Commission documents [2001] OJ L145/43.

particular time to adjust.[149] All these steps, it is submitted, amount to good legislative practice, but they appear to have no place in the practice of the Australian rule-making bodies in this case.

## *ii. Content*

In light of the above concerns, it is all the more important that the substance of the Amendment Rule, and the recommendation of the Council of Chief Justices which led to it, should be carefully examined. The remainder of this chapter focuses on three aspects of the reforms. First, the question (addressed with respect to the former Supreme Court Rules in *Agar v Hyde*) of the evidential requirements for a plaintiff to bring his claim within the grounds for service outside Australia.[150] Secondly, the elements of the new supplemental rule (r 11.5) allowing originating process to be served outside Australia with the prior leave of the Court in a case falling outside those provided for in sch 6.[151] Thirdly, the extension of the connecting factors to support the existence of adjudicatory jurisdiction based upon connections to Australia, Australian law or Australian courts even in the absence of a connection to New South Wales, New South Wales' law or New South Wales courts.[152]

### a. The Evidential Requirement

It is regrettable, in light of the doubts that have arisen as to the status and precise effect of the reasoning of the plurality in *Agar v Hyde*,[153] that the new rules do not expressly address questions concerning the evidential basis of adjudicatory jurisdiction.

That omission is all the more unfortunate, given that r 11.5(5) requires that the Court be 'satisfied' of the matters set out in the following three subparagraphs before granting leave to serve out. That wording, and the evaluative nature of the enquiries called for, support the conclusion that it will not suffice under this sub-rule for the plaintiff simply to allege in his statement of claim facts and matters that suggest a real and substantial connection with Australia under r 11.5(5)(a).[154] If that is the correct understanding, one might wonder whether a different, less onerous requirement should continue to apply to a case in which the plaintiff asserts the power to serve originating process out of the jurisdiction without leave (r 11.4) and then seeks leave to proceed (r 11.8AA).

[149] Brussels I Regulation, art 81.
[150] Text to nn 107–21.
[151] UCPR, r 11.5(5) (see text to nn 132–33).
[152] Text to nn 137–38.
[153] Text to nn 116–20.
[154] See *Agar v Hyde* (n 8) [108] (Callinan J), referring to *Vitkovice Horni a Hutni Tezirstvo v Korner* [1951] AC 869.

Why should an absent defendant be less well protected for claims falling within sch 6 than claims falling outside it?

The omission appears is even more perplexing once it is realised that the Harmonisation of Rules Committee directed its mind to the point, and rejected any qualification or narrowing of the approach taken by the plurality in *Agar*. The explanatory memorandum accompanying the Council of Chief Justices' recommendation contains the following statement:[155]

> Rule X.02 enables service out of Australia if one of 18[156] paragraphs of the Rules … is satisfied. …
>
> In broad terms, the criteria involve particular types of connection between the claim *as pleaded* and Australia. Accordingly, it is anticipated that generally speaking the principles stated in *Agar v Hyde*[157] and *Madden International v Lew Footwear Holdings Ltd*[158] will apply.

The explanatory memorandum was before the Uniform Rules Committee when it resolved to act upon the Council of Chief Justices' recommendation.[159] It is nonetheless doubtful whether this document, which is not referred to in the Amendment Rule and is not in the public domain, may be relied on as an aid to construction of the rule. It is hoped that the High Court will take the earliest opportunity to consider this question, and to revisit the decision in *Agar v Hyde*.

### b. The Elements of the New Prior Leave Rule

The three requirements in r 11.5(5) must be examined separately, although there will inevitably be a degree of overlap between the enquiries. As to the requirement in r 11.5(5)(a) that the Court be satisfied that 'the claim has a real and substantial connection with Australia',[160] it is to be noted that the required connection is with the 'claim'[161] and not with the dispute or with the proceedings. This, therefore, is a different enquiry from that undertaken by courts in England, New Zealand and elsewhere (but not in Australia) to identify the 'natural forum' for a dispute, ie 'that with which the action has the most real and substantial connection',[162] and the two should not be confused or conflated.[163]

[155] Emphasis as original. See Paul Le Gay Brereton, ch 13, text to n 12–13.

[156] There are, in fact, 19 sub-paragraphs.

[157] (n 8).

[158] (n 119).

[159] Section III.C.

[160] As to the reference to Australia, see section III.E(ii)(c) below.

[161] The approach of the High Court in *Agar v Hyde* suggests that 'claim' should be understood as referring to each cause of action pleaded by the plaintiff individually, but *cf Club Resorts v Van Breda* (n 11) [99], focusing on 'the factual and legal situation' giving rise to the claim (Le Bel J).

[162] *Spiliada Maritime Corp v Cansulex Ltd* [1987] AC 460, 478 (Lord Goff, UKHL). *Cf Voth v Manildra Flour Mills Pty Ltd* (1990) 171 CLR 538, 558 (Mason CJ, Deane J, Dawson J, Gaudron J).

[163] This is a temptation to which the New Zealand courts have on occasion yielded (see eg *Exportrade Corp v Irie Blue New Zealand Ltd* [2013] NZCA 675, [31], [46]–[50]).

The Supreme Court of Canada has strongly emphasised the concept of a 'real and substantial connection' as being fundamental to understanding and defining the limits of the adjudicatory jurisdiction of Canadian courts.[164] The Supreme Court was, nevertheless, not content to leave that term undefined. As LeBel J noted:[165]

> The real and substantial connection test is now well established. However, it is clear that dissatisfaction with it and uncertainty about its meaning and conditions of application have been growing, and that there is now a perceived need for greater direction on how it applies. …
>
> Judicial discretion has an honourable history, and the proper operation of our legal system often depends on its being exercised wisely. Nevertheless, to rely completely on it to flesh out the real and substantial connection test in such a way that the test itself becomes a conflicts rule would be incompatible with certain key objectives of a private international law system. …
>
> Given the nature of the relationships governed by private international law, the framework for the assumption of jurisdiction cannot be an unstable, ad hoc system made up 'on the fly' on a case-by-case basis – however laudable the objective of individual fairness may be. … Justice and fairness are undoubtedly essential purposes of a sound system of private international law. But they cannot be attained without a system of principles and rules that ensures security and predictability in the law governing the assumption of jurisdiction by a court.

To address these concerns, the Supreme Court emphasised the need to develop, over time, a list of objective connecting factors linking particular legal situations to the court seised.[166] Those factors (labelled as 'presumptive connecting factors') were not to be absolute or unchallengeable, and might be argued to be inappropriate as a basis for establishing jurisdiction in the circumstances of a particular case.[167]

It remains to be seen whether the Australian courts will develop similar guidelines, or whether they be content to deal with the matter in individual cases 'on the fly'.[168]

Next, r 11.5(5)(b) requires that the Court be satisfied that 'Australia is an appropriate forum for the trial'.[169] This provision may be contrasted with the corresponding provision in the New Zealand High Court Rules, which refers to New Zealand being 'the appropriate forum for the trial'.[170] The difference, of course, can be traced to Australia's singular approach to the *forum conveniens*

[164] *Club Resorts v Van Breda* (n 11).
[165] ibid [67], [70], [73].
[166] ibid [75], [82]–[94].
[167] ibid [76], [95]–[100].
[168] There appears to be no inclination, as yet, among the New Zealand judiciary to elaborate upon the requirement of a 'real and substantial connection with New Zealand' in r 6.28(5)(a) of the New Zealand High Court Rules (see *Exportrade Corp v Irie Blue* (n 163)).
[169] As to the reference to Australia, rather than New South Wales, see section III.E(ii)(c) below.
[170] New Zealand High Court Rules 2016, r 6.28(5)(c).

doctrine, by its adoption of a 'clearly inappropriate forum' test focused on the suitability of the Australian court rather than a 'clearly more appropriate' test (as applied by the courts of England, New Zealand and elsewhere) requiring a comparison of the suitability of the forum court and a suggested alternative, available forum.[171] For these purposes, the adjective 'appropriate' appears to be the obverse of 'inappropriate' (or 'clearly inappropriate')[172] and the same considerations should guide the enquiry as to whether the local forum is 'appropriate' as guide the enquiry under what is now r 11.6(2)(b) as to whether it is 'inappropriate'.[173] The onus will nevertheless be upon the plaintiff to prove facts and matters which justify the conclusion that it is appropriate (ie not clearly inappropriate[174]) to bring proceedings in Australia.

It is, nonetheless, unclear why this requirement has been introduced as an element of the enquiry at the leave stage when the Harmonisation of Rules Committee was otherwise content to follow the approach of the High Court in *Agar v Hyde*.[175] The High Court in that case ruled that questions concerning the appropriateness of the Australian forum (as well as merits issues[176]) were to be dealt with at the stage of considering a defendant's forum application, and not as an element within the leave to proceed enquiry.[177] Requiring the plaintiff to address questions of the appropriateness of the Australian forum at this stage, when the ultimate shape of the trial will likely be hazy at best, introduces an unnecessary element of complication and duplication into the process. The precise relationship between r 11.5(5)(b), which refers to the appropriateness of 'Australia' as a forum, and r 11.6(2)(b), which refers to the inappropriateness of 'the court' as a forum, is also unclear, and will need to be examined.

Finally, r 11.5(5)(c) requires that the Court be satisfied that 'in all the circumstances the court should assume jurisdiction'. It is not immediately obvious on first reading what this requirement adds to the first two sub-paragraphs, considered above. With respect to the equivalent provision in the New Zealand High Court Rules (r 6.28(5)(d)), the New Zealand Court of Appeal commented, unhelpfully, that:[178]

> This serves to emphasise that the assumption of jurisdiction ultimately involves an evaluation of a range of considerations which are very much fact dependent.

[171] *Voth v Manildra Flour Mills* (n 162). *cf Spiliada Maritime v Cansulex* (n 162).

[172] *Regie Nationale des Usines Renault v Zhang* (2002) 210 CLR 491, [25] (Gleeson CJ, Gaudron, McHugh, Gummow and Hayne JJ).

[173] Douglas and Bath (n 19), 169–70 are also of this view.

[174] *CSR Ltd v Cigna Insurance Australia Ltd* (1997) 189 CLR 345, 397 (Dawson, Toohey, Gaudron, McHugh, Gummow and Kirby JJ).

[175] Text to n 155.

[176] Note that, consistently with *Agar v Hyde*, r 11.5, unlike its New Zealand counterpart (r 6.28(5)(d)) does not require the plaintiff to satisfy the court that 'there is a serious issue to be tried on the merits'.

[177] Text to n 114.

[178] *Wing Hung Printing Co Ltd v Saito Offshore Pty Ltd* [2010] NZCA 502, [2011] 1 NZLR 754, [47].

Nevertheless, the broad formulation of sub-para (b), considered above, may suggest a useful function for sub-para (c).[179] The former refers to 'Australia' (not New South Wales) being an appropriate forum for the trial. This opens up the possibility that the New South Wales court is not itself an appropriate forum or that another court in Australia has a stronger claim to take the case forward to trial. In such a case, the New South Wales court considering an application under r 11.5 may conclude that the circumstances are such that (if service were allowed, leading to the claim becoming pending) it would likely be required to transfer the proceedings under the provisions of s 5 of the Jurisdiction of Courts (Cross-Vesting) Act 1987 (NSW) or, in cases to which that section does not apply, that an application by the defendant for a stay under s 20 of the Service and Execution of Process Act 1992 (Cth) would likely be successful.[180] If so, the appropriate course would be to refuse leave on the ground that the requirements of this sub-paragraph are not satisfied.

### c. The Nature of the Connections Required

Upon first reading of the new sch 6, one is left with the impression that something has gone wrong: that the quest for harmonisation has been taken too far and that the separate identity and territorial jurisdiction of the legal systems within the Commonwealth of Australia has been overlooked. One might, for example, contrast the EU's Brussels I Regulation,[181] which substantially harmonises the rules of jurisdiction to be applied by Member State courts in determining disputes in civil and commercial matters but uses connecting factors that refer to a particular Member State. The United Kingdom legislation implementing the Regulation, which allocates the jurisdiction granted to the United Kingdom courts between its legal systems, also uses connecting factors which refer to a particular part of the United Kingdom.[182] One may also contrast the recent reform of the service out rules in the Australian Capital Territory which, although for the most part in line with the Council's harmonised rules, relies on connections to the ACT, and not to Australia.[183]

A few examples may serve to illustrate the startling consequences of this jurisdictional excess: under the newly formulated sch 6, the New South Wales courts have the power to adjudicate a claim brought by a Japanese tourist against a German bus driver arising from a road traffic accident in Perth (or for which medical

[179] Note also r 11.5(4), which requires the plaintiff's affidavit to state 'any facts or matters related to the desirability of the court assuming jurisdiction, including the place or country in which the person to be served is or possibly may be found, and whether or not the person to be served is an Australian citizen'. It is unclear what relevance, if any, these facts have to the enquiry under r 11.5(5)(c).

[180] See also Trans-Tasman Proceedings Act 2010, s 17.

[181] (n 148).

[182] Civil Jurisdiction and Judgments Act 1982, s 16 and sch 4.

[183] Court Procedures Rules 2006 (ACT) rr 6502 and 6503.

treatment was received by the tourist on arriving in Perth);[184] a claim brought by a Korean company against an Argentinian company arising from a contract which was partly to be performed in Darwin,[185] or a claim by an Indonesian citizen against an individual domiciled in Queensland (but resident in Bali) arising from conduct in a Balinese nightclub.[186]

It is no comfort that the New South Wales court would be a clearly inappropriate forum for the determination of these disputes, for that question could only be considered upon an application made by the defendant in accordance with r 11.6, requiring the defendant to take the time to instruct legal counsel and to incur significant expense to avoid a default judgment upon a claim that has absolutely nothing to do with New South Wales. It is also of little comfort to note the potential existence of an obligation on the part of the Supreme Court to transfer the proceedings to another Australian court under the cross-vesting legislation.[187] The existence of adjudicatory jurisdiction is one thing, its exercise another.[188] Moreover, in many cases (such as the second or third examples above), no Australian court will be an appropriate forum: it seems far from obvious that it is in the 'interests of justice'[189] to transfer proceedings from one Australian court to another as the venue for a challenge by the defendant to the latter court's jurisdiction on clearly inappropriate forum grounds. Finally, the cross-vesting legislation only facilitates transfer between Supreme Courts. For inferior courts, s 20 of the Service of Execution and Process Act 1992 (Cth) enables the defendant to seek a stay if a court of another State or Territory is 'the appropriate court' to determine 'all the matters in issue between the parties'. That may not be the case, as the above examples show.

It is, however, clear that the result was intended by the Harmonisation of Rules Committee. In a letter to Justice Nye Perram, the Committee's convener, the members of the sub-committee charged with the task of drafting the rules stated:[190]

> The subcommittee agrees that the references within the paragraphs to a place should be to Australia and not to an individual State or Territory of whose Rules the rules form part. This is because State and Territory courts now have Australia wide jurisdiction pursuant to section 4 of the uniform Jurisdiction of Courts (Cross Vesting) Acts. The real issue will be a potential contest between the action being heard and determined in Australia as opposed to another country. If it should be heard and determined in Australia, the question which Court in which State or Territory or the Federal Court should hear and determine the matter is best addressed under section 5 of the Jurisdiction of Courts (Cross Vesting) Act.

[184] UCPR, sch 6, sub-para (a)(i) (or (ii)).

[185] UCPR, sch 6, sub-para (b)(iii).

[186] UCPR, sch 6, sub-para (g).

[187] (n 180).

[188] *Club Resorts v Van Breda* (n 11) [101] (Le Bel J: '*Forum non conveniens* comes into play when jurisdiction is established. It has no relevance to the jurisdictional analysis itself.').

[189] Jurisdiction of Courts (Cross-Vesting) Act 1987 (NSW) s 5(2).

[190] Letter of 15 October 2015 (extract kindly provided by John Mathieson, Secretary to the Harmonisation of Rules Committee).

This reasoning is troubling, to say the least. It does not engage at all with the conflict of authority on the question whether the provisions of the cross-vesting legislation are concerned only with subject-matter jurisdiction or extend to the jurisdiction to adjudicate with respect to particular persons. In *David Syme & Co Ltd v Grey*,[191] the Federal Court (Neaves, Gummow and Higgins JJ) held that the provisions of the cross-vesting legislation were concerned with the cross-vesting of subject-matter jurisdiction, not what was described as 'personal jurisdiction'.[192]

Gummow J expressed the same opinion in the High Court in *BHP Billiton Ltd v Schultz*.[193] The opposite view had been taken by Rogers CJ of the New South Wales Supreme Court in *Seymour-Smith v Electricity Trust of South Australia*,[194] but Gummow J in *David Syme* rejected the submission founded on that decision for reasons which, it is submitted, are compelling. The two leading Australian works on private international law concur with him.[195]

Secondly, the sub-committee's reasoning disregards limits on the cross-vesting of jurisdiction, such as those contained in s 4(4) of the NSW cross-vesting legislation and the exclusion of State jurisdiction below Supreme Court level.

Thirdly, the sub-committee's cross-vesting argument, if accepted, renders the cross-vested forum's rules of adjudicatory jurisdiction (including, in New South Wales, the Amendment Rule) irrelevant.

Finally, the argument appears to rest on an assumption (demonstrably false both at the time of adoption of the Amendment Rule and today) that all of Australia's legal systems will subscribe to a common set of rules of adjudicatory jurisdiction. The proposition, for example, that a New South Wales court has jurisdiction to determine a tort claim on the basis that some damage has occurred in Western Australia[196] because it has been cross-vested with the adjudicatory jurisdiction of the Western Australian Supreme Court is manifestly false on any view of the effect of the cross-vesting legislation, as the latter court does not claim such jurisdiction.[197]

If the sub-committee's supposed justification for the extension of jurisdiction of the New South Wales Supreme Court to situations connected to Australia but not to the State disappears, the question of constitutional validity considered by the New South Wales Court of Appeal in *Flaherty v Girgis*[198] re-emerges. The Court of Appeal's reasoning would, of course, be equally favourable to the Amendment Rule. The doubts expressed above as to the correctness of that reasoning might put

[191] *David Syme & Co Ltd v Grey* (1992) 38 FCR 303.

[192] ibid 310 (Neaves J), 331–33 (Gummow J), 348 (Higgins J).

[193] [2004] HCA 61, (2004) 221 CLR 400, [44]–[45], with the agreement of Hayne J (at [177]).

[194] (1989) 17 NSWLR 640.

[195] Mortensen, Garnett and Keyes (n 100) [2.31]–[2.34]; Nygh (n 97) [6.11] fn 17.

[196] UCPR, sch 6, sub-para (a)(ii).

[197] *Cf* Rules of the Supreme Court 1971 (WA) ord 10, r 1(1)(k), referring only to a 'tort committed within the jurisdiction'.

[198] Text to nn 98–101.

the question back in the balance if the matter were to be raised before the High Court.

Putting the constitutional question to one side, one cannot escape the conclusion that the Harmonisation of Rules Committee and the rules committees in New South Wales and elsewhere in Australia which followed its line would have benefited greatly from wider consultation with practitioners, academics and other interested parties on this and other points, and that the outcome of the reform process might well have been different if that consultation had taken place.

## IV. Conclusion

Few would contest the proposition that the harmonisation of rules of adjudicatory jurisdiction in Australia is, in principle, a 'good thing' and long overdue. That does not mean, however, that any harmonisation of those rules is of unquestionable benefit. The Amendment Rule, and the corresponding rules adopted elsewhere (but not everywhere) in Australia, provide a very good example of this. This chapter has raised concerns as to both the legislative processes and the substantive content of the reform package. With those concerns in mind, it is to be hoped that the Amendment Rule and its counterparts do not constitute the final settlement of Australian rules of adjudicatory jurisdiction, and that those charged with the responsibility of developing the law will adopt procedures that are more open and receptive than those followed in this instance.

# 3

# The Exercise of Jurisdiction and the Role of Enforcement

VIVIENNE BATH*

## I. Introduction

This chapter considers the relationship between the exercise of jurisdiction by a court and the potential enforceability of either a judgment of the court overseas or of a competing overseas judgment in Australia. How relevant are the prospects of enforceability to the exercise of jurisdiction or the issue of interim measures? How relevant should the prospects of enforcement be, if at all? These questions have arisen in a number of recent cases decided by Australian courts which have looked at the question of the relevance of enforceability. They are highlighted by recent developments in Australian private international law relating to jurisdiction and new and potentially conflicting initiatives on jurisdiction and enforcement at the international level.

In Australia, the effect of the recent revisions (based on provisions in effect in New Zealand)[1] to the Uniform Civil Procedure Rules 2005 (NSW)[2] and associated amendments in Victoria, Tasmania, the Australian Capital Territory and South Australia[3] is to expand the circumstances in which these courts can take jurisdiction over foreign defendants. These revisions widen the gap between the potential scope of the jurisdiction of these Australian courts and the more limited 'international jurisdiction' of foreign courts which is a prerequisite for the enforcement of judgments by Australian courts under both common law and the

* This chapter is based on a presentation at the conference, 'Commercial Issues in Private International Law', held on 16 February 2018 at Sydney Law School.

[1] High Court Rules 2016 (NZ) pt 6-4.

[2] Uniform Civil Procedure (Amendment No 83) Rule (NSW) 2016; see also M Douglas and V Bath, 'A New Approach to Service Outside the Jurisdiction and Outside Australia under the Uniform Civil Procedure Rules' (2017) 44 *Australian Bar Review* 160 and A Dickinson, ch 2 of this volume.

[3] See Supreme Court Civil Rules 2006 (SA) pt 4; Supreme Court (General Civil Procedure) Rules 2015 (Vic) Ord 7; Supreme Court Rules 2000 (Tas) div 10; and Court Procedures Rules 2006 (ACT) div 6.8.9. In relation to the Australian Capital Territory, see Dickinson, ibid, text to n 183.

Foreign Judgments Act 1991 (Cth).[4] They also thus potentially further increase the potential for foreign courts to refuse to recognise Australian judgments, at least in cases where the foreign court also applies its own rules relating to jurisdiction.[5] At the same time, the Australian Government has announced its intention to accede to the Hague Convention on Choice of Court Agreements (the Hague Choice of Court Convention),[6] which legislates a strong link between jurisdiction and enforcement in relation to exclusive jurisdiction agreements. Australia is also an active participant in The Hague Conference on Private International Law Judgments Project,[7] which aims to facilitate enforcement by standardising the jurisdictional issues which may be used as a prerequisite to recognition and enforcement of foreign judgments.[8] The provisions on jurisdiction in the 2018 Draft Convention of this project do not coincide either with the current 'long-arm' jurisdiction rules referred to above or to Australian common law or statutory requirements in relation to the jurisdiction of a foreign court which issued a judgment under consideration for enforcement in Australia.[9]

In view of these differing approaches to local and international jurisdiction, the question arises: to what extent, if any, should a domestic court consider the question of enforcement in relation to the exercise of its own jurisdiction? Should the ability (prospective or otherwise) of a party ultimately to enforce a judgment overseas be relevant to the exercise of jurisdiction in the first instance, or to a decision to refuse to exercise jurisdiction? To what extent should the enforceability of a potential judgment in a foreign proceeding which is parallel to or overlaps with an Australian proceeding either overseas or in Australia play a role in the decision of an Australian court to proceed with or grant a stay in a case, or to grant interim protection? This chapter focuses on the facts and decisions in a number of recent cases in which this issue has arisen, briefly considers some of the potential implications of international initiatives and draws some tentative conclusions in relation to these questions.

The discussion in this chapter focuses on cross-border commercial litigation. Although one of the leading cases on parallel litigation in Australia which addresses the question of potentially conflicting court orders is the family law case of *Henry v Henry*,[10] this chapter does not deal with the specialist issues presented in cases on family law and related issues.

[4] See discussion in M Davies, AS Bell and PLG Brereton, *Nygh's Conflict of Laws in Australia*, 9th edn (Sydney, LexisNexis, 2014) 896 and 945–48.

[5] R Brand, 'New Challenges in the Recognition and Enforcement of Judgments' PittLaw, Legal Studies Research Paper Series, Working Paper No 2018–29, September 2018, https://papers.ssrn.com/sol3/papers.cfm?abstract_id=3246053, fn 84.

[6] Entered into force on 1 October 2015. See also M Keyes, ch 12 of this volume, fn 2.

[7] Hague Conference on Private International law, The Judgments Project, www.hcch/net/en/projects/legislative-projects/judgments (Hague Judgments Project).

[8] ibid. See also Brand, 'New Challenges in the Recognition and Enforcement of Judgments' (n 5).

[9] ibid, art 5.

[10] *Henry v Henry* [1996] HCA 51, (1996) 185 CLR 571.

# II. Recent Cases

This section considers the facts and decisions in a number of recent cases in Australia and England in which the question has arisen of the relevance of the enforceability of a foreign judgment in the domestic court and enforceability (or unenforceability) of a domestic or foreign judgment overseas. The cases referred to arise in a range of contexts subject to varying tests and a range of considerations – stays of proceedings in the context of *forum non conveniens* claims, exclusive jurisdiction clauses and other application for the exercise of discretion and applications for anti-suit and other injunctions.[11] For purposes of space, the detailed background and differing legal considerations which apply to applications of these different kinds are not discussed.

## A. The Relevance to Australian Proceedings of the Enforceability or Unenforceability in Australia of a Judgment of a Foreign Court

The Australian rule is that the court, in deciding an application for a stay on *forum non conveniens* grounds, must determine whether the Australian court is a 'clearly inappropriate forum'.[12] However, it is accepted that the existence, or prospect, of proceedings dealing with what are contended to be the same or overlapping issues before both an Australian court and a foreign court does necessarily involve some consideration of the foreign court proceedings and, potentially, the consequences of the foreign court's decisions. Thus, in *Oceanic Sun Line Special Shipping Company Inc v Fay*,[13] Deane J included effective enforcement of a judgment in an Australian forum in his summary of matters which could constitute a '[l]egitimate and substantial advantage to the plaintiff…which would not be available in proceedings in the foreign tribunal which the defendant claims is the appropriate one for their determination'.[14]

The basic issue of the relevance of enforcement when there are conflicting orders was directly presented in case of *Henry v Henry*:[15]

> However, if both have jurisdiction, it will be relevant to consider whether each will recognise the other's orders and decrees. If the orders of the foreign court will not be recognised in Australia, that will ordinarily dispose of any suggestion that the local

[11] The considerations in relation to the issue of an anti-suit injunction or other interim relief are of course not the same as those in a determination on *forum non conveniens* grounds. Nevertheless, some of the practical implications are relevant in considering the overall question of the relationship between jurisdiction and enforcement.

[12] See *Nygh's Conflict of Laws in Australia* (n 4) 192–95.

[13] *Oceanic Sun Line Special Shipping Company Inc v Fay* [1988] HCA 32, (1988) 165 CLR 197.

[14] ibid [5].

[15] See n 10, 592–93.

> proceedings should not continue. However, if the orders of the foreign court will be recognised in Australia, it will be relevant to consider whether any orders may need to be enforced in other countries and, if so, the relative ease with which that can be done. As well, it will be relevant to consider which forum can provide more effectively for complete resolution of the matters involved in the parties' controversy.

The principle set out in *Henry v Henry* in relation to the implications of the unenforceability of a foreign judgment is relatively clear. It can, however, be practically difficult to consider and apply it in different situations, as a number of recent cases illustrate.

The relevance of the unenforceability of a foreign judgment was discussed in *Centrebet Pty Limited v Baasland.*[16] Baasland was a habitual gambler, who engaged in online gambling activities on Centrebet's website. Centrebet is an Australian registered company licensed to operate as a sports bookmaker in the Northern Territory and operating out of Australia. The electronic account form which customers were obliged to complete before engaging in online betting contained a link to standard terms and conditions which included provisions for the application of the law of the Northern Territory, submission of all disputes to the Northern Territory Government's Racing Commission and submission to the jurisdiction of the courts of the Northern Territory. In this case, Centrebet had initiated the litigation in the Northern Territory in response to a case brought by Baasland in Norway against Centrebet alleging breach of a 'non-statutory rule of negligence' and 'non-statutory strict liability'.[17] In Norway, contested proceedings relating to jurisdiction had been finally decided in Baasland's favour, and equally contested proceedings in relation to the law applicable to the case were still underway at the time of the Australian hearing.[18]

The purpose of Centrebet's successful application before the Supreme Court of the Northern Territory was therefore to seek negative declarations that it had no liability to Baasland under the gaming contract nor owed any money in Baasland's account with Centrebet. If successful, this would essentially forestall any subsequent attempt by Baasland to engage in further litigation in the Northern Territory (or enforce a judgment).[19] In deciding whether to issue the declarations, Hiley J included as one of the factors for his refusal to grant a stay on *forum non conveniens* grounds the unenforceability under the Foreign Judgments Act 1991 (Cth) of a judgment resulting from the proceedings in Norway.[20]

[16] *Centrebet Pty Limited v Baasland* [2013] NTSC 59, [41] (Hiley J).

[17] ibid [44].

[18] ibid [53].

[19] Hiley J's judgment referred to a similar case brought by another betting company (Hillside) against Baasland in the English High Court in which Hillside successfully obtained negative declarations to the effect that Hillside had no liability for any loss or damage that Baasland may have suffered by reason of his gambling activities with Hillside: *Hillside (New Media) Ltd v Baasland* [2010] 2 CLCQB 986; ibid [127]–[128].

[20] See n 16 [161], [163]. Note that Hiley J seemed to conclude that a Norwegian judgment might be enforceable at common law on the ground that Centrebet had participated in the Norwegian proceedings (referring to *Emanuel v Symon* [1908] I KB 302).

The recent case of *Central Petroleum Limited v Geoscience Resource Recovery LLC*,[21] which also arose from an application for a negative declaration, dealt in more detail with the issue of enforcement of a foreign judgment in Australia. The underlying dispute in this case was whether there was an agreement between the parties pursuant to which Central Petroleum had agreed to pay Geoscience a success fee for introducing a French company (Total) to Central Petroleum. The alleged agreement included a provision that '[t]his agreement shall be governed by the laws of the State of Texas and any dispute will be resolved by suit either in Texas or California'.[22] Geoscience brought proceedings against Central Petroleum in Texas in July 2015. Central Petroleum unsuccessfully attempted to enter a 'special appearance' for the purpose of contesting jurisdiction before the Texas court and subsequently appealed this decision in Texas.[23] While awaiting a decision from the Texas Court of Appeals on this point, Central brought proceedings against Geoscience in the Supreme Court of Queensland seeking declaratory relief, including a claim for a declaration 'to the effect that Central did not enter into, and is not bound by, the 2012 agreement'. Geoscience in response contested the jurisdiction of the Queensland Supreme Court and sought a temporary or permanent stay of the Queensland proceedings pending the resolution of the proceedings in Texas.

After determining the jurisdictional point in Central Petroleum's favour,[24] Bowskill J turned to the question whether, in view of the Texas proceedings, the Queensland Supreme Court was a clearly inappropriate forum and thus the proceedings should be stayed. Bowskill J was not persuaded that Queensland was a clearly inappropriate forum for the dispute.[25]

Bowskill J held, based principally on the judgment of the High Court in *Oceanic Sun Line Special Shipping Co Inc v Fay*[26] and the Federal Court of Australia in *Trina Solar (US) Inc v Jasmin Solar Pty Ltd*,[27] that there was a good argument that the law applicable to determine whether a contract had in fact been entered into was the law of Queensland, as the law of the forum. This was a very significant factor in refusing a stay of the proceedings.[28] The judge held that the plaintiff might obtain a legitimate advantage from proceeding in Queensland which could not be obtained in Texas – that is, a determination whether the Texas court had jurisdiction 'in

[21] *Central Petroleum Limited v Geoscience Resource Recovery LLC* [2017] QSC 223 (Bowskill J). Appeal against the decision of Bowskill J on the applicability of Uniform Civil Procedure Rules 1999 (Qld) r124(1)(g) dismissed in *Geoscience Resource Recovery LLC v Central Petroleum Limited* [2018] QCA 216.

[22] *Central Petroleum Limited v Geoscience Resource Recovery LLC* (n 21) [3].

[23] ibid [1]–[7].

[24] ibid [9]–[32].

[25] ibid [81].

[26] See n 13.

[27] *Trina Solar (US) Inc v Jasmin Solar Pty Ltd* [2017] FCAFC 6, (2017) 247 FCR 1 and the judgment of Edelman J at first instance in *Jasmin Solar Pty Ltd v Trina Solar Australia Pty Ltd* [2015] FCA 1453, (2015) 331 ALR 108.

[28] See n 16, [49].

the international sense' without which no Texas judgment could be enforced in Queensland where, it was found, all of Central Petroleum's assets were located.[29] In order to make this determination, the Queensland court would have to decide whether Central Petroleum had entered into the alleged contract.[30]

Similarly, the judge held that the grant of a stay pending the determination of the appeal on jurisdiction in Texas, was not appropriate, in part because the determination of the issue in the Queensland proceeding might affect Central Petroleum's decision whether to defend on the merits in Texas. If the outcome of the Queensland proceedings was a determination that Central Petroleum had not entered into the alleged contract 'it is in both parties' interests to know that, because if there is no likelihood of any judgment against Central in the Texas proceedings being enforceable in Australia, it may be that the whole proceedings are a waste of time and money'.[31] There was therefore something to be gained by Central Petroleum in bringing the Queensland proceedings which it could not gain in the Texas proceedings.

The issue for a party contesting jurisdiction in an overseas court is fairly presented by this case: if Central Petroleum failed before the Texas court in its argument relating to jurisdiction,[32] in order to preserve its position in Australia in relation to enforcement, it would have to withdraw from the US proceedings and accept the risk that Geoscience would obtain a default judgment against it. Even if this judgment was not enforceable in Australia, it could potentially be enforced elsewhere if Central Petroleum ever acquired assets overseas. (The application for a negative declaration, if successful, could also potentially establish a *res judicata* on the substantive issue as to whether the alleged agreement did or did not exist. Although not addressed in the case, this would be another benefit, in addition to the potential advantage to Central Petroleum of having a ruling which would make clear that a subsequent Texas judgment would be unenforceable in Queensland.)

At the time of writing, the substantive issues relating to the issue of a negative declaration have not yet been resolved in *Central Petroleum*. However *Centrebet*[33]

[29] ibid [79].
[30] ibid [78].
[31] ibid [84].
[32] In a substitute opinion filed 8 March 2018 (after the decision of Bowskill J in the Queensland case) (*Central Petroleum v Geoscience Resource Recovery, LLC* 543 S.W.3d 901 (2018)), the Texas Court of Appeals upheld the decision of the trial judge in relation to the jurisdiction on the Texas court. The trial judge had found that, for the purpose of determining jurisdiction, the alleged agreement, containing a forum-selection clause, had been signed by an officer of Central Petroleum and operated as a consent to jurisdiction. In relation to the Australian litigation, the Court held that 'In sum, Central has not shown that under Australian law in general, or under the Australian court's opinion in particular, a Texas judgment would be unenforceable or that the parties would be required to relitigate the case in Australia'. ibid 926.
[33] Hiley J (n 16) was influenced by the view of UK authority in relation to the use of negative declaration in situations where the law of the forum, in combination with an exclusive jurisdiction clause, applied to the underlying contract. Bowskill J referred to the applicability of Queensland law in relation to the determination whether or not there was a contract.

and *Central Petroleum* are both cases which deal with the use of negative declarations in parallel proceedings. The issue of resisting enforcement of an overseas judgment is a significant part of the case in both cases. Whether this is consistent with High Court authority which refers disapprovingly to the possibility for negative declarations to be used in order to prevent 'another party from pursuing remedies available in the courts of another country and not available in this country'[34] or with international initiatives to facilitate enforcement of judgments is another question. Setting this aside, these cases highlight the difficult choice for a party which is brought before a foreign court which it claims to have no jurisdiction. The party must be careful not to engage in substantive argument on the merits if it wishes – for purposes of enforcement abroad – to preserve its right to claim that it has not submitted to the jurisdiction of the foreign court. The determination in *Central Petroleum* that there could be a relatively quick decision on the case, which would thus allow Central Petroleum to decide whether to participate in the Texas proceedings, potentially provides one solution to this problem. A point which was relevant to the judge in her considerations was the fact that the Texas proceedings had not, at that stage, advanced beyond the argument on jurisdiction.[35] A similar consideration in relation to the rival Norwegian proceedings was considered relevant in *Centrebet v Baasland*.[36] Other factors relevant to the question, such as costs, expenses and so on, were not as significant.

The reverse situation – that is, the question of the significance of enforcement where a final judgment of a foreign court in related or parallel proceedings *could* be enforced in Australia – does not seem to have been addressed in many cases, at least in the commercial context. The principle laid down in *Henry v Henry* is that if the overseas judgment or order would be enforced in Australia, the court would have to look at the enforceability of the Australian orders overseas. But is this a factor which would contribute to a determination that the Australian proceedings are vexatious or oppressive? In *Centrebet*, Hiley J commented generally that the question whether 'orders of one forum are enforceable or are recognised in the other forum is a relevant consideration'[37] but did not go beyond finding that the cause of action relied on in the Norwegian proceedings would not provide Baasland with a cause of action in Australia.[38] In *Global Partners Fund Limited v Babcock & Brown Limited (In Liquidation)*,[39] the second, third and fourth defendants listed as one of the relevant factors in their ultimately successful claim for a

[34] *CSR Ltd v Cigna* [1997] HCA 33, (1997) 189 CLR 345, 401 (Dawson, Toohey, Gaudron, McHugh, Gummow and Kirby JJ). See discussion in R Garnett, 'Stay of Proceedings in Australia: A "Clearly Inappropriate" Test?' (1999) 23(1) *Melbourne University Law Review* 30, text to fn 136ff.

[35] See n 22, [50]–[54].

[36] See n 16, [158].

[37] See n 16, [158], relying on *Henry v Henry*, n 10.

[38] ibid [163].

[39] *Global Partners Fund Limited v Babcock & Brown Limited (In Liquidation)* [2010] NSWSC 270, [1519] para (w).

permanent stay of the Australian proceedings the fact that the English judgments in the parallel proceedings would be enforceable in Australia under the Foreign Judgments Act 1991(Cth). Similarly, in *Henry v Henry*, the majority felt that it was a relevant consideration in determining whether the Australian court was an inappropriate forum that the wife had instituted ongoing proceedings in a Monaco court, which had jurisdiction, and could make an order that would be enforceable in Australia.[40]

It is arguably implicit in a discussion of the undesirability of multiple conflicting proceedings that the prospect of a multiplicity of conflicting judgments, which may or may not be enforceable, is equally undesirable. Yet in *CSR Ltd v Cigna Insurance Australia Ltd*,[41] for example, although the majority considered that the possibility of an award under the Sherman Act, which was not available in NSW, was an advantage for Cigna in proceeding with the relevant proceedings in the US, the majority judgment, in ordering a stay of the Australian proceedings, did not discuss the question of enforceability of such an award in Australia. The issue was, however, raised and discussed in oral argument before the Court, and it may have been that the majority was satisfied that enforceability in Australia was not relevant.[42] A strong dissent by Brennan CJ on the inappropriateness of the exercise of jurisdiction by a US court under the Sherman Act over conduct in Australia similarly did not refer directly to the question of enforcement.[43]

## B. The Relevance of the Enforceability of a Judgment Overseas

Since in *forum non conveniens* applications the party seeking a stay of a proceeding brought before an Australian court must show that the Australian court is a clearly inappropriate forum, there is a question whether enforceability of the Australian judgment is or should be at all relevant to the Australian court's considerations. The majority of the High Court in *Voth v Manildra Flour Mills Pty Ltd*[44] indicated that the fact that there is a foreign court which could grant relief should be taken into account: '[T]he availability of relief in a foreign forum will always be a relevant factor in deciding whether or not the local forum is a clearly inappropriate one'. Against this should be set the reluctance of the Australian court to assess or compare the merits of foreign legal systems and foreign courts. Indeed,

[40] [1996] HCA 51, (1996) 185 CLR 571.

[41] *CSR Ltd v Cigna Insurance Australia Ltd* [1997] HCA 33, (1997) 189 CLR 345.

[42] See discussion in *CSR Limited v Cigna Insurance Australia Limited* S119/1996 [1996] HCATrans 449 (14 November 1996).

[43] (1997) 189 CLR 345, 378.

[44] *Voth v Manildra Flour Mills Pty Ltd* [1990] HCA 55, (1990) 171 CLR 538, [37] (Mason CJ, Deane, Dawson and Gaudron JJ).

the Australian court can be a clearly inappropriate forum even if there is no foreign forum which is competent to hear the case.[45] The question of enforceability does not appear to feature in these considerations.

Since it is the plaintiff which makes the decision to institute its suit in Australia and – having successfully shown jurisdiction – has a *prima facie* right to insist on the case being heard there,[46] it is also logical to argue that the plaintiff should bear the responsibility for enforcing the judgment, even if it must be enforced overseas. The argument for separation of the considerations relating to the exercise of jurisdiction and subsequent enforcement overseas is supported by the comments of Brennan J in *Oceanic Sun*:

> If we be confident of the quality of justice administered in Australian courts, there is no reason why we should defer to other fora, who have it within their power to grant or refuse recognition to and enforcement of the judgments of Australian courts according to their municipal laws.[47]

This question was directly addressed in the recent judgment of Garling J in *Wilson v Addu Investments Pte Ltd*.[48] This case related to injuries suffered by the NSW plaintiffs in the Maldives while on holiday there. The defendants were an international company and a company located in the Maldives. As part of their argument for a stay of the proceedings before the NSW Supreme Court on *forum non conveniens* grounds, the defendants contended that a judgment obtained in NSW would not be enforceable in the Maldives. This was contested by the plaintiffs. However, Garling J took the view was that it was unnecessary to resolve the question of enforceability, because it was 'difficult to imagine' that the defendants would not give effect to a judgment of the NSW court (on the basis that Addu Investments was a company which advertised for business in Australia) and also because both Addu Investments and the second defendant were presumably insured, and the insurer would not ignore a judgment of the NSW court.

> Secondly, and persuasively, if there be an inability to enforce the judgment of this Court in the Maldives, that is a direct consequence of the fact that the plaintiffs have chosen to litigate the matters in this Court. It is they who are prepared to bring their claim, and maintain it, in this Court, thereby taking the risk on the issue of enforceability. If the ultimate judgment is unenforceable and the defendants decline to comply with it, then it is hard to see that the defendants are able to say that the proceedings would be seriously and unfairly burdensome, prejudicial or damaging.[49]

A similar issue was raised in the earlier Federal Court case of *Anglo-Australian Foods v Von Planta*,[50] which involved a claim of misleading and deceptive conduct

[45] ibid [37]–[39].
[46] ibid [30].
[47] *Oceanic Sun Line Special Shipping Company Inc v Fay* (n 13) [32].
[48] *Wilson v Addu Investments Pte Ltd* [2014] NSWSC 381.
[49] ibid [131].
[50] *Re Anglo-Australian Foods Limited v Peter Von Planta* [1988] FCA 382.

under the then Trade Practices Act 1974 (Cth). The first respondent argued in support of an application for a stay that the judgment would probably be unenforceable in Switzerland, which would render the action futile. Lee J commented[51] that this might be regarded as being a separate ground for the exercise of discretion to stay proceedings and not an element of the doctrine of *forum non conveniens*. The judge distinguished between a case where the judgment or decree of the court 'depends upon the assistance of a foreign court for its fulfilment' (such as an order or decree for specific performance or acts of restraint) and a judgment for a money sum.

> The lack of prospect of recovery on a money judgment can be no more a cause for declining to exercise jurisdiction where an applicant seeks judgment against a foreign resident than it would where both parties were domiciled within the jurisdiction of the court.[52]

The judge was in any event not satisfied that the judgment would be unenforceable, and the stay was refused. (The emphasis which Lee J put in this case on the right of a plaintiff which had shown the jurisdiction of the forum to be heard by the court was criticised in *Voth*,[53] but not in the context of his comment on enforcement.)

The issue of the relevance of unenforceability was, however, resolved in a different way in the recent Victorian case of *Bendigo and Adelaide Bank Ltd v Quine*.[54] This case involved an attempt by Bendigo Bank to enforce a debt against an elderly defendant who lived, and all of whose assets were located, in England. Croft J was satisfied that since service was effected out of the jurisdiction, a judgment issued in Victoria would not be enforced in England under the Foreign Judgments (Reciprocal Enforcement) Act 1933 (UK). Croft J decided in this case to grant a stay. The decision was not, however, made on the basis that the Court was an inappropriate forum for the purposes of r 7.04(2)(b) of the Supreme Court (General Civil Procedure) Rules 2015.[55] The judge, after going through the relevant case law, felt that the Victorian Supreme Court was not an inappropriate forum. The judge exercised his residual discretion in the defendant's favour under r 7.04(1) on the basis that he was constrained by s 7 of the Civil Procedure Act 2010 (Vic). This provides that effect must be given to the overarching purpose of the Act, which is the facilitation of 'the just, efficient, timely and cost effective resolution of the real issues in the dispute'. Since the real issue underlying the case was whether the defendant must *pay* the alleged debt, rather than whether the plaintiff was entitled to the sum owed, a decision by the Court to take jurisdiction in circumstances where the

[51] ibid [61], citing Nygh, *Conflict of Laws in Australia*, 4th edn (Sydney, Butterworths, 1976) 64–65.
[52] ibid [62].
[53] *Voth v Manildra Flour Mills Pty Ltd* (n 44).
[54] *Bendigo and Adelaide Bank Ltd v Quine* [2018] VSC 272.
[55] ibid [5]–[13].

judgment would not be enforceable in England would not facilitate resolution of the real issue in dispute.[56]

The relevance of enforceability, in this case the enforceability of a foreign judgment overseas, was also discussed in the dispute between Sunland and Prudentia,[57] in the context of an application for an anti-suit injunction. Sunland Waterfront (BVI) Ltd brought a civil case against Prudentia and two individuals (collectively, Prudentia) in the Victorian Supreme Court alleging misrepresentation and deceit in relation to certain transactions involving Dubai. Sunland subsequently also brought a so-called 'civil right' case in a criminal proceeding in Dubai brought against Prudentia and several Australian citizens. Both cases arose from the same facts and involved substantially the same claims for relief. Prudentia made two applications in Australia seeking anti-suit injunctions preventing Sunland from bringing the civil right case in Dubai. In determining whether the proceedings in Dubai were vexatious or oppressive, the Court considered that it was necessary for Sunland – in resisting the application – to show that there was a legitimate advantage to be gained in maintaining the Dubai proceedings in addition to the Australian proceedings.[58] As part of its argument on this point, Sunland contended that it would be a juridical advantage for it to obtain 'a judgment enforceable in places where an Australian judgment is not enforceable'.[59] This was dismissed by both the trial judge and the Court of Appeal.

> In the absence of any assets in the UAE (or it appears in any of the jurisdictions which such a judgment could reach) any benefit that such a judgment could confer would be insubstantial. Though Sunland submits that this may change if assets are brought into the jurisdiction, we agree with the trial judge that this submission is entirely speculative. Beyond stating that a UAE judgment would enable it to recover in the event that assets were brought into a jurisdiction in which a UAE judgment may be enforced, Sunland did not, in its submissions, articulate what the advantage to it consists in.[60]

This case is similar to *Bendigo and Adelaide Bank v Quine* in that the Court was able to satisfy itself that the relevant judgment would be unenforceable due to the

[56] A similar analysis was adopted in *Marque Lawyers Pty Ltd v Ryer Development Ltd* [2017] NSWSC 1397 in which the Court looked at a similar provision in s 56(1) of the Civil Procedure Act 2005 (NSW), which states that the overriding purpose of the Act and rules of court is to facilitate 'the just, quick and real resolution' of the real issues. Accordingly, the Court refused an application for it to use its discretion to order the transfer of proceedings from the Supreme Court to the Local Court of NSW on the basis that this would mean that enforcement of any judgment made against the defendant (a Hong Kong based company) in Hong Kong would have to be made under the more cumbersome and less convenient common law process rather than under the Hong Kong statutory regime for the enforcement of judgments.

[57] *Sunland Waterfront (BVI) Ltd v Prudentia Investments Pty Ltd (No 2)* [2010] FCA 312; *Sunland Waterfront (BVI) Ltd v Prudentia Investments Pty Ltd* [No 1] [2012] VSC 1 (Croft J); *Sunland Waterfront (BVI) Ltd v Prudentia Investments Pty Ltd* [2013] VSCA 237.

[58] *Sunland Waterfront (BVI) Ltd v Prudentia Investments Pty Ltd* [2013] VSCA 237, [461] (Warren CJ, Osborn JA and Macaulay AJA).

[59] ibid [473] (i).

[60] ibid [476].

lack of assets against which it could be enforced and there would therefore be no clear juridical advantage for Sunland if such a judgment was obtained. As noted above, the prospect of assets subsequently being brought into the jurisdiction was considered to be 'entirely speculative'.

The judgments in the *Impala* litigation discussed below, which also deal with anti-suit injunctions arising from a breach of an exclusive jurisdiction clause, raise a number of related issues in connection with enforceability. In the much-cited judgment of Brandon J in *The Eleftheria*,[61] which dealt with the case of parties suing in England in breach of an exclusive jurisdiction clause, the inability of a party to enforce a judgment in a foreign court was included in the list of issues which a judge could take into account in deciding whether or not the court should use its discretion to grant a stay of proceedings. Although the question of the significance of this factor has not been much discussed, it was argued in detail in the recent litigation between Impala Warehousing and Logistics (Shanghai) Company Ltd (Impala Shanghai) and Wanxiang Resources (Singapore) Pte Ltd (Wanxiang).[62] In this case, Wanxiang sued Impala Shanghai in Shanghai under a contract (a warehousing receipt) which the English courts held incorporated an exclusive jurisdiction clause nominating the courts of England.[63] Impala responded by seeking, first, an interim anti-suit injunction against Wanxiang, and, then, when the Shanghai proceedings continued, a final anti-suit injunction and a mandatory injunction ordering Wanxiang to discontinue the final proceedings.[64] Wanxiang (the party which had brought proceedings in China in breach of the exclusive jurisdiction clause) presented a number of arguments as to why it would suffer prejudice if it was compelled to litigate in England, one of which was that it would be disadvantaged because an English judgment would not be enforceable in China.

In the trial before Teare J, he refused the application for permanent injunctions, refused the application to discharge the anti-suit injunction and referred the matter for trial. The judge discussed and dismissed a range of matters relied on by Wanxiang in attempting to show that the exclusive jurisdiction clause should be relied upon.[65]

> Lastly, it was said that Wanxiang would suffer prejudice if they had to litigate in England because any judgment of the English court would not be enforceable in China. ....

[61] *The Eleftheria* [1970] P 94, 100.

[62] *Impala Warehousing and Logistics (Shanghai) Company Ltd v Wanxiang Resources (Singapore) Pte Ltd* [2015] EWHC 25 (Comm) ('trial before Teare J') (Teare J, following the grant of a preliminary anti-suit injunction on 19 September 2014: refused Impala Shanghai's application for a final anti-suit injunction, and for an interim mandatory injunction requiring Wanxiang to discontinue the Shanghai proceedings; refused Wanxiang's application to discharge the preliminary anti-suit injunction granted on 19 September 2014; and granted Wanxiang's application for a speedy trial). In *Impala Warehousing and Logistics (Shanghai) Company Ltd v Wanxiang Resources (Singapore) Pte Ltd* [2015] EWHC 811 (Comm) ('trial before Blair J'), following the full trial, Blair J granted a final prohibitory injunction and a final mandatory injunction.

[63] Trial before Blair J, ibid [103].

[64] See statement of facts [2015] EWHC 25 (Comm) [5].

[65] Trial before Teare J, n 62, [28].

> I did not consider that the point then made was a strong reason for not enforcing the jurisdiction clause because I expected the parties to respect a decision of this court. However, an inability to enforce a judgment is a form of prejudice specifically mentioned by Brandon J. in *The Eleftheria*. The question which therefore arises is whether Wanxiang's inability to enforce any judgment of this court in its favour against Impala Shanghai in China would be a strong reason for not giving effect to the exclusive jurisdiction clause. Having reflected upon this matter, and in the absence of any suggestion as to how this prejudice could be reliably avoided, I have reached the conclusion that it would be such a reason.[66]

In the trial before Blair J, the question of enforceability and its relevance in the context of the issue of an anti-suit injunction as a way of enforcing the exclusive jurisdiction clause was again brought up by Wanxiang. In response, Impala made various offers in order to mitigate the potential prejudice resulting from unenforceability. Thus, Wanxiang asked for security; Impala offered to arbitrate the dispute (although the parties could not agree on terms for the arbitration) and a proposal was made about an agreement to pay (which would not, however, be enforceable in China). Blair J finally concluded as follows:

> On the point of principle, neither party cited a case where the fact that an English judgment is not enforceable in a particular foreign country has been treated as a 'strong reason' for refusing to grant an anti-suit injunction based on an English exclusive jurisdiction clause. However, Impala Shanghai's submission to the effect that it can never be a strong reason cannot be correct: see *The Eleftheria* as approved in *Donohue v Armco Inc* .... I do however accept that the circumstances in which it may amount to a 'strong reason' may be rare, not least because non-enforceability may be foreseen or foreseeable as a risk when the exclusive jurisdiction clause is agreed.
>
> In my view, a situation which could potentially arise as a 'strong reason' for refusing to grant an anti-suit injunction is where the claim involves property, particularly a claim to recover property, and a judgment of the English court would not be recognised or enforced by the courts of the situs to the defendant's detriment. As a practical matter, the courts of the situs will decide what happens to property situated there.[67]

Blair J finally concluded that it was 'not commercially unreasonable'[68] to hold the parties to the exclusive jurisdiction clause and grant a permanent injunction (although Impala did agree to the imposition of conditions, such as the obligation to arbitrate).

This litigation highlights the difficulties with placing too much emphasis on the potential relevance of enforceability of a judgment. In particular, as Blair J's comments above make clear, Wanxiang, which, according to the decision of the English court, agreed to a contract which contained an exclusive jurisdiction clause and then instituted litigation in China in breach of the clause, should

[66] ibid [29].
[67] [2015] EWHC 811 (Comm) [137]–[138].
[68] ibid [142].

not be in a good position to argue in support of its application for a stay of the English proceedings that an English judgment against Impala Shanghai would be unenforceable.[69]

However, notwithstanding the Court's final conclusion on this point, the Court gave the issue of enforceability weight by issuing (by consent) conditional final orders with the form to be settled subsequently, and, in particular, by hearing the parties' detailed arguments on how to compensate for the unenforceability of the English judgment against Impala Shanghai. This clearly indicates the risk that the court could become closely involved in engaging with the question of how to ensure that a judgment can be enforced instead of merely taking the issue of enforceability into account.

## C. International Agreements and Initiatives

The discretion of the common law courts in relation to exclusive jurisdiction clauses (and thus the relevance of *The Eleftheria* factors) is being increasingly affected by legislation and international initiatives.[70] Under s 7(4)(b) of the Foreign Judgments Act 1991 (Cth), a foreign judgment will not be registered if – except in cases of submission to jurisdiction – the bringing of proceedings was 'contrary to an agreement under which the dispute in question was to be settled otherwise than by proceedings in the courts of the country of that court'. The Hague Choice of Court Convention similarly removes the discretion of the courts to refuse to give effect to such an agreement.[71] There is, however, a strong link between jurisdiction and enforcement in both the Foreign Judgments Act and the Hague Choice of Court Convention, as non-enforcement of a judgment obtained in breach of an agreement covered by the Act or the Convention is the sanction for non-compliance. The implications of this non-discretionary approach have yet to be fully worked out in practice.[72]

[69] On the question of parties utilising the unenforceability of Chinese judgments as a litigation tool generally, see V Bath, 'Overlapping Jurisdiction and the Resolution of Disputes before Chinese and Foreign Courts' (2015–16) 17 *Yearbook of International Private Law* 111, 144–45.

[70] See also discussion on the Trans-Tasman Proceedings Act 2010 (Cth) in M Keyes, ch 12 of this volume.

[71] Although it does not clearly resolve the issue of submission to jurisdiction. See B Marshall and M Keyes, 'Australia's Accession to the Hague Convention on Choice of Court Agreements' (2017) 41(1) *Melbourne University Law Review* 246.

[72] See, however, the fact situation in *Zeta-PDM Ltd v Petro Technology Australia Pty Ltd* [2011] WASC 338, in which the judgment debtor had refused to appoint an arbitrator under a domestic arbitration clause in the UK and similarly did not participate in the following UK court proceedings. It succeeded in contesting registration of the judgment in Australia by arguing that the proceedings were contrary to s 7(4)(b) of the Foreign Judgments Act 1991 (Cth) (which provides that the original court will be deemed not to have jurisdiction 'if the bringing of the proceedings in the country of the original court was contrary to an agreement under which the dispute in question was to be settled otherwise than by proceedings in the courts of the country of that court') and the judgment debtor had not submitted to the jurisdiction of the UK court.

The question of the relationship between jurisdiction and enforcement is raised more directly by the 2018 Draft Convention. Article 5 deals with the issue of the jurisdiction of a court which gives a judgment (the 'state of origin') for which enforcement is subsequently sought abroad in a court of a requested state by setting out a list of factors which would be considered by the court of a requested state to establish a connection between the court of the state of origin and either the defendant or the subject-matter of the case. These are not described as jurisdictional requirements in the Convention but as 'bases for recognition and enforcement'. The requirements focus on the residence of the defendant in the jurisdiction, either personally or through a business presence and require a link between the location of the court in the state of origin and the defendant (in the form of residence or business presence) and the location of immovable property in the state of origin.

This list may well not reflect the bases upon which the domestic court involved generally takes jurisdiction over cross-border disputes. They do not, for example, mirror the revised NSW long-arm jurisdictional provisions.[73] The Draft Convention makes clear (in art 16) that these grounds are not intended to cover the field in relation to the criteria on which a state may enforce foreign judgments.[74] They do, however, as in the Hague Choice of Court Convention, limit the grounds on which a court of a contracting party may refuse to recognise or enforce a judgment given in a state of origin. Article 7 sets out grounds which deal primarily with lack of due process, fraud or public policy (including procedural unfairness and infringements of security or sovereignty of the requested state) or an inconsistent prior judgment of a court of the requested state or another state. Thus if the Draft Convention (in its current form) achieves significant coverage, a domestic court would, at the early stages of a case, potentially be better able to assess whether a foreign judgment given in a parallel proceeding could be enforceable in that court, or whether a domestic court judgment had a strong chance of being enforced in a specified overseas court without asking for detailed expert evidence on this point. This additional degree of certainty could then arguably allow enforceability to be given more consideration at an earlier stage, particularly in deciding whether the court should exercise jurisdiction over a case where to do so is bound to result in an unenforceable judgment. Since the definition of 'judgment' includes final non-monetary judgments, however, the nature of potentially enforceable orders is wider than under the current common law and statutory regimes,[75] which could increase the difficulty of considering them early in the proceedings.

[73] See eg the content of the NSW rules on service out of the jurisdiction: Uniform Civil Proceedings Rules, pts 11 and 11A. See also Bath and Douglas, 'A New Approach' (n 2).

[74] See also discussion in FJ Garcimartín Alférez and G Saumier, 'Judgments Convention: Revised Preliminary Explanatory Report' Fourth Meeting of the Special Commission on the Recognition and Enforcement of Foreign Judgments 24–29 May 2018, No 10 of 2018 assets.hcch.net/docs/7cd8bc44-e2e5-46c2-8865-a151ce55e1b2.pdf, 72–73.

[75] See generally *Nygh's Conflict of Laws in Australia* (n 4) 895–950.

The Draft Convention is, however, at an early stage. There is a long list of exclusions from its application, which is effectively restricted to commercial cases (art 2). The way in which it could or would be incorporated into domestic law is unclear – whether its impact would be limited to statutory enforcement within the context of the Convention, whether it would extend more widely to statutory enforcement generally or whether it would have an impact on common law enforcement by changing the whole concept of 'international jurisdiction'. It could also be an impetus for further reform of the rules on service outside the jurisdiction to conform to the bases set out in art 5 and bring Australia's domestic and international jurisdictional rules into line with each other. Its effect on the consideration of enforcement in the context of jurisdictional and related determinations is therefore very difficult to predict.

## III. Discussion

The cases summarised above highlight both the disinclination of many judges to delve into the specifics of potential enforcement and the fact-specific nature of those cases in which the court has done so. The cases discussed in this chapter also indicate the difficulties for the court in attempting to do so. (As noted above, this discussion focuses on commercial cases and does not examine the issue of competing divorce and other family orders, in which the court may have no option but to do so.)

Although the cases range across considerations of *forum non conveniens*, the enforcement of exclusive jurisdiction clauses, anti-suit injunctions and negative declarations, there are several points which can be drawn from the cases.

First, there is the view that the question of enforceability of a domestic judgment outside the jurisdiction does not need to be taken into account because, as Garling J commented in *Wilson v Addu Investments*,[76] a party can be expected to obey the judgment of the court. In *Wilson*, this was on the grounds that 'an international organisation such as the defendant' would surely, for reputational reasons, satisfy an Australian court judgment. Teare J commented in his decision in *Impala*[77] that he initially did not consider unenforceability to be significant because he expected the parties to obey the decision of the Court. The numerous cases in which defendants contest enforcement even if they have actively participated in the proceedings, of course, casts doubt on this as a general proposition. The *Central Petroleum* litigation in Queensland, in fact, is based on Central Petroleum's calculation that its best defence to the US litigation might well be to rely entirely on non-enforcement of any Texas judgment against it. A hopeful comment by Geoscience in the Queensland proceedings that it doubted that 'Central would not voluntarily

[76] [2014] NSWSC 381.
[77] [2015] EWHC 25 (Comm) [29].

satisfy any Texas judgment against it' was dismissed by the judge because Central Petroleum's 'clear position' was that it well might not do so.[78]

Related to this is the principle that '[a] party who has regularly invoked the jurisdiction of a competent court has a prima facie right to insist upon its exercise and to have his claim heard and determined'.[79]

In practice, this is by no means an absolute principle.[80] However, the logical consequence of this right of the plaintiff to choose its forum is that the plaintiff must bear the consequences of the choice, as Garling J held in *Wilson v Addu Investments*.[81] The view that the plaintiff's inability to enforce a judgment against the defendant is a separate ground for arguing for a stay rather than an argument that it would be vexatious or oppressive to proceed is supported by the view taken by Lee J in *Anglo-Australian Foods v Von Planta*[82] and by Garling J in *Bendigo and Adelaide Bank Ltd v Quine*[83] (dealing with the concept of an 'inappropriate forum' under the rules of court).

This concept of choice is particularly relevant in relation to the enforcement of exclusive jurisdiction clauses, where the parties must be taken to have made up their own minds in advance in relation to the appropriate forum, and should generally be held to their bargain.[84] In this case, the assumption is that the parties have considered the matter before signing the agreement and, therefore, should have made their own assessment in relation to enforceability (subject to statutory protective provisions for consumers and others in need of protection).[85] This hard-line approach to jurisdiction clauses is supported by s 7(4)(b) of the Foreign Judgments Act 1991 (Cth) and more recently the Hague Choice of Court Convention, which backs it up by limiting the circumstances in which enforcement of a judgment given under the Convention by a court in the territory of a party can be refused by the court of another party to the Convention. This would thus remove the discretion of the adjudicatory court described in *The Eleftheria*,[86] which suggests that one relevant factor in a decision not to apply such a clause might be the unenforceability of a judgment of the nominated court. As noted above,[87] the *Impala* litigation appears to be one the few examples where this consideration

[78] *Central Petroleum Limited v Geoscience Resource Recovery LLC* (n 21) [79].

[79] *Oceanic Sun Line* [1988] HCA 32, (1988) 165 CLR 197, [1] (Deane J).

[80] See *Voth* (n 49) [54] (Mason CJ, Deane, Dawson and Gaudron JJ). See also discussion in *Nygh's Conflict of Laws in Australia* (n 4) 193.

[81] See n 76, [131]. See also text to n 49.

[82] *Re Anglo-Australian Foods Limited v Peter Von Planta* [1988] FCA 382.

[83] [2018] VSC 272.

[84] For a recent decision applying this principle, see *Parnell Manufacturing Pty Ltd v Lonza Ltd* [2017] NSWSC 562 (Ball J): permanent stay of NSW proceedings granted in view of exclusive jurisdiction clause in favour of Delaware.

[85] See comments of Spigelman J on possible exceptions for small businesses; JJ Spigelman, 'The Hague Choice of Court Convention and International Commercial Litigation' (2009) 83 *Australian Law Journal* 386, 391; cited M Douglas, 'Choice of Court Agreements under an International Civil Law Act (2018) 34 *Journal of Contract Law* 186, 209.

[86] [1970] P 94.

[87] See text to n 62.

was examined and applied in some detail and, after examining the relevance of unenforceability of an English judgment in China in considerable detail, Blair J ultimately concluded that the 'circumstances in which [unenforceability] may amount to a "strong reason" may be rare, not least because non-enforceability may be foreseen or foreseeable as a risk when the exclusive jurisdiction clause is agreed'.[88] Certainly, *Impala* is a good example of the complexities in which a court can become enmeshed when attempting to resolve the issue of unenforceability.

The approach of courts to the relevance to a decision on jurisdiction of the fact that the plaintiff may well be unable to enforce the court's decision in a specified (or competing) jurisdiction overseas may also be subject to consideration of the circumstances of the case. In *Addu*, the plaintiff (Wilson) was an individual and was bringing a case against a multinational enterprise with many locations – and presumably assets – worldwide. In *Bendigo and Adelaide Bank Ltd v Quine*,[89] however, the judge took the view that the question of enforceability of any Australian judgment in England was a relevant – and, in fact, the deciding – consideration in his decision to stay the Australian case. Although he did not consider it relevant to the exercise of his discretion under the relevant Victorian rules of court (that is, the question whether the court was an inappropriate forum), it was relevant to the exercise of his residual discretion to refuse jurisdiction which was guided by the provisions of the Civil Procedure Act 2010 (Vic). In *Quine*, unlike *Addu*, the defendant was an individual, resident in England, whose only assets were located in England. The Court was therefore able to satisfy itself that an Australian judgment in which the court had taken jurisdiction under the long-arm rules would not be enforceable in England, which was the only venue available for enforcement. The judge did, however, express some concern about the implications of this conclusion:

> I reach this conclusion with some concern that while it is required by the CPA as it may reduce unnecessary costs in the present case, it adds another layer of complexity to the question of whether the Court ought to exercise jurisdiction in respect of a claim. Ordinarily, of course, parties do not commence proceedings seeking monetary relief where success in the proceeding will not result in recovery of at least part of the sum claimed. Indeed, it is not unusual for a defendant not to appear, even to contest jurisdiction, in respect of a claim where the defendant is of the view that the ultimate relief sought by the plaintiff in the proceeding will not be obtainable because the resulting judgment will be unenforceable[90]

This case highlights a number of significant issues in the discussion: first, the question whether the court should essentially second-guess the plaintiff's decision to institute proceedings; secondly, whether it is necessary to do so, since the defendant can presumably (with appropriate advice) make a decision whether or

[88] [2015] EWHC 811 (Comm) [137]–[138].
[89] [2018] VSC 272.
[90] ibid [26].

not to defend the proceedings, including by consideration of the question whether the decision is likely to be unenforceable against the defendant, and, thirdly, the degree to which the court can be satisfied that the judgment would indeed be unenforceable against the defendant. All of this was relatively straightforward in *Quine*, due to the circumstances of the defendant. The basis of the decision is not, however, inconsistent with the view of Garling J that unenforceability is not relevant in relation to the question of the appropriateness of the forum.

In fact, Garling J's comments are supported by practical considerations. In an increasingly internationalised world, prospects for international enforcement of judgments should also increase as parties hold assets in more locations than their seat of business or their residence. The supportive approach taken by Australian courts in relation to the grant of freezing orders over Australian assets in support of overseas litigation – both current and pending[91] – where a judgment could subsequently be enforceable in Australia, on grounds of comity between courts[92] underlines the fact that in enforcing judgments in cross-border matters, the judgment creditor may not be limited to assets in one or two jurisdictions. A party may hold assets in numerous jurisdictions; it may sign cross-border contracts which offer further prospects of attachment of income streams; it may subsequently acquire inventory, receivables, debts and other interests which can be the basis for an enforcement action. Proving that a judgment would or would not be enforceable overseas may well require expensive expert evidence to be produced to the court. This tends to support the view taken by the courts in the cases above that enforceability overseas should not generally be a major factor in the court's considerations when deciding whether to stay domestic proceedings in favour of overseas litigation or to give orders in support of domestic proceedings – it is the plaintiff's responsibility to decide where to bring an action if it has a basis to bring it and, similarly, its responsibility to pursue enforcement internationally, wherever it may be available.

The question of the relevance of the enforceability of a foreign judgment in Australia where there are parallel or overlapping proceedings in both a foreign and a domestic court presents slightly different questions. Among other things, it raises the issue whether a court can determine to its own satisfaction that a foreign judgment will not ultimately be enforceable in Australia given that this relies on a number of factors which are subject to change as the cases proceed. In *Central Petroleum*, the Court noted that all Central Petroleum's assets were in Queensland. This was a relevant consideration in determining that Central Petroleum did indeed have something to gain by obtaining judicial confirmation that an overseas judgment would not be enforceable against it. The Court was confident

[91] See eg *PT Bayan Resources TBK v BCBC Singapore Pte Ltd* [2015] HCA 36, (2015) 258 CLR 1 (freezing order in relation to proceedings pending in Singapore); *FremantleMedia Ltd v Yu* [2016] NSWSC 1167 (freezing order in relation to proceedings pending in Beijing).

[92] J Allsop, 'Comity and Commerce' (FCA) [2015] *Federal Judicial Scholarship* 27.

(at the preliminary stage) that, as long as Central Petroleum did not participate in the merits in the Texas proceedings, the Australian court would not recognise the jurisdiction of the Texas courts for the purposes of enforcement.

Indeed, the consequences of a decision not to participate in one set of the proceedings in order to avoid future enforcement are potentially very significant. A striking example of this is the English case of *Spliethoff's Bevrachtingskantoor BV v Bank of China Limited*,[93] in which a Chinese court (the Qingdao Maritime Court) decided to hear a case brought by Spliethoff's Chinese contractual partner against it in China despite what the English courts held was an effective arbitration clause. Since Splietfhoff had defended the case against it on the merits before the Chinese courts, and had thereby submitted to the jurisdiction of the Chinese courts, the Chinese judgment was held to be enforceable against it in England.[94] It is not clear, however, that the court is bound to – or should – assist in a decision by a party whether to undertake the defence of the overseas action. Certainly, as the majority stated clearly in *CSR v Cigna*, the High Court is not prepared to assist a party in litigation the 'dominant purpose' of which was to prevent the other party from pursuing in a foreign court remedies not available in Australia.[95] (The final decision on the merits in Central Petroleum has of course not been issued. It is not clear that the Queensland court will look favourably on an application for a negative declaration in the admittedly unusual fact situation of this case (where the existence of the underlying contract is called into question.))

Generally, it should be observed that a decision to litigate is not necessarily principally directed at enforcement. A case in Australia may be brought for predominantly defensive purposes in order to head off litigation or to obtain a judgment which could preclude enforcement of future overseas litigation (as in *Central Petroleum*). This can be regarded as a legitimate litigation tactic or it can, as in *CSR*, attract strong criticism from the court. A case can be brought requesting non-monetary orders which are currently not enforceable outside the jurisdiction. Domestic courts are not bound to give effect to anti-suit injunctions of a foreign court, for example.[96] A case can be brought in order to establish a precedent in relation to future similar litigation, even though the plaintiff is fully aware that there is little chance of enforcing a judgment overseas. It can be brought in the hope or expectation that there may in the future be assets upon which a judgment can be enforced. It can be brought entirely for personal reasons, or simply to prove a point. In all of these cases, the decision is the plaintiff's and so, presumably, the consequences in relation to enforcement should also be the plaintiff's.

[93] [2015] EWHC 999 (Comm) (Carr J).

[94] ibid [110]–[128]. Fortunately for Spliethoff, however, it was able to enforce against the Bank of China guarantees made under English law in respect of the repayment of its upfront payments to the Chinese shipbuilder.

[95] *CSR Ltd v Cigna Insurance Australia Ltd* [1997] HCA 33, (1997) 189 CLR 345, 402 (Dawson, Toohey, Gaudron, McHugh, Gummow and Kirby JJ).

[96] *Commonwealth Bank of Australia v White [No 3]* [2000] VSC 25; *Telesto Investments Ltd v UBS AG* [2012] NSWSC 44, [90]–[115] (Ward J).

An important practical factor in attempting to take enforceability into account at an early stage in proceedings is the unpredictability of the outcome, particularly where multiple courts and proceedings are involved. Judges may comment on the undesirability of multiple proceedings and the risk of inconsistent findings, particularly where it is likely that the cases will deal with the same issues,[97] and the consequent costs and expenses. Clearly the courts consider it undesirable for proceedings to result in conflicting or overlapping judgments. Ward J set this out clearly in the 2012 case of *Telesto Investments Ltd v UBS AG*:

> It seems to me that .... it would be vexatious and oppressive of the Telesto parties (in the sense of the objective effect on UBS AG of their conduct) now to pursue a course of conduct that will have the inevitable result of exposing UBS AG to the risk of conflicting judgments across two jurisdictions.[98]

Cases with fact situations as clear cut in *Bendigo and Adelaide Bank Ltd v Quine*[99] (and *Henry v Henry)* should, however, be distinguished from complex, long drawn-out multi-jurisdictional proceedings, where attempting to assess and then rely on the possibility of a judgment being unenforceable may well come within the scope of 'speculative' submissions criticised in the *Prudentia and Sunland* litigation.[100]

In addition, as predicted by the judge in *Quine*, delving too deeply into the issue and implications of unenforceability potentially involves the court in a range of considerations and issues which are removed from the underlying dispute. The arguments in *Impala* provide a good example of this.[101] The discussion before the Court as to the steps that could be taken to deal with the potential unenforceability of a judgment of the English court in China supports the view that the court should not become too deeply involved in this issue. Parties argued about the issue of providing security to support the judgment (rejected on the basis that this would put a party that had breached the exclusive jurisdiction clause in a better position than it would be in if the judgment were enforceable); entering into an arbitration agreement (since an award would be enforceable) (rejected because the parties could not come to terms on the substance of the arbitration) or a side agreement on payment (rejected because it would be unenforceable in China). The final decision of the judge was to issue a final prohibitory injunction and a final mandatory injunction but with the parties to make submissions as to the terms of the injunction, including conditionality. This does not, with respect, seem to be a very satisfactory solution.

Finally, Australia's potential accession to the Hague Choice of Court Convention and the Draft Convention does not assist in relation to this question.

[97] See eg *Henry v Henry* (n 10), discussed in *CMA CGM SA v Ship 'Chou Shan'* [2014] FCAFC 90, (2014) 224 FCR 384, [29]–[30] (Allsop CJ, Besanko and Pagone JJ).

[98] [2012] NSWSC 44, [210].

[99] *Bendigo and Adelaide Bank Ltd v Quine* (n 54).

[100] See n 57.

[101] See text to n 58ff.

The Hague Choice of Court Convention, consistently with the Foreign Judgments Act, links jurisdiction firmly with enforcement but moves Australian practice in relation to exclusive jurisdiction clauses away from judicial discretion to a mandated approach. The issue of enforceability presented in *Impala* would not have been relevant under the Hague Choice of Court Convention.

The Draft Convention is still at a relatively early stage, but incorporation into domestic law will undoubtedly present a challenge for both civil and common law systems. Ways in which the Draft Convention could be incorporated into Australian law and practice range from minor changes to the Foreign Judgments Act to cover states which accede to the Convention to comprehensive changes to enforcement both under statute and under common law, as well as modifications to current rules on long-arm jurisdiction. Whichever option is adopted, there would also be a question whether the adoption of the Draft Convention could or should change the approach of the courts in relation to the exercise of jurisdiction. In theory, within the context of the Draft Convention, a court could have increased certainty in predicting whether a foreign judgment given by a court in a state which is a party to the Convention could be enforced in Australia (based on the minimum criteria set out in the Draft Convention). Similarly, it might assist the court in determining whether a domestic judgment could be enforced in another Contracting State, without the requirement for detailed expert evidence.

In practice, since the Draft Convention establishes a minimum standard for enforcement under art 16, an argument that a domestic judgment could *not* be enforced in a competing jurisdiction would still need to be supported by detailed examination and expert evidence.[102] This would therefore seem to be a strong argument why the party bringing the case in an Australian court against a foreign defendant should take its own risks in relation to enforcement. In relation to assessing the likelihood of enforcement, the Draft Convention does not resolve the issues presented by future actions of the parties, particularly by submission to jurisdiction or participation in the overseas proceedings on the merits.[103] The prospect of enforcement of non-monetary judgments also adds to the issues on this point.

In few of the cases looked at (with the exception of *Quine*, *Impala* and *Central Petroleum*) has enforceability played a major role in the arguments or the ultimate decision. The recent cases in which enforceability was considered in detail tend to be fact-specific and decided accordingly. Thus, *Quine* was decided pursuant to the principles set out in the Civil Procedure Act rather than the 'inappropriate forum' test; *Central Petroleum* involves the relatively unusual fact situation of a dispute over the very existence of an agreement and in *Impala*, one of the litigants decided to test the viability of the factors set out in *The Eleftheria*. In other cases, such as

[102] See discussion in J Hogan-Doran and D Hogan-Doran on issues relating to proof of foreign law, ch 10 of this volume.

[103] Draft Convention, arts 7(1) (e) and (f).

*Addu,* the judge applied the common-sense principle that a plaintiff who brings a case thereby also makes its own determination in relation to enforceability. Given the various factors discussed above, particularly the unpredictability of enforcement due not just to the complexity of different national rules but also to the effect that actions of the litigants themselves may have upon enforceability, an approach which places only limited weight on enforceability has much to recommend it.

## IV. Conclusion

There is a logical attraction to the idea that the enforcement of the final judgment should be considered by a court at the time that proceedings are commenced. Similarly, one might anticipate that the enforceability of a prospective foreign judgment could be taken into account when the court decides whether to take jurisdiction or to grant interim relief. The cases discussed tend to be fact-specific but, with some exceptions, indicate that Australian courts adhere to the principle that the parties should make their own litigation decisions, which include taking risks in relation to enforceability, and are cautious in giving weight to factors of enforceability in making determinations at the early stage of proceedings. Rules on enforcement differ across jurisdictions (unless and until they are harmonised by the Draft Convention). The actions of the litigants themselves can affect the enforceability of a judgment. The cases also raise the question as to the degree to which the court – as opposed to the parties – should become involved in attempting to deal with the implications of unenforceability (as in *Impala*) or the litigation tactics of the parties (as in *Central Petroleum*).

On the whole, it is argued that a review of the facts and decisions in the recent cases discussed in this chapter, as well as a quick survey of recent international developments, support the view that, unless the question of enforceability is immediate and easily resolved and giving weight to it is clearly in the interests of justice (as in *Quine*), the courts should continue, in making a determination on jurisdiction or interim relief, to take a cautious approach in assessing the relevance of the enforceability of a prospective judgment.

# 4

# The Case Management Stay in Private International Law

REID MORTENSEN*

## I. Introduction

Since the late 1990s, the power to stay civil proceedings temporarily on case management grounds has emerged in commercial litigation as a supplement to more established powers for addressing concurrent litigation or arbitrations in other countries. This has been overwhelmingly an English development. As such, 'the case management stay' developed a legal profile that reflects the complex relationship between the common law and European Union law – the *acquis communautaire* – that for the time being at least has effect in England.[1] It has also been successfully exported, with recognition throughout the Anglo-common law world, although in no country have courts rushed to order case management stays where there is concurrent litigation or arbitrations. However, the unique status of the temporary stay as an exercise of a common law court's managerial power, and the broad discretion that it gives to judges, means that, inside and outside the EU, it has potential to be used to sidestep existing limitations on courts' powers to address, in particular, the problem of *lis pendens* – a term that, perhaps too loosely, is taken to include concurrent litigation or a concurrent arbitration.

In this chapter, I give an account of the case management stay and its use in cross-border commercial litigation. This involves, in section II, a discussion of the origins of the case management stay in England and the shape it has taken in common law courts in the EU. It includes consideration of the unique place that the case management stay holds in the uneasy and ambiguous relationship

* I thank Adeline Chong, Sarah McKibbin, Mary Keyes and Michael Douglas for comments on this chapter. Any errors are inevitably my own.

[1] This chapter was written in 2018, before the anticipated date for the United Kingdom's exit from the EU. Assuming that Brexit takes place on 29 March 2019, it is intended that, for the most part, the *acquis* will from that day be patriated as UK law but, potentially, be subject to parliamentary and judicial modification: see European Union (Withdrawal) Act 2018 (UK). It is not entirely clear what effect this might have on the existing law of civil jurisdiction.

between, on the one hand, the common law and, on the other, the Brussels I Regulation Recast,[2] the parallel Lugano II Convention[3] and their forerunners.[4] The European Court of Justice's decision in *Owusu v Jackson*[5] outlawing stays of proceedings on the ground of *forum non conveniens* in Brussels I litigation looms large in this analysis. The common law of England, nevertheless, also continues to lead and influence the development of the common law in countries outside the EU, particularly in the Commonwealth (and recent Commonwealth). In section III, consequently, the recognition of the case management stay in commercial litigation in Australia, Canada, Hong Kong, New Zealand and Singapore is discussed. The effect that the *acquis* might have had in shaping the case management stay in England is naturally siphoned from any reception of the case management stay in common law countries outside the EU. And while any strictures that the *acquis* has placed on the exercise of the managerial power in the EU are irrelevant in these countries, the case management stay still has potential outside the EU for bypassing different limits in the law dealing with *lis pendens*.

# II. The Case Management Stay in Europe

## A. The Managerial Power

The established powers of a court to stay cross-border proceedings have been expanded over the last two decades by the court's use of a temporary stay to give effect to principles of case management. This power was first recognised in 1998 when, in *Reichhold Norway ASA v Goldman Sachs International*,[6] Moore-Bick J held that the High Court of Justice in England and Wales had an inherent jurisdiction to stay proceedings on the ground, in *Reichhold* itself, that there was an arbitration in Norway that should be determined first. The Court of Appeal comprehensively affirmed Moore-Bick J's decision, in both the result and the reasoning that

[2] Regulation (EU) No 1215/2012 of the European Parliament and of the Council of 12 December 2012 on jurisdiction and the recognition and enforcement of judgments in civil and commercial matters (Recast) [2012] OJ L351/1 (Recast).

[3] Convention on jurisdiction and the recognition and enforcement of judgments in civil and commercial matters, Lugano, 30 October 2007 [2007] OJ L339/3 (Lugano II).

[4] For the predecessors of the Recast, see Convention on jurisdiction and the enforcement of judgments in civil and commercial matters, Brussels, 27 September 1968 (Brussels Convention) [1998] OJ C27/1; Council Regulation (EC) No 44/2001 of 22 December 2000 on jurisdiction and the recognition and enforcement of judgments in civil and commercial matters [2001] OJ L12/1 (Brussels I Regulation). Any provisions that are effectively uniform in the Brussels Convention, the Brussels I Regulation and the Recast are referred to as Brussels I. The predecessor of Lugano II was the European Community-European Free Trade Association Convention on jurisdiction and the recognition and enforcement of judgments in civil and commercial matters, Lugano, 16 September 1988 [1988] OJ L319/9 (Lugano I). Any provisions that are effectively uniform in Lugano I and Lugano II are referred to as Lugano.

[5] Case C-281/02 *Owusu v Jackson* [2005] ECR I-1383.

[6] [1999] 1 All ER (Comm) 40.

led to it.[7] It has recognised *Reichhold*'s authority in later decisions,[8] as has the Northern Ireland Court of Appeal.[9] Indeed, apart from later recognition that the principles for the granting of a case management stay would have to respond to developments in the *acquis*, Moore-Bick J's decision is a remarkably complete statement of the principles of the case management stay to this day. The decision was without precedent, but the power to order a temporary stay did not emerge *ex nihilo*. It was a necessary implication of a recently evolved understanding of the court as having inherent powers to manage litigation before it.[10]

As will be seen,[11] this managerial power to grant a stay is available when a court is not able to grant a stay on grounds allowing it to decline a jurisdiction that it is entitled to exercise. These jurisdictional grounds for the granting of stays include powers that arise in relation to vexatious or oppressive proceedings, *forum non conveniens*, *lis alibi pendens*, the enforcement of a choice of court agreement or the enforcement of an arbitration agreement under the Arbitration Act 1996 (UK). It seems that the managerial power has developed as a consequence of the changing role of the court itself – and not in response to the introduction of specific rules of 'caseflow management' that enable the judge to supervise how proceedings will move through the litigation process from the time of initiation to the point of final disposition.[12] In *Reichhold*, the Norwegian claimant argued that it had 'an absolute right' to bring a 'legitimate claim' against a defendant in England, even if there was also an entitlement to claim against others in other countries.[13] Moore-Bick J replied that the court's jurisdiction to stay proceedings relied only on the need to give effect to the interests of justice and was otherwise 'unfettered'. The court's inherent jurisdiction was the sole source he drew on to reach that conclusion.[14] It was not a matter of who could sue or be sued in England; it was a matter (in *Reichhold*) of deciding whether English litigation or a Norwegian arbitration should run first. The English judge had powers to manage that.[15]

[7] *Reichhold Norway ASA v Goldman Sachs International* [2000] 1 WLR 173 (Lord Bingham CJ and Otton and Robert Walker LJJ).

[8] *Racy v Hawila* [2004] EWCA Civ 209, [25]–[27] (Thorpe, May and Parker LJJ); *Konkola Copper Mines Plc v Coromin Limited* [2006] 1 All ER (Comm) 437, 453 (Sir Anthony Clarke MR and Rix and Richards LJJ); *Amlin Corporate Member Ltd v Oriental Assurance Corporation* [2012] EWCA Civ 1341, [19] (Longmore, Rimer and Tomlinson LJJ).

[9] *HSBC Bank Plc v Robinson* [2017] NICA 64 (Gillen and Stephens LJJ). The Northern Irish courts have nevertheless only used the *Reichhold* temporary stay in purely domestic cases involving possession of land: *Barclays Bank Plc (t/a The Woolwich) v Boyd* [2015] NICh 16 (Deeny J); *HSBC Bank Ltd v Robinson* [2017] NICh 7 (McBride J).

[10] The inherent jurisdiction to order a temporary stay is preserved by legislation: Senior Courts Act 1981 (UK) s 49(3); Civil Procedure Rules 1998 (UK) r 3.1(2)(f); *Goldman Sachs International v Novo Banco SA* [2015] EWHC 2371 (Comm), [117] (Hamblen J).

[11] See text accompanying below nn 56–62.

[12] M Solomon and D Somerlot, Caseflow Management in the Trial Court: Now and for the Future (Chicago, American Bar Association, 1987) 3.

[13] [1999] 1 All ER (Comm) 40, 46.

[14] ibid 46–47.

[15] ibid 47.

Similarly, in the Court of Appeal, Lord Bingham CJ accepted that 'forensic practice was changing' and that this meant that the court was more actively involved in managing proceedings.[16] In short, in *Reichhold* it meant that a judge could use a temporary stay of proceedings to put the hearing of local litigation and a foreign arbitration into a more efficient sequence.[17]

## B. Brussels I and the Common Law

As early as *Reichhold* itself,[18] the courts carefully delineated the roles of the managerial and jurisdictional powers to grant a stay of proceedings. The clarification was probably needed because the powers have some apparent similarities; both amount to an exercise of a judicial discretion not to deal with litigation before the court, albeit that the breadth of that discretion for the jurisdictional power differs from ground to ground. The large role of discretion in litigation about where to litigate, and the flexibility that it gives to the judge, are important characteristics of the modern common law. They give the common law a distinctive capacity to deal with commercial litigation in cost-effective and cost-efficient ways,[19] and they assist in elevating the importance of achieving a commercial outcome to the dispute (even above that of securing a technically correct judgment).[20] These discretions evidently allow greater pre-trial skirmishing in common law courts about the best venue for the litigation, and this can certainly undermine the common law's claims to being cost-efficient in its handling of commercial litigation. However, even here the discretions can, somewhat perversely, assist in securing a commercial outcome.[21] As Staughton J famously observed in *The Spiliada*,[22] litigation about where to litigate is often better understood as litigation about which legal system will give the backdrop for negotiating a commercial settlement.[23]

The role of discretion in common law procedure has inevitably created tension with the more rules-based approach that is taken to jurisdictional questions in Brussels I and – by implication – Lugano. In many respects, Europe was not ready for the common law and has not learned how it works. The original 1968 Brussels Convention, naturally, exemplified the codified civil law traditions of the original six Member States of the European Economic Community. It was only when (with Denmark) the United Kingdom and Ireland acceded to the

[16] [2000] 1 WLR 173, 184–85.
[17] ibid.
[18] See text accompanying below nn 56–62.
[19] See generally R Fentiman, *International Commercial Litigation*, 2nd edn (Oxford, Oxford University Press, 2015) 12–17.
[20] ibid 14.
[21] ibid 24.
[22] *Spiliada Maritime Corp v Cansulex Ltd* [1987] AC 460.
[23] ibid 468.

Convention in 1978,[24] that the Brussels I scheme was first adopted for legal systems that rested on developed systems of 'grown and growing law'. The depth of the difference was not appreciated. Professor Schlosser's report on the revision of the Brussels Convention to accommodate the accessions of 1978 recognised the different positions that the common law had reached in relation to the enforcement of judgments,[25] remedies[26] and adjudicative jurisdiction.[27] Schlosser also noted the use of discretion in the then distinctive doctrine of *forum non conveniens* in Scots law.[28] However, more important differences in the method, the basic character and the juridical attitude[29] of the common law received no recognition. The Brussels I regime did not contemplate, and has never accommodated, the organic evolution of the doctrinal positions of the common law.

In *The Spiliada*[30] in 1986, four years after the Brussels I regime came into force in the United Kingdom,[31] the Scottish doctrine of *forum non conveniens* was adopted as law in England and Wales. This is a 'convenience-suitability approach' to declining jurisdiction,[32] when a stay will be granted if 'there is some other available forum, having competent jurisdiction, which is the appropriate forum for trial of the action, ie in which the case may be tried more suitably for the interests of all the parties and the ends of justice'.[33] The same year saw the principles for granting anti-suit injunctions against foreign proceedings aligned with those of *forum non conveniens*.[34] Together, these jurisdictional powers enable common law courts to compel litigation to be heard in the place where its centre of gravity rests – whether that is a local or foreign court.

These powers originated in litigation that was not captured by Brussels I but, despite early reservations that they were incompatible with it,[35] English courts eventually toyed with the idea that these discretionary powers could be reconciled

[24] Convention of Accession of the Kingdom of Denmark, of Ireland and of the United Kingdom of Great Britain and Northern Ireland to the Convention on jurisdiction and enforcement of judgements in civil and commercial matters and to the Protocol on its interpretation by the Court of Justice, Luxembourg, 9 October 1978 [1978] OJ L304/1.

[25] Report on the Convention on the Association of the Kingdom of Denmark, Ireland and the United Kingdom of Great Britain and Northern Ireland to the Convention on jurisdiction and the enforcement of judgments in civil and commercial matters and to the Protocol on its interpretation by the Court of Justice [1979] OJ C59/71, 78–79.

[26] ibid 80.

[27] ibid 99, 100.

[28] ibid 97.

[29] A Dickinson and E Lein (eds), *The Brussels I Regulation Recast* (Oxford, Oxford University Press, 2015) 5.

[30] *Spiliada Maritime Corp v Cansulex Ltd* (n 22).

[31] Civil Jurisdiction and Judgments Act 1982 (UK).

[32] AT von Mehren, 'Theory and Practice of Adjudicatory Authority in Private International Law: A Comparative Study of the Doctrine, Policies and Practices of Common- and Civil-Law Systems' (2002) 295 *Recueil des Cours* 326.

[33] *Spiliada Maritime Corp v Cansulex Ltd* (n 22) 476 (Lord Goff of Chieveley).

[34] *Société Nationale Industrielle Aerospatiale v Lee Kui Jak* [1987] 1 AC 871. See also *Airbus Industrie GIE v Patel* [1999] 1 AC 119.

[35] *S&W Berisford v New Hampshire Insurance Co* [1990] 2 QB 631; *Arkwright Mutual Insurance Co v Bryanston Ince* [1990] 2 QB 649.

with the Brussels I system.[36] That assumption was scuttled when, in 2004, the European Court of Justice ruled that an English anti-suit injunction could not be issued against proceedings elsewhere in the EU even when those proceedings were intentionally brought to frustrate the English litigation.[37] Even more relevant to the question of stays of proceedings was the European Court's decision the following year in *Owusu v Jackson*.[38] The application of the Brussels I system has always been conditioned on the defendant (in proceedings in the EU) being domiciled in a country of the EU.[39] *Owusu* demonstrated how strong that rule is when determining the scope of Brussels I, as the case was a domestic English personal injuries claim between two English domiciliaries. The injury was, nevertheless, suffered in Jamaica and, in addition, Jamaican corporate defendants were joined to the action against the principal English defendant. At trial, a plea to stay proceedings in favour of a Jamaican court was rejected. On appeal, the Court of Appeal referred the question of the availability of the doctrine of *forum non conveniens* in matters arising under Brussels I to the European Court of Justice. The central question was whether the plea of *forum non conveniens* was available when the competition was between a court in the EU and a court outside the EU. The Grand Chamber held it was not. Brussels I applied whenever a defendant was domiciled in a Member State of the EU, and it did not require the claimant to have come from a different Member State. It would apply in purely domestic proceedings within a single EU country.[40] That being so, the Grand Chamber then found that legal certainty and predictability, pillars of the *acquis*, would be compromised if a court seised of a Brussels I jurisdiction was allowed a discretion not to exercise it.[41] It held that:[42]

> the Brussels Convention precludes a court of a Contracting State from declining the jurisdiction conferred on it by [the Brussels Convention] on the ground that a court of a non-Contracting State would be a more appropriate forum for the trial of the action even if the jurisdiction of no other Contracting State is in issue or the proceedings have no connecting factors to any other Contracting State.

The Court of Appeal in Owusu had also asked the European Court whether the doctrine of *forum non conveniens* was banned in all cases that were captured by Brussels I. Although the Grand Chamber's reasoning had rested on the general principle that discretionary powers affecting the exercise of jurisdiction introduced legal uncertainty and unpredictability, it baulked in *Owusu* at stating the natural consequence of that principle – potentially banning any exercise of a jurisdictional

[36] *Re Harrods (Buenos Aires) Ltd* [1992] Ch 72.
[37] Case C-159/02 *Turner v Grovit* [2004] ECR I-3565.
[38] *Owusu v Jackson* (n 5).
[39] Brussels Convention, art 2; Brussels I Regulation, arts 2, 4; Recast, art 4. Similarly, Lugano applies whenever the defendant is domiciled in the European Economic Area (the EU with Iceland, Norway and Switzerland): Lugano I, art 3; Lugano II, art 2.
[40] [2005] ECR I-1383, [24]–[36].
[41] ibid [37]–[43].
[42] ibid [46].

discretion in litigation within the scope of Brussels I. As a result, it dismissed the Court of Appeal's question as hypothetical.[43] This is ironic, of course, because the Grand Chamber's response to the Court of Appeal's question itself compounded the uncertainty and unpredictability of the place of discretionary powers relating to the exercise of jurisdiction in Brussels I cases. It was especially unclear in genuine *lis pendens* cases, where the proceedings outside the EU preceded or began at the same time as those being addressed inside it.[44] *Owusu* and the European Court's dislike of the anti-suit inunction[45] led to significant – and justified – criticism that the European Court was more invested in the public law infrastructure of the EU than in the needs of commercial litigants.[46] This collision revealed profound differences in the juridical cultures of common law courts and of the *acquis communautaire*. It reinforces Brussels I's 'seemingly uncommercial orientation';[47] and the assessment that it is 'too unsophisticated, too un-commercial in its assumptions, to regulate substantial commercial disputes'.[48] However, the case management stay was one means by which the common law was shaped by, and yet developed around, the constraints on the conduct of commercial litigation that had emerged in the *acquis*.

## C. After *Owusu*: Features of the Case Management Stay

Although the contours of the case management stay have remained unchanged since *Reichhold*,[49] the European Court's reasoning in *Owusu*[50] has seen adjudication put those contours into sharper relief. To an extent, adjudication in England

[43] ibid [47]–[52].

[44] eg *Goshawk Dedicated Ltd v Life Receivables Ireland Ltd* [2009] IESC 7; *Lucasfilm Ltd v Ainsworth* [2010] 1 Ch 503, 533–4; *Ferrexpo v Gilson Investments Ltd* [2012] EWHC 721 (Comm) (Andrew Smith J); *Lungowe v Vedanta Resources Plc* [2016] EWHC 975 (TCC), [57]. The Recast, arts 33–34, subsequently gave an express power to stay proceedings in these *lis pendens* cases. *Owusu* was held inapplicable to stays based on an exclusive choice of court agreement derogating from English jurisdiction: *Konkola Copper Mines plc v Coromin* (n 8) 448–49, 455–56.

[45] *Turner v Grovit* (n 37) was followed by *Allianz SpA v West Tankers Inc* [2009] ECR I-00663, where an English court issued an anti-suit injunction against an Italian court that was hearing a marine insurance claim in breach of an arbitration agreement. The injunction was issued to enforce the agreement, but the European Court of Justice held that it was incompatible with 'the trust which the Member States accord to one another's legal systems and judicial institutions': [2009] ECR I-00663, [39].

[46] In *West Tankers* this was explicit; the rights of courts were given clear priority over certainty of contractual relations and holding parties to their bargains: see ibid. For more general criticisms, see T Hartley, 'The Modern Approach to Private International Law: International Litigation and Transactions from a Common Law Perspective: General Course on Private International Law' (2006) 319 *Recueil des Cours* 9, 183; J Harris, 'The English Response to the Europeanisation of Private International Law' (2008) 4(3) *Journal of Private International Law* 347, 369, 377; A Briggs, *Private International Law in English Courts* (Oxford, Oxford University Press, 2014) Preface.

[47] Fentiman, *International Commercial Litigation* (n 19) 28.

[48] ibid 29.

[49] [1999] 1 All ER (Comm) 40.

[50] *Owusu v Jackson* (n 5).

and Wales, Northern Ireland and Ireland has also clarified the utility of the stay in commercial litigation. A number of characteristics of the case management stay have emerged.

First of all, of necessity the case management stay may only be made temporarily. The order is made to manage litigation before the court and, as a result, the court must retain its control over the proceedings.[51] Its purpose is for 'the efficient marshalling of multi-jurisdictional and multi-party proceedings but which does not involve the court declining jurisdiction'.[52] This leads to a second quality of the stay, and that is its availability in proceedings captured by Brussels I. Although Richard Fentiman considers that *Owusu* cast a shadow over the use of a temporary stay in Brussels I litigation,[53] it has not been questioned in national common law courts in the EU.[54] The recognition that, even if the stay is granted, the court suspending the trial of the proceedings nevertheless continues to control them, means that the ordering of a case management stay maintains a Brussels I jurisdiction that is properly claimed. It merely defers trial of the merits. In this respect, the case management stay does not engage the general principle of *Owusu* that a discretion should not defeat a jurisdiction to which litigants in the EU have an entitlement. Having said that, the Brussels I regime, and specifically the decision in *Owusu*, have conditioned how the case management stay is applied in Brussels I litigation, and beyond.[55]

Thirdly, the English courts have, at least in a formal sense, carefully confined the availability of the case management stay to proceedings where there is not a jurisdiction to grant a stay on other grounds. It does not seem to be available if proceedings are characterised as vexatious, oppressive, an abuse of process or being brought in bad faith,[56] or if a stay is sought under the Arbitration Act 1996 (UK).[57] It is not available when *lis pendens* is being addressed by enforcing an exclusive choice of court agreement.[58] Most importantly, the courts have treated the principles of case management and the doctrine of *forum non conveniens* as, in effect, mutually exclusive.[59] The difference is that, given its requirement that there be an alternative forum for the determination of a dispute, the doctrine of *forum non conveniens* deals with the prior question of whether jurisdiction over the

[51] *Jefferies International Limited v Landsbanki Islands HF* [2009] EWHC 894 (Comm) [28]–[29] (Cooke J).

[52] *Autoridad Del Canal De Panamá v Sacyr, SA* [2017] EWHC 2228 (Comm) [149] (Blair J).

[53] Fentiman (n 19) 466.

[54] *ET Plus SA v Welter* [2005] EWHC 2115 (Comm) [91]; *Equitas Limited v Allstate Insurance Company* [2008] EWHC 1671 (Comm) [64] (Beatson J); *Jefferies International Limited v Landsbanki Islands HF* (n 51) [26]; *Ferrexpo v Gilson Investments Ltd* [2012] EWHC 721 (Comm) [199]; *Lungowe v Vedanta Resources Plc* (n 44) [84] (Coulson J); *Autoridad Del Canal De Panamá v Sacyr, SA* (n 52) [149].

[55] See text accompanying below nn 63–75.

[56] *Reichhold Norway ASA v Goldman Sachs International* [2000] 1 WLR 173, 185.

[57] *J&W Sanderson Ltd v Fenox (UK) Ltd* [2014] EWHC 4322 (Ch) [9]-[10], [12]–[15] (Pymont QC); *Autoridad Del Canal De Panamá v Sacyr, SA* (n 52) [151].

[58] *Konkola Copper Mines plc v Coromin* (n 8) 452.

[59] *Racy v Hawila* (n 8) [61].

proceedings in England should be exercised. A question concerning how proceedings should be managed, instead, addresses the time at which they are best to be heard. *Forum non conveniens*, as Moore-Bick J put it in *Reichhold*, 'is not a question of when but whether the plaintiff should be allowed to pursue the action here'.[60] For that reason, a permanent stay of proceedings is available when the English court is a *forum non conveniens* but only a temporary stay is available when case management principles are in play.[61] Lord Bingham concluded that there is a similar distinction between a permanent stay made on the ground of *lis alibi pendens*, and the temporary stay made to co-ordinate the timing of parallel proceedings.[62]

Fourthly, there is the question as to how the case management stay relates to the ban on stays of proceedings made in *Owusu* and the more general reservation expressed by the Grand Chamber that discretionary stays of proceedings undermine the *acquis* pillars of certainty and predictability. *Reichhold* itself was held to be untouched by Brussels I or Lugano.[63] However, the decision in *Owusu* was looming when Lawrence Collins J decided *Mazur Media Limited v Mazur Media GmbH*,[64] a case that was squarely within a Brussels I jurisdiction.[65] Although *Mazur Media* did not involve an application for a *Reichhold*-style case management stay, the judge expressed serious reservations about the granting of a stay of any kind that edged towards considering factors that were typically relevant to a question of *forum non conveniens*.[66] These included the cost of proceedings, the limited effect that any judgment would have in the foreign proceedings, the availability of the foreign court, and the possibility of incompatible judgments.[67] The application for a stay in *Mazur Media* was not made on the ground of *forum non conveniens*, but Lawrence Collins J considered that Brussels I created a deep prohibition on considering any aspects of the doctrine. So long as a factor was something that was relevant to a question of *forum non conveniens*, it could not be legitimately considered in a Brussels I jurisdiction.[68]

Lawrence Collins J's emphasis on the substance of the application for a stay, rather than the tag given to it in submissions, was reinforced after *Owusu*. If a stay was sought on either case management or *forum non conveniens* grounds, there was the possibility that the question of exercising managerial powers might slip into one of jurisdictional powers.[69] In Brussels I jurisdictions, the courts were therefore unwilling to grant a temporary stay on case management grounds if, in effect, the issues that arose shadowed those arising in the outlawed *forum non*

[60] *Reichhold Norway ASA v Goldman Sachs International* [1999] 1 All ER (Comm) 40, 51.
[61] ibid 51.
[62] *Reichhold Norway ASA v Goldman Sachs International* [2000] 1 WLR 173, 185.
[63] *Reichhold Norway ASA v Goldman Sachs International* [1999] 1 All ER (Comm) 40, 51.
[64] [2004] 1 WLR 2966.
[65] ibid 2970.
[66] ibid 2983–84.
[67] ibid.
[68] ibid 2984.
[69] *Konkola Copper Mines plc v Coromin* (n 8) 452, 455.

*conveniens* application.[70] However, not every English or Irish judge has been as scrupulous – and there are instances where the location of the parties, witnesses and documentary evidence;[71] governing law;[72] the enforceability of the judgment;[73] and the risk of incompatible judgments[74] have been considered relevant to the question of case management. The mutual exclusion of the principles relating to managerial and jurisdictional stays also means that, if a jurisdictional plea is allowed, no question of a case management stay can be considered.[75]

Fifthly, an application to a court to exercise its managerial powers has an important similarity to an application for the exercise of jurisdictional powers: it is litigation about where to litigate, albeit that for the temporary stay it is where to litigate *first*. The effect of the different orders can be the same. For instance, a permanent stay granted in England on the ground of *forum non conveniens* may be made on condition that the foreign limitation period is waived.[76] Evidently, despite a permanent stay, the English proceedings might be properly re-activated if the condition cannot be fulfilled.[77] Equally, the decision to grant a temporary stay in *Reichhold* was made in part because Moore-Bick J considered that the Norwegian arbitration could deal with issues earlier than they could be dealt with in England, and it could do so relatively cheaply.[78] In these conditions, the possibility that the foreign tribunal's decision will create an issue estoppel or even make the matter *res judicata* must be contemplated.[79] Indeed, in *Klockner Holdings GmbH v Klockner Beteilegungs GmbH*,[80] Gloster J considered that a reason *not* to grant a temporary stay was that 'the other proceedings will not even bind the parties to the action stayed, let alone finally resolve all the issues in the case to be stayed'.[81] In litigation

[70] *CNA Insurance Company Limited & Ors* [2005] EWHC (Comm) 456, [26] (Langley J); *Blomqvist v Zavarco Plc* [2016] Ch 128, 145; *Autoridad Del Canal De Panamá v Sacyr, SA* (n 52) [144].

[71] *Innovia Films Limited v Frito-Lay North America, Inc* [2012] EWHC 790 (Pat) [129]–[131] (Arnold J).

[72] ibid [132]; *Bankhaus Wolbern & Co (AG & CO KG) v China Construction Bank Corporation, Zhejiang Branch* [2012] EWHC 3285 (Comm) [16], [20].

[73] *Bankhaus Wolbern & Co (AG & CO KG) v China Construction Bank Corporation, Zhejiang Branch* (n 72) [16], [20].

[74] *Kalix Fund Ltd v HSBC Institutional Trust Services (Ireland) Ltd* [2010] 2 IR 581, [43] (Clarke J); *Innovia Films Limited v Frito-Lay North America, Inc* (n 71) [133]; *Ferrexpo v Gilson Investments Ltd* (n 44) [200]; *Citigroup Global Markets Ltd v Amatra Leveraged Feeder Holdings Ltd* [2012] EWHC 1331 (Comm) [73]; *Stemcor UK Ltd v Global Steel Holdings Ltd* [2015] EWHC 363, [43]–[44] (Comm) (Hamblen J).

[75] *Innovia Films Limited v Frito-Lay North America, Inc* (n 71) [127]; *cf Racy v Hawila* (n 8) [61]; *Citigroup Global Markets Ltd v Amatra Leveraged Feeder Holdings Ltd* (n 74) [80].

[76] *Spiliada Maritime Corp v Cansulex Ltd* (n 22) 483–84; *Baghlaf Al Zafer Factory Co BR for Industry Ltd v Pakistan National Shipping Co* [1998] 2 Lloyd's Rep 229, 237, 239.

[77] eg *Baghlaf Al Zafer Factory Co BR for Industry Ltd v Pakistan National Shipping Co (No 2)* [2000] 1 Lloyd's Rep 1.

[78] *Reichhold Norway ASA v Goldman Sachs International* [1999] 1 All ER (Comm) 40, 52; cf *J&W Sanderson Ltd v Fenox (UK) Ltd* (n 57) [13].

[79] *Blomqvist v Zavarco Plc* (n 70) 145.

[80] [2005] EWHC 1453 (Comm).

[81] [2005] EWHC 1453 (Comm) [21]; see also *Isis Investments Ltd v Oscatello Investments Ltd* [2013] EWHC 7 (Ch) [22] (Asplin J); *Stemcor UK Ltd v Global Steel Holdings Ltd* [2015] EWHC 363, [44].

over the Channel Tunnel, Gross J granted a temporary stay in favour of a French arbitration – while openly recognising that the arbitration might be 'ultimately decisive' of the claims.[82] The deference to the foreign litigation or arbitration will inevitably narrow the issues to be dealt with locally once the suspension of the local proceedings is lifted.[83] The temporary stay may therefore have the same effect as a permanent stay; and just as a *forum conveniens* decision about where to litigate may merely identify a legal system that narrows the terms that will direct the settlement of a claim, a managerial decision about where to litigate first could have exactly the same result.

A number of cases suggest that, at least initially, litigants might apply for a case management stay as an alternative to a jurisdictional stay for that very reason. So, litigants in England and Ireland have applied for a case management stay alongside a simultaneous application to stay or set aside proceedings permanently on the ground of *forum non conveniens*,[84] *lis alibi pendens*,[85] an abuse of process,[86] an arbitration agreement[87] or an exclusive choice of court agreement[88] – or an objection to an application for an anti-suit injunction.[89] And most importantly, when *Owusu* means that, in Brussels I litigation, the plea of *forum non conveniens* is simply unavailable, a stay granted on case management grounds might well be an alternative way of securing the outcome that the stay on forum grounds would have given. This surreptitious use of the case management stay to bypass the limitations of the *acquis* was evidently what Lawrence Collins J was warning against in *Mazur Media*,[90] and it was confirmed by Beatson J in *Equitas Limited v Allstate Insurance Company*.[91] A stay should not be granted in the exercise of the court's case management powers where the effect of doing so would in substance be permanent; *Owusu* outlaws that.

But leaving the formal principles to one side, the judge cannot predict precisely what the effect will be of deferring temporarily to a foreign court or arbitration.

[82] *ET Plus SA v Welter* (n 54) [91].

[83] *Reichhold Norway ASA v Goldman Sachs International* [1999] 1 All ER (Comm) 40, 49; *ET Plus SA v Welter* (n 54) [91].

[84] *Racy v Hawila* (n 8); *Pacific International Sports Clubs Ltd v Soccer Marketing International Ltd* [2009] EWHC 1839 (Ch) [30]–[34], [114]–[115] (Blackburne J); *Innovia Films Limited v Frito-Lay North America, Inc* (n 71); *Bankhaus Wolbern & Co (AG & CO KG) v China Construction Bank Corporation, Zhejiang Branch* (n 72); *P Elliot & Co Ltd v FCC Elliot Construction Ltd* [2012] IEHC 361, [23] (MacEochaidh J); *Ferrexpo v Gilson Investments Ltd* (n 44); *Blomqvist v Zavarco Plc* (n 70) 136, 145; *Lungowe v Vedanta Resources Plc* (n 44) [65]–[72].

[85] *P Elliot & Co Ltd v FCC Elliot Construction Ltd* (n 84) [23]; *Ferrexpo v Gilson Investments Ltd* (n 44); *Blomqvist v Zavarco Plc* (n 70) 136, 145.

[86] *Pacific International Sports Clubs Ltd v Soccer Marketing International Ltd* (n 84) [114]-[115], [122]; *Ferrexpo v Gilson Investments Ltd* (n 44), [192]–[198]; *cf Lungowe v Vedanta Resources Plc* (n 44) [73]–[82].

[87] *J&W Sanderson Ltd v Fenox (UK) Ltd* (n 57) (Pymont QC); *Autoridad Del Canal De Panamá v Sacyr, SA* (n 52).

[88] *Konkola Copper Mines plc v Coromin* (n 8).

[89] *CNA Insurance Company Limited & Ors* (n 70).

[90] [2004] 1 WLR 2966. See text accompanying above nn 64–70.

[91] [2008] EWHC 1671 (Comm) [64].

In many cases, the probability that a temporary stay will have the same outcome as a permanent stay means it may make it worth a litigant's while to pursue. While it has been recognised since *Reichhold* that courts have to guard against ulterior uses of the managerial power,[92] its exercise has plainly been sought in some cases to sidestep *Owusu*. Jonathan Harris has observed how the case management stay 'constitutes another important, flexible weapon' for limiting the effect of *Owusu*.[93] It is another example of the Schlosser Report's failure to account for the constant evolution of the common law[94] and, when combined with the pressure that, in particular, litigants in the London Commercial Court have put on the *acquis*, its ability to develop powers that have outpaced or stepped around the 'uncommercial' Brussels I system.[95]

This is not to claim that national common law courts in the EU have allowed extensive avoidance of *Owusu* through the case management stay. There is formally a heavy burden on the defendant to make out the grounds for a stay, and to satisfy the court that the interests of justice are better served by granting the temporary stay. Lord Bingham said the case management stay should only be granted in rare and compelling circumstances,[96] and in general this seems to be how common law courts in the EU have approached the managerial power.[97] Since its genesis in *Reichhold*, the reported instances of successful applications for case management stays are minute when compared with the incidence of applications for permanent jurisdictional stays.

## III. The Case Management Stay Outside Europe

The recognition in *Reichhold* that the sole source of the power to grant a stay on case management grounds was the inherent jurisdiction of the court improved the possibility that the power would be recognised outside England and Wales. Although 'caseflow management' has been widely adopted in the civil procedure

[92] *Reichhold Norway ASA v Goldman Sachs International* [2000] 1 WLR 173, 186; *Jefferies International Ltd v Landsbanki Islands HF* (n 51) [25].

[93] Harris, 'The English Response to the Europeanisation of Private International Law' (n 46) 393.

[94] See text accompanying above nn 25–29.

[95] Fentiman (n 19) 28.

[96] *Reichhold Norway ASA v Goldman Sachs International* [2000] 1 WLR 173, 186; see also *CNA Insurance Company Limited v Office Depot International* (n 70) [26]; *Amlin Corporate Member Ltd v Oriental Assurance Corporation* [2012] EWCA Civ 1341, [19]; *HSBC Bank Plc v Robinson* [2017] NICA 64, [33]–[35]; *Lungowe v Vedanta Resources Plc* (n 44) [85]. If jurisdiction is based on an exclusive choice of court agreement the court will be much less likely to stay proceedings even temporarily: *Equitas Limited v Allstate Insurance Company* (n 54) [65]–[66]; *Citigroup Global Markets Ltd v Amatra Leveraged Feeder Holdings Ltd* (n 74), [75]; *P Elliot & Co Ltd v FCC Elliot Construction Ltd* (n 84) [73]; *Amlin Corporate Member Ltd v Oriental Assurance Corp* [2013] 1 All ER (Comm) 495, [22]; *Autoridad Del Canal De Panamá v Sacyr, SA* (n 52) [159]–[160]; *cf Amlin Corporate Member Ltd v Oriental Assurance Corporation* [2012] EWCA Civ 1341, [22].

[97] eg *Konkola Copper Mines plc v Coromin* (n 8) 453; *Equitas Limited v Allstate Insurance Company* (n 54) [54].

rules of courts outside the EU, the managerial power to grant a stay was not generated by any network of legislation that was peculiar to England. Adjudication in Australia,[98] Canada,[99] Hong Kong,[100] New Zealand[101] and Singapore[102] has expressly recognised the managerial power to order a temporary stay in the inherent jurisdiction of the court. Appeal courts in Hong Kong,[103] New Zealand[104] and Singapore[105] have simply assumed that *Reichhold* represents the law, and accept that local courts have managerial powers.

There are nevertheless differences between the inherent jurisdiction as exercised in the English and Irish courts and the inherent jurisdiction as exercised in different countries outside the EU. The absence of any *Owusu*-effect, differences in the law and practice that predated the recognition of a *Reichhold*-style stay and, inevitably, the different evolution of the common law in independent court systems has seen nuances develop in the different approaches taken to the case management stay outside the EU.

As would be expected, nothing in the *acquis*, including *Owusu v Jackson*,[106] has received any mention in adjudication on the case management stay outside the EU. This has two implications. First, to the extent that *acquis* shaped principles for the exercise of the managerial power in England and Wales and in Ireland, doubts must be expressed as to how relevant those principles could be for case management stays outside the EU. This certainly includes the limits stated in *Mazur Media*,[107] in which Lawrence Collins J thought that any factors that are relevant to the plea of *forum non conveniens* should never be considered in Brussels I litigation. Although this strict position has not always been maintained,[108] it is difficult to know whether this has influenced the sharp distinction made in common law countries in the EU between jurisdictional and managerial stays in general. Secondly, it seems that, being unable to plead *forum non conveniens* in Brussels I jurisdictions, litigants in the common law countries of the EU have had a greater incentive to apply for a stay on case management grounds when, in the

[98] *UDP Holdings Pty Ltd (Rec and Mgr Apptd) v Ironshore Corporate Capital Ltd* [2016] VSC 400, [25] (Hargrave J).
[99] *Jardine Lloyd Thompson Canada Inc v Western Oil Sands Inc*, 2006 ABQB 933, [22] (Wittman ACJ).
[100] 厦門新景地集團有限公司 *v Eton Properties Limited* [2010] HKCFI 236, [151], [153] (Fok J).
[101] *Danone Asia Pacific Holdings Pte Ltd v Fonterra Co-Operative Group Limited* [2014] NZHC 1681, [33], [39], [50], [54] (Venning J); *Openyd Limited v GJ Lawrence Dental Limited* [2018] NZHC 1618, [22] (Cooke J).
[102] *Shanghai Construction (Group) General Co Singapore Branch v Tan Poo Seng* [2012] SGHC 265, [13], [14], [16]-[20], [26] (Chua AR); *Maybank Kim Eng Securities Pte Ltd v Lim Keng Yong* [2016] SGHC 68, [13], [19]- [21], [23], [32]-[33], [37] (Steven Chong J).
[103] *Ghossoub v Team Y&R Holdings Hong Kong Ltd* [2017] HKCA 296, [52] (Lam VP and Kwan JA).
[104] *Danone Asia Pacific Holdings Pte Limited v Fonterra Co-Operative Group Limited* [2014] NZCA 536, [15] (White, French and Cooper JJ).
[105] *Tomolugen Holdings Ltd v Silica Investors Ltd* [2016] 1 SLR 373, [164], [186]–[188] (Sundaresh Menon CJ, Chao Hick Tin JA and Chan Sek Keong SJ).
[106] *Owusu v Jackson* (n 5); see text accompanying above nn 38–48.
[107] *Mazur Media Limited v Mazur Media GmbH* [2004] 1 WLR 2966.
[108] See text accompanying above nn 64–75.

upshot, it might lead to the same outcome.[109] All of these countries outside the EU, other than Australia, have adopted *Spiliada*'s 'convenience–suitability' approach to the doctrine of *forum non conveniens*.[110] This is also available, when successfully pleaded, to defeat the exercise of jurisdiction in all cross-border commercial litigation in these countries, other than Australia, and so there is less need to find a practical substitute for it than there is in the EU. There are few applications for a case management stay in these countries. In some, the temporary stay has been sought alongside an application for a stay to prevent an abuse of process,[111] enforce an arbitration agreement[112] or enforce an exclusive choice of court agreement[113] – or again to defend against an anti-suit injunction.[114] There is no reported instance of a case management stay being sought outside the EU as an alternative to a permanent stay on the ground of *forum non conveniens*. Furthermore, in all cases outside the EU – bar one[115] – the application has been made to address a concurrent arbitration rather than litigation, suggesting that the established means of addressing foreign litigation through *forum non conveniens* or *lis alibi pendens* have not needed the supplement of the managerial power.[116] It is compatible with the suspicion that, inside the EU, litigants might contemplate the temporary stay as a means of avoiding *Owusu*.

There is slippage between managerial and jurisdictional powers in a small number of cases, although this may result more from pre-existing differences in the law dealing with cross-border litigation than from the siphoning of the *Owusu*-effect when the case management stay has been recognised outside the EU. In Australia, the blending of managerial and jurisdictional powers has at times been explicit. The exercise of a jurisdictional power to transfer proceedings has been described as 'a "nuts and bolts" management decision as to which court, in the pursuit of the interests of justice, is the more appropriate to hear and determine the substantive dispute'.[117] Here, the transfer replaces the stay for dealing with *forum non conveniens* (according to *Spiliada* standards) in interstate

[109] See text accompanying above nn 76–83.

[110] Canada: *Amchem Products Inc v British Columbia (Workers Compensation Board)* [1993] 1 SCR 897; Hong Kong: *The Adhiguna Meranti* [1988] 1 Lloyd's Rep 384; New Zealand: *Wing Hung Printing Co Ltd v Saito Offshore Pty Ltd* [2011] 1 NZLR 754; Singapore High Court: *Brinkerhoff Maritime Drilling Corp v PT Airfast Services Indonesia* [1992] 2 SLR 776. See text accompanying above nn 30–34. For the Singapore International Commercial Court, see Rules of Court (Sg), ord 110 r 8(1).

[111] *Danone Asia Pacific Holdings Pte Ltd v Fonterra Co-Operative Group Limited* [2014] NZHC 1681.

[112] 厦門新景地集團有限公司 *v Eton Properties Limited* (n 100) [123]–[154]; *Gorthy Anil Kumar v Pacific Alliance Investment Management (HK) Ltd* [2017] HKFI 1287 (Saunders DJ); *Openyd Limited v GJ Lawrence Dental Limited* (n 101); *Tomolugen Holdings Ltd v Silica Investors Ltd* (n 105).

[113] *Ghossoub v Team Y&R Holdings Hong Kong Ltd* (n 103).

[114] *Gorthy Anil Kumar v Pacific Alliance Investment Management (HK) Ltd* (n 112).

[115] *Ghossoub v Team Y&R Holdings Hong Kong Ltd* (n 103) [52] (Lam VP and Kwan JA).

[116] This was expressly held to be the case in the Singapore International Commercial Court, where in *BNP Paribas Wealth Management v Jacob Agam* [2017] 3 SLR 27, [36] Steven Chong J considered that different conditions applied to a case management stay for a concurrent arbitration and to one for concurrent litigation, where *forum non conveniens* and questions of comity might arise.

[117] *Bankinvest v Seabrook* (1988) 14 NSWLR 711, 714 (Street CJ); *BHP Billiton v Schultz* [2004] HCA 61, (2004) 221 CLR 400, [13] (Gleeson CJ, McHugh and Heydon JJ).

or federal-state litigation,[118] but the decision is both managerial and jurisdictional. Australian courts had also earlier recognised the availability of a temporary stay for the purposes of managing litigation before them, although this was only in cases where there was concurrent foreign litigation.[119] In *UDP Holdings v Ironshore Corporate Capital*,[120] Hargrave J in the Supreme Court of Victoria was asked to stay proceedings temporarily to allow the completion of an earlier arbitration, and drew on both the existing power to grant a temporary stay on *lis pendens* grounds and the case management stay. *Reichhold* was relied on explicitly to justify an extension of the existing Australian powers relating to *lis pendens* to a concurrent arbitration.[121] Similarly, Canadian courts had taken different approaches to stays of proceedings in favour of foreign or local arbitrations[122] but, in Alberta, Court of Appeal authority restricted the stay to circumstances where the issues in the litigation and arbitration were substantially the same and, in addition, the litigation was oppressive, vexatious or an abuse of process and the stay would not cause an injustice to the plaintiff.[123] The additional conditions relied on the early twentieth century principles for stays of proceedings that, in *forum non conveniens* cases, had been superseded by *Spiliada* and dismissed by the Supreme Court of Canada when it followed *Spiliada*.[124] They nevertheless lingered in Alberta when addressing a concurrent arbitration, and in *Jardine Lloyd Thompson Canada Inc v Western Oil Sands Inc*[125] Wittman ACJ evidently considered that it would strain precedent if he was to stay the litigation before him in favour of an earlier arbitration involving the plaintiff and insurance underwriters. However, he also considered that *Reichhold* was applicable,[126] and preferred the more flexible approach taken in Ontario to a concurrent arbitration.[127] It is evident that the broad discretion available in *Reichhold* could have served independently to justify a temporary stay, but Wittman ACJ chose instead, formally at least, to blend it with the Alberta approach. Holding that, regardless of his personal preference, he had to apply the Court of Appeal precedent, the judge said that 'it is appropriate to apply that test in the context and the spirit of [*Reichhold* and the Ontario approach]'.[128]

[118] Jurisdiction of Courts (Cross-vesting Act) 1987 (Cth) s 5 (and comparable legislation in all States and Territories); *BHP Billiton v Schultz* (n 117). For a similar jurisdictional power of transfer between the Singapore High Court and the Singapore International Commercial Court on the ground that the other court is 'more appropriate for the case to be heard', see Rules of Court (Sg) ord 110, r 12(1).

[119] *Sterling Pharmaceuticals Pty Ltd v Boots Company (Australia) Pty Ltd* (1992) 34 FCR 287 (Lockhart J); *Henry v Henry* (1996) 185 CLR 571, 590; *CSR Ltd v Cigna Insurance Australia Ltd* (1997) 189 CLR 345, 390.

[120] [2016] VSC 400.

[121] ibid [34].

[122] *Boart Sweden Ab v Nya Stromnes Ab* [1988] OJ No 2839; *BWV Investments Ltd v Saskferco Products Inc* [1994] SJ No 629.

[123] *Province of Alberta v Alberta, Union Provincial Employees* (1984) 53 AR 277, [9]–[10]; see also *Bank of British Columbia v Sitko* (1986) 68 AR 65.

[124] ie the standard set by Scott LJ in *St Pierre v South American Stores (Gath & Chaves) Ltd* [1936] 1 KB 382, 398. See *Amchem Products Inc v British Columbia (Workers Compensation Board)* (n 110).

[125] 2006 ABQB 933.

[126] ibid [20]–[22].

[127] ie *Boart Sweden Ab v Nya Stromnes Ab* [1988] OJ No 2839. See 2006 ABQB 933, [12], [23].

[128] 2006 ABQB 933, [23].

In *UDP Holdings*, the Victorian Supreme Court merely used *Reichhold* to justify the incorporation of concurrent arbitrations in the power to order the temporary stay in *lis pendens* cases. In contrast, *Jardine Lloyd Thompson* is the clearest instance, outside the EU, of the *Reichhold*-style stay being used blatantly to sidestep existing limitations in the law addressing concurrent proceedings. In his application of the strict Alberta approach to a concurrent arbitration, Wittman ACJ passed over, *sub silentio*, the fact that the defendant in the litigation would not be bound by the arbitration.[129] He did not bother to consider whether the defendant was suffering oppression, vexation or an abuse of process by the litigation – as was required by the Alberta approach before a stay could be granted.[130] A stay, pending the finalisation of the arbitration, was granted.[131] Alberta Court of Appeal precedent was just given lip-service, but was in substance ignored.

The common law courts outside the EU agree that the managerial power is exercised 'in the interests of justice'[132] and, as a result, that judges are invested with the broad discretion needed to put concurrent litigation or arbitrations in the most cost-efficient and effective sequence. As will be seen,[133] the phrase 'interests of justice' has particular significance for the possible expansion of approaches to *lis pendens* in Australia. However, the more significant development in the export of the *Reichhold*-style stay beyond the EU is the specific content that has been given to 'the interests of justice' standard. In *Danone Asia Pacific Holdings Pte Ltd v Fonterra Co-Operative Group Limited*,[134] an arbitration began in Singapore and, the next day, litigation was initiated before the New Zealand High Court. The defendant applied for the litigation to be stayed until completion of the arbitration and, then, to re-commence 'in light of the findings of the arbitration'.[135] Venning J approved *Reichhold* without any qualification.[136] In deciding whether or not there were case management grounds to justify a stay, he said:[137]

> it is necessary to consider in more detail the relationship between the parties to the proceedings and the arbitration and, in particular, the claims in the arbitration and proceedings and the issues they raise, together with other relevant factors such as issue estoppel, the risk of inconsistent findings, delay and cost.

[129] ibid [24].
[130] ibid [25].
[131] ibid [33].
[132] *UDP Holdings Pty Ltd (Rec and Mgr Apptd) v Ironshore Corporate Capital Ltd* (n 98) [40]; *Jardine Lloyd Thompson Canada Inc v Western Oil Sands Inc* (n 99) [20]; *Gorthy Anil Kumar v Pacific Alliance Investment Management (HK) Ltd* (n 112) [53]; *Openyd Limited v GJ Lawrence Dental Limited* (n 101) [38]; *Danone Asia Pacific Holdings Pte Ltd v Fonterra Co-Operative Group Limited* [2014] NZHC 1681, [39], [46], [55], [94], [97]; *Tomolugen Holdings Ltd v Silica Investors Ltd* (n 105) [164], [179], [188]; *Shanghai Construction (Group) General Co Singapore Branch v Tan Poo Seng* (n 102) [20].
[133] See text accompanying below nn 161–170.
[134] [2014] NZHC 1681.
[135] ibid [29].
[136] ibid [45]–[55].
[137] ibid [56].

Each criterion was considered in turn, but there was a substantial degree of overlap between the issues being considered in the Singapore arbitration and the New Zealand litigation which made it undesirable that they be conducted concurrently and that, as a result, the resources dedicated to dispute resolution be duplicated.[138] Incompatible findings were a risk which, if arising, would further delay the litigation.[139] Again, the underlying relationship between the exercise of discretions in litigation and the realising of commercial outcomes was reinforced by the expectation that the Singapore arbitration would either create issue estoppels or 'at the very least clarify the landscape for the remaining issues'.[140]

Venning J's decision in *Danone* is, after *Reichhold*, the most influential authority for the case management stay in common law countries outside the EU. It was confirmed on appeal by the New Zealand Court of Appeal,[141] and it supported the recognition of the managerial power in the Supreme Court of Victoria in *UDP Holdings*.[142] In *Tomolugen Holdings Ltd v Silica Investors Ltd*,[143] the Singapore Court of Appeal thought that Venning J's statement of criteria (as outlined above) 'offer[ed] a comprehensive (although by no means exhaustive) and instructive guide' to courts when they were confronted by overlapping issues in litigation and a concurrent arbitration.[144] *Tomolugen* also involved multi-party litigation in which only two of the parties had agreed to dispute resolution by arbitration. An application was made to stay the litigation under the International Arbitration Act 2002 (Sg), but to capture the litigants who were not subject to the arbitration agreement a stay on case management grounds was also sought.[145] The Court of Appeal undertook a comprehensive survey of the approach taken in Commonwealth jurisdictions to concurrent arbitrations that overlapped with local litigation, but settled on *Reichhold*[146] and *Danone*[147] as properly recognising the lead that the court should take 'as the final arbiter … ensuring the efficient and fair resolution of the dispute'.[148] Orders were made allowing the plaintiff to opt out of some of the claims it made in the litigation but, if failing to do so, also staying proceedings under the International Arbitration Act and temporarily on case management grounds.[149]

[138] ibid [94].
[139] ibid [94].
[140] [2014] NZHC 1681, [96].
[141] *Danone Asia Pacific Holdings Pte Limited v Fonterra Co-Operative Group Limited* [2014] NZCA 536, [7], [15].
[142] [2016] VSC 400, [36]–[39].
[143] [2016] 1 SLR 373.
[144] ibid [188]; see also *Maybank Kim Eng Securities Pte Ltd v Lim Keng Yong* (n 102) [21].
[145] *Tomolugen Holdings Ltd v Silica Investors Ltd* (n 105) [7].
[146] ibid [164]–[174].
[147] ibid [175]–[185].
[148] ibid [186].
[149] ibid [190].

*Tomolugen* also exemplifies how, outside the EU, the threshold for granting a temporary stay has been modified. Lord Bingham had insisted that the stay should only be granted in 'rare and compelling circumstances'.[150] Although this standard was stated long before *Owusu*, it is possible that the threshold was subsequently reinforced by common law courts in the EU to avoid trespassing into the general principle of *Owusu*. It may also explain why there has been some departure from this standard outside the EU. As a trial judge decision, *UDP Holdings*[151] may not represent anything more than an idiosyncratic gloss on the phrase 'rare and compelling', but Hargrave J merely considered that the case for a stay had to be 'convincing'.[152] He held that, when the factors are evenly balanced, the stay should be refused,[153] but in doing so the circumstances in which Hargrave J considered that a stay is to be granted hardly appear to be rare. In *Tomolugen*,[154] the Singapore Court of Appeal rejected the 'rare and compelling' threshold altogether.[155] The test to use is more elaborate, recognising that the plaintiff's right to sue wherever it wants to is fundamental, but is not absolute and is only modestly qualified by ordering a temporary stay.[156] Menon CJ said:[157]

> This does not mean that if part of a dispute is sent for arbitration, the court proceedings relating to the rest of the dispute *will* be stayed as a matter of course. The court must in every case aim to strike a balance between three higher-order concerns that may pull in different considerations: first, a plaintiff's right to choose whom he wants to sue and where; second, the court's desire to prevent a plaintiff from circumventing the operation of an arbitration clause; and third, the court's inherent power to manage its processes to prevent an abuse of process and ensure the efficient and fair resolution of disputes. The balance that is struck must ultimately serve the ends of justice.

Hong Kong and New Zealand courts have maintained the requirement of 'rare and compelling circumstances' before the managerial power can be exercised,[158] although the Hong Kong Court of First Instance has left open the question of following the Singapore Court of Appeal in *Tomolugen* on this point.[159] It has, naturally, also been followed in Singapore.[160]

[150] *Reichhold Norway ASA v Goldman Sachs International* [2000] 1 WLR 173, 186; see text accompanying above nn 95–96.
[151] [2016] VSC 400.
[152] ibid [41].
[153] ibid [41].
[154] [2016] 1 SLR 373.
[155] ibid [187].
[156] ibid [187]. See also the comments in *Maybank Kim Eng Securities Pte Ltd v Lim Keng Yong* (n 102) [33] and *BC Andaman Co Ltd v Xie Ning Yun* [2017] SGHC 64, [102] (Quentin Loh J).
[157] *Tomolugen Holdings Ltd v Silica Investors Ltd* (n 105) [188].
[158] 厦門新景地集團有限公司 *v Eton Properties Limited* (n 100) [154]; *Ghossoub v Team Y&R Holdings Hong Kong Ltd* (n 103) [52]; *Danone Asia Pacific Holdings Pte Ltd v Fonterra Co-Operative Group Limited* [2014] NZHC 1681, [49].
[159] *Gorthy Anil Kumar v Pacific Alliance Investment Management (HK) Ltd* (n 112) [55].
[160] *Maybank Kim Eng Securities Pte Ltd v Lim Keng Yong* (n 102) [21]–[22].

The adequacy of broad discretionary jurisdictional powers to deal with *lis pendens* may explain the limited uptake of *Reichhold*'s managerial power outside the EU and, in general, its being adopted in cases involving a concurrent arbitration rather than litigation.[161] Indeed, the only jurisdictional power where it may seem that the managerial power could potentially be used to overcome juridical weaknesses is the Australian approach to *forum non conveniens*. For international litigation (other than any competing with New Zealand courts)[162] the Australian doctrine of *forum non conveniens* remains an 'abuse of process approach' rather than a 'convenience-suitability approach' to the question of venue for litigation.[163] It formally requires vexation and oppression before proceedings will be stayed or dismissed, although that is satisfied if the local court regards itself as a clearly inappropriate forum.[164] The test therefore prohibits any comparison of the relative advantages of the Australian and foreign courts when determining whether or not to grant a stay;[165] a restriction that is also found in English approaches to the *Reichhold*-style stay.[166] When *lis pendens* questions arise in Australian *forum non conveniens* cases the courts seem less reluctant to stay proceedings,[167] but then the possibility must be conceded that broader recognition of the temporary case management stay in Australia will, in some cases, help to overcome the entrenched abuse-of-process approach to stays of proceedings. There is longstanding recognition in Australia that, where a statute uses the phrase 'interests of justice' in relation to the exercise of a jurisdictional power, it imports the *Spiliada* convenience-suitability approach to the question of *forum non conveniens*. As a result, when jurisdictional powers allow the transfer of proceedings in the interests of justice in interstate and federal-state litigation, the transfer can take place when another court is, simply, the more appropriate for the litigation.[168] As has been seen, the managerial power of *Reichhold* is also exercised outside the EU 'in the interests

[161] See text accompanying above n 115. Indeed, in *BNP Paribas Wealth Management v Jacob Agam* (n 116) [36] Steven Chong J in the Singapore International Commercial Court drew a sharp distinction between the case management stay where there was a concurrent arbitration and one where there is concurrent litigation (and so where *forum non conveniens* issues might become relevant).

[162] Trans-Tasman Proceedings Act 2010 (Cth) s 19.

[163] von Mehren, 'Theory and Practice of Adjudicatory Authority in Private International Law' (n 32) 326.

[164] *Voth v Manildra Flour Mills Pty Ltd* (1990) 171 CLR 538, 558. The Singapore International Commercial Court also still holds jurisdiction when another court might be the *forum conveniens*, as it only stays proceedings 'if it is not appropriate for the action to be heard in the Court': Rules of Court (Sg) ord 110, r 8(1).

[165] *Voth v Manildra Flour Mills Pty Ltd* (1990) 171 CLR 538, 558–61.

[166] *Racy v Hawila* (n 8) [61].

[167] *Henry v Henry* (n 119).

[168] *Bankinvest v Seabrook* (n 117) 730 (Rogers AJA); *BHP Billiton v Schultz* (n 117) [14] (Gleeson CJ, McHugh and Heydon JJ).

of justice'.[169] It has been used in the EU to sidestep restrictions on jurisdictional powers that have been imposed by the *acquis*.[170] Even though ordered temporarily, the case management stay can help achieve precisely the same commercial outcome that a permanent stay on the ground of *forum non conveniens* (according to *Spiliada* criteria) might secure. There is no reason why it may not be used in similar strategic ways to sidestep the more restrictive doctrine of *forum non conveniens* in Australia.

[169] *UDP Holdings Pty Ltd (Rec and Mgr Apptd) v Ironshore Corporate Capital Ltd* (n 98) [40]; *Jardine Lloyd Thompson Canada Inc v Western Oil Sands Inc* (n 99) [20]; *Gorthy Anil Kumar v Pacific Alliance Investment Management (HK) Ltd* (n 112) [53]; *Openyd Limited v GJ Lawrence Dental Limited* (n 101) [38]; *Danone Asia Pacific Holdings Pte Ltd v Fonterra Co-Operative Group Limited* [2014] NZHC 1681, [39], [46], [55], [94], [97]; *Tomolugen Holdings Ltd v Silica Investors Ltd* (n 105) [164], [179], [188]; *Shanghai Construction (Group) General Co Singapore Branch v Tan Poo Seng* (n 102) [20].

[170] See text accompanying nn 76–97.

# PART II

# Foreign Judgments

# 5

# The 2005 Hague Convention

## *A Panacea for Non-Exclusive and Asymmetric Jurisdiction Agreements Too?*

BROOKE MARSHALL*

The 2005 Hague Convention on Choice of Court Agreements (the Hague Choice of Court Convention or the Convention)[1] needs little introduction. It is what emerged from the first round of noble attempts to create a convention providing bases on which courts globally should exercise jurisdiction, and recognise and enforce foreign judgments:[2] the so-called 'Judgments Project'. The Hague Conference on Private International Law actively resumed work on that project in 2016. The Hague Choice of Court Convention seeks to ensure the uniform treatment internationally of 'exclusive' jurisdiction agreements and of judgments rendered by courts, the jurisdiction of which was based on an exclusive agreement. Under the Convention, an exclusive jurisdiction agreement is one which designates, to the exclusion of all others, the jurisdiction of the courts of a single country. The Convention is in force in all European Union (EU) Member States, Mexico, Singapore and Montenegro.[3] The United States of America, Ukraine and China have

* I thank Michael Douglas and Vivienne Bath as well as Maria Hook and Bevan Martin for inviting me to speak at the conference at Sydney Law School and participate in the workshop at the Victoria University of Wellington, where I explored various issues presented in this chapter.

I am grateful to the participants of the Wellington workshop and to Andrew Dickinson for their invaluable remarks on earlier drafts, to Nicola Nygh and Eike Hosemann for their questions on several points made in this chapter, and to Max Winterhalder for proof-reading and editing assistance. Any errors are my own.

Parts of section I.A and all of section I.C of this chapter are extracted from my doctoral thesis, submitted to the University of Hamburg.

[1] Convention on Choice of Court Agreements, opened for signature 30 June 2005, 44 ILM 1294.

[2] See generally LE Teitz, 'The Hague Choice of Court Convention: Validating Party Autonomy and Providing an Alternative to Arbitration' (2005) 53 *American Journal of Comparative Law* 543, 544–50.

[3] See Council Decision of 4 December 2014 on the Approval, on Behalf of the European Union, of the Hague Convention of 30 June 2005 on Choice of Court Agreements [2014] OJ L 353/5; Choice of Court Agreements Act 2016 (Singapore). The Convention entered into force for all EU Member States

also signed but not ratified it.[4] In November 2016, the Joint Standing Committee on Treaties recommended that Australia should accede to the Convention.[5] The Commonwealth Government proposes to implement the Convention in an International Civil Law Act.[6]

The Hague Choice of Court Convention only applies to jurisdiction arising out of *exclusive* jurisdiction agreements.[7] But the Convention allows Contracting States to extend the provisions in Chapter III of the Convention governing recognition and enforcement[8] to judgments rendered by courts which had jurisdiction under a non-exclusive jurisdiction agreement. The Convention provides for states to do so by making a reciprocal declaration under art 22 of the Convention.[9] Where two states whose courts are involved have made a declaration, the court addressed[10] shall recognise the judgment of the court of origin,[11] provided certain conditions are satisfied. Non-exclusive jurisdiction agreements of different types

(except Denmark) and Mexico on 1 October 2015, for Singapore on 1 October 2016, for Montenegro on 1 August 2018 and for Denmark on 1 September 2018: Hague Conference on Private International Law, 'Status Table: 37 – Convention of 30 June 2005 on Choice of Court Agreements' www.hcch.net/en/instruments/conventions/status-table/?cid=98.

[4] Hague Conference on Private International Law, 'Status Table: 37' (n 3). Ontario (Canada), Tunisia and Brazil are reportedly considering acceding to the Convention: Permanent Bureau of the Hague Conference on Private International Law, 'Suggested Further Work in Support of Forum and Law Selection in International Commercial Contracts' (Preliminary Document No 5, January 2017) [5]–[7]. The United Kingdom intends to accede independently to the Convention after Brexit: Explanatory Memorandum to The Civil Jurisdiction and Judgments (Hague Convention on Choice of Court Agreements 2005) (EU Exit) Regulations 2018 [2.12] (Ministry of Justice, 13 September 2018) www.gov.uk/eu-withdrawal-act-2018-statutory-instruments/the-civil-jurisdiction-and-judgments-hague-convention-on-choice-of-court-agreements-2005-eu-exit-regulations-2018: see also nn 73, 195). The Convention currently applies to the UK via the EU's approval of it, meaning that on Brexit, the Convention will lose force of law in the United Kingdom: A Dickinson, 'Back to the Future – the UK's EU Exit and the Conflict of Laws' (2016) 12 *Journal of Private International Law* 195, 197–98.

[5] Joint Standing Committee on Treaties, Parliament of Australia, Implementation Procedures for Airworthiness – USA; Convention on Choice of Courts – Accession; GATT Schedule of Concessions – Amendment; Radio Regulations – Practical Revision (Report No 166, November 2016) [3.21].

[6] National Interest Analysis: Australia's Accession to the Convention on Choice of Court Agreements [2016] ATNIA 7 [21].

[7] Hague Choice of Court Convention, art 1(1).

[8] Recognition denotes giving effect 'to the determination of the legal rights and obligations' made by the court that rendered judgment. Enforcement refers to 'the application of the legal procedures' of the enforcing court to ensure compliance with the judgment rendered: T Hartley and M Dogauchi, *Explanatory Report on the Convention of 30 June 2005 on Choice of Court Agreements* in Permanent Bureau of the Conference, *Proceedings of the Twentieth Session*, Tome III (Antwerp, Intersentia, 2010) 783 [825].

[9] Hague Choice of Court Convention, art 22. See also Minutes of the Special Commission of April 2014, Minutes No 9, Meeting of Monday 26 April (afternoon) in ibid 473. These minutes, as well as others referred to in this chapter, relate to the meetings of the Hague Conference on Private International Law preceding the conclusion of the Convention.

[10] ie the court called upon to recognise the judgment.

[11] ie the court that rendered the judgment.

feature in Australian case law,[12] which may explain why Australia was one of the delegations which proposed that art 22 be included in the Convention.[13]

This chapter contributes to the literature by examining the content and effect of the reciprocal declaration mechanism in art 22 of the Convention and exactly which types of 'non-exclusive jurisdiction agreements' to which it applies.[14] The purpose of the chapter is to consider whether a reciprocal declaration is something which Australia, in consultation with the EU,[15] Singapore, Mexico and Montenegro,[16] should make.[17] This chapter comprises three sections.

[12] eg *Babcock & Brown DIF III Global Co-Investment Fund, LP v Babcock & Brown International Pty Ltd* [2016] VSC 623, [8]; *Re Douglas Webber Events Pty Ltd* (2014) 291 FLR 173, [6] (which were both cases in which the clause designated the courts of a single jurisdiction and was described as non-exclusive). See also *Centrebet Pty Ltd v Baasland* [2013] NTSC 59; *Armacel Pty Ltd v Smurfit Stone Container Corp* [2008] FCA 592, (2008) 248 ALR 573; *Green v Australian Industrial Investment Ltd* (1989) 25 FCR 532, (1989) 90 ALR 500; *Telesto Investments Ltd v UBS AG* [2012] NSWSC 44, (2012) 262 FLR 119; *Bagsfirst Global Pty Ltd v Global Brands (Football) Pty Ltd* [2010] NSWSC 988; *Autotrop Sdn Bhd v Powercrank Batteries Pty Ltd* [2006] VSC 401.

[13] This provision originated as a proposal of the USA during the Hague Conference on Private International Law's Special Commission of 2004: Minutes No 9, Meeting of Monday 26 April (afternoon) in Permanent Bureau of the Conference (n 8) 473. It was revived as a proposal of the USA and Australia and adopted by the second commission of the Diplomatic Session: Working Document No 28, Distributed on Monday 20 June 2006 [sic] in Permanent Bureau of the Conference (n 8) 517; Minutes No 20 of 27 June 2005 (afternoon) in Permanent Bureau of the Conference (n 8) 709.

[14] The most comprehensive analysis of art 22 is by RA Brand and PM Herrup: *The 2005 Hague Convention on Choice of Court Agreements: Commentary and Documents* (Cambridge, Cambridge University Press, 2008) 153–59 critiqued by P Beaumont: 'Hague Choice of Court Agreements Convention 2005: Background, Negotiations, Analysis and Current Status' (2009) 5 *Journal of Private International Law* 125, 154–56. The other leading commentary on the Convention does not mention it: T Hartley, *Choice of Court Agreements under the European and International Instruments* (Oxford, Oxford University Press, 2013). Some recent articles on the Convention refer to art 22 in passing: A Mills, 'The Hague Choice of Court Convention and Cross-Border Dispute Resolution in Australia and the Asia-Pacific' (2017) *Melbourne Journal of International Law* 15; S Reuter and G Wegen, 'Das Haager Übereinkommen über Gerichtsstandsvereinbarungen vom 30.6.2005 – Entstehung, Charakteristika, Erfolgschancen' (2017) *Zeitschrift für Vergleichende Rechtswissenschaft* 382, 396; M Ong, 'Rethinking Jurisdiction Clauses in New Zealand: The Hague Convention and Beyond' (2013) 219 *Auckland University Law Review* 245, 239, fn 114; T Kruger, 'The 20th Session of the Hague Conference: A New Choice of Court Convention and the Issue of EC Membership' (2006) 55 *International and Comparative Law Quarterly* 447, 449; Teitz, 'The Hague Choice of Court Convention' (n 2) 555–56; G Tu, 'The Hague Choice of Court Convention – A Chinese Perspective' (2007) 55 *American Journal of Comparative Law* 347, 355.

[15] The EU has refrained from making a declaration until other Contracting States have expressed a view: Proposal for a Council Decision on the approval on behalf of the EU of the Hague Convention 30 January 2014 [3.2.1].

[16] At the time of writing, the EU, Mexico, Singapore and Montenegro had not made a reciprocal declaration: Hague Conference on Private International Law, 'Status Table: 37' (n 3).

[17] If Australia were to make a declaration on accession to the Hague Choice of Court Convention, both the Convention and the declaration would enter into force three months after Australia has deposited the instrument of accession: Hague Choice of Court Convention, arts 31(2)(a), 32(3). For the EU, Singapore, Mexico and Montenegro, the declaration would take effect three months after the depositary in the Netherlands has been notified of the declaration: Convention, art 32(4). It is at the discretion of each declaring Contracting State as to whether the declaration 'covers choice of court agreements concluded, proceedings commenced, or judgments given in the State of origin before the declaration enters into force for the requested State [ie the declaring Contracting State]': Hartley and Dogauchi, *Report on the 2005 Hague Convention (Final)* (n 8) [254]. For criticism, see C Kessedjian, 'Convention de la Haye du 30 juin 2005 sur l'élection de for' (2006) 133 *Journal du droit international* 813, 845.

It examines, first, what constitutes a non-exclusive jurisdiction agreement under the Convention. It will be argued that the recent claim that asymmetric agreements are exclusive is flawed, demonstrating that such agreements are non-exclusive for the purposes of the Convention. Secondly, the chapter scrutinises the content and effect of the conditions that a judgment, based on a non-exclusive jurisdiction agreement, must fulfil before it can be recognised, highlighting several drawbacks. The final section evaluates whether, despite those drawbacks, a reciprocal declaration between Australia and existing Convention Contracting States would be an improvement on the current law in Australia on recognition and enforcement.

## I. What are Exclusive and Non-Exclusive Jurisdiction Agreements under the Convention?

An agreement that is exclusive and governed by the jurisdictional provisions of the Convention evidently cannot, at the same time, be one which is non-exclusive and therefore only subject to the Convention at the recognition and enforcement stage, if a reciprocal declaration is made. Article 3(b) of the Convention deems a jurisdiction agreement to be exclusive, unless the parties 'expressly provided otherwise'.[18] Article 3(a) defines an *exclusive* jurisdiction agreement as one which 'designates … the courts of one Contracting State … to the exclusion of the jurisdiction of any other courts'.[19] Any form of agreement that, by its express terms, does not conform with that definition will be non-exclusive and thus outside the scope of the Convention, at the *jurisdictional* stage. For the purposes of *recognition and enforcement, non-exclusive* jurisdiction agreements are also defined by the Convention in art 22(1). A non-exclusive agreement is one which designates a court or the courts of *one or more* Contracting States.[20] It is the converse of the definition of exclusivity which requires that the agreement designate the courts of *one* Contracting State 'to the exclusion of the jurisdiction of any other courts'[21] and which does not allow parties to choose the courts of *more* than one Contracting State or those of a Contracting State and a third state. Presumably, a definition of non-exclusivity was included to make clear that jurisdiction agreements designating the courts of one Contracting State could be either exclusive or non-exclusive

[18] The introduction of this deeming rule is an improvement on the current Australian law. Often it is not express on the face of a jurisdiction clause designating the courts of a single territorial unit or country whether the parties intended the clause to be exclusive or non-exclusive. Accordingly, Australian courts regularly engage in a lengthy interpretative process to determine the character of such a clause. See BA Marshall and M Keyes, 'Australia's Accession to the Hague Convention on Choice of Court Agreements' (2017) 41 *Melbourne University Law Review* 246, 251–52.

[19] The agreement must also comply with the formal requirements of art 3(c).

[20] Hague Choice of Court Convention, art 22(1). Again, the agreement must also comply with the formal requirements of art 3(c).

[21] ibid, art 3(a).

depending on whether or not the parties intended to exclude the jurisdiction of other courts.[22]

As an agreement cannot at once be exclusive and non-exclusive for the purposes of the Convention, it is important to determine which types of jurisdiction clauses will be exclusive and which will be non-exclusive. The first subsection (I.A) examines which choice of law rules, if any, will apply to this determination. The second (I.B) will consider how different variants of symmetric agreements – those which regulate jurisdiction identically, irrespective of the procedural positions of the parties – will be characterised for the purposes of the Convention. The third (I.C) will investigate the more complex question of how asymmetric jurisdiction agreements – those which provide for one party to make a deferred decision as to the court in which it will sue – will be characterised.

## A. Choice of Law Rule(s)

Article 3(a) and (b) and art 22(1) of the Hague Choice of Court Convention are silent as to the law that applies to the characterisation of a clause as exclusive or non-exclusive, respectively. Does this mean that the courts of a Contracting State are free to apply the choice of law rules of the forum to determine whether, by reference to the applicable law those rules designate, the jurisdiction clause in question complies with the definition of exclusivity in art 3(a)? On the one hand, it could be argued that the answer is clearly 'no': the applicable law *is* the Convention, the definition of exclusivity being complete and autonomous. On the other hand, it could be argued that while it is clear that the Convention mandates *what* exclusivity is, via its definition, the Convention does not mandate *how* a court is to determine whether a given clause is exclusive and the choice of law to be applied in making that determination.[23] The latter argument is, nonetheless, undermined if one recognises that the Convention does regulate *how* a court is to determine whether a given clause is exclusive: art 3(b) *deems* the agreement to be exclusive unless the parties have *expressly* provided otherwise, in which case it will not be exclusive. The fact that the Convention contains a deeming rule strongly suggests that characterisation on the question of exclusivity is regulated wholly by the Convention itself: the parties have either expressly provided that their agreement is otherwise than exclusive or they have not and no reference to a governing national

[22] Though one could arrive at the same conclusion simply by applying the definition of exclusivity and by reference to the rebuttable deeming rule of exclusivity, meaning that an additional definition of non-exclusive agreements is somewhat superfluous.

[23] By analogy to the reasoning adopted in *Trina Solar (US) Inc v Jasmin Solar Pty Ltd* [2017] FCAFC 6, (2017) FCR 1, [179] (Beach J with whom Dowsett J agreed) (observing, in relation to an agreement governed by the International Arbitration Act 1974 (Cth), which implements the New York Convention in Australia, that although *what* an arbitration agreement is may be unconstrained by an applicable law, the New York Convention does not mandate '*how* that mutual consensus is to be determined and the choice of law to be made relevant to that determination'). See generally M Douglas, '*Trina Solar (US) Inc v Jasmin Solar Pty Ltd* [2017] FCAFC 6' (2017) 91 *Australian Law Journal* 201.

law is needed.[24] That view is consistent with the growing perception, in respect of the similar wording to art 3(b) in the recast EU Regulation on Jurisdiction and the Recognition and Enforcement of Judgments (recast Brussels I Regulation),[25] that no recourse to an applicable law is needed in determining the character of a jurisdiction clause.[26]

Notwithstanding these arguments, it seems likely that Australian courts would apply forum choice of law rules to the question of characterisation. This seems probable in light of recent Australian case law interpreting the International Arbitration Act 1974 (Cth), which implements the New York Convention.[27] In *Trina Solar (US) Inc v Jasmin Solar Pty Ltd*, the Full Court of the Federal Court held the choice of law rule to determine whether a party is bound to an arbitration agreement is dictated by the forum's choice of law rules, because art 7(2) of the International Arbitration Act 1974 (Cth) (art II(3) of the New York Convention) is 'silent on choice of law'.[28] Given that art 3(b) of the Convention is at least in part 'silent on choice of law', Australian courts may be inclined to adopt the same approach, by applying Australian choice of law rules to determine which law governs the question of whether the parties have expressly agreed for the clause to be otherwise than exclusive. Some support for applying that approach to the Convention by analogy can arguably be found in the Convention itself: art 26(1) requires Contracting States to interpret the Convention 'so far as possible' to be compatible with other international treaties in force in Contracting States. Beaumont explains that 'so far as possible' interpretation is naturally precluded, where it is contradicted by the text of the Convention itself.[29] Given the partial silence of the Convention on the law applicable to the exclusivity issue, it may be open

[24] Cp Brand and Herrup, *The 2005 Hague Convention on Choice of Court Agreements* (n 14) 42–43 (stating that the word 'deemed' rather than 'presumed' in art 3(b) was a deliberate attempt to avoid the application of national, evidentiary law) and D Joseph, *Jurisdiction and Arbitration Agreements and their Enforcement*, 3rd edn (London, Sweet & Maxwell, 2015) [6.52] with R Fentiman, *International Commercial Litigation*, 2nd edn (Oxford, Oxford University Press, 2015) [2.73] (stating that '[t]he reference to the provision's deemed effect maintains the position that interpretation is theoretically a matter for national law').

[25] Regulation (EU) No 1215/2012 of the European Parliament and of the Council of 12 December 2012 on Jurisdiction and the Recognition and Enforcement of Judgments in Civil and Commercial Matters [2012] OJ L 351/1, art 25(1) (which provides that the jurisdiction of an EU Member State court designated in an agreement 'shall be exclusive unless the parties have agreed otherwise'. Unlike the Hague Choice of Court Convention, the Regulation does not provide that the parties should have 'expressly' agreed otherwise.)

[26] A Mills, *Party Autonomy in Private International Law* (Cambridge, Cambridge University Press, 2018) 110 (stating that 'interpretation (as to exclusivity)' is purely a matter for European (autonomous) rules); Fentiman, *International Commercial Litigation* (n 24) [2.71] (although suggesting that recourse to an applicable, national law is equally conceivable). See also A Briggs, 'The Hidden Depths of the Law of Jurisdiction' [2016] *Lloyd's Maritime and Commercial Law Quarterly* 236, 249 referring to the European Court of Justice's ruling in Case C-352/13 *Cartel Damage Claims (CDC) Hydrogen Peroxide SA v Akzo Nobel NV* [2015] ECLI:EU:C:2015:335, which suggests that no national law applies to determine, at least the outer limits of, the scope of a jurisdiction clause.

[27] Convention on the Recognition and Enforcement of Foreign Arbitral Awards, opened for signature 10 June 1958, 330 UNTS 38 (entered into force 7 June 1959) art II(1) (New York Convention).

[28] See *Trina Solar (US) Inc v Jasmin Solar Pty Ltd* (n 23) [182] (Beach J with whom Dowsett J agreed).

[29] Beaumont, 'Hague Choice of Court Agreements Convention 2005' (n 14) 140–41.

to Australian courts to interpret the Convention in a way which the Full Court of the Federal Court of Australia would perceive to be consistent with the New York Convention, unless the deeming rule in art 3(b) indicates that no national law at all should apply.

Even if Australian courts and the courts of other Contracting States were to apply forum choice of law rules to art 3(b), this would make no practical difference as far as most variants of symmetric jurisdiction agreements are concerned.[30] As subsection I.B will demonstrate, application of the deeming rule and the definition of exclusivity to symmetric jurisdiction agreements means that the role left to play for national law (if applicable) is, at most, limited to several variants of non-exclusive clauses. But as far as asymmetric jurisdiction agreements are concerned, recourse to choice of law rules which designate the national law of a common law jurisdiction, especially in connection with the definition of exclusivity in art 3(a), may lead to different results than simply applying the Convention, as section I.C will show.

## B. Symmetric Jurisdiction Agreements

How a symmetric jurisdiction clause will be characterised under the Hague Choice of Court Convention will turn on the deeming rule of exclusivity and the clarity of any wording intended to displace it, and on the extent to which the clause complies with the definition of exclusivity. In other words, exclusivity or non-exclusivity can be established simply by reference to the provisions of the Convention. For instance, an agreement providing that 'the courts of Singapore have exclusive jurisdiction' will be exclusive under the Convention, because it designates the courts of one Contracting State to the exclusion of the jurisdiction of all others.[31] An agreement providing that 'the forum is New South Wales for the conduct of any dispute'[32] would also be exclusive for the purposes of the Convention, by operation of the deeming rule.[33] An agreement providing that 'the courts of New Zealand have non-exclusive jurisdiction'[34] or 'proceedings … may be brought only in the

[30] Joseph also alludes to this point: 'It is … largely unnecessary in the context of the … Convention to consider whether or not, on a true construction of the agreement, it provides for exclusive jurisdiction. It will be deemed exclusive unless the agreement expressly provides otherwise': (n 24) [6.52].

[31] Hague Choice of Court Convention, art 3(a).

[32] Which was the clause in *Anderson Formrite Pty Ltd v Baulderstone Hornibrook Pty Ltd* [2004] WASC 115, [11].

[33] Hague Choice of Court Convention, art 3(b).

[34] Which was the clause in *Re Douglas Webber Events Pty Ltd* (2014) 291 FLR 173, 175–76, [6], a case concerning the Trans-Tasman Proceedings Act 2010 (Cth). For a discussion of the Act, see M Keyes, 'Developing Australian Private International Law: The Hague Choice of Court Convention & The Hague Principles of Choice of Law in International Commercial Contracts', pp 280–282 in ch 12 of this volume). See also *Babcock & Brown DIF III Global Co-Investment Fund, LP v Babcock & Brown International Pty Ltd* (n 12) 623, [8] '[this agreement] is governed by the laws in force in the State of Victoria, Australia. The parties submit to the non-exclusive jurisdiction of Courts exercising jurisdiction there'.

courts of Korea or the courts of China'[35] would be non-exclusive. The former would be non-exclusive, because the parties have made express provision for the courts of a single state to have jurisdiction that is otherwise than exclusive.[36] The latter would be non-exclusive because the clause, in designating the courts of more than one Contracting State, does not satisfy the definition of exclusivity.[37]

Clauses the character of which cannot easily be resolved solely by reference to the Convention are those in which it is unclear whether the language used is intended to rebut the deeming rule of exclusivity and those which designate one or more territorial units *within* a Contracting State. As to the first, assume a clause states that 'either party may bring proceedings in the courts of New South Wales'. Is the use of the permissive verb 'may' a sufficient (and express) counter-indication of exclusivity for the purposes of art 3(1)(b)? It might be argued, in relation to a clause such as this one, that it is permissible to refer to case law of the law designated by the forum's choice of law rule in order to show that the use of permissive rather than obligatory language rebuts the presumption of exclusivity. The risk with that approach is that this case law may have developed in a context where there is no presumption of exclusivity[38] and in which the use of permissive language is merely one factor among others that may instead tell against the conclusion that the parties intended the clause to be non-exclusive.[39] If those competing factors are too allowed to enter the fray, there is a risk that national law will render redundant the Convention's deeming rule. The most compelling solution to this problem resides with the parties themselves. The deeming rule leaves it 'reasonably open to the parties to demonstrate'[40] through their words what they intend, and they would be well-advised to do so.[41] For example, if the parties intend to add the courts of New South Wales to the pool of courts that are, absent an agreement, competent but assign no *preference* for litigation in New South Wales, a clause providing that 'The courts of New South Wales have jurisdiction but not to the exclusion of the jurisdiction of any other courts' may suffice.[42] If, instead, the parties intend to give preference to proceedings in New South Wales, irrespective of when they are commenced, they should say so. A clause in the following terms might be apt to achieve that result: providing that 'either party may bring proceedings in the courts of New South Wales. This clause does not prevent either party

[35] Which is an example given in the Hartley and Dogauchi (n 8) [247].

[36] Hague Choice of Court Convention, art 3(b).

[37] *Cf* ibid, art 3(a).

[38] Which is the case under Australian law.

[39] For a description of those factors under Australian law, see B Marshall, 'Australia: Inconsistencies in the Treatment of Optional Choice of Court Agreements' in M Keyes (ed), *Optional Choice of Court Agreements in Private International Law* (Springer, forthcoming), text accompanying fnn 68–79.

[40] See Mills, *Party Autonomy* (n 26) 99.

[41] Concerns about 'surrender[ing] to formalism' (*FAI General Insurance Co Ltd v Ocean Marine Mutual Protection and Indemnity Association* (1997) 41 NSWLR 117, 126 (Giles CJ)) may have been overstated.

[42] Such words make clear that the agreement does not comply with the definition of exclusivity in art 3(a) of the Convention.

from bringing proceedings in other competent courts unless or until one of them seises the courts of New South Wales'. To hold that the parties both had *ex ante* an implied intention to achieve *that* result with a clause providing 'either party may bring proceedings in the courts of New South Wales' risks imputing to both an intention which one of them regrets *ex post* they did not have.[43]

In an international case, the character of a clause which designates all territorial units or more than one territorial unit *within* a Contracting State will be established by reference to both the Convention and national law. Take, for instance, a clause providing that 'the parties agree to submit to the jurisdiction of any competent court in a State or Territory of Australia'[44] and a clause providing 'the parties submit to the jurisdiction of the courts of New South Wales and the Commonwealth of Australia'.[45] Such clauses will be deemed exclusive under art 3(b) of the Convention because the parties have not expressly rebutted the rule and although the clauses designate more than one court, they designate the courts of only one Contracting State. It follows that if a Singaporean court were seised, it would be required to suspend or dismiss those proceedings.[46] So far as Australian proceedings are concerned, this issue is somewhat more complex. Masato Dogauchi and Trevor Hartley, in their Explanatory Report to the Convention, state that it is for the national law of the Contracting State to allocate jurisdiction in such a case, although the application of national law is tempered by the obligation in art 5(3)(b) of the Convention of the 'chosen court' to give due consideration to 'the choice of the parties' in deciding whether to transfer a case.[47] That obligation will obviously not apply to a clause which designates 'any competent court in a State or Territory of Australia' because any Australian court is the chosen court for the purposes of that provision. The question of which Australian court pursuant to a clause of that type should hear the case would, it seems, be resolved by the legislation that applies in intra-national cases.[48] There is a requirement under cross-vesting legislation

[43] The suggestion, based on the exceptional case of *Sabah Shipyard v Government of Pakistan* [2002] EWCA Civ 1643, [2003] 2 Lloyd's Rep 571, that non-exclusive clauses, absent special wording, should generally be given such effect on the grounds that this is the implied intention of the parties, has been called into question: see *Deutsche Bank AG v Highland Crusader Offshore Partners LP* [2009] EWCA Civ 725, [2010] 1 WLR 1023 [64], [105], [120]; Mills (n 26) 150–51. For the suggestion, see A Briggs, *Agreements on Jurisdiction and Choice of Law* (Oxford, Oxford University Press, 2008) [4.20]–[4.21] ('version (3)' of Briggs' interpretations.); R Fentiman, *International Commercial Litigation*, 2nd edn (Oxford, Oxford University Press, 2015) [2.67], [2.240], [16.52].

[44] Which was the clause in *ACE Insurance v Moose Enterprise Ltd* [2009] NSWSC 724, [11].

[45] This example is a modified version of the clause in *Open Universities Australia Pty Ltd v TAFE Commission* [2017] VSC 617, [6]. In that case, the clause was described as 'non-exclusive'.

[46] Hague Choice of Court Convention, art 6.

[47] Hartley and Dogauchi (n 8) [107], [128]–[131], [258]–[260]. The obligation in art 5(3)(b) will, unfortunately, not apply in cases involving transfers of proceedings between Australian courts where all parties reside in Australia, the relationship of the parties as well as all elements relevant to the dispute are connected only with Australia, and the jurisdiction agreement designates one or more Australian courts. Such intra-national cases fall outside the scope of the Convention: Hague Choice of Court Convention, arts 1(1), 25(2); Hartley and Dogauchi (n 8) [261]–[262].

[48] See eg Jurisdiction of Courts (Cross-Vesting) Act 1987 (Cth) s 5 (applicable to superior courts); Service and Execution of Process Act 1992 (Cth) s 20(4)(d) (applicable to lower courts).

for a superior court to *transfer* proceedings to another Australian court where it appears that the other court is the 'more appropriate court',[49] or the transfer is in the 'interests of justice'.[50] The obligation to give due consideration to the choice of the parties will, however, apply to a clause nominating 'the courts of New South Wales and the Commonwealth of Australia'. Under that clause, other State courts such as the Supreme Court of Victoria are not chosen courts.[51] Again, it appears that the question of whether one Australian court should *transfer* proceedings to another Australian court will be resolved by the cross-vesting legislation. Under current principles, a jurisdiction clause – exclusive or non-exclusive – will be one among a number of factors relevant to the question of whether a transfer is in the interests of justice. Little turns on the distinction between exclusive and non-exclusive clauses for the purposes of a transfer.[52] If the Convention's characterisation of the clause as exclusive were to apply for the purposes of the cross-vesting legislation, the obligation under the Convention to give due consideration to the parties' choice in deciding whether to transfer a case should mean that one of the chosen courts (the Supreme Court of New South Wales, for example) would give significant weight to the choice of the parties if called upon to transfer the case to a State court not chosen in the clause (for example, Supreme Court of Victoria).[53] An impetus for a chosen Australian court to give greater weight to the choice of the parties in deciding whether to allow a transfer to a non-chosen Australian court can be found in Chapter III of the Convention: a court addressed in another Contracting State will be able to refuse to recognise and enforce a judgment from a non-nominated Australian court against a party who had 'objected to the transfer in a timely manner'.[54]

## C. Asymmetric Jurisdiction Agreements

Whether and, if so, how the Convention applies to asymmetric jurisdiction clauses is opaque. Although asymmetric jurisdiction clauses[55] are of various types, for the

[49] *BHP Billiton Ltd v Schultz* [2004] HCA 61, (2004) 221 CLR 400, [175].

[50] ibid [14], [175]. See M Keyes, 'Improving Private International Law' in A Dickinson, M Keyes and T John (eds), *Australian Private International Law for the 21st Century: Facing Outwards* (Oxford, Hart Publishing, 2014) 15, 27.

[51] See *Open Universities Australia Pty Ltd v TAFE Commission* (n 45) [7].

[52] Marshall, 'Australia: Inconsistencies in the Treatment of Optional Choice of Court Agreements' in Keyes (ed), *Optional Choice of Court Agreements in Private International Law* (n 45), text accompanying fn 175.

[53] Hague Choice of Court Convention, art 5(3)(b). Whether a jurisdiction clause is exclusive or non-exclusive for the purposes of the cross-vesting legislation is currently determined by common law principles: *Asciano Services Pty Ltd v Australian Rail Track Corp Ltd* [2008] NSWSC 652, [16]-[17].

[54] ibid, art 8(5).

[55] For the most recent analyses on the subject, see L Merrett, 'The Future Enforcement of Asymmetric Jurisdiction Agreements' (2018) 67 *International and Comparative Law Quarterly* 37; H Wais, 'Einseitige Gerichtsstandsvereinbarungen und die Schranken der Parteiautonomie' (2017) 81 *Rabels Zeitschrift für ausländisches und internationales Privatrecht* 815.

purposes of the present discussion, I will focus on the most common type of asymmetric clause.[56] This type requires one party[57] (the non-option holder) to sue in the jurisdiction named in the clause but allows the other party[58] (the option holder) to sue there and/or elsewhere.[59] It provides for one party to make a deferred decision as to which court or courts it will seise. For example:

> Any dispute which arises between the client and the Bank will be submitted to the exclusive jurisdiction of the courts of Luxembourg. The Bank nonetheless reserves the right to proceed against the client in the courts of the client's domicile or before any other court with jurisdiction in default of an election of the preceding jurisdiction.[60]

Different variants of this type of clause can be found in the case law. For instance, many provide for the option holder to bring an action in the court named in the clause *and/or* 'in the courts of any other jurisdiction' without referring expressly to the courts of the non-option holder's domicile.[61] Others make express provision for the option holder to sue in the court named in the clause and in several optional fora simultaneously.[62] Some are much narrower, providing for the option

[56] There is nonetheless a significant question mark over how other types of asymmetric jurisdiction agreements will be treated for the purposes of the Hague Choice of Court Convention.

[57] Or group of parties.

[58] Or group of parties.

[59] In other words, it 'purports to have a derogation effect for [proceedings *against*] the beneficiary' of the clause: Mills (n 26) 164.

[60] Cass civ, 1ère, 26.9.2012, *Madame X v Banque Privée Edmond de Rothschild*, No 11-26.022, Publié au bulletin [publicised by the court]; D Bureau, 'Clause attributive de juridiction potestative et pluralité de défendeurs dans des actions fondées sur des loi différentes, Cour de cassation (Civ 1re) – 26 septembre 2012, D 2012 2876' (2013) 102 *Revue critique de droit international privé* 256. It is unclear from the face of the clause whether 'in default of an election of the *preceding jurisdiction*' refers to the courts of the client's domicile or also to an election of the courts of Luxembourg. The clause in the French original reads: 'Les litiges éventuels entre le client et la banque seront soumis à la juridiction exclusive des tribunaux de Luxembourg. La banque se réserve toutefois le droit d'agir au domicile du client ou devant tout autre tribunal compétent à défaut de l'élection de juridiction qui précède'. It would not have been possible, in light of the *lis pendens* rule in the predecessor to the recast Brussels I Regulation, for the bank to have seised the courts of Luxembourg *and* either the courts of the client's domicile in Barcelona or another EU Member State court with jurisdiction under that Regulation, though it would have been possible for the Bank to have seised the courts of Luxembourg *and* another court elsewhere with jurisdiction under its own rules.

[61] eg the clause in *Barclays Bank plc v Ente Nazionale di Previdenza* [2015] EWHC 2857 (Comm Ct), [2015] 2 Lloyd's Rep 527, [30]:

> … [E]ach of the parties irrevocably: (a) agrees for [C's] benefit that the courts of England shall have jurisdiction to settle any suit, action or other proceedings relating to this Agreement ('Proceedings') and irrevocably submits to the jurisdiction of such courts (provided that this shall not prevent us from bringing an action *in the courts of any other jurisdiction*) … (emphasis added).

[62] eg the clause in Loan Market Association, Investment Grade Loan Market Association Single Currency Term and Revolving Facilities Agreement, cl 40.1 (provided by the Loan Market Association): The courts of England have exclusive jurisdiction to settle any dispute arising out of or in connection with this Agreement …

> …
> This [c]lause … is for the benefit of the Finance Parties only. As a result, no Finance Party shall be prevented from taking proceedings relating to a Dispute in any other courts with jurisdiction. To the extent allowed by law, the Finance Parties may take concurrent proceedings in any number of jurisdictions.

holder to bring an action in either the court named in the clause or one optional court.[63] What is common to all variants of this type of clause is that they contain two principal limbs: a limb nominating the jurisdiction of an '"anchor" court',[64] applicable to proceedings brought by both parties,[65] and a limb giving one party an option to seise another court or other courts. As a clause of this type was in issue in the widely-discussed French Cour de cassation *Rothschild* case,[66] clauses of this type are referred to in the following discussion as 'Rothschild clauses'. Rothschild clauses are widespread in Europe,[67] especially in England[68] and can also be found in Australian case law.[69]

Until recently, it had been undisputed that asymmetric clauses of this type did not have an exclusive character for the purposes of the Convention.[70] It was thought that the only way in which the Convention might affect them would be at the stage of recognition and enforcement of judgments, if a reciprocal declaration had been made under art 22. Despite their apparent exclusion from the Convention at the jurisdictional stage, the English High Court has recently suggested that asymmetric jurisdiction agreements, specifically, Rothschild clauses, are

[63] eg the clause in Cass civ 1ère, 25.05.2016, No 15-10.163 Non publié au bulletin [not publicised by the court] ('the courts of the city of Luxembourg shall have exclusive jurisdiction, unless the bank prefers to choose the courts of your [the client's] head office' (my translation)).

[64] Fentiman (n 24) [2.127].

[65] The language of some clauses found in the case law could suggest that the first limb is intended to prorogate the jurisdiction of the anchor court only for proceedings brought *against* the non-option holder; not for proceedings which the non-option holder brings: see eg *Marks v Australia and New Zealand Banking Group Ltd* [2014] QCA 102 (Unreported 26 February, 6 May 2014) [31] ('The Guarantor irrevocably submits to the non-exclusive jurisdiction of the courts of Singapore or of any other court as the Bank may elect'); *Commerzbank Aktiengesellschaft v Liquimar Tankers Management Inc* [2017] EWHC 161 (Comm Ct), [2017] 1 WLR 3497, [9]; *Continental Bank NA v Aeakos Compania Naviera SA* [1994] 1 WLR 588 (CA) 591–92; *Ocarina Marine Ltd v Marcard Stein & Co* [1994] 2 Lloyd's Rep 524 (Comm Ct) 526. The English High Court has on several occasions rejected that construction, holding that the jurisdiction of the anchor court applies to proceedings brought by both parties (*Ocarina Marine Ltd v Marcard Stein & Co* [1994] 2 Lloyd's Rep 524 (QB) 529; *Mauritius Commercial Bank Ltd v Hestia Holdings Ltd* [2013] EWHC 1328 (Comm Ct) (QB), [2013] 2 All ER 898, [40]–[41]) but has also on several recent occasions adopted it, preventing the non-option holder from relying on the clause at all: *In re Van Gansewinkel Groep BV* [2015] EWHC 2151 (Ch), [2015] Bus LR 1046, [49]; *In the Matter of Global Garden Products Italy SpA* [2016] EWHC 1884 (Ch) [31] (*obiter*).

[66] n 60.

[67] K Bälz und P Stompfe, 'Asymmetrische Streitbeilegungsklauseln in internationalen Wirtschaftsverträgen' (2017) 15 *Zeitschrift für Schiedsverfahren* (*SchiedsVZ*) 157, 158.

[68] R Fentiman, 'Unilateral Jurisdiction Agreements in Europe' (2013) *Cambridge Law Journal* 24, 24; S Garvey, 'Hybrid Jurisdiction Clauses: Time for a Rethink' (2016) 31 *Butterworths Journal of International Banking and Financial Law* 6, 6.

[69] eg *Telesto Investments Ltd v UBS AG* [2013] NSWSC 503, 94 ACSR 29, [5] ('the exclusive place of jurisdiction … shall be the jurisdiction in which the Account is booked. Notwithstanding this, the Bank shall have the right, but not the duty or obligation, to take legal action against the Client in the jurisdiction in which UBS e-banking Services is offered, in the Client's place of residence or domicile or any other jurisdiction'). See also *Reinsurance Australia Corporation Ltd v HIH Casualty & General Insurance Ltd (in liq)* [2003] FCA 56, (2003) 254 ALR 29, [339], [341], [343]–[346] (in which Jacobson J held that a Rothschild clause had exclusive effect as far as the non-option holder was concerned).

[70] See eg M Keyes and BA Marshall, 'Jurisdiction Agreements: Exclusive, Optional and Asymmetrical' (2015) 11 *Journal of Private International Law* 345, 366; J Barbet and P Rosher, 'Les clauses de résolution de litiges optionnelles' (2010) *Revue de l'arbitrage* 45, 80, fn 102.

nonetheless exclusive jurisdiction clauses for the purposes of the Convention.[71] It is conceivable that the court made this suggestion with an eye on Brexit: once the United Kingdom leaves the European Union, EU Member State courts will no longer be obliged by the recast Brussels I Regulation to recognise and enforce judgments rendered by English courts,[72] including where they had jurisdiction under a Rothschild clause. If Rothschild clauses are not 'exclusive' agreements under the Hague Choice of Court Convention, EU Member State courts will not be obliged to recognise and enforce judgments rendered by English courts with jurisdiction under such clauses under that Convention either.[73]

There are five conceivable ways in which the Convention could apply to a Rothschild clause at the jurisdictional stage: either by the definition of exclusivity, irrespective of where proceedings are brought; if the non-option holder brings proceedings in the anchor court; if only the option holder brings proceedings and only in the anchor court; if only the option holder sues and only pursuant to its option; or if only the option holder is considered to be bound by the clause. The following subsections will examine and reject these possibilities in turn, arguing that most variants of Rothschild clauses can fall within the Convention only at the recognition and enforcement stage.

### i. *Exclusive Irrespective of the Proceedings Brought*

The 2017 English High Court decision of *Commerzbank Aktiengesellschaft v Liquimar Tankers Management Inc*[74] concerned a standard variant of Rothschild clause. It relevantly provided:

> For the exclusive benefit of the Lender, the Guarantor irrevocably agrees that the courts of England are to have jurisdiction to settle any disputes which may arise out of or in connection with this Guarantee and Indemnity … Nothing contained in this Clause shall limit the right of the Lender to commence any proceedings against the Guarantor in any other court of competent jurisdiction nor shall the commencement of any proceedings against the Guarantor in one or more jurisdictions preclude the commencement of any proceedings in any other jurisdiction, whether concurrently or not') (emphasis added).[75]

There, Cranston J observed in *obiter* that '[t]here are good arguments … that the words of the definition of exclusive jurisdiction clauses in article 3*a)* of the …

[71] *Commerzbank Aktiengesellschaft v Liquimar Tankers Management Inc* (n 65) [74].

[72] See J Basedow, 'Brexit und das Privat- und Wirtschaftsrecht' (2016) 24 *Zeitschrift für Europäisches Privatrecht* 567, 572.

[73] They would be obliged to enforce judgments rendered by English courts where they had jurisdiction under an exclusive jurisdiction agreement under the Hague Choice of Court Convention, provided the United Kingdom independently ratifies the Convention after Brexit, as it intends to do: see further n 195.

[74] *Commerzbank Aktiengesellschaft v Liquimar Tankers Management Inc* (n 65).

[75] ibid [9].

Convention cover asymmetric jurisdiction clauses'.[76] As has been seen, art 3(a) of the Convention defines an exclusive jurisdiction agreement as one designating the courts of one jurisdiction to the exclusion of all others.[77] Masato Dogauchi and Trevor Hartley, in their first Explanatory Report to the preliminary draft convention, had suggested that 'it might be desirable' to add to the definition of exclusivity that 'Such an agreement must be exclusive irrespective of the party bringing the proceedings'.[78] The crux of Cranston J's argument is that because this was not done, Rothschild clauses are exclusive under the Convention.[79] With respect, this argument is unpersuasive. Hartley and Dogauchi made that suggestion in the context of making clear that Rothschild clauses 'would *not* be covered by the Convention' (emphasis added).[80] The Informal Working Group on the Convention had excluded them, because like symmetric non-exclusive clauses, Rothschild clauses would have necessitated rules dealing with parallel proceedings,[81] which the Convention does not contain.[82] (It is plain that a clause which provides for the jurisdiction of the courts of more than one state creates a risk of concurrent proceedings.) The final version of the Explanatory Report states in unambiguous terms that Rothschild clauses 'are not exclusive choice of court agreements for the purposes of the Convention'.[83] The Explanatory Report also states that '[i]t was agreed by the Diplomatic Session that, in order to be covered by the Convention, the agreement must be exclusive irrespective of the party bringing the proceedings'.[84] Indeed, the Diplomatic Session, which concluded the Convention,[85] had rejected a proposal of the Swiss delegation that Rothschild clauses should be brought within the scope of the Convention.[86] The Swiss had suggested amending the definition of an exclusive choice of court agreement to one which 'designates, *for some or all of the parties*

[76] ibid [74].

[77] Text to n 19.

[78] M Dogauchi and TC Hartley, *Preliminary Draft Convention on Exclusive Choice of Court Agreements: Explanatory Report* (Preliminary Document No 25 of March 2004) [49].

[79] *Commerzbank Aktiengesellschaft v Liquimar Tankers Management Inc* (n 65) [37]–[39], [73]–[74].

[80] Dogauchi and Hartley, *First Report on the Preliminary Draft Convention* (n 78) [49].

[81] A Schulz, *Report on the Work of the Informal Working Group on the Judgments Project, in particular on the Preliminary Text Achieved at its Third Meeting – 25 to 28 March 2003* (Preliminary Document No 22 of June 2003) in Permanent Bureau of the Conference (n 8) 87 at [51], [63].

[82] Dogauchi and Hartley note that 'this would have raised issues of *lis pendens* that would have been difficult to resolve in an acceptable way': (n 78) [9]; M Dogauchi and TC Hartley, *Preliminary Draft Convention on Exclusive Choice of Court Agreements: Explanatory Report* (Preliminary Document No 26 of December 2004) [14].

[83] Hartley and Dogauchi (n 8) [106].

[84] ibid.

[85] ibid 787.

[86] Minutes No 2, Meeting of Tuesday 14 June 2005 (afternoon) in Permanent Bureau of the Conference (n 8) 574; Minutes No 3, Meeting of Wednesday 15 June 2005 (morning) in Permanent Bureau of the Conference (n 8) 578: 'The chair … not[ed] that there was no support for the proposal to amend Article 3 *a)* [and] … that the view of the Commission was that asymmetric agreements were not covered by the Convention and that the Convention was not designed for clauses of this sort. … [T]he issue remained on the table for the purposes of [the then] Article 9 [on the recognition of judgments arising out of non-exclusive agreements]'.

*to the agreement*, … the courts of one Contracting State … to the exclusion of the jurisdiction of any other courts'.[87]

It may be that the decision of the Diplomatic Session not to amend the definition of exclusivity expressly to encompass Rothschild clauses can be considered, for the purposes of interpreting the Convention under public international law, an 'agreement' among all Contracting States in connection with the conclusion of the Convention and therefore part of the 'extrinsic context'[88] against which the courts of Contracting States *must* interpret the Convention in good faith.[89] Even if that decision is not an agreement which binds the Contracting States, it is a highly cogent supplementary means of confirming the ordinary meaning of the definition of exclusivity, given the proximity of the decision to the conclusion of the Convention.[90] That definition, when read in the context of the rest of the Convention, which does not contain rules regulating parallel proceedings, must apply in the same manner to both parties.[91] All of that being so, the claim that the words of the definition of exclusive jurisdiction clauses in art 3(a) of the Convention cover Rothschild clauses seems difficult to sustain. But it is not impossible. If the decision of the Diplomatic Session is not an agreement but rather a supplementary means of interpretation, Contracting States are not obliged to have recourse to it.[92] And if Contracting States' courts can find a way to bring Rothschild clauses within the definition of exclusivity without them resulting in parallel proceedings, then arguably that course is open to them. The remaining four subsections consider possible ways in which that might occur.

### *ii. Exclusive if the Non-Option Holder Sues in the Anchor Court*

The Convention could conceivably apply to a Rothschild clause at the jurisdictional stage in circumstances where the non-option holder in fact brings proceedings in the anchor court. As has been explained, the anchor court is where the non-option holder *must* sue and where the option holder *can* sue.[93] In their first report to the preliminary draft convention, Hartley and Dogauchi observed that '[i]t might be thought' that a Rothschild clause designating the courts of State X as

[87] Working Document No 3, Distributed on Tuesday 14 June 2005 in Permanent Bureau of the Conference (n 8) 510.

[88] See generally O Dörr in O Dörr and K Schmalenbach, *Vienna Convention on the Law of Treaties: A Commentary*, 2nd edn (Berlin, Springer, 2018) art 31, [61]–[66].

[89] Vienna Convention on the Law of Treaties (opened for signature 23 May 1969, entered into force 27 January 1980) 1155 UNTS 331, art 31(1)(2)(a).

[90] See O Dörr in Dörr and Schmalenbach, *Vienna Convention on the Law of Treaties* (n 88) art 32, [20].

[91] Vienna Convention, arts 31–32.

[92] 'Recourse *may* be had to supplementary means of interpretation' (emphasis added): Vienna Convention, art 32.

[93] Text to nn 64–65, though as noted there, there are conflicting English authorities on the effect of the anchor part of the agreement on the non-option holder.

the anchor courts[94] 'would be covered by the Convention when the proceedings were brought by the [*non-option holder*], but not when they were brought by the [*option holder*]'.[95] The authors dismissed this scenario on the basis that it 'would produce unacceptable results'. Assuming the option holder seised a court of State Y *first*, pursuant to its option, that court would be entitled to hear those proceedings because they 'would not be covered by the Convention'.[96] Presumably, the option holder's proceedings in State Y would not be covered by the Convention, because proceedings that the option holder brings are not proceedings to which an exclusive jurisdiction agreement, as defined by the Convention, applies: the option holder is not bound by an agreement to sue in one jurisdiction to the exclusion of all others.[97] The courts of State X (the anchor courts bound by the Convention), on the other hand, would be required to hear any proceedings that the non-option holder *subsequently* brings. The non-option holder's proceedings would be covered by the Convention, because the courts of State X have jurisdiction to the exclusion of all other courts for proceedings brought by the non-option holder.[98] The Convention now provides some architecture for resolving whether the judgment of the courts of State Y or State X would prevail,[99] which it did not at the time Hartley and Dogauchi wrote their first, draft report.[100] But the Convention still contains no mechanism for resolving the question of which set of proceedings should proceed at the jurisdictional stage. The result is the risk that the non-option holder's proceedings in State X and the option holder's proceedings in State Y inefficiently proceed in parallel,[101] possibly to the point of judgment, or at least to the point of trial, if the parties choose to stop short of multiple trials on the merits in both sets of proceedings.[102]

[94] eg a clause providing: 'Proceedings by the borrower [non-option holder] against the lender [option holder] may be brought exclusively in the courts of State X; proceedings by the lender [option holder] against the borrower [non-option holder] may be brought in the courts of State X or in the courts of any other State having jurisdiction under their own law': Dogauchi and Hartley (n 78) [49].

[95] ibid [50].

[96] ibid.

[97] *Cf* Hague Choice of Court Convention, art 3(a). In other words, State Y would not be required, in accordance with art 6 of the Convention, to suspend or dismiss its proceedings, because those are not proceedings to which an exclusive jurisdiction agreement applies.

[98] Dogauchi and Hartley (n 78) [50].

[99] The courts of another state (eg State Z) would have the discretion to refuse to recognise State X's judgment if State Y's had been issued first and vice versa: Hague Choice of Court Convention, art 9(g). But neither State X nor State Y would be required to recognise the other's judgment irrespective of which judgment was issued first: Hague Choice of Court Convention, art 9(f).

[100] Dogauchi and Hartley (n 78) [50].

[101] Inefficiency is one of several problems resulting from an absence of rules controlling parallel proceedings. See generally C McLachlan, *Lis Pendens in International Litigation* (Leiden, Martinus Nijhoff, 2009) 21, 82–83.

[102] Cp R Fentiman, *International Commercial Litigation*, 1st edn (Oxford, Oxford University Press, 2010) [8.39] (observing that 'the likelihood that proceedings will advance significantly in both places is in practice remote') with *Royal Bank of Canada v Centrale Raiffeisen Boerenleenbank* [2004] EWCA Civ 7, [2004] 1 Lloyd's Rep 471, [50] (where Mance LJ reasoned that 'proceedings once begun are normally intended to be pursued to trial').

What if, contrary to the suggestion in Hartley and Dogauchi's draft, the option holder's proceedings in State Y *are* proceedings to which an exclusive jurisdiction agreement in favour of the courts of State X applies? It could be argued that a Rothschild clause, designating the courts of State X in the anchor limb, is an exclusive jurisdiction agreement for the purposes of art 3(a) of the Convention, even though at the time the clause is concluded, the option holder is not under a present obligation to bring disputes only in State X. This argument could be made in respect of narrow variants of Rothschild clauses which allow for the option holder to sue in the anchor court (in State X) *or* a court pursuant to its option (in State Y). For instance, 'the courts of State X shall have exclusive jurisdiction, unless the bank prefers to choose the courts of your head office in State Y'. That is because such a clause arguably obliges the option holder, once it initiates proceedings in State X, to continue proceedings in that court; it cannot change its mind and bring proceedings in the other court instead or as well. It could therefore be said that the option holder, although not under a present obligation at the time of contracting to sue in State X, is under a future obligation to sue there, and only there (just as much as the non-option holder), if it initiates proceedings there.[103] The Singaporean Court of Appeal recently upheld a decision accepting such an argument in the context of an asymmetric hybrid arbitration litigation clause.[104] The clause provided 'at the election of Dyna-Jet, the dispute may be referred to and personally settled by means of arbitration proceedings'.[105] Vinodh Coomaraswamy J of the court below reasoned that although the clause did not expressly refer to litigation, 'its effect is to confer on Dyna-Jet an unfettered right to elect arbitration and also to decline to elect arbitration with respect to any specific dispute'.[106] His Honour arrived at this conclusion by applying either English law (as the proper law of the arbitration agreement) or Singaporean law (as the law of the forum).[107] The contractual effect of the clause, assessed *ex ante*, is that Dyna-Jet is under a future obligation to arbitrate because if Dyna-Jet were elect to arbitrate, it would be bound to arbitrate its claims (just as much as its counterparty).[108] It followed that there was an agreement to arbitrate even though Dyna-Jet *ex post* had declined to elect to arbitrate, initiating litigation instead.

[103] (This argument could not be made in respect of standard variants of Rothschild clauses which empower an option holder to bring proceedings in the anchor and an optional court or the anchor and several optional courts, because at no point in time can it be said that the option holder is obliged to bring proceedings only in the anchor court.)

[104] *Wilson Taylor Asia Pacific Pte Ltd v Dyna-Jet Pte Ltd* [2017] SGCA 32, [2017] 2 Lloyd's Rep 104, [13].

[105] *DynaJet v Wilson Taylor Asia Pacific* [2016] SGHC 238, [2017] 1 Lloyd's Rep 59, [10].

[106] ibid [134]. See also [138]: 'the parties are in litigation *pursuant to*, and not despite, the contractual operation of their arbitration agreement'.

[107] Vinodh Coomaraswamy J observed that 'there is no material difference between Singapore law and English law' on the relevant points and therefore found it unnecessary to specify which law he was applying: ibid [32].

[108] See ibid [135]–[137].

Assume for the moment that the analogy with asymmetric hybrid arbitration litigation agreements and the Singaporean courts' reasoning were thought persuasive in the context of the Hague Choice of Court Convention,[109] at least if Contracting States are free to resolve the question of whether a jurisdiction clause complies with the definition of exclusivity in art 3(a) by reference to an applicable national law.[110] The court in State Y would be required to suspend or dismiss the option holder's proceedings, in favour of the proceedings in State X subsequently brought by the non-option holder, unless one of the five narrow exceptions in art 6 of the Convention applies,[111] which, in this scenario, would not appear to be the case, or unless the proceedings, which the option holder has first chosen to litigate in State Y, are not 'proceedings to which an exclusive choice of court agreement [designating the courts of State X] applies',[112] which is arguable. Again, this approach finds support in the decision of the Singaporean Court of Appeal in the *DynaJet* case. The Court held that a dispute which Dyna-Jet had not elected to resolve by arbitration but rather 'elected otherwise by commencing [litigation]' was not a dispute which fell within the scope of the arbitration agreement.[113] By analogy of reasoning, it could be said that a dispute which the option holder has not elected to resolve by proceedings in the courts of State X but has elected otherwise by commencing proceedings in the courts of State Y is not a dispute within the scope of the exclusive choice of court agreement designating the courts of State X. The result is that the courts of State Y could retain the option holder's proceedings.

Applying the Singaporean Court of Appeal's approach by analogy is an ambitious way to bring a Rothschild clause within the jurisdictional ambit of the Convention, only to conclude that proceedings brought pursuant to the clause are

[109] Which is conceivable given that the Singaporean case was decided pursuant to the International Arbitration Act (Singapore) (Ch 143A, 2002 rev edn) (Singapore) ss 2A(1), 6, which echo the definition of an arbitration agreement and the obligation of a court to stay legal proceedings between parties to an arbitration agreement in art II of the New York Convention: *DynaJet v Wilson Taylor Asia Pacific* (n 105) [21]. Art 26(1) of the Hague Choice of Court Convention, as mentioned at text to n 29, requires the courts of Contracting States, of which Singapore is one, to interpret the Convention 'so far as possible to be compatible with other international treaties in force for Contracting States'. The New York Convention is likely to have particular relevance for the purposes of art 26(1) given that the overarching aim of the Hague Convention Choice of Court Convention is to achieve for jurisdiction agreements and resulting judgments what the New York Convention has achieved for arbitration agreements and resulting arbitral awards: Hartley and Dogauchi (n 8) 787.

[110] Section I.A.

[111] The exceptions allowing a non-chosen court (in my example, State Y) to retain jurisdiction are where: the agreement is null and void according to the law of the state of the chosen court; one party lacked contractual capacity under the law of the court seised; 'giving effect to the agreement would lead to a manifest injustice or would be manifestly contrary to the public policy' of the law of the forum; the agreement cannot be performed because of 'exceptional reasons beyond the control of the parties'; or 'the chosen court has decided not to hear the case': Hague Choice of Court Convention, art 6(a)–(e).

[112] Hague Choice of Court Convention, art 6: 'A court of a Contracting State other than that of the chosen court shall suspend or dismiss proceedings to which an exclusive choice of court agreement applies'.

[113] *Wilson Taylor Asia Pacific Pte Ltd v Dyna-Jet Pte Ltd* [2017] SGCA 32, [2017] 2 Lloyd's Rep 104, [14]–[24]. The quote is at [24].

in fact outside of the clause's scope. Although it is not untenable, it is not clear that this is a conceptually sound approach,[114] or that State X and State Y's courts would arrive at the same result, whether because one would characterise the issue as one of scope whereas the other would not, or because the choice of law rule that each state would apply to the issue of scope would lead to the application of different substantive laws. (Again, the Convention is silent as to the law which a court should apply to determine whether the proceedings before it are proceedings to which a jurisdiction agreement applies.[115]) This approach would also not solve the problem of parallel proceedings in State Y and State X, unless the court of State X equally considers that the dispute brought before it by the non-option holder is, by virtue of the option holder's prior election to bring proceedings in State Y, no longer 'a dispute to which the agreement applies' under art 5(1) of the Convention.[116]

It is also difficult to see how approaching the issue as one of scope would work if the order of the proceedings were reversed. Assume the non-option holder were first to bring proceedings in State X and the option holder were subsequently to bring proceedings pursuant to its option in State Y. After the non-option holder has already commenced proceedings, is a dispute which the option holder now decides to litigate elsewhere than in the anchor court, retrospectively, not a dispute within the scope of the exclusive jurisdiction agreement designating the courts of State X? It seems improbable that the courts of both State X and State Y would answer that question in the same way.[117] The court of State X is prevented by art 5(2) of the Convention from 'declin[ing] to exercise jurisdiction on the ground that the dispute should be decided in a court of another State', unless the dispute before it is not one 'to which the agreement applies'[118] which, at least at the time the court of State X is seised of proceedings, the dispute plainly is.

[114] There is some indication that the Privy Council might agree: in a case concerning an option for either party to elect that proceedings be brought to arbitration, Lord Mance and Lord Clarke of Stone-cum-Ebony JJSC, handing down the judgment of the board, observed at [8] that '[e]ven if one could in loose terms describe a conditional agreement to arbitrate as an arbitration agreement, the Board would not regard it as such within the meaning of section 6(2)': *Hermes One Ltd v Everbread Holdings Ltd* [2016] UKPC 1, [2016] 1 WLR 4098. The Board held that an arbitration agreement is triggered when either of the parties with the option to arbitrate insists on it: at [34]–[35]. The legislation in question was s 6(2) of the Arbitration Ordinance 1976 (Cap 6) which is in materially the same terms as s 6 of the International Arbitration Act (Singapore) which the Singaporean courts applied in the *Dyna-Jet* case. Both of these provisions are materially the same as s 9 of the Arbitration Act 1996 (England and Wales) and s 7(2), (4), (5) of the International Arbitration Act 1974 (Cth).

[115] n 112.

[116] Hague Choice of Court Convention, art 5(1): 'The court or courts of a Contracting State designated in an exclusive choice of court agreement shall have jurisdiction to decide *a dispute to which the agreement applies*, unless the agreement is null and void under the law of that State' (emphasis added).

[117] Cp the opposite approaches taken by common law and German courts to the retrospective exercise of an option under an asymmetric hybrid arbitration litigation agreement: BGH 24.09.1998 – III ZR 133/97, NJW 1999, 282 [Bundesgerichtshof (Federal Court of Justice of Germany)]; *NB Three Shipping Ltd v Harebell Shipping Ltd* [2004] EWHC 509 (QB), [2005] 1 Lloyd's Rep 509, [11]; *Law Debenture Trust Corp plc v Elektrim Finance* [2005] EWHC 1412 (Ch), [2005] 2 Lloyd's Rep 755, [45].

[118] Hague Choice of Court Convention, art 5(1), extracted at n 116.

One could instead perhaps make the argument that the agreement designating the courts of State X, if it can be separated from the option designating State Y, is null and void under the law of State X, or the law designated by its choice of law rules.[119] This is the only other basis on which the court in State X could decline to entertain the non-option holder's proceedings under the Convention.[120] If waiver of the right to rely on a jurisdiction agreement is properly to be characterised as an issue of 'null and voidness' (which is a fairly substantial 'if'),[121] it could be argued the non-option holder has waived its right to insist that it or the option holder bring suit in the courts of State X if and when the option holder brings proceedings in the court of State Y. That argument would require some conduct on the part of the non-option holder which is, under the applicable law, inconsistent with the maintenance of its rights to sue or be sued exclusively in State X, such as counterclaiming in the option holder's proceedings in State Y.[122] It would also require the courts of State X to assess the validity of the agreement not at the time the agreement is concluded, or at the time proceedings are commenced before it, but rather at the time the option holder commences proceedings in State Y, which tends to suggest waiver is not relevant to the inherent validity of a jurisdiction agreement with which art 5(1) of the Convention appears to be concerned.

A possible solution would be for parties to draft around this problem. It is open to them to make clear on the face of their clause that the non-option holder must discontinue proceedings in the courts of State X and bring cross-claims in State Y if and when the option holder initiates proceedings in State Y, *if* those are in fact their intentions. One of the risks of implying such an intention in the absence of clear wording was already mentioned above.[123]

### *iii. Exclusive if Only the Option Holder Sues and Only in the Anchor Court*

A further way in which the Convention could conceivably apply to any variant of Rothschild clause at the jurisdictional stage is where only the option holder brings proceedings and only in the anchor court.[124] As Brand and Herrup put it, 'the agreement *ipso facto* is exclusive'.[125] But this approach requires the character

[119] Hartley and Dogauchi (n 8) [125].

[120] ibid.

[121] The Convention is silent as to the law which applies to characterisation of this question. Brand and Herrup (n 14) 81–82 appear to suggest that the applicable law itself applies to characterise an issue as falling within or outside of the '"null and void" category'. If the applicable law were Australian law, waiver would not render the agreement null and void and would therefore not be relevant: see Marshall and Keyes, 'Australia's Accession to the Hague Convention on Choice of Court Agreements' (n 18) 260.

[122] See *Bogart Lingerie Ltd v Steadmark Pty Ltd* [2013] VSC 212 [36], [50]; *Steadmark Pty Ltd v Bogart Lingerie Ltd* [2013] VSC 402 [36], [45]; Marshall and Keyes (n 18) 274–275.

[123] Text to and in n 43.

[124] Dogauchi and Hartley (n 82) [72].

[125] Brand and Herrup (n 14) 44.

of the clause to be assessed at the time proceedings are commenced, based on the conduct of the parties, rather than at the time of the clause's conclusion, based on the terms of the clause. Given that jurisdiction clauses appear to have a contractual nature under the Convention,[126] the character of a jurisdiction clause must be determined under the Convention at the time it is concluded; not at the time a dispute arises. Even if this temporal question were to be determined by an applicable national law, and that were the law of a common law system, the proper construction of the jurisdiction clause would still need to be conducted by reference to the time of its conclusion, just like any other contractual clause,[127] even if the clause only has effect from the time a dispute arises.[128] If that is right, then even if the option holder only brings proceedings in the anchor court, the fact that the agreement expressly empowers it to bring proceedings in other courts means that it is not an exclusive agreement.

Even if it were consistent with the Convention to assess the clause at the time of proceedings rather than at the time it is concluded, most variants of Rothschild clause[129] would still not comply with the definition in art 3(a); the fact that the option holder has brought proceedings in the anchor court does not prevent it from later bringing proceedings *in addition* in a court pursuant to its option.[130] Moreover, if the clause expressly provides in the optional limb for the option holder to bring proceedings concurrently, as the clause did in *Commerzbank Aktiengesellschaft v Liquimar Tankers Management Inc*,[131] the fact that the option holder has brought proceedings in the anchor court does not prevent it from later bringing proceedings in addition in *several* courts pursuant to its option. In other words, whether the clause is assessed at the time of its conclusion or at the time of proceedings, the non-option holder has not, contrary to Merrett's argument, 'agreed to be sued in a particular jurisdiction and only that jurisdiction'.[132] Quite the opposite; the non-option holder has agreed to be sued in a particular jurisdiction and in many other jurisdictions, even simultaneously.

[126] Briggs, *Agreements on Jurisdiction and Choice of Law* (n 43) [13.13]; A Briggs, 'The Brussels I bis Regulation Appears on the Horizon' [2011] *Lloyd's Maritime and Commercial Law Quarterly* 157, 161–62.

[127] On this principle of contractual interpretation, see eg *Wood v Capita Insurance Services Ltd* [2017] UKSC 24, [2017] AC 1173, [10] (Lord Hodge with whom Lords Neuberger, Mance, Clarke and Sumption agreed).

[128] See Joseph, *Jurisdiction and Arbitration Agreements and their Enforcement* (n 24) [4.09] (stating that in common law systems, a jurisdiction agreement 'will have legal effect from the time that disputes have arisen (if not from the date of the agreement)').

[129] An exception would be the narrow variant of Rothschild clause quoted at n 63 and, possibly, the clause in the Rothschild case itself, depending on how the words 'in default of an election of the *preceding jurisdiction*' are understood: see n 60.

[130] See 'Minutes No 3, Meeting of Wednesday 15 June 2005 (morning)' in Permanent Bureau of the Conference (n 8) 578.

[131] *Commerzbank Aktiengesellschaft v Liquimar Tankers Management Inc* (n 65) [9] quoted at text to n 75.

[132] *Cf* Merrett, 'The Future Enforcement of Asymmetric Jurisdiction Agreements' (n 55) 58 (discussing the clause in ibid).

### iv. *Exclusive if Only the Option Holder Sues and Only Pursuant to its Option*

A further way in which the Convention could apply to a Rothschild clause at the jurisdictional stage is where only the option holder sues and only pursuant to its option. It could be argued that once exercised, the optional limb of the clause itself is potentially capable of meeting the criterion in art 3(a) because it excludes the jurisdiction of the anchor court. This latter argument could prevail in respect of a narrow variant of Rothschild clause of which the optional limb designates a specific court. For instance, 'the courts of the city of Luxembourg shall have exclusive jurisdiction, *unless* the bank prefers to choose the courts of your [the client's] head office' (emphasis added).[133] Such a clause makes clear that the bank can choose to sue in the courts of Luxembourg *or* the courts of the client's head office, and that the choice of one means the other is no longer available. It would not, however, prevail in respect of standard variants of Rothschild clauses of which the optional limb designates 'other courts with jurisdiction', because bringing proceedings pursuant to that part of the clause does not preclude the option holder from subsequently also bringing proceedings in the anchor court.[134] Nor would it prevail in respect of those variants of Rothschild clauses which expressly provide for the option holder to bring proceedings pursuant to its option concurrently.[135]

### v. *Exclusive because Only One Party is Bound*

The final way in which the Convention could apply to a Rothschild clause is by reference to Hartley's view that '[t]here would … seem to be no reason why it should not be agreed by the parties to the contract that only some of them will be bound by the choice-of-court agreement'.[136] Recent first instance English decisions have interpreted Rothschild clauses as applying only to proceedings brought by the *option holder* (that is, as preventing the non-option holder from relying on the clause at all, instead requiring the non-option holder to rely on a default head of jurisdiction in order to bring proceedings against the option holder).[137] Taken one step further, this reasoning could suggest that, on application of English law,

[133] Cass civ 1ère, 25.05.2016, No 15-10.163 Non publié au bulletin [not publicised by the court].

[134] Again, the clause in the Rothschild case itself may be an exception, depending on how the words 'in default of an election of the *preceding jurisdiction*' are understood: see n 60.

[135] n 62; text to n 75.

[136] Hartley, *Choice of Court Agreements under the European and International Instruments* (n 14) [8.13].

[137] *In re Van Gansewinkel Groep BV* [2015] EWHC 2151 (Ch), [2015] Bus LR 1046, [49], [50]–[51]; *In the Matter of Global Garden Products Italy SpA* [2016] EWHC 1884 (Ch) [29], ([31] (*obiter*)). In these cases, the relevant head of default jurisdiction was art 8(1) of the recast Brussels I Regulation. This provision allows a defendant, domiciled in an EU Member State, to be sued before the courts of its co-defendant's domicile where the claims against both are closely connected, provided certain conditions are satisfied: see generally Fentiman (n 24) [9.90]–[9.99].

only *option holders* are 'bound' by a Rothschild clause. (Again, the Convention does not deal with which law should apply to determine which of the 'two or more parties'[138] will be bound by the jurisdiction agreement, presumably because it assumes that the 'two or more parties' that concluded the agreement will be bound by it.) Even if English law were applicable to this question and the line of reasoning recently taken by the English High Court were right,[139] Rothschild clauses could still not be enforced under the Convention because the *option holder*, the 'only' party 'bound' by the clause, has not, neither at the time of contracting nor at the time of proceedings, agreed to sue in a particular jurisdiction and only that jurisdiction as required by art 3(a) of the Convention.[140]

### D. Conclusion

In sum, a jurisdiction agreement that designates the courts of one Contracting State will be exclusive and thus governed by the jurisdictional provisions of the Convention unless the parties, by their words, make clear that the agreement does not exclude the jurisdiction of any other courts, in which case it will be non-exclusive. A jurisdiction clause designating two or more Contracting States, but not two or more territorial units within a Contracting State, will be non-exclusive. It is probable that asymmetric jurisdiction clauses, particularly Rothschild clauses, will also be non-exclusive for the purposes of the Convention, though Contracting States' courts may try to treat them, or at least some variants of them, as exclusive. It is improbable that the Convention intends them to do so, although parties themselves could solve the problem of parallel proceedings which Rothschild clauses create in the context of the Convention through suitable drafting.

## II. Conditions for Recognition and Enforcement of Judgments Rendered by Courts with Non-Exclusive Jurisdiction

As already foreshadowed, Contracting States that wish to allow for a judgment – rendered by a court with jurisdiction under an agreement that is non-exclusive – to be recognised and enforced under the Convention have the possibility to do so by declaration on reciprocal terms. Where the state of the court addressed and the state of the court of origin have made a declaration, the court addressed

[138] Hague Choice of Court Convention, art 3(a).

[139] Or even if it were wrong but an English court were to apply it anyway, the English court taking the view that art 3(b) requires recourse to an applicable law, that being English law (whether as the law of the forum or the proper law of the jurisdiction agreement) in the circumstances.

[140] Text to n 132.

must recognise and enforce the judgment of the court of origin, provided five cumulative[141] conditions are satisfied,[142] unless one of the bases for refusal exists under Chapter III of the Convention.[143]

The first condition under art 22 of the Convention for recognition and enforcement is satisfaction of the Convention's definition of a non-exclusive agreement: an agreement consented to[144] by two or more parties in writing or a form that can be subsequently consulted, which designates a court or courts of *one or more* Contracting States.[145] It has already been seen in section I which types of jurisdiction agreement will satisfy that definition, assuming they have been consented to and satisfy the requisite formal requirements. The second condition is that the court that rendered the judgment must have been 'designated' in the non-exclusive agreement.[146] Third, there cannot already be a *judgment* from a court in which proceedings were permitted by the non-exclusive agreement.[147] Fourth, there must be no *proceedings pending* between the same parties on the same cause of action in a court permitted by the non-exclusive agreement.[148] Finally, the court which rendered the judgment must have been the court first seised.[149]

[141] Kessedjian, 'Convention de la Haye du 30 juin 2005 sur l'élection de for' (n 17) 846.

[142] See Brand and Herrup (n 14) 154. Art 22 of the Hague Choice of Court Convention is in the following terms:

> Reciprocal declarations on non-exclusive choice of court agreements
>
> (1) A Contracting State may declare that its courts will recognise and enforce judgments given by courts of other Contracting States designated in a choice of court agreement concluded by two or more parties that meets the requirements of Article 3, paragraph *c)*, and designates, for the purpose of deciding disputes which have arisen or may arise in connection with a particular legal relationship, a court or courts of one or more Contracting States (a non-exclusive choice of court agreement).
>
> (2) Where recognition or enforcement of a judgment given in a Contracting State that has made such a declaration is sought in another Contracting State that has made such a declaration, the judgment shall be recognised and enforced under this Convention, if –
>
> (a) the court of origin was designated in a non-exclusive choice of court agreement;
>
> (b) there exists neither a judgment given by any other court before which proceedings could be brought in accordance with the non-exclusive choice of court agreement, nor a proceeding pending between the same parties in any other such court on the same cause of action; and
>
> (c) the court of origin was the court first seised.

[143] Hague Choice of Court Convention, art 9(a)–(g); Hartley and Dogauchi (n 8) [240] fn 279. Art 9(f) is concerned only with *inconsistent* judgments and art 9(g) only with inconsistent judgments that fulfil the conditions necessary for recognition in the requested state. They are therefore narrower than the corresponding condition in art 22(2)(b), so any ground for refusal on these bases would have already been weeded out by art 22(2)(b); *cf* Brand and Herrup (n 14) 157 (arguing, although acknowledging the awkwardness of the argument, that art 22(2)(b) should not be read more broadly than arts 9(f) and (g)).

[144] Hartley and Dogauchi (n 8) [242].

[145] Hague Choice of Court Convention, art 22(1), art 3(c). The definition contains additional elements not relevant to the present discussion.

[146] ibid, art 22(2)(a).

[147] ibid, art 22(2)(b) first phrase.

[148] ibid, art 22(2)(b) second phrase.

[149] ibid, art 22(2)(c).

The critique in this section focuses on the latter two conditions.[150] It will argue, first, that the requirement that there must be no *proceedings pending* in a court permitted by the non-exclusive agreement, before a court can recognise a judgment, may carry the risk of abuse (section II.A), and, secondly, that the requirement that the court which rendered the judgment must have been the court first seised means that art 22 will not facilitate the recognition of judgments rendered by courts designated in a non-exclusive clause where prior proceedings, permitted by the clause, have been dismissed on *forum non conveniens* grounds. For the same reasons, art 22 will not facilitate the recognition of judgments rendered by courts designated in service of suits clauses; a type of asymmetric jurisdiction clause used in common law jurisdictions in international reinsurance contracts (section II.B).[151]

## A. Are there Proceedings Pending in a Court with Non-Exclusive Jurisdiction?

Article 22(2)(b) of the Convention provides that the courts of a Contracting State cannot recognise and enforce a judgment under the Convention if there are *proceedings pending* between the same parties on the same cause of action in a court 'before which proceedings could be brought in accordance with the non-exclusive choice of court agreement'.[152] The effect of this condition, applied to a symmetric non-exclusive agreement providing for the 'non-exclusive jurisdiction of the courts of New South Wales', is that the party that loses in New South Wales could initiate proceedings in any court with jurisdiction under its own rules in

[150] That is not to say that the other conditions do not warrant reflection: further exploration of the concept of 'designat[ion]' in ibid, art 22(2)(a), in particular, would be welcome. This provision requires the court of origin to have been 'designated' in the agreement. It is unclear whether 'designated' refers only to a court named in the agreement or also any court 'before which proceedings could be brought in accordance with the non-exclusive choice of court agreement', which is the language used in art 22(2)(b). Brand and Herrup assert that it encompasses the latter; 'a court that is capable of hearing a case under the non-exclusive choice of court agreement': (n 14) 156. Kessedjian asserts that this must be a 'court competent by virtue of the parties' autonomy': (n 17) 846 (my translation). Hartley and Dogauchi (n 8) do not provide any detail on art 22(2)(a): [241]. It is also not entirely clear whether the words 'between the parties … on the same cause of action' in the second phrase of art 22(2)(b) are also intended to apply to the first phrase of art 22(2)(b). In other words, does the existence of a judgment given by any other court before which proceedings could be brought in accordance with the non-exclusive jurisdiction agreement prevent recognition and enforcement or only if the judgment of that other court disposes of a dispute between the same parties on the same cause of action?

[151] The EU declaration, which excludes from the scope of the Convention certain types of insurance contracts, does not apply to reinsurance contracts: Declaration/Reservation/Notification', HCCH (Web Page) [2(a)] www.hcch.net/en/instruments/conventions/status-table/notifications/?csid=1044&disp=resdn. This means that if Australia and the European Union were to make a reciprocal declaration, judgments rendered by courts with jurisdiction under a service of suits clause in a reinsurance contract would fall within the scope of art 22 of the Convention.

[152] Hague Choice of Court Convention, art 22(2)(b).

order to thwart the recognition and enforcement of the judgment against it[153] in a Contracting State that has made a reciprocal declaration under the Convention. That is because any court with jurisdiction under its own rules is a court before which proceedings 'could be brought' in accordance with the agreement, unless the parties have expressly provided in the agreement that once the named court is seised, no proceedings elsewhere are permitted, or a court holds that the parties had an implied intention to achieve that result.[154] Absent an express provision or implication of this kind, this condition in art 22 creates a risk of abuse. A party with a legitimate judgment from one declaring Contracting State cannot enforce it in another declaring Contracting State until the abusive proceedings brought by the judgment debtor in any competent court, to thwart that judgment, have been dismissed. If a judgment debtor brings those proceedings in Italy, their dismissal might take a decade.

The fact that the Working Group responsible for drafting art 22 was alive to this problem, but nonetheless chose to proceed, suggests that art 22 is less concerned with facilitating the recognition and enforcement of judgments based on *symmetric* non-exclusive jurisdiction agreements. Instead, it seems that the real intention underlying art 22 is to allow option holders, awarded judgment under a Rothschild or similar clause, to benefit from enforcement under the Convention.[155] It was explained above that the option holder is the party which can sue in the jurisdiction named in the anchor part of a Rothschild clause and elsewhere, whereas the non-option holder can sue only in the jurisdiction named in the anchor.[156] If an option holder were to be awarded judgment by the anchor court and then a non-option holder sought to prevent enforcement of that judgment by commencing proceedings in another court with jurisdiction, the judgment could nonetheless be enforced under art 22, because the proceedings by the non-option holder are not permitted under the agreement.[157] But if a non-optional holder has received a judgment rendered by the anchor court, it cannot enforce that judgment if the option holder chooses to exercise its option to bring proceedings on the same cause of action in another court. The example from the Convention's Explanatory Report is illustrative:

> Assume that a lender and a borrower enter into a loan agreement. The agreement contains a choice of court clause that provides, 'Proceedings by the borrower against the lender may be brought only in the District Court of Seoul, but proceedings by the lender against the borrower may be brought either in that court or in any other court having jurisdiction under the law of the State in which it is located'.

[153] Minutes No 20 of 27 June 2005 (afternoon) in Permanent Bureau of the Conference (n 8) 709–10; see also Hartley and Dogauchi (n 8) [246].

[154] See text preceding, to and in n 43.

[155] See Minutes No 20 of 27 June 2005 (afternoon) in Permanent Bureau of the Conference (n 8) 709–10 (David Goddard of the New Zealand delegation, on behalf of the Working Group, cited asymmetric agreements as a qualification which prevented this condition from 'being fatally flawed'.)

[156] Text to nn 56–64.

[157] *Cf* Hague Choice of Court Convention, art 22(2)(b) second phrase.

> The District Court of *Seoul grants a judgment and proceedings are brought to enforce it in China*, both States having made declarations under Article 22. Proceedings under the loan agreement are also pending before a court in Australia. If the latter proceedings were brought by the lender against the borrower, they would preclude enforcement of the Korean judgment in China under Article 22, since they were in accordance with the non-exclusive choice of court agreement. If, on the other hand, they had been brought by the borrower against the lender, this would not be the case; consequently, they would not preclude enforcement of the Korean judgment in China (emphasis added).[158]

The passive construction in italics conceals the possibility that the Seoul judgment is granted in favour of the non-option holder (the borrower) and that it is the non-option holder which has brought enforcement proceedings in China.[159] The option holder (the lender) can, if the Seoul proceedings are progressing unfavourably for it, thwart the effect of the forthcoming judgment by commencing proceedings in Australia with respect to the same cause of action. If the Australian proceedings culminate in a judgment first, it will prevent China from recognising the Seoul judgment under art 22 of the Convention because of the third condition of art 22, namely that there cannot already be a judgment from a court in which proceedings were permitted by the non-exclusive agreement.[160] Indeed, the option holder could, at least arguably, call upon China to recognise the Australian judgment, in place of the non-option holder's Seoul judgment which art 22 of the Convention would require China to do.[161] Moreover, the option holder can, even after the non-option holder has its Seoul judgment and has commenced enforcement proceedings in China, thwart the effect of that judgment by commencing proceedings in Australia. The Convention's Explanatory Report makes clear that the Australian proceedings need not have been initiated before the court in Seoul delivers its judgment or before the Chinese proceedings are initiated,[162] suggesting that the point in time at which the art 22(2)(b) condition is to be satisfied is the time at which recognition and enforcement of the judgment is sought rather than the date of the Seoul judgment. While, in this constellation, any judgment in the Australian proceedings would not benefit from enforcement under art 22 because there is already a *judgment* from a court in which proceedings were permitted by the non-exclusive agreement,[163] until such a time as the Australian proceedings are struck out or culminate in a judgment, the non-option holder cannot enforce its judgment in China.

[158] Hartley and Dogauchi (n 8) [250].

[159] Why else would there be an issue of enforcement under art 22? In other words, a lender is not going to seek to enforce the Seoul judgment in China if it is, at the same time, pressing on with proceedings on the same cause of action in Australia.

[160] Hague Choice of Court Convention, art 22(2)(b) first phrase.

[161] This argument assumes that the Hague Choice of Court Convention conceptualises Rothschild clauses as 'designating', for the purposes of art 22(2)(a), all possible courts in which the option holder can bring suit, not just the anchor court: Brand and Herrup (n 14) 156. See n 150.

[162] Hartley and Dogauchi (n 8) [250], fn 291.

[163] *Cf* Hague Choice of Court Convention, art 22(2)(b) first phrase.

The net result is that art 22 allows option holders to benefit from the recognition and enforcement provisions of the Convention in a similar manner as they would, had they concluded an exclusive jurisdiction agreement. But it does not allow non-option holders to similarly so benefit, which is incongruous given that it is the non-option holder, not the option holder, which must sue in one Contracting State court to the exclusion of all others.

## B. Was the Court of Origin the Court First Seised?

For a judgment to be recognised under art 22 of the Convention, the court of origin must have been the court first seised.[164] It must have been the court first seised from among the courts not excluded by the non-exclusive jurisdiction agreement[165] which are, consistent with the condition just discussed, at the time of recognition no longer seised.[166] This condition implements a 'court first seised priority rule' of jurisdiction at the recognition and enforcement stage, for non-exclusive agreements, by refusing to enforce the judgment of a court which, although having non-exclusive jurisdiction, was not the court first seised in accordance with the non-exclusive agreement. This condition, which was introduced to satisfy the European Commission, representing the Member States of the European Union,[167] does not specify the time at which a court is 'seised' for the purposes of the Convention.[168] Moreover, the condition reduces the attractiveness of the art 22 declaration for common law jurisdictions. Hartley and Dogauchi explain that it 'was intended to apply where there were proceedings before the other court but … they were dismissed under the doctrine of *forum non conveniens*'.[169] This condition would prevent the judgment of a court nominated in the jurisdiction agreement second seised from being recognised and enforced if a court first seised, whose jurisdiction was not excluded by the agreement, had stayed its

[164] ibid, art 22(2)(c).

[165] Hartley and Dogauchi (n 8) [252]; Brand and Herrup (n 14) 158.

[166] Hartley and Dogauchi (n 8) [251]; Kessedjian (n 17) 846.

[167] Minutes No 20 of 27 June 2005 (afternoon) in Permanent Bureau of the Conference (n 8) 709. Absent the rule, it was thought that 'a *defendant* who only wanted to *bring* proceedings in one Contracting State could be exposed to proceedings in a Contracting State where [it] did not wish to litigate' (emphasis added). The concern of the European Commission does not make much sense: the very nature of a non-exclusive jurisdiction clause is that a defendant is exposed to proceedings in any number of states. Presumably, the actual concern of the European Commission was to secure a rule which encouraged non-exclusive jurisdiction agreements that operate in the same way they do within the European Union, which is by allocating jurisdiction to the court first seised, be that the court designated in the non-exclusive clause or some other court with jurisdiction under the recast Brussels I Regulation.

[168] Brand and Herrup suggest that this question will be dealt with under the law of the court addressed: (n 14) 157.

[169] Hartley and Dogauchi (n 8) [251]. On the *forum non conveniens* doctrine under residual English private international law rules, see R Mortensen, 'The Case Management Stay in Private International Law' p. 73 in ch 4 of this volume.

proceedings on *forum non conveniens* grounds[170] in favour of the designated court or, presumably, if it had dismissed its proceedings on other grounds, for example if the proceedings before the court first seised are an abuse of its processes.[171]

It is difficult to see what this rule achieves and seems to misunderstand how non-exclusive jurisdiction agreements operate according to common law rules, as contrasted with the autonomous regime applied within the European Union under the recast Brussels I Regulation. Under that Regulation, where a clause confers non-exclusive jurisdiction on the courts of an EU Member State, the question of which court will exercise jurisdiction when proceedings are pending before two Member State courts involving the same parties and the same cause of action will be resolved by the *lis pendens* rule,[172] whose operation is 'objective and automatic'.[173] A court, designated in a non-exclusive jurisdiction agreement, which is first seised must exercise that jurisdiction.[174] A court designated in a non-exclusive agreement, but second seised, will (if the jurisdiction of the first court is established) be required to decline jurisdiction in favour of a court first seised,[175] provided the proceedings involve the same parties and the same cause of action (that is, they have the same factual and legal basis[176] and 'the same end in view').[177]

By contrast, in common law systems in which the existence of jurisdiction is a separate enquiry from its exercise, the relevance of a foreign non-exclusive jurisdiction is a factor in the *forum non conveniens* analysis which determines whether a court seised of jurisdiction will exercise it.[178] In fact, the scenario of

[170] *VTB Capital plc v Nutritek International Corp* [2013] UKSC 5, [2013] 2 AC 337 [12]; *Spiliada Maritime Co v Cansulex Ltd* [1987] AC 460 (HL) 476, 480; *cf* the Australian iteration of the doctrine (*Voth v Manildra Flour Mills Pty Ltd* (1990) 171 CLR 538, adopting at 564 the reasoning of Deane J in *Oceanic Sun Line Special Shipping Co Inc v Fay* (1988) 165 CLR 197, 247).

[171] *R v Sang* [1980] AC 402, 423.

[172] See recast Brussels I Regulation, art 29(1), (3) and recital (22); Joseph (n 24) [4.06].

[173] Case C-111/01 *Gantner Electronic GmbH v Basch Exploitatie Maatschappij BV* [2013] ECR-I 4225, [30].

[174] *Cf* recast Brussels I Regulation, art 29(3).

[175] ibid, art 29(3). See Joseph (n 24) [4.06].

[176] Recast Brussels I Regulation, art 29(1); Case C-406/92 *The Tatry* [1994] ECR I-5439, [39] (ie 'the facts and the rule of law relied on as the basis of the action').

[177] P Rogerson, '*Lis Pendens* and Related Actions' in A Dickinson and E Lein (eds), *The Brussels I Regulation Recast* (Oxford, Oxford University Press, 2015) art 29, [11.16]. See Case C-406/92 *The Tatry* (n 176) [41].

[178] Some English decisions hold it to be a particular factor which prevents a court from considering other factors of appropriateness; other English decisions treat it as one factor, albeit a very significant one, among others: A Mills and U Grušić, 'Jurisdiction under the Brussels/Lugano System' in P Torremans and JJ Fawcett (eds), *Cheshire, North & Fawcett: Private International Law*, 15th edn (Oxford, Oxford University Press, 2017) 191, 399. *Cf* the position in Australia: in no published decision to date has the 'clearly inappropriate forum' test led to an Australian court staying proceedings in favour of a court named in a non-exclusive jurisdiction agreement: *Bagsfirst Global Pty Ltd v Global Brands (Football) Pty Ltd* (n 12) [35]; *Green v Australian Industrial Investment Ltd* (n 12) 512; *Autotrop Sdn Bhd v Powercrank Batteries Pty Ltd* (n 12) [27]–[33]; *Parnell Manufacturing Pty Ltd v Lonza Ltd* [2017] NSWSC 562, [29]–[31] (*obiter*).

a competent court first being seised and subsequently staying its proceedings on *forum non conveniens* grounds, if and when the option holder exercises its option, is one which is contemplated by a service of suit clause. '[C]ommon place'[179] in transatlantic reinsurance contracts,[180] service of suit clauses are a type of asymmetric jurisdiction clause. They give an option to the US reinsured, which when exercised, requires the English reinsurer to submit to the jurisdiction of a US court if the English reinsurer fails to pay a claim. The approach English courts have taken to service of suit clauses is that a reinsurer is not prevented from bringing proceedings in a court competent under its own rules of private international law.[181] But, if and when the reinsured calls upon the reinsurer to defend proceedings, the reinsurer must discontinue any proceedings it had previously initiated elsewhere and bring proceedings afresh before the designated US court. This is the direct effect of the English court, in which the reinsurer had first initiated proceedings, staying proceedings on *forum non conveniens* grounds.[182] Applying the Convention to this scenario, the judgment of the court designated in the service of suit clause will not benefit from recognition and enforcement under the Convention if the reinsurer has commenced litigation before the reinsured exercises its option,[183] unless, like the optional limb of the narrow variant of Rothschild clause discussed in section I.C.iv, the reinsurer's option once exercised is capable of being characterised as an 'exclusive clause'. If it is, then recognition and enforcement will occur under Chapter III of the Convention.

Especially relevant to Australian judgments is the question of how the art 22(2)(c) condition works where there were prior proceedings before the court of another Australian State or Territory, which had been stayed or transferred pursuant to the relevant legislation.[184] For example, assume that a jurisdiction clause provides for the 'non-exclusive jurisdiction of the courts of Western Australia'.[185]

[179] *BP plc v National Union Fire Insurance Co* [2004] EWHC 1132 (Comm Ct) [39].

[180] Briggs (n 43) [1.29]. They are also used in Australian reinsurance and insurance policies: eg *Ace Insurance Ltd v Moose Enterprise Pty Ltd* [2009] NSWSC 724, [11]. As a matter of current law, if a service of suit clause nominating foreign courts were to come before an Australian court in an insurance contract within the scope of the Insurance Contracts Act 1984 (Cth), which prevents parties to insurance contracts from excluding application of the Act via a jurisdiction agreement, it will not be enforced: ss 9(1)(a), 52; *Akai Pty Ltd v The People's Insurance Co Ltd* (1996) 188 CLR 418, 447–48. As explained above, if Australia accedes to the Hague Choice of Court Convention, it also seems unlikely that an Australian court would give effect to a service of suit clause nominating foreign courts in an insurance policy: National Interest Analysis (n 6) [25]; *cf* Hague Choice of Court Convention, art 6(c)). The Insurance Contracts Act 1984 (Cth) does not apply to reinsurance contracts: s 1(a).

[181] *Excess Insurance v Allendale Mutual Insurance Co* [2001] 1 Lloyd's Rep 524 (CA).

[182] See eg *Catlin Syndicate Ltd v Adams Land & Cattle Co* [2006] EWHC 2065 (Comm Ct), [2006] 2 CLC 425, [28]; *Ace Insurance SA-NV v Zurich Insurance Co* [2001] EWCA Civ 173, [2001] 1 Lloyd's Rep 618, 631 (Rix LJ, with whom Kennedy LJ and Jacob J agreed).

[183] *Cf* Hague Choice of Court Convention, art 22(2)(c).

[184] n 48.

[185] See *Mineralogy Pty Ltd v Sino Iron Pty Ltd* [2013] NSWSC 466, [27] although the clause is paraphrased rather than quoted in the judgment. A further example is the clause in *Commissioner of Taxation (Cth) v Arnold (No 2)* (2015) 324 ALR 59, 73, which provided '[t]he parties agree to the non-exclusive jurisdiction of the Courts of New South Wales, the Federal Court of Australia, and of Courts entitled to hear appeals from those courts'.

If proceedings commenced first in the Supreme Court of New South Wales are subsequently transferred to the Supreme Court of Western Australia,[186] would a Singaporean court recognise and enforce a judgment of the latter court under art 22 if Singapore and Australia had each made a reciprocal declaration? It is uncertain whether it could do so under art 22. Article 25(1)(c) of the Convention provides that 'any reference to the court or courts of a State shall be construed as referring, where appropriate, to the court or courts in the relevant territorial unit'. Given that art 22 refers to the need for 'the court of origin'[187] to have been 'the court first seised', those references to 'court' appear to refer, consistently with art 25(1)(c), to the court of the relevant territorial unit, namely the Supreme Court of Western Australia (the court of origin) and the Supreme Court of New South Wales (the court first seised). If that is right, it would prevent a Singaporean court from recognising and enforcing the Western Australian judgment under art 22 of the Convention.

## III. Evaluation: Recognition and Enforcement under the Convention Versus the Status Quo

From Australia's perspective, the principal reason which militates in favour of making a reciprocal declaration with other Contracting States, under art 22 of the Convention, is increased certainty that judgments rendered by her courts, the jurisdiction of which was based on a non-exclusive jurisdiction clause, will be recognised and enforced in foreign courts.

Recognition and enforcement in Australia of judgments rendered by foreign courts which had exercised jurisdiction based on a non-exclusive jurisdiction clause is currently governed by the Foreign Judgments Act 1991 (Cth)[188] or by common law rules,[189] although neither the Act nor the common law draws a distinction between exclusive and non-exclusive clauses, designating the foreign court, for the purposes of recognition or enforcement.[190] A foreign judgment to

[186] Which is what occurred in *Mineralogy Pty Ltd v Sino Iron Pty Ltd* (n 185) [30].

[187] *Cf* '*State* of origin' which is the term used in art 8(5) of the Hague Choice of Court Convention (emphasis added). This provision concerns the recognition or enforcement of a judgment where there had been a transfer between the territorial units of a Contracting State in circumstances where the parties had expressly chosen in their jurisdiction clause more than one territorial unit *within* a Contracting State. As explained above, jurisdiction clauses designating more than one territorial unit will be treated as exclusive under the Convention: text to nn 44–54.

[188] s 7(3)(a)(i). See also R Mortensen, 'The Hague and the Ditch: The Trans-Tasman Judicial Area and the Choice of Court Convention' (2009) 5 *Journal of Private International Law* 213, 236. A separate legislative regime applies to recognition and enforcement in Trans-Tasman cases, which is not considered here: Trans-Tasman Proceedings Act 2010 (Cth) pt 7.

[189] See generally M Davies, A Bell and P Le Gay Brereton, *Nygh's Conflict of Laws in Australia*, 9th edn (Chatswood, LexisNexis Butterworths, 2014) 895–96.

[190] *Cf* Foreign Judgments Act 1991 (Cth) s 7(4)(b), which allows, subject to limited exceptions, for a registered judgment to be set aside on application of the judgment debtor, if the foreign court rendered judgment in circumstances where there was an exclusive jurisdiction agreement designating another court.

which the Act applies that is registered under the Act will be enforced unless the judgment debtor successfully applies to have the judgment set aside.[191] A judgment given by a foreign court which had jurisdiction 'in the international sense'[192] will, unless a defence applies, be recognised at common law and enforced in Australia.

Provided the judgment satisfies the requirements of the Foreign Judgments Act, including (on the present state of the law) that the judgment be one to pay a sum of money, an Australian court must register a foreign judgment from the courts of a country listed in the Foreign Judgments Regulations 1992.[193] The inclusion of superior courts of a country in that list is conditional upon the Governor-General being satisfied that a judgment, rendered by an Australian court which had jurisdiction under a non-exclusive jurisdiction clause, will be enforced by the countries listed in those Regulations.[194] Of the countries that are currently Contracting States to the Hague Choice of Court Convention,[195] five EU Member States and Singapore are listed in the Regulations.[196] An art 22 reciprocal declaration under the Convention between Australia and Singapore would, therefore, not increase certainty that the judgments of one will be enforced in the other, though it would produce some gain, by narrowing the criteria for non-enforcement, in allowing for a non-money judgment of a Singaporean court to be enforced in Australia and a non-money judgment of an Australian court to be enforced in Singapore.[197]

[191] ibid, s 7. eg s 7(2): If the judgment debtor was not given sufficient notice of the foreign proceedings, the judgment was obtained by fraud, or its enforcement would be contrary to public policy, and if a competent court had, prior to the court of origin, already rendered judgment in the matter in dispute.

[192] ie jurisdiction in the perception of the common law as opposed to the perception of the foreign court itself. See generally A Dickinson, 'Schibsby v Westenholz and the Recognition and Enforcement of Judgments in England' (2018) 134 *Law Quarterly Review* 426, 430; P Kutner, 'Recognition and Enforcement of Foreign Judgments – The Common Law's Jurisdiction Requirement' (2019) 83 *Rabels Zeitschrift für ausländisches und internationales Privatrecht* 1.

[193] Foreign Judgments Act 1991 (Cth) ss 3(1) (definition of 'money judgment') 6; Foreign Judgments Regulations 1992, s 4, Schedule.

[194] ibid, s 5(1).

[195] As mentioned above at n 73, on the United Kingdom's withdrawal from the European Union, the Hague Choice of Court Convention will no longer have force of law in the United Kingdom. The UK plans to accede separately to the Convention, which would come into force three months after Brexit (Convention, arts 27, 31) – the European Union has exclusive competence to negotiate treaties concerning judicial co-operation, meaning that the UK cannot accede to the Convention before Brexit: J Basedow, 'BREXIT and Business Law' (2017) 5 *China-EU Law Journal* 101, 116. A draft statutory instrument has been prepared containing legislation to implement the Convention in the UK. It contains provisions governing the treatment by UK courts of '"transitional" cases to which the 2005 Hague Convention currently applies, and agreements entered into during any period between disapplication of the 2005 Hague Convention to the UK by virtue of EU Exit, and the Convention coming into force for the UK once again following accession': Explanatory Memorandum (n 4) [2.16]; The Civil Jurisdiction and Judgments (Hague Convention on Choice of Court Agreements 2005) (EU Exit) Regulations 2018, SI Draft, regs 4–5.

[196] Those are France, Germany, Italy, Poland, the United Kingdom: Foreign Judgments Regulations 1992, s 4, sch items 9, 10, 15, 19A, 24, 27.

[197] Apart from the Choice of Court Agreements Act 2016 (Singapore), which gives effect to the Hague Choice of Court Convention, 'there is no authority in Singapore law for the enforcement of a foreign

Nor would a declaration between Australia and the EU increase certainty, if the aim is to facilitate the recognition and enforcement of money judgments between Australia, on the one hand, and France, Germany, Italy, Poland or the United Kingdom, on the other. But again, some gain would be produced to the extent that non-money judgments of those countries would, following a declaration, be enforced in Australia. Certainty will also be increased by the knowledge that non-money judgments of Australian courts will be enforced in those countries.

There are, however, another 23 EU Member States[198] that are Contracting States to the Hague Choice of Court Convention the judgments of which do not benefit from recognition under the Foreign Judgments Act.[199] The number of commercial relationships between Australian businesses and businesses in these countries is likely to increase if a Free Trade Agreement between the European Union and Australia is concluded.[200] With more commerce will come more disputes and, in the absence of an arbitration agreement or settlement, more court judgments. The frequency with which judgment creditors will call upon EU Member State courts to recognise and enforce Australian judgments is therefore likely to increase. Although common law rules already require Australian courts[201] to enforce judgments from those countries, on the basis that their courts were competent by reason of the fact the judgment debtor had contracted to be subject to the jurisdiction of the foreign court[202] by non-exclusive agreement,[203] there is no certainty that all 23 of those countries would recognise and enforce the judgment of an Australian court in reciprocal circumstances;[204] a position which an art 22 declaration by Australia and the EU under the Convention would clarify. The same can be said, albeit speculatively, of all states that have signed but not yet ratified

judgment ordering non-monetary relief': A Chong, 'Country Report: Singapore' in A Chong (ed) *Recognition and Enforcement of Foreign Judgments in Asia* (Singapore, Asian Business Law Institute, 2017) 163, 167. On the common law rule that only foreign monetary judgments can be enforced, see M Douglas, 'Choice of Court Agreements under an International Civil Law Act' (2018) 34 *Journal of Contract Law* 186, 207; Davies, Bell and Brereton, *Nygh's Conflict of Laws in Australia* (n 189) 910–12.

[198] Those are: Austria, Belgium, Bulgaria, Croatia, Cyprus, Czech Republic, Denmark, Estonia, Finland, Greece, Hungary, Ireland, Latvia, Lithuania, Luxembourg, Malta, the Netherlands, Portugal, Romania, Slovakia, Slovenia, Spain and Sweden.

[199] The same can be said of Mexico and Montenegro.

[200] Negotiations began on 18 June 2018: Department of Foreign Affairs and Trade, 'Australia–European Union Free Trade Agreement' http://dfat.gov.au/trade/agreements/aeufta/pages/aeufta.aspx. See generally Council of the European Union, 9102/18, Outcome of the Council Meeting, 3618th Council Meeting, Foreign Affairs Trade and Development Issues (Brussels, 22 May 2018) www.consilium.europa.eu/media/34837/st09102-en18.pdf.

[201] See generally R Mortensen, R Garnett and M Keyes, *Private International Law in Australia*, 3rd edn (Chatswood, LexisNexis, 2015) [5.15].

[202] *Copin v Adamson* (1873–74) LR 9 Ex 345, 354 aff *Copin v Adamson* (1875–76) LR 1 Ex D 17 (CA) 18–19; Dickinson, '*Schibsby v Westenholz*' (n 192) 430; Kutner, 'Recognition and Enforcement of Foreign Judgments' (n 192) 42–48.

[203] See *Telesto Investments Ltd v UBS AG* [2013] NSWSC 503, 94 ACSR 29, [266]–[272].

[204] That said, even in Sweden, which has a restrictive approach to the recognition of foreign judgments in civil and commercial matters that prevents a Swedish court from recognising a foreign judgment absent explicit legislative rules, an exception is made for jurisdiction agreements: M Hellner, 'Sweden' in J Basedow et al (eds), *Encyclopedia of Private International Law* (Cheltenham, Edward Elgar Publishing, 2017) vol 3, 2535, 2546.

the Convention, including China and the United States of America,[205] whose judgments, under common law rules, Australia ought to enforce, with no guarantee that the courts of those countries will reciprocate. To date, it appears that no Australian judgment has been recognised in China, though there is a possibility that if an Australian court first recognises an equivalent Chinese judgment (which it is yet to do),[206] Chinese courts might 'follow suit'.[207] To facilitate the recognition and enforcement of the judgments of Australian courts in China, which is reportedly likely soon to ratify the Convention,[208] a declaration would be in Australia's interests.

The principal reasons weighing against making a declaration under the Convention are the problems to which several pre-conditions for recognition and enforcement under art 22 give rise. As demonstrated in section II.A, the condition that a Contracting State cannot recognise and enforce a judgment under the Convention, if there are *proceedings pending* between the same parties on the same cause of action in a court 'before which proceedings could be brought in accordance with the non-exclusive choice of court agreement',[209] may give rise to several problems. The first is that it creates a risk of abuse by judgment debtors in cases involving symmetric non-exclusive jurisdiction clauses. The second is that it appears to produce considerable unfairness to non-option holders, if they eventuate to be judgment creditors, in cases involving Rothschild clauses. As explained in section II.B above, art 22(2)(c) of the Convention requires that for a judgment to be recognised and enforced, the court of origin must have been the court first seised. This condition prevents the recognition and enforcement of a judgment of a court designated in a symmetric non-exclusive agreement or service of suit clause, if another court had first been seised but stayed its proceedings. Accordingly, this condition necessarily limits the number of judgments based on non-exclusive jurisdiction agreements which would benefit from recognition and enforcement under the Convention and thus the utility of making a declaration. It is also unclear how a judgment of an Australian court to which another Australian court had transferred the case would be treated by foreign courts for the purposes of this condition.

The significance of these problems is diminished if a court addressed is not prevented from recognising or enforcing a foreign judgment, to which the Convention applies, under its national law if any one of the cumulative conditions

[205] See text to n 4. Though it is doubtful whether the USA will ever ratify the Hague Choice of Court Convention given the dispute between Democrats and the Republicans as to whether the Convention falls within federal or state competence: J Basedow, 'EU-Kollisionsrecht und Haager Konferenz – Ein schwieriges Verhältnis' (2017) *Praxis des Internationalen Privat- und Verfahrensrechts (IPRAX)* 194, 197.

[206] See Y Guo, 'Country Report: The People's Republic of China' in Chong, *Recognition and Enforcement of Foreign Judgments in Asia* (n 197) 57.

[207] W Zhang, 'Sino–Foreign Recognition and Enforcement of Judgments: A Promising "Follow-Suit" Model?' (2017) 16 *Chinese Journal of International Law* 515, 537–40.

[208] Guo, 'Country Report: The People's Republic of China' (n 206) 67.

[209] Hague Choice of Court Convention, art 22(2)(b).

set out in art 22 is not satisfied. If, as the literature suggests,[210] a reciprocal declaration does not preclude recognition or enforcement under national law, there is little incentive for a judgment debtor to bring baseless proceedings to prevent the recognition and enforcement of a judgment in a Contracting State that has made the declaration, *if* that state under its national law could nonetheless recognise or enforce the judgment. That would be the case, for example, if Singapore and Australia were both to make an art 22 declaration and an Australian court were called upon to recognise and enforce a Singaporean judgment, in circumstances where the judgment debtor had since brought proceedings to thwart the effect of that judgment in China.[211] The Australian court could not recognise and enforce the judgment under art 22 of the Convention, though it could recognise it under national law.[212] Equally, the fact that a judgment of a court nominated in a non-exclusive jurisdiction agreement but second seised (even, seemingly, in a case involving a transfer between Australian courts) cannot be recognised under art 22 is of less import.

One conclusion might be that the benefit of the increased certainty that Australian judgments would be recognised and enforced in the 25 Contracting States to the Convention, not listed in the Foreign Judgments Act,[213] and potentially in China, outweighs the risk of abusive proceedings and unfairness, as well as the increased complexity generated by having multiple legal regimes governing recognition and enforcement, assuming Contracting States' national laws continue to apply. Of course, it is likely that not all those states' national laws provide for the recognition or enforcement of judgments based on non-exclusive jurisdiction agreements. It is clear that China's, for instance, does not.[214] If a judgment creditor seeks to recognise an Australian judgment under art 22 of the Convention in a state whose national law does not provide for recognition of a judgment rendered by a court of origin with jurisdiction under a non-exclusive agreement (for example, by reason of a lack of formal reciprocity), then the risk that a judgment debtor will seek to torpedo that recognition by bringing proceedings in a dilatory jurisdiction is evidently heightened.

In the case of doubt, it may be wise for Contracting States to refrain from making a reciprocal declaration until the future of the revived Hague Conference 'Judgments Project' becomes clear. The project, in its current form,[215] seeks to

[210] Hartley and Dogauchi (n 8) [251], fn 293. See also Brand and Herrup (n 14) 157.

[211] In this example, it is immaterial whether or not China is a Contracting State to the Hague Choice of Court Convention.

[212] Foreign Judgments Act 1991 (Cth) s 7(3)(a)(iii); Foreign Judgments Regulations 1992, s 4, sch item 24. See text to nn 193–196.

[213] ie the 23 EU Member States listed in n 198 as well as Montenegro and Mexico.

[214] Text to n 206. See also G Tu and Z Huang, 'Optional Choice of Court Agreements in the People's Republic of China (PRC)' in M Keyes (ed), *Optional Choice of Court Agreements in Private International Law* (Springer, forthcoming), text accompanying and immediately following fn 82.

[215] The project may also be expanded to develop an instrument providing bases on which courts globally should exercise jurisdiction: Permanent Bureau of the Hague Conference on Private International Law, 'Conclusions and Recommendations Adopted by the Council' (13–15 March 2018) 1, [5].

develop a global convention on the recognition and enforcement of judgments rendered by courts whose jurisdiction is based on grounds other than an exclusive jurisdiction agreement. Recognition and enforcement of judgments rendered by courts which had jurisdiction under a symmetric non-exclusive jurisdiction clause is provided for in the current draft of that convention; recognition and enforcement may be provided for judgments rendered by courts which had jurisdiction under a Rothschild clause.[216] If the project does not culminate in a ratifiable convention, or if it does but China and the United States are disinclined to accede to it, it may be better to have some harmonised mechanism for the recognition and enforcement of judgments based on Rothschild and non-exclusive jurisdiction clauses, flawed as it may be, than none. If Australia takes that view, it should consult with existing Contracting States to the Convention and clarify any substantive concerns that they have about art 22[217] before including it in the International Civil Law Act.

# IV. Conclusion

The jurisdictional provisions of the 2005 Hague Convention on Choice of Court Agreements only apply to one category of jurisdiction agreements: those that designate, to the exclusion of all others, the jurisdiction of the courts of a single country. Relevantly for Australia, a jurisdiction clause designating the courts of two or more of her States or Territories will be treated as exclusive for the purposes of the Convention. The Convention nonetheless provides for Contracting States to extend, by reciprocal declaration, the Convention's provisions governing recognition and enforcement to judgments rendered by courts which had jurisdiction

[216] Hague Conference on Private International Law, Special Commission on the Recognition and Enforcement of Foreign Judgments (24–29 May 2018), *2018 Draft Convention*, art 5(1)(m); FJ Garcimartín Alférez and G Saumier, *Judgments Convention: Revised Preliminary Explanatory Report* (Preliminary Document No 7 of April 2018, Hague Conference on Private International Law) [189–90].

[217] As already mentioned, the EU has refrained from making a declaration until other Contracting States have expressed a view. The European Commission also indicated, however, that it did not propose making a declaration at the time of approving the Hague Choice of Court Convention, because 'the recognition and enforcement of judgments given on the basis of non-exclusive choice of court agreements would lead to the result that the courts of EU Member States in general could not take jurisdiction in situations where they would be seised by one of the parties after a judgment based on a non-exclusive choice of court agreement had already been given by the court of another Contracting Party which had made a declaration under Article 22': Proposal for a Council Decision on the approval on behalf of the EU of the Hague Convention, 30 January 2014 [3.2.1]. It is difficult to see why the fact that an EU Member State could not take jurisdiction after a judgment based on a non-exclusive jurisdiction agreement had already been given is a problem in proceedings on the same cause of action between the same parties. This fact could suggest that the European Commission understands the two phrases in art 22(2)(b) to be disjunctive: in other words, the existence of any judgment rendered by a court before which proceedings could be brought in accordance with the non-exclusive jurisdiction agreement, even one in respect of a different cause of action, would, in the eyes of the European Commission, prevent an EU Member State court from assuming jurisdiction in respect of proceedings on a different cause of action: see n 150.

under a non-exclusive jurisdiction agreement. Asymmetric jurisdiction clauses, and specifically, Rothschild clauses, which require one party to sue in the jurisdiction named in the clause but allow the other party to sue there and/or elsewhere, will also (notwithstanding arguments to the contrary) likely be characterised as non-exclusive.

Ultimately the decision as to whether to use the reciprocal declaration mechanism, allowing Contracting States to recognise and enforce judgments based on non-exclusive jurisdiction agreements under the Convention, turns on a policy preference. That is, whether states prefer to avoid the problems generated by a partially flawed provision by not making a declaration, or whether they prefer the possibility of providing for greater recognition and enforcement in spite of them. The likelihood of the revived Hague Conference 'Judgments Project' resulting in a ratifiable convention to which their key trading partners will be inclined to accede, ought to inform states' preferences.

# 6

# Reciprocal Recognition and Enforcement of Foreign Judgments in China

## *The Proposal of a Registration System*

JIE (JEANNE) HUANG*

## I. Introduction

2016 and 2017 witnessed unprecedented developments for reciprocal recognition and enforcement of foreign judgments in China: Chinese courts recognised and enforced two commercial monetary judgments rendered in Singapore and the US based upon reciprocity.[1] However, this development should not be over-estimated because of its prospective institutional, doctrinal and practical challenges. The main institutional challenge is that the Chinese courts in charge of the recognition and enforcement of foreign judgments (JRE) are Intermediate People's Courts, which are lower lever courts in China's judicial system.[2] The current Chinese Civil Procedural Law (CPL)[3] and Supreme People's Court (SPC) judicial interpretations fail to provide sufficient guidance for them. The doctrinal challenge lies in the controversial values and ambiguous content of reciprocity, which heightens the practical challenges of putting JRE based upon reciprocity into practice.

* This chapter is part of a research project which has received support from the China National Social Science Fund (No 16BF18).

[1] *Kolmar v Jiangsu Textile Industry (Group) Import & Export Co*, Case No (2016) Su-01 Xie Wai Ren 3 Civil Judgment, Intermediate People's Court, Nanjing City, Jiangsu Province, People's Republic of China; *Liu Li v Tao Li and Tong Wu* (2015) Yue Wuhan Zhong Min Shang Wai Chu Zi No 00026, Intermediate People's Court of Wuhan City, Hubei Province, People's Republic of China.

[2] Interpretation of the Supreme People's Court on the Application of the Civil Procedure Law of the People's Republic of China (SPC Judicial Interpretation of CPL), as adopted at the 1636th meeting of the Judicial Committee of the Supreme People's Court 18 December 2014, effective 4 February 2015, art 544.

[3] Civil Procedure Law of the People's Republic of China, adopted at the 4th Session of the Seventh National People's Congress on 9 April 1991, as amended 27 June 2017.

This chapter scrutinises the recent promising development of JRE based upon reciprocity in China. It analyses prospective challenges and, more importantly, proposes a registration system to resolve these challenges. It is a timely effort to help develop the Chinese JRE system.[4] It also has potentially broad international implications. First, the values, content and practical regime required to realise JRE based upon reciprocity have been much debated since the American Law Institute drafted and disseminated a draft Foreign Judgments Recognition and Enforcement Act (ALI Proposed Federal Statute) in 2005.[5] However, the proposed Act has not been enacted in the US, demonstrating the controversial nature of reciprocity.[6] Therefore, JRE based upon reciprocity is not a unique issue for China. It has wide implications for other jurisdictions across the world. Second, studies have shown that JRE between civil law and common law systems is more difficult than between the same legal tradition.[7] Although China has concluded 32 effective bilateral JRE treaties, all have been with civil law countries.[8] Reciprocity may open a door for judgments rendered in common law countries to be recognised and enforced in China.

[4] The SPC is currently drafting a judicial interpretation on JRE based upon reciprocity in order to guide lower courts. See SPC Specialist News Group, 'The statement of Liu Guixiang on the Establishment of a Just, Efficient and Convenient Transnational Dispute Resolution Mechanism for the "One Belt One Road" Initiative at the Silk Road Judicial Assistance International Form', www.court.gov.cn/fabu-xiangqing-61912.html.

[5] American Law Institute, *Recognition and Enforcement of Foreign Judgments: Analysis and Proposed Federal Statute* (2006). A digital version is available at www.ali.org/publications/show/recognition-and-enforcement-foreign-judgments-analysis-and-proposed-federal-statute/. For debates about reciprocity, see LJ Silberman, 'Some Judgments on Judgments: A View from America' (2008) 19 *Kings Law Journal* 235, 235; B Elbalti, 'Reciprocity and the Recognition and Enforcement of Foreign Judgments: A Lot of Bark but Not Much Bite' (2017) 13 *Journal of Private International Law* 184.

[6] JB Bellinger and RR Anderson, 'Tort Tourism: The Case for a Federal Law on Foreign Judgment Recognition' (2013) 54 *Virginia Journal of International Law* 501, 542.

[7] See P Trooboff, 'Ten (and Probably More) Difficulties in Negotiating a Worldwide Convention on International Jurisdiction and Enforcement of Judgments: Some Initial Lessons' in J Barcelo and KM Clermont (eds), *A Global Law of Jurisdiction and Judgments: Lessons from The Hague* (The Hague, Kluwer Law International 2002), 276 (analysing the difficulties coming from conflicts between different legal traditions when negotiating a broad scope JRE convention at the Hague); AT von Mehren, *Adjudicatory Authority in Private International Law: A Comparative Study* (The Hague, Martinus Nijhoff, 2007) 57–75 (comparing different designs of jurisdiction rules and norms in the US and Germany); J Huang, 'Conflicts between Civil Law and Common Law in Judgment Recognition and Enforcement: When Is the Finality Dispute Final' (2011) 29 *Wisconsin International Law Journal* 7 (demonstrating the sharply different understanding of finality between civil law Mainland China and common law Hong Kong).

[8] As of 5 September 2018, China has concluded 36 bilateral judicial assistance treaties in civil, commercial or criminal affairs. For a list of China judicial assistance treaties, see Foreign Ministry of the People's Republic of China, 'Status Quo of China Treaties on Judicial Assistance and Extradition', www.fmprc.gov.cn/web/ziliao_674904/tytj_674911/wgdwdjdsfhzty_674917/t1215630.shtml. Combing the two lists, 32 effective treaties have JRE clauses (Chinese JRE treaties). For a list of these treaties, see ZS Tang, YP Xiao and ZX Huo, *Conflict of Laws in the People's Republic of China* (Cheltenham and Northampton, Edward Elgar, 2016) 150–51. Besides bilateral treaties, China signed the Hague Convention on Choice of Court Agreements (the Hague Choice of Courts Convention), which entered into force on 1 October 2015, on 12 September 2017, but has not ratified it. For the status table of the Convention, see the HCCH website, www.hcch.net/en/instruments/conventions/status-table/?cid=98.

This chapter has six sections. The second section analyses the recent breakthrough of JRE based on reciprocity between China and Singapore and the US respectively. Section III proposes a registration model to address the institutional design of JRE. It suggests that the SPC should compile a list of countries that recognise and enforce Chinese judgments, so judgments rendered in these countries can also be recognised and enforced in China. The registration system contains two consecutive parts. The first is *ex parte* proceedings where the judgment creditor applies to register the judgment in the JRE court while the debtor is not heard. The second part involves the JRE court notifying the debtor, who can apply to set aside the registration by invoking one or more defences to JRE. Section IV discusses which judgments can be registered. It covers three issues: which judgments would be covered by the proposed registration system; what law should be applied to determine the finality of a foreign judgment in Chinese JRE proceedings, and what the statute of limitations for an application to register a foreign judgment should be. Section V addresses the question when registration must be set aside on jurisdiction grounds. Section VI concludes the chapter.

## II. Promising Developments

Chinese domestic law for recognition and enforcement of foreign judgments is comprised of arts 280 to 282 of the CPL and Chapter 22 of the SPC Judicial Interpretation of CPL. These provisions provide that recognition and enforcement of foreign judgments should be conducted according to treaties ratified by China or on the principle of reciprocity.[9] For judgments beyond the scope of treaties, reciprocity is the only legal basis available.[10]

For comments, see GJ Tu, 'The Hague Choice of Court Convention – A Chinese Perspective Comment' (2007) 55 *American Journal of Comparative Law* 347, 347–65. China is a Member State to the International Convention on Civil Liability for Oil Pollution Damage (Oil Pollution Convention), adopted on 29 November 1969, entered into force on 19 June 1975, being replaced by 1992 Protocol, adopted on 27 November 1992, entered into force on 30 May 1996. The Oil Pollution Convention provides for recognition and enforcement of relevant civil and commercial judgments. See Annex. The only common law jurisdiction that has an effective and binding bilateral JRE arrangement with Mainland China is Hong Kong, but this is the interregional JRE under the constitutional framework of 'One Country, Two Systems'. This chapter focuses on international JRE, which is significantly different from interregional JRE. See the Arrangement between the Mainland and the Hong Kong Special Administrative Region on Reciprocal Recognition and Enforcement of the Decisions of Civil and Commercial Cases under Consensual Jurisdiction signed 14 July 2006, which entered into force in Hong Kong by the Mainland Judgment (Reciprocal Enforcement) Ordinance (Cap 597) in 2008 and in Mainland China by the Supreme People's Court Judicial Interpretation on Reciprocal Recognition and Enforcement of the Decisions of Civil and Commercial Cases under Consensual Jurisdiction between Mainland China and Hong Kong in 2008.

[9] CPL, art 282.

[10] ibid.

Although Chinese judgments have been recognised and enforced in foreign countries by reciprocity,[11] Chinese courts have often refused JRE on the basis of lack of reciprocity.[12] However, recent years have witnessed several positive breakthroughs.

In 2006, German Züblin International Co applied to the Court of Appeal of Berlin to recognise and enforce an arbitral award rendered in China. The opposing party, Wuxi Walker General Engineering Rubber Co, Ltd, argued that a court in the city of Wuxi, which was the seat of arbitration, had held that the relevant arbitration clause was invalid so the award should not be recognised and enforced.[13] The Court of Appeal of Berlin recognised the Wuxi court judgment on the principle of reciprocity and refused to recognise and enforce the arbitral award.[14] In 2012, Sascha Rudolf Seehaus applied to the Wuhan Intermediate People's Court for recognition of a Germany bankruptcy judgment issued in 2009 by the Montabaur Regional Court (*Sascha Rudolf Seehaus*).[15] The German judgment nominated Sascha Rudolf Seehaus as the trustee of the bankrupt SP Management GmbH. The Wuhan Intermediate People's Court decided to recognise the German judgment. It held that reciprocity existed between Germany and China considering the decision in *Züblin*, and recognised that the German judgment did not infringe the basic principles of Chinese law, state sovereignty, security and social and public interests.[16]

In 2014, in *Giant Light Metal Technology (Kunshan) Co Ltd v Aksa Far East Pte Ltd*, the High Court of Singapore recognised and enforced a Chinese commercial monetary judgment under common law.[17] The Chinese judgment was rendered by the Intermediate People's Court of Suzhou City in Jiangsu Province on 16 December 2010 in a contractual dispute brought by Giant Light Metal Technology (Kunshan) Co Ltd, a Chinese company, against Aksa Far East Pte Ltd, a Singaporean company. Two years after the High Court of Singapore recognised and enforced the Chinese judgment, on 9 December 2016, the Intermediate People's Court of Nanjing City in Jiangsu Province reciprocated: in *Kolmar v Jiangsu*

[11] Besides Singapore and the US, courts in South Korea, Israel, New Zealand, Germany and the UK have recognised or enforced Chinese commercial judgments. For South Korea, see HF Zhu, 'Most Recent Cases: Chinese Courts Unprecedentedly Recognize and Enforce a Judgment Rendered in Singapore', chuansong.me/n/1498096641835. See also ASIL Private International Law Interest Group, 'Commentaries on Private International Law', the PILIG Newsletter, Vol 2(2), Spring 2016, p 9, available at www.asil.org/sites/default/files/documents/PIL_vol3_issue1_v2%20%281%29.pdf. For New Zealand, see *Yang Chen v Jinzhu Lin* [2016] NZCA 113. For Germany, see nn 13–15. For the UK, see n 56.

[12] J Huang, *Interregional Recognition and Enforcement of Civil and Commercial Judgments* (Oxford, Bloomsbury Publishing, 2014) 59.

[13] Vgl. Urteil des Kammergerichts Berlin vom 18.05.2006, Aktenzeichen 20 Sch 13/04. This case has been widely covered by scholarship. See eg Wenliang Zhang, 'Sino–Foreign Recognition and Enforcement of Judgments: A Promising "Follow-Suit" Model?' (2017) 16 *Chinese Journal of International Law* 515, 523; Elbalti, 'Reciprocity and the Recognition and Enforcement of Foreign Judgments' (n 5) 194–95.

[14] For an English-language summary of the decision, see P Beckers, 'German Court Takes First Step on Road to Mutual Recognition with China', International Law Office Newsletter, 31 May 2007.

[15] (2012) E Wuhan Zhong Minshang Wai Chuzi No 16.

[16] ibid.

[17] *Giant Light Metal Technology (Kunshan) Co Ltd v Aksa Far East Pte Ltd* [2014] SGHC 16.

*Textile Industry (Group) Import & Export Co*, it recognised and enforced a commercial monetary judgment issued by the High Court of Singapore according to the principles of reciprocity.[18]

In 2009, in *Hubei Gezhouba Sanlian Industrial Co., Ltd et al v Robinson Helicopter Company, Inc*,[19] the US District Court for the Central District of California recognised and enforced a Chinese monetary judgment pursuant to the Uniform Foreign Money-Judgments Recognition Act (UFMJRA).[20] Eight years after the decision in *Hubei Gezhouba Sanlian*, a Chinese court eventually reciprocated. In 2017, in *Liu Li v Tao Li and Tong Wu*,[21] the Intermediate People's Court of Wuhan city recognised and enforced a monetary judgment issued by the Los Angeles Superior Court in California.

China's grand One Belt One Road Initiative (OBOR) may further encourage Chinese legislators and courts to favourably consider recognising foreign judgments based on reciprocity. OBOR covers 64 countries, and aims to enhance connections between the Asian, European and African continents and their adjacent seas to promote the free flow of economic factors.[22] Ultimately the aim is to make China the global hub connecting the vibrant East Asian and developed European economic circles.[23] In order to facilitate the implementation of OBOR, early in July 2015, the SPC issued the Several Opinions to Provide Judicial Service and Safeguards for the Belt and Road Initiative.[24] Article 6 of the Opinions indicates that for states involved in OBOR which have promised to provide reciprocity but do not have a concluded treaty, China may offer judicial assistance (including JRE). Singapore is included in the OBOR Initiative. Although China has never explicitly included the US in the Initiative, *Liu Li* benefits from and reflects this pro-JRE momentum. On 8 June 2017, the Nanning Statement reached on the second China-ASEAN Justice Forum indicated that, to assist in promoting OBOR, in the circumstance where two states have not concluded a JRE treaty and neither state has rejected JRE due to a lack of reciprocity, there should be a presumption of reciprocity within the limits of the countries' domestic laws.[25]

[18] *Kolmar v Jiangsu Textile Industry (Group) Import & Export Co* (n 1).

[19] *Hubei Gezhouba Sanlian Industrial Co, Ltd v Robinson Helicopter Co, Inc*, US District Court Central District of California, 2009 WL 2190187 (C. D. Cal).

[20] Effective 1 January 2008, California's UFMJRA statutes, s 1713f, was repealed and replaced with a new version, the Uniform Foreign-Country Money-Judgments Recognition Act, s 1724ff. The former UFMJRA applies to all actions commenced prior to 1 January 2008.

[21] *Liu Li v Tao Li and Tong Wu* (n 1).

[22] 'Vision and Actions on Jointly Building Silk Road Economic Belt and 21st Century Maritime Silk Road', issued jointly by the National Development and Reform Commission, Ministry of Foreign Affairs, and Ministry of Commerce with State Council authorisation in March 2015, en.ndrc.gov.cn/newsrelease/201503/t20150330_669367.html.

[23] ibid.

[24] Supreme People's Court, The Several Opinions to Provide Judicial Service and Safeguards for the Belt and Road Initiative, promulgated and effective on 16 June 2015.

[25] Nanning Statement represented the consensus researched among the attendees at the second China-ASEAN Justice Forum, www.court.gov.cn/zixun-xiangqing-47372.html, Arts 2 and 7. The attendees included the chief justices from China, Cambodia, Indonesia, Laos, Malaysia, Burma, the Philippines, Singapore, Thailand, Vietnam, Afghanistan, Bangladesh, Nepal, Pakistan and Sri Lanka.

The decision in *Kolmar* has been strongly endorsed by the SPC by including it in the Second Series of Typical Cases concerning 'One Belt One Road'.[26] *Sascha Rudolf Seehaus*, *Kolmar* and *Liu Li*, although positive breakthroughs, do not resolve prospective challenges to the recognition and enforcement of foreign judgments based upon reciprocity in China. First, they do not address the institutional design of JRE based on reciprocity such as which level of courts should determine that reciprocity exists and what the scope of reciprocity is. Second, *Kolmar* and *Liu Li* also fail to resolve many basic doctrinal and practical issues with JRE based upon reciprocity that Chinese courts may be confronted with in the future. For example, what types of judgments does JRE based upon reciprocity cover? Should Chinese courts examine the jurisdiction of the judgment-rendering court?

## III. Institutional Design: A Foreign Judgment Registration System

This section proposes a registration model to address the institutional design of JRE based on reciprocity in China, administered by the SPC. The SPC should compile a list of countries which *de jure* recognise and enforce Chinese judgments so judgments rendered in these countries can be reciprocally recognised and enforced in China. The registration system should be divided into two consecutive parts, the first part being unilateral *ex parte* proceedings in which a judgment creditor can apply to register a foreign judgment for recognition and enforcement if the judgment was rendered in a listed country. A judgment will not be registered if at the date of the application it has been wholly satisfied or it is unenforceable in the judgment-rendering country. The creditor would need to prove that the judgment is final and conclusive, for a fixed or calculable amount of money, and that registration would not exceed the statute of limitations of the JRE courts. After registration, a foreign judgment will have the same force and effect for the purposes of enforcement as a judgment originally issued on the date of registration by the Chinese court which registered it. The second part of the registration system involves the judgment debtor. After registration, the JRE court should notify the judgment debtor who can then apply to set aside the registration by invoking one or more of defences to JRE under Chinese law. If the debtor fails to apply or set aside the registration, the foreign judgment will be recognised and enforced as a domestic Chinese judgment.

The proposed registration system can bring four major benefits:

First, it will centralise the determinative power over which country (or even which courts in a relevant country) offers reciprocity to Chinese judgments to the SPC. Under the current Chinese CPL, the judgment creditor must apply to

[26] The SPC published the Second Series of Typical Cases concerning 'One Belt One Road' in 2017: www.chinanews.com/gn/2017/05-15/8224293.shtml.

the Intermediate People's Court where the debtor's assets are located.[27] The JRE decision rendered by this Intermediate People's Court will be legally effective once it is served upon the parties.[28] The decision is not appealable.[29] The Chinese court system is constituted of four levels: (1) Basic People's Courts at the level of autonomous counties, towns and municipal districts; (2) Intermediate People's Courts at the level of prefectures, autonomous prefectures and municipalities; (3) Higher People's Courts at the level of the provinces, autonomous regions and special municipalities; and (4) the Supreme People's Court, which is the court of last resort for the People's Republic of China, excluding the Macao and Hong Kong Special Administrative Regions.[30] The Intermediate People's Courts are therefore comparatively low level. Deciding which countries offer reciprocity to Chinese judgments not only involves complex legal issues but also has diplomatic implications in relation to international judicial assistance.[31] Leaving the decision to the Intermediate People's Courts may also create inconsistent judicial practices in different regions. China is still in the preliminary stage of developing laws and policies for reciprocity of JRE, so it is more appropriate for the SPC to determine which countries offer reciprocity to Chinese judgments.

Second, the registration system would help to streamline China's JRE system. Currently, it is unclear which countries provide *de jure* reciprocity to Chinese judgments. The registration system will distinguish countries that offer *de jure* reciprocity to Chinese judgments from those which do not. Therefore, it will give clear guidance to judgment creditors: if the country of the original court is listed in the registration system, the creditors should apply for registration; if the original country has neither concluded a JRE treaty with China nor provided *de jure* reciprocity to Chinese judgments, the foreign judgment will not be recognisable and enforceable in China.

Third, the proposed registration system is cost- and time-saving compared to litigation.[32] The first part of the registration proceeding is *ex parte*, whereby foreign judgment creditors from countries with established reciprocity simply register judgments rather than bringing an action. After registration, the Chinese court in which the judgment is registered should notify the judgment debtor. The debtor can initiate proceedings to set aside registration by proving defences to JRE.

[27] SPC Judicial Interpretation of the CPL, art 544.

[28] ibid, art 548.

[29] Although parties to a foreign judgment cannot appeal the decision of the JRE proceedings, they can bring an action on the substantive dispute in the case to the Chinese courts. ibid, art 544.

[30] CPL, ss 17–20.

[31] See R Brand, 'Enforcement of Foreign Money-Judgments in the United States: in Search of Uniformity and International Acceptance' (1991) 67 *Notre Dame Law Review* 253, 282 (indicating the complexities where a foreign JRE court needs to determine whether a US court offers reciprocity to foreign judgments); RW Hulbert, 'Symposium Articles, Some Thoughts on Judgments, Reciprocity, and the Seeming Paradox of International Commercial Arbitration' (2008) 29 *University of Pennsylvania Journal of International Law* 641, 651 (discussing the uncertainty in determining the existence of reciprocity).

[32] See V Black, 'Canada and the US Contemplate Changes to Foreign-Judgment Enforcement' (2007) 3 *Journal of Private International Law* 1, 2.

However, if the statute of limitation expires without action from the debtor, the foreign judgment can be executed. Registration systems have been adopted under the Foreign Judgments (Reciprocal Enforcement) Act 1933 (UK) and its progenies in such countries as Australia and Hong Kong.[33] A system of registration has also been proposed by the Uniform Law Conference of Canada in its Uniform Enforcement of Foreign Judgments Act (Canada UEFJA)[34] and the ALI Proposed Federal Statute.[35]

Fourth, the current Chinese JRE system relies on judgment creditors to prove whether a foreign country offers reciprocity to Chinese judgments. For example, in 2015, the Tel Aviv District Court in Israel recognised and enforced a monetary judgment issued by the Nantong Intermediate People's Court in China.[36] The Israeli court held that reciprocity existed between China and Israel.[37] While this case was being appealed to the High Court of Justice in Israel,[38] a party applied to an intermediate court in Fuzhou, the capital city of Fujian province in China, to recognise and enforce the Israeli judgment.[39] The Fuzhou court rejected recognition due to lack of reciprocity between China and Israel.[40] In its judgment, the Fuzhou court did not refer to the Tel Aviv court's recognition of the Chinese judgment – possibly

[33] The UK Foreign Judgments (Reciprocal Enforcement) Act 1933 and its progeny are not based on the reciprocity JRE theory where UK courts are urged to recognise a foreign judgment rendered in a situation in which they would *mutatis mutandis* have exercised jurisdiction themselves. They are based upon substantially reciprocal JRE arrangements between the JRE state and the judgment-rendering states. See also the Australian Foreign Judgments Act 1991 (Cth) s 5(1), (3), (6).

[34] Canada UEFJA, s 12, s 14. Canada UEFJA does not require reciprocity for JRE.

[35] ALI Proposed Federal Statute (n 5) s 5(d), s 10.

[36] In 2009, Israeli citizen Itshak Reitmann contracted with China Jiangsu Overseas Group Corporation (Jiangsu Company) to recruit construction workers for work in Ukraine. Jiangsu Company sent workers to Ukraine but found that the work promised by Reitmann did not exist. In March 2009, Jiangsu Company sued Reitmann in the Nantong Intermediate People's Court for the commissions, relevant interest and litigation costs. In December 2009, the Nantong court rendered a judgment in Jiangsu Company's favour, ordering Reitmann to return the commissions of USD551,400 and CNY8,372,615.36 and litigation costs of CNY108,044 (Nantong Judgment). Jiangsu Company applied to the Tel Aviv District court to recognise and enforce the Nantong Judgment. In 2015, the Tel Aviv District Court held that the Nantong Judgment should be recognised and enforced for four reasons. First, there existed a 'reasonable potential' for an Israeli judgment to be enforced in China. Such potential satisfied the condition of 'reciprocity of enforcement' required by Israeli legislation, which aims to promote judicial co-operation between Israel and other countries. Second, co-operation between China and Israel was a new frontier because neither country had enforced or refused to enforce the other's judgments and no JRE treaty existed. Third, Chinese law recognised JRE based on reciprocity. If a country limits recognition and enforcement of foreign judgments to countries which have previously recognised and enforced its own judgments, reciprocity will be inhibited. Fourth, with the development of economic co-operation between China and Israel, judicial assistance could promote business certainty. Therefore, courts should encourage judicial assistance for the benefit of the public interest. People's Court Daily, 'High Court of Justice in Israel Rendered the Final Judgment and Unprecedentedly Recognized and Enforced a Chinese Judgment', 16 August 2017, rmfyb.chinacourt.org/paper/html/2017-08/16/content_129031.htm?div=-1.

[37] ibid.

[38] This judgment was affirmed by the High Court of Justice on 15 August 2017. ibid.

[39] Zhang, 'Sino–Foreign Recognition and Enforcement of Judgments: A Promising "Follow-Suit" Model?' (n 13) 526.

[40] ibid.

because it was not pleaded by the parties in the JRE proceeding.[41] A Chinese professor commented that the Fuzhou court might have reached a different ruling if the Tel Aviv court's recognition had been pleaded.[42]

This case shows that under the current JRE system if a party does not plead or fails to prove that reciprocity exists between China and a certain foreign country, the Chinese JRE court may not raise this issue of its own instance. This may cause inconsistent decisions regarding whether reciprocity exists between China and a foreign country. The existence of reciprocity between China and a certain country should be an objective fact and cannot rely on the strength of a party's evidence. Moreover, this practice is inconsistent with the Law of the Application of Law for Foreign-related Civil Relations,[43] art 10 of which provides that people's courts, arbitration institutions or administrative organs shall prove the foreign law that applies to foreign-related civil relations; parties shall prove the foreign law that they choose. Proving the existence of reciprocity requires proof of the law of the judgment-rendering country. It is not the law that parties chose. Therefore, courts should bear the primary responsibility of proving the law of the judgment-rendering country. Parties can provide assistance in this process. If a judgment creditor does not plead the existence of reciprocity, the JRE court should be able to raise this issue and investigate further itself. This is because the existence of reciprocity is related to national interests, as well as the personal interests of the concerned parties.[44]

A solution is that the SPC should provide a list of countries that offer reciprocity for Chinese judgments. The list will centralise the determinative power over which country (or even which courts in a particular country) offers reciprocity to Chinese judgments to the SPC. It will distinguish countries that offer reciprocity to Chinese judgments from those do not. The first version of this list may include (1) countries that have recognised or enforced Chinese monetary judgments; (2) trading countries along the OBOR that offer *de jure* reciprocity to Chinese judgments. The first group covers the US, New Zealand, Germany, Israel, South Korea and Singapore, who have already recognised or enforced Chinese monetary judgments. Countries that joined China in the Nanning Statement may be included in the second group. The SPC should also look into laws of other countries and decide whether their domestic laws permit recognition and enforcement of Chinese judgments. The SPC should update the list from time to time. This list can resolve the concern that Intermediate People's Courts are inexperienced in deciding complicated legal and political issues related to reciprocity.

[41] ibid.

[42] ibid.

[43] The Application of Law for Foreign-related Civil Relations of the PRC, adopted and promulgated by the Standing Committee of the 11th National People's Congress on 28 October 2010, effective 1 April 2011.

[44] South Korean JRE courts examine whether a guarantee of reciprocity exists between South Korea and the judgment-rendering country *ex officio*. HK Suk, 'Country Report South Korea' in A Chong (ed), Recognition and Enforcement of Foreign Judgments in Asia (2017), abli.asia/LinkClick.aspx?fileticket=I0rTeJ0yljw%3d&portalid=0, 181.

It also does not require parties to plead or prove the existence of reciprocity. This list is important for China to realise a smooth shift from *de facto* reciprocity to *de jure* reciprocity.

Providing a list of countries to facilitate JRE is not a rare practice in the world. For example, the Foreign Judgments (Reciprocal Enforcement) Act 1933 (UK) and its progeny in Australia, Singapore and Hong Kong all provide a list of countries that offer substantial reciprocity of treatment to judgments of the JRE states.[45] For example, in Australia, the Foreign Judgments Act 1991 (Cth) creates an *ex parte* registration system for judgments of the superior courts (and specified inferior courts) of the list of countries that have reciprocal JRE arrangements with Australia.[46] The list can be found in the Foreign Judgments Regulations 1992 (Cth).[47] A country will be added to the list, if it concludes a bilateral or multilateral JRE treaty with Australia, but this is not the only way.[48] As long as the Governor-General of Australia is satisfied that 'substantial reciprocity of treatment will be assured in relation to the enforcement in that country of money judgments given in all Australian superior courts', this country will be added to the list.[49]

## IV. What Judgments can be Registered?

Proper function of the registration system requires clarification of three issues: which judgments can be registered; which laws should be applied to determine the finality of a foreign judgment in Chinese JRE proceedings, and what the statute of limitations for applying to register a foreign judgment is.

### A. Monetary and Non-Monetary Judgments

The registration system should cover monetary judgments, namely judgments that order a debtor to pay a fixed, or readily calculable, sum of money, to the

[45] Notably, the UK Foreign Judgments (Reciprocal Enforcement) Act and its progeny are not based on the reciprocity JRE theory where UK courts are urged to recognise a foreign judgment rendered in a situation in which they would *mutatis mutandis* have exercised jurisdiction themselves. *Sharps Commercials Ltd v Gas Turbines Ltd* [1956] NZLR 819; *Gordon Pacific Developments Pty Ltd v Conlon* [1993] 2 NZLR 760.

[46] Global Legal Group, *The International Comparative Legal Guide to: Enforcement of Foreign Judgments 2016*, 12.

[47] Schedule of Foreign Judgments Regulations 1992 (Cth). The list of countries includes New Zealand, Province of Alberta Canada, Bahamas, Province of British Columbia Canada, British Virgin Islands, Cayman Islands, Dominica, Falkland Islands, Fiji, France, Germany, Gibraltar, Grenada, Hong Kong, Israel, Italy, Japan, South Korea, Malawi, Province of Manitoba Canada, Montserrat, Papua New Guinea, Poland, St Helena, St Kitts and Nevis, St Vincent and the Grenadines, Seychelles, Singapore, Solomon Islands, Sri Lanka, Switzerland, Taiwan, Tonga, Tuvalu, the UK and Western Samoa.

[48] A Bell, 'Country Report Australia' in A Chong (ed) *Recognition and Enforcement of Foreign Judgments in Asia* (2017), abli.asia/LinkClick.aspx?fileticket=I0rTeJ0yljw%3D&portalid=0, 7.

[49] Foreign Judgments Act 1991 (Cth) s 5(1).

creditor. The judgments should result from commercial proceedings. Judgments for the recovery of taxes, fines or penalties, bankruptcy and insolvency, and family matters (eg judgments for divorce, support, maintenance, and custody) should be excluded. Taxes, fines or penalties are disputes involving public laws and should not be enforced in private civil proceedings.[50] Bankruptcy and insolvency differ from typical commercial disputes and should generally be regulated by special laws.[51] Furthermore, JRE reciprocity for commercial judgments may not be established because a foreign state recognises and enforces a Chinese judgment on domestic relations (eg divorce), and vice versa.[52] Distinguishing family law judgments on family relationship from commercial judgments and establishing different JRE regimes is a widely acknowledged international practice. For example, in the EU, the Brussels II bis Regulation[53] regulates the former while the Brussels I Regulation (Recast)[54] governs the latter. Similarly, in the US, the ALI Proposed Federal Statute and the 2005 UFMJRA exclude judgments on domestic relations from their scope of JRE.[55]

Another issue of practical importance is whether the registration system should cover non-monetary judgments that require a defendant to do or abstain from doing something. The contemporary reciprocity practice in China already covers non-monetary judgments. For example, in *Sascha Rudolf Seehaus* the Chinese court recognised a Germany judgment appointing a trustee in bankruptcy. China should be very cautious to include non-monetary judgments into its registration system. This is because, as previously indicated, China is in the preliminary transition period from *de facto* reciprocity or *de jure* reciprocity. It is too early to include

[50] RA Brand 'Federal Judicial Center International Litigation Guide Recognition and Enforcement of Foreign Judgments' (2012) 74 *University of Pittsburgh Law Review* 491, 508.

[51] eg in the EU, bankruptcy is not regulated by Brussels I Regulation (recast) (n 54) but by Council Regulation (EC) No 1346/2000 of May 29, 2000 on Insolvency Proceedings, 2000 OJ (L 160) 1.

[52] eg early in December 2009, the Probate Division of the Circuit Court in Saint Louis Country Missouri in the US recognised and enforced in the State of Missouri a civil money judgment about succession rendered by the Basic People's Court in Chaoyang District, Beijing. The US court decided to give full faith and credit to the Chinese judgment. The Court found that the decedent was not a Missouri resident, had no contact with the State of Missouri, other than an online purchase of assets in a Scottrade Account, so there could not be any probate proceedings in Missouri. The US court ordered the assets in the account to be distributed according to the scheme put forth in the Chinese judgment. This Missouri judgment may establish *de facto* reciprocity between the U.S and China on succession matters but there is no basis for extending reciprocity to commercial disputes, such as sales and corporate governance. Probate Letter sent by Robert C Weis, Commissioner of Probate Division, Circuit Court, Saint Louis Country, Missouri to Mr Jonathan Yao, Director of Asia Pacific Scottrade, Inc on 15 December 2009. On file with the author.

[53] Council Regulation (EC) No 2201/2003 of 27 November 2003 concerning Jurisdiction and the Recognition and Enforcement of Judgments in Matrimonial Matters and Matters of Parental Responsibility, repealing Regulation (EC) No 1347/2000, 2003 OJ (L 338) 1. Council Regulation (EC) No 4/2009 of 18 December 2008 on Jurisdiction, Applicable Law, Recognition and Enforcement of Decisions and Cooperation in Matters relating to Maintenance Obligations, 2009 OJ (L7) 1.

[54] Art 1.2(e) and (f) of Regulation (EU) No 1215/2012 of the European Parliament and the Council on Jurisdiction and the Recognition and Enforcement of Judgments in Civil and Commercial Matters (Recast), 2012 OJ (L 351) 1 (Brussels I Regulation (Recast)).

[55] ALI Proposed Federal Act (n 5) § I(A)(i)-(iii). UFMJRA § 3(b)(3).

the complexity of non-monetary judgments into China's JRE regime. Moreover, there is no uniform approach in the world regarding whether non-monetary judgments can be recognised and enforced as a monetary judgment. In *Spliethoff's Bevrachtingskantoor Bv v Bank of China Limited,* the English court recognised two Chinese judgments that injuncted Bank of China from making payment.[56] However, the English court went ahead and enforced the English law guarantees notwithstanding the injunction, on the basis that illegality under the law of the place of domicile was irrelevant.[57] In Australia, it is a controversial issue whether courts are obliged to give effect to injunctions and other non-monetary judgments of foreign courts.[58] The three criteria adopted by the Supreme Court of Canada in *Pro Swing Inc v Elta Golf Inc* might be of reference for the Chinese SPC, if it ultimately determines to include non-monetary judgments into its JRE regime: first, the foreign judgment should be clear and specific as to the rights, duties and obligations that it imposes on the defendant;[59] second, the judgment should be clear about whether it was intended to apply outside the territory of the judgment-rendering country;[60] and third the proceedings must have a sufficient connection with the JRE country.[61]

## B. Final, Conclusive and Enforceable

The competent foreign judgment should be final, conclusive and enforceable.[62] Finality is an important condition for registration. However, China utilises different criteria from common law countries to determine whether a judgment is final.

China's court system is characterised by 'four levels and two instances of trials'.[63] In the people's courts, a case is decided after two instances of trials at most.

[56] *Spliethoff's Bevrachtingskantoor Bv v Bank of China Limited* [2015] EWHC 999 (Comm). The English court determined that the Chinese court judgments should be recognised because firstly, according to English private international law, the defendant submitted to the jurisdiction of the Chinese courts by defending its case, and secondly, because the defendant submitted to the Chinese courts, the English court should not carry out an evaluative assessment of the Chinese court judgments and no public policy would be offended by recognising it. Nevertheless, the English court held that recognition of the Chinese court judgments did not afford the Bank of China a stay of enforcement of the English guarantees, because China was not the place of performance and Chinese law was not *lex loci solutions*. Moreover, the Bank of China would not have faced any real risk of criminal or civil sanction or double jeopardy in China if it made payments according to the orders of the English court.

[57] ibid.

[58] K Pham, 'Enforcement of Non-Monetary Foreign Judgments in Australia' (2008) 30 *Sydney Law Review* 663, 663–89.

[59] *Pro Swing Inc v Elta Golf Inc* [2006] 2 SCR 612, 629, 653.

[60] ibid 640–42.

[61] ibid 638–89.

[62] R Mortensen, R Garnett and M Keyes, *Private International Law in Australia*, 3rd edn (Australia, LexisNexis Butterworths, 2015) 137.

[63] CPL, art 175.

A party may bring an appeal against a judgment of first instance to the people's court at the next higher level only once. The judgment of the first instance becomes legally effective or 'final' if, within the prescribed period for appeal, no party makes an appeal. Judgments and orders of the court of second instance, and judgments rendered by the Supreme People's Courts as the court of first instance are immediately legally effective.[64] Therefore, under Chinese CPL, a judgment is not final if it is still subject to appeal or the time for appeal has not expired. However, in common law jurisdictions such as Singapore and Hong Kong, a judgment is taken to be final and conclusive even though it may still be subject to appeal or an appeal may be pending against it.[65]

Hong Kong courts apply Hong Kong law to determine the finality of judgments rendered in Mainland China.[66] This has been deeply criticised by Chinese scholars.[67] In the Memorandum of Guidance between the SPC and the Supreme Court of Singapore on Recognition and Enforcement of Money Judgments in Commercial Cases, both parties agree to apply Chinese law to determine the finality of a judgment, regardless of whether it is a Chinese or a Singaporean judgment.[68] The benefits of this arrangement is to guarantee that the finality of Chinese judgment will not be second-guessed in a Singaporean court: if a judgment is considered as final under Chinese law, Singapore should deem this judgment to be final. However, this arrangement will diminish the scope of recognisable and enforceable Singaporean judgments, because a judgment that is final in Singapore may not be considered final in China. The Supreme Court of Singapore can accept this unequal treatment possibly because of two reasons. First, this Memorandum is not binding and does not constitute a treaty or legislation.[69] It does not supersede any existing or future laws, judicial decisions or court

[64] ibid, art 155.

[65] See s 5(5) of the Australia Foreign Judgments Act 1991; § 3(2)(a) and 3(3) of the Hong Kong Foreign Judgments (Reciprocal Enforcement) Ordinance (Cap 319). See *Beatty v Beatty* [1924] 1 KB 807, 815–16 (holding a judgment is no less 'final' just because an appeal is possible or pending, unless a stay of execution has been granted in the foreign court). In other circumstances, Hong Kong courts may stay the proceedings, see *Colt Industries Inc v Sarlie (No 2)* [1966] 3 All ER 85, 88, [1966] 1 WLR 1287, 1293.

[66] *Chiyu Banking Corp Ltd. v Chan Tin Kwun* [1996] 2 HKLR 395 (HC); *Wuhan Zhong Shuo Hong Real Estate Co Ltd v the Kwong Sang Hong Int'l Ltd* [2000] HKC 711 (CFI); *Tan Tay Cuan v Ng Chi Hung* [2001] HKC 164 (CFI). Under the Chinese retrial system, the Chinese court that rendered the original judgment may retry the case in circumstances prescribed by law. This is true regardless of whether the retrial is initiated by the judgment-rendering court or a higher court, a procuratorate, or a party. However, according to Hong Kong, a case is not final if the judgment-rendering court retains the power to retry the case. Therefore, these Hong Kong cases held that the relevant Chinese judgments were not final.

[67] eg Huang, *Interregional Recognition and Enforcement of Civil and Commercial Judgments* (n 12) 197–202.

[68] Arts 7 and 19 of Memorandum of Guidance between the SPC and the Supreme Court of Singapore on Recognition and Enforcement of Money Judgments in Commercial Cases, concluded on 31 August 2018, www.chinajusticeobserver.com/memorandum-of-guidance-between-china-supremecourt-and-singapore-supremecourt-on-recognition-and-enforcement-of-money-judgments.

[69] ibid, art 2.

rules. Second, Singapore is eager to become an international dispute resolution centre. Since Hong Kong and Mainland China concluded the Arrangement on Reciprocal Recognition and Enforcement of the Decisions of Civil and Commercial Cases under Consensual Jurisdiction (the Mainland-Hong Kong Choice of Court Arrangement), Hong Kong judgments can be recognised and enforced in Mainland China.[70] Compared with Singaporean courts, Hong Kong courts are preferred by foreign parties to resolve disputes with Mainland parties. Although not binding, the contents of this Memorandum are broader and more pro-JRE compared with the Mainland-Hong Kong Choice of Court Arrangement. It may make Singaporean courts more attractive than their Hong Kong counterparts for disputes related to Chinese parties.

So, following the SPC approach in the Memorandum, under the proposed registration procedure, the SPC may specify that Chinese law is to be applied in determining the finality of foreign judgments. If an appeal is pending in the judgment-rendering state or the time for appeal in that state has not yet expired, the Chinese court of registration may stay the enforcement until the result of the appeal is rendered.

## C. Statute of Limitations for Registration

Under the current CPL, the statute of limitations for JRE applications is two years, which is the same as applications for the enforcement of domestic Chinese judgments.[71] The two-year statute of limitations is too short for judgment creditors to apply for recognition and enforcement of foreign judgments in China. Unlike creditors of domestic judgments, foreign creditors need to spend time translating judgments and relevant documents (eg proofs of service of process) into Chinese, getting official certifications of the translations from a Chinese embassy in the country of the judgment-rendering court, and locating the debtor's assets in China. Compared with JRE statutes in foreign countries, the two-year statute of limitations is strikingly short. For example, the Australian Foreign Judgments Act 1991 (Cth) and Hong Kong Foreign Judgments (Reciprocal Enforcement) Ordinance both allow a creditor of a foreign judgment six years from the date of the judgment to apply to register the judgment at the appropriate court. Where there have been proceedings by way of appeal against the judgment, it is six years from the date of the last judgment in those proceedings.[72] The 2005 US UFMJRA provides a 15-year

[70] See n 8.

[71] SPC Judicial Interpretation of the CPL, art 547. The statute of limitations starts from the last day of the performance period specified in the foreign judgment, the last day of each specified performance period if a foreign judgment requires performance in instalments or, if the judgment does not specify a period of performance, from the date a foreign judgment becomes effective. CPL, art 239.

[72] Australian Foreign Judgments Act 1991, s 5(6). Hong Kong Foreign Judgments (Reciprocal Enforcement) Ordinance, s 6(1).

statute of limitations running from the effective date of the foreign judgment.[73] In the Canada UEFJA and the ALI Proposed Federal Statute, the statute of limitations for JRE is ten years from the day the judgment first becomes enforceable in the state of origin.[74] Therefore, the SPC should allow a longer statute of limitations for registering foreign judgments.

## V. What are the Jurisdictional Grounds to Set Aside Registration?

After a foreign judgment is registered, the court of registration should inform the judgment debtor and the debtor may apply to the court to set aside the registration in circumstances specified by law. 'A basic rule of judgments recognition in nearly all legal systems is that a court will not recognise a judgment from a court that did not have jurisdiction to hear the case'.[75] However, current Chinese law does not explicitly indicate whether Chinese JRE courts should examine the jurisdiction of the judgment-rendering courts where JRE reciprocity has been established. In *Kolmar* and *Liu Li*, Chinese JRE courts did not review jurisdiction. The benefit of the current Chinese approach is generosity. As long as *de facto* reciprocity is established, courts do not review the jurisdiction of the judgment-rendering court. This approach is usually adopted in two scenarios. First, when a double JRE convention exists between the judgment-rendering state and the JRE state. For example, the 1968 Brussels Convention on Jurisdiction and Enforcement is a double convention that regulates both direct jurisdiction and JRE.[76] As long as a judgment-rendering court decides a case according to the direct jurisdiction rule of the Convention and the 2012 Brussels I Regulation (Recast),[77] its Member States cannot apply their indirect jurisdiction rules to review the jurisdiction of the judgment-rendering court in the JRE proceedings.[78] Second, where the JRE state decides to adopt pro-JRE policies towards the judgment-rendering jurisdiction to encourage benefits such as national integration.[79] For example, arts 15 and 16 of the SPC Regulation

[73] National Conference of Commissioners on Uniform. State Laws, Uniform. Foreign-Country Money Judgments Recognition Act §§ 1–13 (2005).

[74] Canada UEFJA (n 34) s 5; ALI Proposed Federal Statute, s 2(c).

[75] RA Brand, 'Understanding Judgments Recognition' (2014) 40 *North Carolina Journal of International Law* and Commercial Regulation 877, 885.

[76] Brussels Convention on Jurisdiction and the Enforcement of Judgments in Civil and Commercial Matters [1972] OJ L 299/32.

[77] For comments on the differences between Brussels I Regulation and its Recast, see generally SP Baumgartner, 'Recent Reforms in EU Law: Recognition and Enforcement of Foreign Judgments' (2013) 97 *Judicature* 188.

[78] Brussels I Regulation (Recast), Arts 45 and 46. M Zilinsky, 'Mutual Trust and Cross-Border Enforcement of Judgments in Civil Matters in the EU: Does the Step-by-Step Approach Work?' (2017) 64 *Netherlands International Law Review* 115, 118.

[79] See KR Miller, 'Playground Politics: Assessing the Wisdom of Writing a Reciprocity Requirement into US International Recognition and Enforcement Law' (2003–04) 35 *Georgetown Journal of International Law* 239, 242–43.

on Recognition and Enforcement of Civil Judgments issued in Taiwan does not allow Chinese Mainland JRE courts to examine the jurisdiction of the Taiwanese courts unless the jurisdiction conflicts with the exclusive jurisdiction of mainland courts or parties have concluded a valid arbitration clause. The same approach is used in Mainland China in relation to the recognition and enforcement of judgments issued in the Macao Special Administrative Region.[80] However, JRE between Mainland China, Taiwan and Macao is interregional and the legal, political and economic contexts differ significantly from international JRE.[81] Therefore, the Chinese approach of not reviewing jurisdiction once JRE reciprocity has been established does not fit into either of the scenarios.

The proposed registration system should explicitly provide that JRE is to be rejected if the judgment-rendering court has no jurisdiction according to the law of the JRE state. In private international law, jurisdiction can be divided into two categories. One is direct jurisdiction, which determines when a court is seised of a case in the judgment-rendering proceedings and is prescribed by the law of the judgment-rendering country.[82] The other is indirect jurisdiction, which is used by the JRE court to decide whether the judgment-rendering court had jurisdiction to hear the case and is determined by the law of the place where the judgment is sought to be recognised or enforced.[83] There are two approaches to designing indirect jurisdiction. The first is to replicate the direct jurisdiction rules. For example, the US, German and Brazilian indirect jurisdiction rules are identical to their direct jurisdiction rules.[84] The second approach is to design special rules for indirect jurisdiction or international jurisdiction, or jurisdiction for the purposes of enforcement. Where this has occurred, the rules are generally more restrictive than direct jurisdiction rules.[85] For example, the UK Foreign Judgments (Reciprocal Enforcement) Act 1933 and its progeny (ie the Australia Foreign Judgments Act and the Hong Kong Foreign Judgments (Reciprocal Enforcement) Ordinance) list international jurisdiction rules for JRE purposes.[86]

The Chinese CPL provides only direct jurisdiction rules and is silent on indirect jurisdiction rules. Eleven out of thirty-two effective bilateral JRE treaties concluded by China provide indirect jurisdictional rules.[87] Therefore, the second approach may better embody China's international JRE practice. Aside from the JRE treaties concluded by China, the SPC may also consider the growing

[80] Arrangement between the Mainland and the Macao Special Administrative Region on the Mutual Recognition and Enforcement of Civil and Commercial Judgments, effective on 1 April 2006, art 11.

[81] Huang (n 12) 1–29.

[82] See R Michaels, 'Some Fundamental Jurisdictional Conceptions as Applied in Judgment Conventions' in R Michaels et al (eds), *Conflict of Laws in a Globalizing World: A Tribute to Arthur Von Mehren* (Cambridge, Cambridge University Press, 2007) 35–36.

[83] ibid.

[84] Brand, 'Understanding Judgments Recognition' (n 75) 890.

[85] ibid.

[86] See the Australian Foreign Judgments Act, ss 7(3) and (4) and the Hong Kong Foreign Judgments (Reciprocal Enforcement) Ordinance, s 6(2).

[87] See Annex.

international consensus on appropriate judicial jurisdiction, such as the Hague Choice of Court Agreement and the Hague Judgments Project. Based on these considerations, the following list of indirect jurisdiction rules is proposed. The list should be open-ended and allow for the possibility of expansion in the future.

1. The judgment debtor, being the defendant in the judgment-rendering proceedings, was domiciled or habitually resident in the judgment-rendering state at the time (s)he became a party to the proceedings in the judgment-rendering court.

A defendant can be sued in their state of domicile or habitual residence.[88] This rule has been adopted by all the Chinese JRE treaties which have indirect jurisdiction rules. (For the benefit of clear categorisation, this chapter separates the indirect jurisdiction rules for the two judgment debtors, being the defendant and plaintiff in the judgment-rendering proceedings.)

2. The judgment debtor, being the defendant in the judgment-rendering proceedings, maintained a branch, agency or other business representative in the judgment-rendering state at the time the debtor became a party to the proceedings in the judgment-rendering court and the claim on which the judgment is based arose out of the business activities of that branch, agency or other business representative.

This rule is based on art 19.2 of the China-UAE JRE Treaty.[89] Unlike the China-UAE JRE Treaty, most of Chinese JRE treaties with indirect jurisdiction rules provide that the judgment-rendering court should be considered to have jurisdiction if the judgment debtor, being the defendant in the judgment-rendering proceedings, maintained a branch, agency, or other business representative in the judgment-rendering state.[90] Such phrasing is vague and insufficiently predictable. The alleged vagueness stems from the question when the judgment debtor must have maintained a business presence in the judgment-rendering state and whether the lawsuit should arise out of its business activities. It is unreasonable to ascribe jurisdiction to the judgment-rendering court if the business presence was established after the commencement of the original trial or the lawsuit had no real and substantial connection with the business activities.

3. The judgment debtor, being the defendant in the judgment-rendering proceedings, expressly consented to the jurisdiction of the judgment-rendering

[88] eg for EU, see Brussels I Regulation (Recast) art 4.1; for the US, see *Goodyear Dunlop Tires Operations, S.A. v Brown*, 131 S. Ct. 2846, 2853–54 (2011) (although not adopting a simple 'defendant's domicile' rule, the judgment states that '[f]or an individual, the paradigm forum for the exercise of general jurisdiction is the individual's domicile; for a corporation, it is an equivalent place, in which the corporation is fairly regarded as at home').

[89] China-UAE JRE Treaty, art 19.2.

[90] See Treaty for Judicial Assistance in Civil, Commercial and Criminal Affairs between China and Cyprus, entered into force 11 January 1996, art 26.2.

court in writing or by any other means of communication which renders information accessible so as to be available for later reference.

This provision addresses choice of court agreements. As China has signed the Hague Choice of Court Convention, the SPC may refer to art 3(c) of the Convention which provides that the choice of court agreement must be in writing or other forms usable for repeated access and subsequent reference.

4. The judgment debtor, being the defendant in the judgment-rendering proceedings, defended the case on its merits without challenging the jurisdiction of the judgment-rendering court.

If a party defends the substance of the case without any reservation over jurisdictional issues, the party should be deemed to have submitted to the jurisdiction of the judgment-rendering court.

5. The judgment debtor brought the claim on which the judgment is based.

This rule regulates the plaintiff or the party who brought a counter-claim in the judgment-rendering proceedings. In terms of direct jurisdiction, if a court takes jurisdiction over a case against a non-resident defendant solely based on the plaintiff's 'domicile, habitual residence, or place of incorporation', this jurisdictional ground is considered exorbitant.[91] However, in terms of indirect jurisdiction, the conclusion may be different. Because if a plaintiff brings a case against a defendant, the plaintiff should be considered to have voluntarily submitted to the jurisdiction of the judgment-rendering court. If the plaintiff loses the case, it is illogical to allow the plaintiff (the judgment debtor) to argue in the JRE proceedings that the judgment-rendering court had no jurisdiction so the JRE should be rejected. Moreover, Chinese direct jurisdictional rules permit courts to exercise personal jurisdiction on a non-resident defendant solely because the plaintiff's domicile, habitual residence or place of incorporation is in China.[92]

6. The judgment concerned a contractual obligation and the contract was performed or should be performed in the judgment-rendering state, or the subject matter of the dispute was located in the judgment-rendering state.

With the exception of the China-UAE Treaty,[93] all of China's JRE treaties provide that the judgment-rendering court should be considered to have jurisdiction if the contract was concluded in the judgment-rendering state. However, where the

[91] See eg ALI Proposed Federal Statute, s 6(a)(ii).

[92] eg CPL art 28 provides that the Intermediate People's Courts located in the place of infringement can exercise jurisdiction over the infringement. This provision is clarified by art 25 of the SPC Judicial Interpretation of CPL, which indicates that in cases where infringement occurs on the internet, the place of infringement includes where the victim is domiciled. The court of the victim's domicile can therefore exercise personal jurisdiction over the non-resident defendant.

[93] China-UAE JRE Treaty, art 19.3.

contract was concluded may simply be fortuitous and should not be considered the basis for indirect jurisdiction.

7. If the judgment ruled on a non-contractual tort obligation, the place of the act or omission was in the judgment-rendering state.

The place of the harm was in the judgment-rendering state if the tortfeasor directed his or her act to the state or should reasonably have expected that the harm would occur in that state. The controversial issue here is whether the place of the harm should be considered a basis for indirect jurisdiction. The China-UAE JRE Treaty answers in the negative while the other JRE treaties concluded by China give positive answers.[94] If the tortfeasor directed his or her act to the judgment-rendering state or should reasonably have expected that the harm would occur in that state, the state should have jurisdiction. This rule has been adopted by the US,[95] Australia and the EU. It does not run counter to the Chinese CPL either.

8. The judgment ruled on real estate that is located in the judgment-rendering state.

This rule, as an overriding provision, is accepted by all JRE treaties with indirect jurisdiction rules concluded by China. This applies even if one or more of the other heads applies. The exercise of jurisdiction of the judgment-rendering court does not conflict with the exclusive jurisdiction of Chinese courts. Chinese courts have exclusive jurisdiction in the following cases: (1) an action instituted for a dispute over real estate located in China;[96] (2) an action instituted for a dispute arising from harbour operations in China;[97] and (3) actions instituted for disputes arising from the performance of contracts for Chinese-foreign equity joint ventures, Chinese-foreign contractual joint ventures or Chinese-foreign co-operative exploration and exploitation of natural resources in China.[98]

## VI. Conclusion

The OBOR Initiative is pushing Chinese courts to liberalise JRE based on reciprocity. This chapter proposes a registration system to address the institutional design of JRE based on reciprocity in China. It also provides detailed answers to which judgments can be registered and what jurisdictional ground can set aside a registration in this proposed system. Hopefully, this proposal can serve as a humble step to modernise the Chinese law for JRE based on reciprocity.

[94] ibid, art 19.4.

[95] eg *Calder v Jones*, 467 US 783 (1984); *Dow Jones & Company Inc v Gutnick*, [2002] HCA 56, (2002) 210 CLR 575; *Shevill v Presse Alliance SA* (ECJ Case C-68/93, 1995).

[96] CPL, art 33.

[97] ibid.

[98] ibid, art 266.

# Annex: Comparison of Indirect Jurisdiction under Chinese CPL and Chinese Treaties

| Defences to JRE | JRE Based on Reciprocity under Chinese CPL | Bilateral JRE Treaties Concluded by China | Multilateral JRE Treaties Concluded by China: Hague Choice of Court Convention | Multilateral JRE Treaties Concluded by China: Oil Pollution Convention |
|---|---|---|---|---|
| No Jurisdiction | Not explicitly provided | The jurisdiction of the judgment-rendering court shall not impinge on the exclusive jurisdiction of Chinese courts.[99] Twelve JRE treaties provide indirect jurisdiction rules.[100] Six JRE treaties provide that if according to the law of the JRE state, the judgment-rendering court has no jurisdiction, JRE shall be rejected.[101] | A valid choice of court agreement[102] | Where an incident has caused pollution damage in the territorial sea of one or more Contracting States, or preventive measures have been taken to prevent or minimise pollution damage, action for compensation may only be brought in the courts of any such Contracting State(s).[103] |

[99] eg Treaty for Judicial Assistance in Civil and Criminal Affairs between China and Ukraine, entered into force 19 January 1994, art 21.2.

[100] The 12 treaties for judicial assistance are concluded between China and Ethiopia, Cyprus, Kuwait, Italy, Peru, Tunisia, Laos, Spain, Vietnam, Egypt, the United Arab Emirates, and Bosnia and Herzegovina, respectively.

[101] China has concluded treaties for judicial assistance with Bulgaria, Turkey, North Korea, France, Mongolia and Argentina.

[102] Hague Choice of Court Agreement, art 3.

[103] Oil Pollution Convention, art II. This Convention is not applicable to general commercial disputes.

PART III

# Choice of Law

# 7

# Paying Attention to Choice of Law in International Commercial Arbitration

*– or –*

*Why the Conflict of Laws Always Matters*

BENJAMIN HAYWARD*

## I. Introduction

International commercial arbitration is an interesting creature of the dispute resolution jungle. It is ADR, as traditionally defined; an alternative to state court litigation. Yet empirical evidence demonstrates arbitration is a preferred means of international dispute resolution.[1] Like litigation, however, arbitration is a formal process. One or more arbitrators apply the law, to resolve a dispute.[2] In this sense, arbitration has more in common with litigation than other ADR processes such as negotiation, mediation and conciliation.

Right next to this jungle, however, sits the 'swamp'[3] said to constitute private international law. The two environments' borderline is a *particularly* intriguing place to tread.[4] Several arbitration-related paths wind along it, leading to the governing procedural law, procedural rules and substantive law; applicable soft

* Dr Benjamin Hayward is a Senior Lecturer in the Department of Business Law and Taxation, Monash Business School, Monash University. The author extends his thanks to the Sydney Law School's 'Commercial Issues in Private International Law' conference delegates for their helpful comments on an earlier draft of this chapter. Portions of this chapter have been adapted from select passages in B Hayward, *Conflict of Laws and Arbitral Discretion – The Closest Connection Test* (Oxford, Oxford University Press, 2017).

[1] See, eg, the various studies published at School of International Arbitration, 'Research' (*School of International Arbitration*, 2018), www.arbitration.qmul.ac.uk/research/.

[2] G Born, *International Commercial Arbitration*, 2nd edn (Alphen aan den Rijn, Kluwer, 2014) 70 and 1997–98.

[3] W Prosser, 'Interstate Publication' (1952–53) 51 *Michigan Law Review* 959, 971.

[4] M Pryles, 'Choice of Law Issues in International Arbitration' (1997) 15 *The Arbitrator* 250, 260.

law; and the law governing recognition and enforcement (amongst other places).[5] This chapter treads just one, addressing the substantive law governing the merits in international commercial arbitration. It demonstrates that while choice of law and the conflicts of laws are distinct, they have a significant and practically important (but often overlooked) interaction.

Though this path's twists and turns 'may seem to be of interest for professors only',[6] they have real consequences for commercial parties. When agreeing to arbitrate, parties should think carefully about their choice of law clauses; as to their drafting, and their inherent limits.

## II. Definitions and Scope

It is useful to begin with some definitions and matters of scope. *Arbitration* is used as shorthand for *international commercial arbitration. Domestic* commercial arbitration, and international *investment* arbitration, are beyond this chapter's scope.

*Law* is given an inaccurate (but convenient) meaning.[7] In arbitral private international law, law refers to state-promulgated law, contrasted with *rules of law*, also including non-national rules.[8] In this chapter, *law* refers to both concepts; the actual wording of relevant arbitral laws and rules should be consulted to determine which is relevant in any given case.[9]

The terms *choice of law* and *conflicts of laws* are often used interchangeably,[10] though are differentiated here. *Choice of law* describes parties choosing their governing substantive law, as in the following sample clause:

> All questions concerning the construction, validity and interpretation of this Agreement and the performance of the obligations imposed by this Agreement will be governed by the laws of the State of California.[11]

[5] N Blackaby et al, *Redfern and Hunter on International Arbitration*, 6th edn (Oxford, Oxford University Press, 2015) [3.07]; S Greenberg, C Kee and JR Weeramantry, *International Commercial Arbitration – An Asia-Pacific Perspective* (Cambridge, Cambridge University Press, 2011) [3.10].

[6] M Blessing, 'Choice of Substantive Law in International Arbitration' (1997) 14(2) *Journal of International Arbitration* 39, 49.

[7] *Cf* F Blase, 'Proposing a New Road Map for an Old Minefield – The Determination of the Rules Governing the Substance of the Dispute in International Commercial Arbitration' (2003) 20 *Journal of International Arbitration* 267, 269–70.

[8] Blackaby et al, *Redfern and Hunter on International Arbitration* (n 5) [3.189].

[9] B Hayward, *Conflict of Laws and Arbitral Discretion – The Closest Connection Test* (Oxford, Oxford University Press, 2017) [5.35].

[10] See, eg, *TCL Air Conditioner (Zhongshan) Co Ltd v Judges of the Federal Court of Australia* [2013] HCA 5, (2013) 251 CLR 533, [71]; *ICC Case No 5717/1988* (1990) 1(2) ICC Bull 22, 22; L Bergman (ed), *Casebook on Choice of Law in Arbitration* (Sweden, Landa, 2017) 5; A Briggs, 'On Drafting Agreements on Choice of Law' [2003] *Lloyd's Maritime and Commercial Law Quarterly* 389, 392; S Greenberg, 'The Law Applicable to the Merits in International Arbitration' (2004) 8 *Vindobona Journal of International Commercial Law and Arbitration* 315, 315.

[11] Trans-Lex, 'Contract Clauses' (*Principle No XIV.2 – Law Applicable to International Contracts*), www.trans-lex.org/971000/_/law-applicable-to-international-contract.

Though choices of law may be made at any time in arbitration,[12] contractual choices are the most common,[13] so are the focus of this chapter's analysis. *Conflicts of laws* describes arbitrators, rather than parties, identifying the governing substantive law. *Applicable law* and *governing law* are then umbrella terms, describing the law identified through both choice of law and conflicts of laws analyses.

## III. The Problem Stated–Presenting Choice of Law and Conflicts of Laws as Binary Alternatives

The applicable law in arbitration affects the determination of party rights and obligations, the performance of contractual obligations, the ability of parties to present and argue their cases, and decision-making around settlement.[14] It is therefore an important matter for commercial parties. As such, the relationship between the choice and conflicts of laws should be clearly understood. This may seem straightforward; given that arbitrators have a duty to apply the law,[15] and that choice of law must be respected,[16] surely conflicts questions only arise where no party choice is made?

It is true that conflicts analyses are necessary where there is no choice of law.[17] Nevertheless, this dividing line is porous. While an absence of choice implicates conflicts of laws, a presence of party choice does not *necessarily* negate the need for conflicts analyses.

The problem addressed by this chapter arises because choice of law and the conflicts of laws are often (incorrectly) presented as binary alternatives. Lew, Mistelis and Kröll, for example, suggest that '[p]arty autonomy provides contracting parties with a mechanism of avoiding the application of an unfavourable or inappropriate law to an international dispute',[18] and go on to assert that party choice renders arbitrators' own identification of the law 'unnecessary'.[19] Similarly, the authors of *Redfern and Hunter* argue that '[i]f the parties do not wish the arbitral tribunal to have such freedom of action [ie itself identifying the governing law], the remedy is in their own hands: they should agree upon the applicable law',

[12] Greenberg, Kee and Weeramantry, *International Commercial Arbitration* (n 5) [3.22].

[13] See, eg, International Chamber of Commerce, '2016 ICC Dispute Resolution Statistics' [2017] (2) *ICC Dispute Resolution Bulletin* 106, 112. See also Hayward, *Conflict of Laws and Arbitral Discretion* (n 9) [1.44]. At the time of writing, the International Chamber of Commerce's 2017 dispute resolution statistics were not yet published.

[14] Hayward (n 9) [1.47]–[1.85].

[15] Born, *International Commercial Arbitration* (n 2) 1997–99; *SCC Case Code 604 (2011)* in Bergman (ed), *Casebook on Choice of Law in Arbitration* (n 10) 260, 262.

[16] *ICC Case No 1512/1971* (1976) I YBCA 128, [3.A].

[17] E Gaillard and J Savage (eds), *Fouchard, Gaillard, Goldman on International Commercial Arbitration* (The Hague, Kluwer, 1999) [1537].

[18] J Lew, L Mistelis and S Kröll, *Comparative International Commercial Arbitration* (The Hague, Kluwer, 2003) [17-8].

[19] ibid [17-6]; *Cf* ibid 424, fn 50.

and if they fail to do so, 'it will fall to the arbitral tribunal to make a decision that is likely to impact on the outcome of the arbitration'.[20]

It is *sometimes* (possibly often) the case that the parties' chosen law is all that need be referred to.[21] Nevertheless, such commentaries risk implying that choice of law clauses *necessarily* prevent conflicts of laws arising. In other words, commercial parties may presume that choice of law clauses implicate absolute certainty.[22] This is inaccurate, and would be unfortunate, given that certainty is empirically-established as a key factor motivating choices of law.[23]

In actual fact, choices of law interact with conflicts of laws. Existing literature recognises this point to a limited extent,[24] though this chapter analyses this issue in a systematic fashion. Choice of law clauses do not secure absolute certainty – their effectiveness is instead subject to inherent limits, and the parties' own drafting.

It is an 'oddity of modern contractual drafting' that 'considerable energy' is devoted to jurisdiction agreements, while choice of law clauses may be approached 'with an air so casual it may be taken for dismissive'.[25] This chapter argues that commercial parties should pay careful attention to their choices of law, and understand that conflicts of laws can still always matter.

## IV. The Interactions of Choice of Law and Conflicts of Laws in International Commercial Arbitration

Notwithstanding an (apparent) choice of law, arbitrators may still be required to identify a governing law for one, more, or possibly all issues in dispute. Choice of law clauses will not prevent conflicts of laws arising, or otherwise avoid the need for conflicts analyses, in nine categories of case. These categories reflect the inherent limits, and drafting, of choices of law. On the latter point, choice of law clauses

[20] Blackaby et al (n 5) [3.220].

[21] See, eg, *ICC Case No 7375/1996* (1996) 11(12) Mealey's A-1, [242]–[290]; *ICC Case No 8177/1995* (2001) 12(2) ICC Bull 85, [2.5].

[22] See, eg, G Cordero-Moss, 'International Arbitration and the Quest for the Applicable Law' (2008) 8(3) *Global Jurist Advances* [Article 2], 4.

[23] LG Meira Moser, 'Choice of Law in Practice – A Global Empirical Survey' in I Schwenzer (ed), *35 Years CISG and Beyond* (The Hague, Eleven International Publishing, 2016) 9, 14.

[24] See, eg, Lew, Mistelis and Kröll, *Comparative International Commercial Arbitration* (n 18) 424, fn 50; C Croft, C Kee and J Waincymer, *A Guide to the UNCITRAL Arbitration Rules* (Cambridge, Cambridge University Press, 2013) [35.9]–[35.10], [35.12] and [35.14]–[35.15]; M Blessing, 'Mandatory Rules of Law Versus Party Autonomy in International Arbitration' (1997) 14(4) *Journal of International Arbitration* 23, 23–24; Cordero-Moss, 'Quest for the Applicable Law' (n 22) 4; G Cordero-Moss, 'Can an Arbitral Tribunal Disregard the Choice of Law Made by the Parties?' (2005) 1 *Stockholm International Arbitration Review* 1, 10.

[25] A Briggs, 'Contractual Agreements on Choice of Law: Some Notes Towards an Understanding of Their Relative Effect' in A Burrows and E Peel (eds), *Contract Terms* (Oxford, Oxford University Press, 2007) 315, 318.

(like all contractual provisions) are 'subject to the normal criteria for interpreting the intention of the parties'.[26]

These nine categories of case arise where:

- the parties' choice of law does not deal with all matters in dispute;
- the parties' choice of law is only a negative choice;
- disputes arise concerning legal issues not within the scope of the parties' choice of law rights;
- the parties' (apparent) choice of law is actually a choice of private international law;
- the parties' (apparent) choice of law is actually an incorporation of contractual terms by reference;
- there is a battle of forms, and the parties' standard terms include conflicting choice of law clauses;
- statutory provisions require conflicts analyses, irrespective of any party choice of law;
- there is an (apparent) choice of law clause, but it is ineffective for being unclear, invalid or indecisive; and
- mandatory law lays claim to application irrespective of the parties' chosen law.

## A. Where the Parties' Choice of Law Does not Deal with all Matters in Dispute

The first category arises where a choice of law does not deal with all matters in dispute. Notwithstanding that choice, conflicts questions may arise for legal issues beyond its scope. This category reflects limits imposed by party drafting.

### *i. Where a Choice of Law Clause Uses Restrictive Language*

A choice of law clause using restrictive language risks confining its operation, as a matter of interpretation, to particular legal issues. Such clauses are binding, but incomplete, thus conflicts analyses identify the law governing other issues in dispute. That law may or may not be the same as the parties' chosen law; but even if it is, it applies because of the arbitrators' own analysis.

Briggs gives (as a hypothetical example, in the litigation context) a clause providing that '[t]his agreement shall be construed in accordance with Y law'.[27]

[26] M Rubino-Sammartano, *International Arbitration – Law and Practice*, 3rd edn (New York, Juris Publishing, 2014) 634.

[27] Briggs, 'On Drafting' (n 10) 390.

This clause only refers to contractual interpretation, and not the parties' overall obligations. Though being a 'rather worse' drafting example,[28] similar clauses are evident in arbitral practice.

International Chamber of Commerce (ICC) jurisprudence is illustrative. *ICC Case No 9517/1998* is close to this example, where parties chose Dubai law for their contract's 'construction and effect'.[29] The arbitrators ultimately identified Dubai law as applicable to all issues in dispute, supplementing this incomplete choice with their own conflicts analysis.[30] Similarly, *ICC Case No 9479/1999* involved a choice of New York law to 'determine any dispute relating to the validity of this Agreement and Stipulation'.[31] In holding the parties strictly to their language, the tribunal emphasised the importance of careful drafting:

> [The parties] were perfectly aware of the restrictive implication of the language that they were using. Indeed, the first draft of the Agreement … indicates that 'the laws of the State of New York shall be the law pursuant to which this Agreement shall be construed and enforced at any arbitration proceedings brought under this Agreement'. A comparison of this language and of that of Article 12(b) of the Agreement eventually executed in 1987 leads to the conclusion that, after negotiations, the parties agreed to restrict the intervention of the law of the State of New York to questions relating to the validity of the Agreement.[32]

The parties' choice was supplemented with usages and international public policy, it being determined that state law was not intended to apply any further than the clause provided (given the contract's truly international nature).[33] This decision demonstrates the risks of incautious drafting – such norms may run counter to the certainty considerations motivating choices of law in the first place.

Stockholm Chamber of Commerce (SCC) awards are also illustrative. In *SCC Case Code 72 (1996)*, a 'limited' choice of law clause selected Lithuanian law 'with regard to certain enumerated issues', being 'corporate activities and corporate structure'.[34] Given that 'all [contractual] functions of any significance' were to be performed in Lithuania, its law was also applied to the claimant's request for the payment of interest, though as a result of the arbitrators' own analysis rather than the parties' choice of law.[35]

Perhaps the most interesting example here is *ICC Case No 8711/1998*, involving a commercial agency dispute, a choice of Austrian law, and an exclusion of mandatory rules relating to Austrian domestic agents.[36] The overall applicability of Austrian law was 'fundamentally agreed', though the tribunal was required to

[28] ibid.
[29] *ICC Case No 9517/1998* (2002) 13(2) ICC Bull 87, 88.
[30] ibid.
[31] *ICC Case No 9479/1999* (2001) 12(2) ICC Bull 67, 68.
[32] ibid.
[33] ibid 68–69.
[34] *SCC Case Code 72 (1996)* in Bergman (ed) (n 10) 64, 64.
[35] ibid 65–66.
[36] *ICC Case No 8711/1998* (2001) 12(1) ICC Bull 120, 120.

interpret the parties' qualification, given that Austrian law contained no provisions specifically addressing domestic agents.[37] After determining the relevant compensation provision, the tribunal identified two possible ways to proceed (it being unnecessary to choose between them). First, it could check whether the parties' exclusion was permitted under Austrian law; as the provision was non-excludable, it would be applied.[38] Alternatively, were the exclusion effective, there would be 'no choice of law for this area', requiring the law for that particular point to be arbitrally-identified via the Austrian Private International Law Act – Italian law would govern.[39] In this second scenario, rather than the parties excluding the legal rule *simpliciter*, a gap would be created, which private international law would fill. Though both Austrian and Italian law were ultimately to the same effect,[40] the case is an interesting example as to how restrictive language might present in practice.

### *ii. Where a Choice of Law Clause Governs Contractual Issues only*

A choice of law's language might also restrict its operation to contractual issues. Even if contractually comprehensive, it may be inapplicable to related tortious claims.[41]

This issue arose in the arbitration underlying *Abu Dhabi Investment Authority v Citigroup, Inc*, a US court decision declining to vacate an arbitral award.[42] The parties' investment agreement provided that '[t]he Transaction Documents will be governed by and construed in accordance with the laws of the State of New York applicable to contracts made and to be performed entirely within such State'.[43] Its language did not extend to the 'non-contract, common law tort claims' (fraud and misrepresentation) raised in the arbitration, and the arbitrators themselves identified the law governing those issues.[44] The award debtor's challenge to the award based on that determination ultimately failed, as the arbitrators had properly discharged their conflicts function under the applicable arbitration rules.[45]

This issue also arose in *ICC Case No 13641/2007*.[46] The parties had concluded a shareholder agreement, and the claimant accused the respondent of breaching

[37] ibid.
[38] ibid 121.
[39] ibid.
[40] ibid.
[41] Croft, Kee and Waincymer, *A Guide to the UNCITRAL Arbitration Rules* (n 24) [35.12].
[42] *Abu Dhabi Investment Authority v Citigroup, Inc* (US Dist Ct, SD NY, No 12 Civ 283 (GBD), 4 March 2013) 9; affd *Abu Dhabi Investment Authority v Citigroup, Inc*, 557 Fed Appx 66, 67–68 (2nd Cir, 2014).
[43] *Abu Dhabi Investment Authority v Citigroup, Inc* (US Dist Ct, SD NY, No 12 Civ 283 (GBD), 4 March 2013) 1, fn 1.
[44] ibid 1–2.
[45] ibid 1 and 5–7.
[46] *ICC Case No 13641/2007* (2014) 25(1) ICC Bull 56.

fiduciary obligations under German law.[47] The respondent argued that the claim was time-barred under New York law, in accordance with the parties' choice.[48] As the parties' choice governed '[t]his Agreement', the tribunal confined its operation to contractual matters; noting that if New York law were to govern the 'entire relationship', there were 'a myriad of alternative formulations' that could have achieved that result.[49]

As with the restrictive language example, however, this is always a matter of interpretation. *ICC Case No 9651/2000* is an interesting counter-example, where a choice of law ostensibly confined to the parties' contract *did* extend to misrepresentation and fraud, given a hypothetical-reasonable-businessperson's interpretation of the clause.[50]

### *iii. Where a Choice of Law is in Favour of a Non-Comprehensive Body of Law*

The first two examples in this category of case implicate incompleteness deriving from the parties' language. By way of contrast, choices in favour of non-comprehensive bodies of law are *necessarily* incomplete, given their subject-matter.

This example does not arise where parties choose state law. State law is necessarily complete, even if the resolution of particular cases requires analogous reasoning, or the application of general principles.[51] Incompleteness does arise, however, where parties choose an international convention, or non-national rules. Such choices must be respected, but are necessarily finite in scope. For example, Art 4 of the United Nations Convention on Contracts for the International Sale of Goods (CISG) limits the Convention's subject-matter scope to contract formation, and party rights and obligations.[52] Where parties choose the CISG, as opposed to the Convention applying as part of state law, there must still be 'a second set of rules of law for those issues which the CISG does not address'.[53] This, in turn, implicates private international law;[54] being the arbitrators' own conflicts analysis.

Two SCC awards involving the CISG illustrate this point. In *SCC Case Code 359 (2005)*, a tribunal concluded that Russian law supplemented the CISG, given the case's 'strong connection to Russia';[55] while in *SCC Case Code 604 (2011)*,

[47] ibid 56.
[48] ibid.
[49] ibid [68]–[69].
[50] *ICC Case No 9651/2000* (2001) 12(2) ICC Bull 76, [23]. See generally ibid [20]–[24].
[51] *Cf* Gaillard and Savage (eds), *Fouchard, Gaillard, Goldman on International Commercial Arbitration* (n 17) [1512].
[52] W Khoo, 'Article 4' in CM Bianca and MJ Bonell (eds), *Commentary on the International Sales Law* (Milan, Giuffrè, 1987) 44, [2.4].
[53] Blase, 'Proposing a New Road Map for an Old Minefield' (n 7) 275.
[54] P Schlechtriem, 'Requirements of Application and Sphere of Applicability of the CISG' (2005) 36 *Victoria University of Wellington Law Review* 781, 788.
[55] *SCC Case Code 359 (2005)* in Bergman (ed) (n 10) 197, 197.

the tribunal made a direct choice of Swedish law to supplement the CISG in relation to interest.[56] Similarly, in *SCC Case Code 114 (1998)*, the CISG's application was agreed at the hearing; Ukrainian law was determined as the supplemental law by the tribunal based on Swedish conflicts rules.[57]

A final (though unusual) example is given by *ICC Case No 9797/2000*, the well-known *Andersen Award*, where the tribunal itself decided to apply the *lex mercatoria*.[58] Quite apart from the content of that determination, however, those general principles applied where the parties' chosen rules of law were 'silent' – the parties had adopted (as governing) the necessarily non-comprehensive Andersen group Member Firm Interfirm Agreements, and the AWSC Articles and Bylaws.[59]

## B. Where the Parties' Choice of Law is only a Negative Choice

When agreeing to arbitrate, parties may make negative (as well as positive) choices of law. Negative choices *exclude* one or more laws, and may be express or implied.[60] They may also operate alongside positive choices, as in *ICC Case No 7375/1996* (an implied negative choice of both parties' home state laws, and an implied positive choice of a-national principles),[61] and as under the *tronc commun* (an implied negative choice of rules differing in each party's home state, and an implied positive choice of rules common to both, with general principles and usages 'filling any gaps').[62]

This second category of case arises where parties *only* make a negative choice. Arbitrators must respect that choice, but must themselves determine the law that *is* applicable. The parties' choice narrows (but doesn't eliminate) a tribunal's residual conflicts discretion.[63]

This category may give rise to considerable difficulty, depending upon the conflicts methodology at issue. For example, what should be done under Art 23(2) of the DIS Rules 1998 (and similar rules) where parties make a negative choice of all laws connected to the dispute?[64] How would a tribunal 'apply the law of the State with which the subject-matter of the proceedings is most closely connected'?[65]

[56] *SCC Case Code 604 (2011)* in Bergman (ed) (n 10), 260, 260–62.

[57] *SCC Case Code 114 (1988)* in Bergman (ed) (n 10), 93, 93–96.

[58] *ICC Case No 9797/2000* (2000) 15(8) Mealey's A-1, A-3.

[59] ibid.

[60] Gaillard and Savage (eds) (n 17) [1442]; Blessing, 'Choice of Substantive Law' (n 6) 43–45.

[61] *ICC Case No 7375/1996* (1996) 11(12) Mealey's A-1, [273]–[290].

[62] JF Poudret and S Besson, *Comparative Law of International Arbitration*, 2nd edn (S Berti and A Ponti trs, London, Sweet & Maxwell, 2007) [687]. See also Rubino-Sammartano, *International Arbitration* (n 26) 673–75.

[63] Croft, Kee and Waincymer (n 24) [35.14].

[64] *Cf* Blase (n 7) 282–83.

[65] DIS Rules 1998, Art 23(2). See also Swiss Rules 2012, Art 33(1). *Cf* DIS Rules 2018, Art 24(2).

A tribunal might need to treat the parties as contractually derogating from the requirement that a connected law be applied, that state law be applied, or both.[66] Opportunities for uncertainty abound.

Even this category of case is evidenced in arbitral practice. In *SCC Case Code 289 (2006)*, the parties' dispute resolution clause provided for arbitration in Sweden, and contained the following stipulation as to the applicable law:

> The Contract shall be construed and interpreted according to such law as determined by the arbitration committee ... however, the law of the Seller's or Buyer's country shall not apply.[67]

The tribunal noted that this clause made the closest connection test in Art 4(1) of the Rome Convention 'redundant', given that the parties' home state laws 'would ordinarily have been considered most closely connected', and ultimately applied Swedish law; though whether this was based on choice or conflicts of laws considerations is not entirely clear.[68] What is clear, however, is that complex interactions between choice of law and conflicts of laws arise where only a negative choice is made.

## C. Where Disputes Arise Concerning Legal Issues not within the Scope of the Parties' Choice of Law Rights

Some commentary suggests that conflicts analyses are only necessary where parties do not choose the law, or only make a limited choice.[69] The first two categories conform to this description, but others, including this third category, do not. Sometimes, an issue in dispute may be beyond the scope of party autonomy. Even a comprehensive choice of law clause will not preclude conflicts analyses with respect to these specific legal issues, which include the parties' 'personal status and capacity to contract'.[70]

### *i. Capacity and Authority*

Capacity (to enter into a contract) and authority (to represent a corporation) attract particular applicable law considerations in arbitration. This is not novel. Under Art VI(2) of the European Convention,[71] where the validity of an arbitration agreement is at issue, questions concerning the parties' capacity are dealt with

[66] Blase (n 7) 283.
[67] *SCC Case Code 289 (2006)* in Bergman (ed) (n 10) 175, 175.
[68] ibid 176–77.
[69] Greenberg, Kee and Weeramantry (n 5) [3.26].
[70] J-L Delvolvé, G Pointon and J Rouche, *French Arbitration Law and Practice: A Dynamic Civil Law Approach to International Arbitration*, 2nd edn (Alphen aan den Rijn, Kluwer, 2009) [258].
[71] European Convention on International Commercial Arbitration (adopted 21 April 1961, entered into force 7 January 1964) 484 UNTS 364.

'under the law applicable to them'. Applying a party's personal law to these issues, irrespective of any chosen law, remains the approach taken today.[72] Effectively, a unique conflicts rule is applied, rather than the more general methodologies used to identify the *lex contractus* at large.[73]

This approach aims to reduce transaction costs; capacity and authority are determined consistently, by a stable law, rather than varying according to the law chosen in any particular case.[74] The law governing these issues may have a significant impact in arbitration – as arbitral jurisdiction is consent-based, an absence of capacity or authority is a basis upon which that jurisdiction (and any resulting award) may be challenged.[75]

### a. Capacity

Disputes concerning both capacity to contract and capacity to enter into an arbitration agreement may require conflicts analyses, even if the parties choose a law.[76] This proposition is not universally accepted,[77] though capacity is generally seen as the classic manifestation of this category of case.[78]

In *SCC Case Code 80 (1995)* (a loan agreement dispute), the parties' contract chose Swedish law, though the respondent Russian party argued it was not bound – under Russian law, the agreement required two signatures (only one person had signed), and that person was not competent in any event.[79] Authority (the second point) is addressed below; the tribunal applied Russian law to both matters.[80] Under Russian law, it was 'at least doubtful' that a binding agreement was initially concluded, though binding relations were ultimately established by the parties' later conduct.[81]

[72] *ICC Case No 6474/1992* (2004) 15(2) ICC Bull 102, [150]; Greenberg, Kee and Weeramantry (n 5) [3.15]; P Burckhardt and P Groz, 'The Law Governing the Merits of the Dispute and Awards *Ex Aequo et Bono*' in E Geisinger, N Voser and A Petti (eds), *International Arbitration in Switzerland: A Handbook for Practitioners*, 2nd edn (Alphen aan den Rijn, Kluwer, 2013) 153, 163–64.

[73] *Cf ICC Case No 13954/2007* (2010) XXXV YBCA 218, [23]; Burckhardt and Groz, 'The Law Governing the Merits of the Dispute and Awards *Ex Aequo et Bono*' (n 72) 164.

[74] J Basedow, '*Lex Mercatoria* and the Private International Law of Contracts in Economic Perspective' (2007) 12 *Uniform Law Review* 697, 700; Y Derains, 'Choice of the Law Applicable to the Contract and International Arbitration' (1995) 6(1) *ICC International Court of Arbitration Bulletin* 10, 16.

[75] New York Convention, Art V(1)(a); Model Law 2006, Art 34(2)(a)(i). See, eg, *ICC Case No 6474/1992* (2004) 15(2) ICC Bull 102, [139]–[141].

[76] Greenberg, Kee and Weeramantry (n 5) [3.15]; Cordero-Moss, 'Disregard the Choice' (n 24) 10; Cordero-Moss (n 22) 4.

[77] M Lehmann, 'Liberating the Individual From Battles Between States: Justifying Party Autonomy in Conflict of Laws' (2008) 41 *Vanderbilt Journal of Transnational Law* 381, 424. See also J Waincymer, *Procedure and Evidence in International Arbitration* (Alphen aan den Rijn, Kluwer, 2012) 151.

[78] See, eg, Croft, Kee and Waincymer (n 24) [35.5]; T Zuberbühler, K Muller and P Habegger, *Swiss Rules of International Arbitration: Commentary* (The Hague, Kluwer, 2005) [11].

[79] *SCC Case Code 80 (1995)* in Bergman (ed) (n 10) 73, 73.

[80] ibid 74.

[81] ibid 74–75.

*SCC Case Code 292 (2007)*[82] and *SCC Case Code 480 (2010)*[83] both address capacity regarding arbitration agreements, similarly finding the respondents' capacities were governed by the law of their places of incorporation, choice of law notwithstanding. UAE law governed the contract (with the law of the People's Republic of China and Yemeni law governing capacity) in the former;[84] Ukrainian law governed the contract (with Delaware law governing capacity) in the latter.[85] The delineation of capacity from the merits is particularly well demonstrated by *SCC Case Code 292 (2007)*; the law of each party's place of incorporation governed whether they were bound to arbitrate as non-signatories (a genuine capacity issue),[86] while agency arguments addressing the same factual circumstances were governed by the contractually-chosen UAE law (agency being a matter going to the merits, rather than a capacity or authority matter as defined here).[87]

#### b. Authority

Authority questions may also relate to the parties' contract, or their arbitration agreement. In *SCC Case Code 507 (2009)*, the parties' contract chose New Jersey law, though the authority of the respondent's signatory to the arbitration agreement was assessed under Nevada law (Nevada being the respondent's place of incorporation).[88] Similarly, in *SCC Case Code 170 (2000)*, Russian law (the respondent's home law) determined whether there was authority to bind the respondent to the main contract, notwithstanding a Swedish choice of law.[89]

That this analysis goes to the inherent limits of choice of law clauses, as opposed to their interpretation, is confirmed by *SCC Case Code 215 (2001)*.[90] That case involved fishing industry contracts, governed by Swedish law, with an argument raised that the Russian respondent's signatory did not have the right to represent it, or sign on its behalf.[91] Russian law resolved those issues,[92] even though the parties' choice of law clauses selected Swedish law 'as to all matters'.[93]

### *ii. Whether a Party to the Arbitration is a Party to the Contract*

Another example of this category of case arises where a party to the arbitration argues that they are not party to the commercial contract at issue. This is

[82] *SCC Case Code 292 (2007)* in Bergman (ed) (n 10) 178.
[83] *SCC Case Code 480 (2010)* in Bergman (ed) (n 10) 229.
[84] *SCC Case Code 292 (2007)* in Bergman (ed) (n 10) 178, 185–87.
[85] *SCC Case Code 480 (2010)* in Bergman (ed) (n 10) 229, 230.
[86] *SCC Case Code 292 (2007)* in Bergman (ed) (n 10) 178, 185–87.
[87] ibid 183–85.
[88] *SCC Case Code 507 (2009)* in Bergman (ed) (n 10) 239, 239–40.
[89] *SCC Case Code 170 (2000)* in Bergman (ed) (n 10) 117, 117 and 121.
[90] *SCC Case Code 215 (2001)* in Bergman (ed) (n 10) 153.
[91] ibid 153–54.
[92] ibid 154.
[93] ibid 153.

not, however, a universally accepted example. Pursuant to Art 8(1) of the Rome Convention and Art 10(1) of the Rome I Regulation on the law applicable to contractual obligations (Regulation (EC) No 593/2008), a contract's 'existence and validity' is determined by its putatively chosen law.

This issue arose in *ICC Case No 6268/1990*.[94] There, the parties' contract identified New York law as governing, though it was disputed whether the clause was properly construed as a choice of law.[95] Party Y argued that it was not party to the contract, and the tribunal explained that in resolving this issue, 'we would not resort to a choice of law in the contract itself to determine in the first instance whether that contract binds Y'.[96] New York law was ultimately applied, but on the basis of the tribunal's own conflicts analysis, and its conclusion that 'the locus of the transaction [is] in New York'.[97]

### *iii. The Legal Status of a Party*

The rationale for subjecting the laws governing capacity and authority to their own conflicts analysis, notwithstanding party choice of law, lies in the need for stability in that law's identity. This same rationale explains this final example – a party's legal status, regarding the effects of insolvency.[98]

*SCC Case Code 525 (2010)* addressed this issue, involving a choice of Swedish law, and a respondent subject to German insolvency proceedings.[99] As explained by the tribunal, German law was consulted to determine the effects of those proceedings:

> As neither Swedish law, applicable in the case at hand, nor German law, applicable to the Respondent's legal status, rules that an insolvency proceeding will automatically suspend an arbitration proceeding, the Arbitral Tribunal repeatedly inquired whether the Receiver intended to participate in the present proceeding.[100]

## D. Where the Parties' (Apparent) Choice of Law is Actually a Choice of Private International Law

The fourth category of case returns to interpretation. An (apparent) choice of law will not eliminate conflicts of laws where interpreted as a choice of private international law. At issue is whether the parties' choice includes the chosen law's conflicts rules; a question of *renvoi*.[101]

[94] *ICC Case No 6268/1990* (1990) 1(2) ICC Bull 23.
[95] ibid 23.
[96] ibid.
[97] ibid.
[98] Derains, 'Choice of the Law Applicable to the Contract and International Arbitration' (n 74) 16.
[99] *SCC Case Code 525 (2010)* in Bergman (ed) (n 10) 248, 248–49.
[100] ibid 249.
[101] Croft, Kee and Waincymer (n 24) [35.12].

As explained by Blessing, parties '[o]ccasionally' (but 'very rarely') cannot agree on a governing law, but do agree on conflicts rules instead.[102] Arbitrators are bound by such agreements,[103] constituting exercises of party autonomy.[104] Cases such as *ICC Case No 6560/1990*, involving express agreement on conflicts methodology,[105] reflect this point. More difficult are those cases involving clauses appearing to be choices of substantive law on their face, which are nevertheless interpreted as referring to private international law.

If express choices of private international law are rare, choices *interpreted* as referring to private international law are surely rarer, as arbitral laws and rules generally exclude *renvoi*. Some specify that *renvoi* is inapplicable, by presuming that references to state law exclude conflicts rules.[106] This presumption's generally-accepted nature is evidenced by inclusion in the Trans-Lex Principles[107] and in Art 8 of the Hague Principles on Choice of Law in International Commercial Contracts (Hague Principles), and though not all arbitral laws and rules contain express anti-*renvoi* provisions,[108] *renvoi* is often considered excluded in any event.[109]

Choices of law sometimes contractually exclude *renvoi*,[110] though in principle, this should not be required to ensure a choice of substantive law. Merely *interpreting* clauses as choosing conflicts rules 'would very seldom accord with

[102] M Blessing, 'Regulations in Arbitration Rules on Choice of Law' in AJ van den Berg (ed), *Planning Efficient Arbitration Proceedings / The Law Applicable in International Arbitration (ICCA Congress Series Vol 7, Vienna, 1994)* (The Hague, Kluwer, 1996) 391, 393.

[103] K Hobér, 'Arbitration Reform in Sweden' (2001) 17 *Arbitration International* 351, 374.

[104] Waincymer, *Procedure and Evidence in International Arbitration* (n 77) 986.

[105] *ICC Case No 6560/1990* (1992) XVII YBCA 226, [4].

[106] See, eg, Model Law 2006, Art 28(1); Arbitration Act 1996, s 46(2); British Columbia International Commercial Arbitration Centre Rules 2000, Art 30(2); Dubai International Arbitration Centre Rules 2007, Art 33(2); Hungarian Chamber of Commerce and Industry Rules 2011, Art 14(1); Hong Kong International Arbitration Centre Rules 2013, Art 35(1); International Commercial Arbitration Court Rules 2017, Art 23(1); Stockholm Chamber of Commerce Rules 2017, Art 27(2); Vienna International Arbitral Centre Rules 2018, Art 27(1). At the time of writing, the Dubai International Arbitration Centre Rules and the Hong Kong International Arbitration Centre Rules were under revision, but those revisions had not yet been finalised or come into effect. Also at the time of writing, promulgation of the Hungarian Chamber of Commerce and Industry Rules 2018 had been reported in the legal press, though the institution's website still contained only the 2011 version of its rules.

[107] Trans-Lex Principles, Art XIII.4.1(a). See Trans-Lex, 'Principle' (*Principle No XIII.4.1 – Rules Applicable to Merits; Decision Ex Aequo et Bono*) www.trans-lex.org/970020/_/rules-applicable-to-merits-decision-ex-aequo-et-bono.

[108] See, eg, French Arbitration Law 2011, Art 1511; Swiss Private International Law Act 1987, Art 187(1); United Nations Commission on International Trade Law Arbitration Rules 2010, Art 35(1); Australian Centre for International Commercial Arbitration Rules 2016, Art 39(1); Milan Chamber of Arbitration Rules 2010, Art 3(1); Danish Institute of Arbitration Rules 2013, Art 17(3); German Arbitration Institute Rules 2018, Art 24(1); International Chamber of Commerce Rules 2017, Art 21(1); International Centre for Dispute Resolution Rules 2014, Art 31(1); JAMS Rules 2016, Art 19(1); Japan Commercial Arbitration Association Rules 2015, Art 60(1); London Court of International Arbitration Rules 2014, Art 22(3); Netherlands Arbitration Institute Rules 2015, Art 42(2); Resolution Institute Rules 2016, Art 35(1); Singapore International Arbitration Centre Rules 2016, Art 31(1); Swiss Rules 2012, Art 33(1).

[109] Born (n 2) 2736. See, eg, Croft, Kee and Waincymer (n 24) [35.10] – with respect to the United Nations Commission on International Trade Law Arbitration Rules 2010, Art 35(1).

[110] See, eg, *ICC Case No 13641/2007* (2014) 25(1) ICC Bull 56, [68]; *ICC Case No 9479/1999* (2001) 12(2) ICC Bull 67, 68; *SCC Case Code 680 (2012)* in Bergman (ed) (n 10) 283, 283.

the expectations of commercial parties', given the certainty motivations at play.[111] In these circumstances, it is unsurprising that choices of private international law are typically 'made explicit'.[112] Nevertheless, the question is always one of interpretation,[113] and awards evidencing this category of case do exist.

*ICC Case No 6360/1990*[114] is one example. The parties' contract provided that disputes would be given 'into the hands of the International Chamber of Commerce in The Hague Holland based on Dutch law'.[115] The tribunal applied Dutch private international law, leading to 'Dutch law as it would apply in the Netherlands Antilles'.[116] It noted that this decision did not conflict with an interpretation of the clause as referring to substantive law,[117] though such conflict could easily arise if a chosen state's conflicts rules did not (coincidentally) lead back to that same state's substantive law.

Another example is *ICC Case No 5607/1989*, where the parties' choice of law provided 'Austrian law will be applicable'.[118] The tribunal noted that this clause could be interpreted as a choice of conflicts rules, or a choice of substantive law, and explained why only conflicts rules had been chosen (with quite remarkable reasoning, illustrating the difficult nature of these cases, as mentioned above):

> The Arbitral Tribunal considered that the choice of Vienna – and incidentally of Austrian jurisdiction – was in all likelihood governed by considerations of subsequent enforcement of the award; it also considered that the dispute had no other connection with Austria; in view of the circumstances, there were in its opinion no reasonable grounds for supposing … that the parties had wished to provide for more than the application of Austrian civil procedure and Austrian conflict rules[.][119]

## E. Where the Parties' (Apparent) Choice of Law is Actually an Incorporation of Contractual Terms by Reference

An (apparent) choice of law will also not avoid the need for conflicts analyses where interpreted as incorporating contractual terms by reference.

Waincymer explains that respecting choice of law 'makes sense' as '[t]he whole essence of contract is that the parties may agree on the terms and conditions of their commercial relationship'.[120] Waincymer notes that parties could simply reproduce a desired law's rules into their contract, but this is 'time consuming

[111] Born (n 2) 2736.
[112] N Natov, 'The Autonomy of Arbitrators in Determining the Law Applicable to the Merits of a Case' in A Bělohlávek and N Rozehnalová (eds), *Czech (& Central European) Yearbook of Arbitration vol II – Party Autonomy Versus Autonomy of Arbitrators* (New York, Juris Publishing, 2012) 171, [9.06].
[113] Croft, Kee and Waincymer (n 24) [35.12].
[114] *ICC Case No 6360/1990* (1990) 1(2) ICC Bull 24.
[115] ibid 24.
[116] ibid.
[117] ibid.
[118] *ICC Case No 5607/1989* (2002) 13(2) ICC Bull 55, 55.
[119] ibid 55–56.
[120] Waincymer (n 77) 985.

and costly', and can be avoided with a 'shorthand' choice of law.[121] Nevertheless, important differences exist between contractual terms and the applicable law. At least according to the common law's world view, contracts are contracts only because the law recognises them and gives them legal effect.[122] As summarised by Born, in the arbitration context:

> [T]he arbitrator's mandate is not simply to apply the terms of the parties' contract … but *instead to apply the applicable law*, including any relevant provisions of mandatory law, in order to resolve the parties' dispute in accordance with the law.[123]

There is a crucial conceptual difference, therefore, between 'incorporation' and 'choice'.[124] Incorporating contractual terms is *subject to* the law and its mandatory provisions.[125] Where parties only incorporate contractual terms by reference, their contract remains in need of a governing law, identified by arbitrators through conflicts analyses. The very same legal provisions may govern as law – though this follows from the arbitrators' analysis, rather than the parties' choice.

This category of case might arise where parties choose non-national bodies of rules. The CISG, and the Principles of International Commercial Contracts promulgated by the International Institute for the Unification of Private Law (UNIDROIT Principles), have been described as 'wonderful source[s] of off-the-shelf provisions which can be incorporated into a contract as part of its terms'.[126] Where the CISG is incorporated as contractual terms, its operation is subject to mandatory provisions in the otherwise applicable law, identified via conflicts analyses.[127] Though not directly applicable in arbitration,[128] the Rome I Regulation recognises that parties may incorporate non-national rules as contractual terms, separately to any question as to a contract's governing law.[129] The matter is one of interpretation. Have the parties genuinely chosen particular rules as rules of law, or merely incorporated them as contractual terms?

This question arose, concerning the CISG, in *ICC Case No 7585/1992*.[130] The parties' sales contract, addressing a production line of foamed boards, provided 'this agreement shall be governed by and construed in accordance with the United Nations Convention on Contracts for the International Sale of Goods of

[121] ibid.

[122] *Amin Rasheed Shipping Corp v Kuwait Insurance Co (The Al Wahab)* [1984] 1 AC 50, 65.

[123] Born (n 2) 1997–98.

[124] U Drobnig, 'The UNIDROIT Principles in the Conflict of Laws' (1998) 3 *Uniform Law Review* 385, 386.

[125] C Bisping, 'The Common European Sales Law, Consumer Protection and Overriding Mandatory Provisions in Private International Law' (2013) 62 *International and Comparative Law Quarterly* 463, 465.

[126] P Finn, 'National Contract Law and Transnational Norms and Practices' (Cross-Border Collaboration, Convergence and Conflict conference, Sydney, February 2010) 12.

[127] Bisping, 'The Common European Sales Law, Consumer Protection and Overriding Mandatory Provisions in Private International Law' (n 125) 476.

[128] G Carducci, 'The Impact of the EU "Rome I" Regulation on International Litigation and Arbitration, A-National Law, Mandatory and Overriding Rules' (2011) 22(2) *ICC International Court of Arbitration Bulletin* 31, 32–34 and 42.

[129] Rome I Regulation, Recital (13).

[130] *ICC Case No 7585/1992* (1995) 6(2) ICC Bull 60.

April, 11, 1980'.[131] The tribunal differentiated the CISG's contractual and legal application, describing it as 'useful to examine whether, irrespective of the express choice … the Convention would have been applicable in any case'.[132] The matter had practical importance – Italy (one party's state) had adopted the CISG without reservation, but Finland (the other's) had an active declaration (since withdrawn) that the CISG's contract formation rules were inapplicable.[133] The parties' choice was interpreted as incorporating the CISG's provisions as contractual terms, with Italian law otherwise governing on a conflicts analysis, meaning the CISG (in its entirety) also had a 'statutory character' in the case.[134]

## F. Where there is a Battle of Forms, and the Parties' Standard Terms Include Conflicting Choice of Law Clauses

The sixth category of case involves battles of forms. The 'battle of forms', a classic contract formation problem, arises where two parties each purport to contract on their own standard terms.[135] Where they contain different choices of law, arbitrators may need to employ conflicts analyses to determine which set of terms prevails, and what law (if any) the parties have chosen.[136] In other words, an anterior conflicts analysis resolves the battle of forms, allowing the chosen law to take effect; there is a 'conflict of the choice of law clauses'.[137]

Where two sets of standard terms choose different laws, the position is both 'complicated and controversial'.[138] Different legal systems provide different (sometimes uncertain) approaches to resolving this question.[139] A contemporary and 'novel' solution is provided by Art 6(1)(b) of the Hague Principles:[140]

- if the same standard terms prevail under both chosen laws, the law designated in those terms applies; and
- if different standard terms prevail under both chosen laws, or if under one or both of the chosen laws no standard terms prevail, there is no choice of law.

Each chosen law's solution to conflicting substantive contract terms, rather than conflicting choice of law clauses, is therefore compared.[141] Though this provision

[131] ibid 60.
[132] ibid 60–61.
[133] ibid 60. See generally CISG, Art 92(1).
[134] *ICC Case No 7585/1992* (1995) 6(2) ICC Bull 60, 61.
[135] See, eg, H Beale (ed), *Chitty on Contracts*, 32nd edn (London, Sweet & Maxwell, 2015) [37-051].
[136] T Kadner Graziano, 'Solving the Riddle of Conflicting Choice of Law Clauses in Battle of Forms Situations: The Hague Solution' (2012–13) 14 *Yearbook of Private International Law* 71, 72–73.
[137] ibid 73.
[138] ibid 81. See also Hague Principles, Commentary [6.11].
[139] Hague Principles, Commentary [6.3]; Kadner Graziano, 'Solving the Riddle of Conflicting Choice of Law Clauses in Battle of Forms Situations' (n 136) 99.
[140] Hague Principles, Commentary [6.12].
[141] B Marshall, 'The Hague Choice of Law Principles, CISG, and PICC: A Hard Look at a Choice of Soft Law' (2018) 66 *American Journal of Comparative Law* 175, 210.

is of interest for this chapter's analysis given the Hague Principles' intended application in arbitration,[142] the power of parties to choose *rules of law* in arbitration limits its potential utility. As recently explained by Marshall, international conventions and non-national rules do not always take a clear position on battles of forms, with their substantive provisions also not necessarily intended to address conflicting choice of law clauses.[143] This makes Art 6(1)(b) of the Hague Principles potentially more difficult to apply in arbitration where non-state rules are selected.

This category of case is evidenced in *SCC Case Code 465 (2008)*, involving an oral sales contract between Swedish and German parties, and standard terms referring to their own laws.[144] Both states had adopted the CISG, though it could not automatically be applied to determine whether the contract was formed (and whether it included the claimant's terms' arbitration clause) as Sweden had an active declaration (since withdrawn) precluding application of the Convention's contract formation rules.[145] This battle of forms thus implicated the conflict of laws.

The tribunal referred to Art 8(1) of the Rome Convention, providing that the existence and validity of a contract or any contractual term is determined by the law that would govern, under the Convention, if it were valid.[146] The tribunal therefore looked to the effect of both German and Swedish law. Under German law, the differing choices would cancel each other out, leaving no effective choice; Art 4(2) of the Rome Convention would then lead to the seller's (Swedish) law applying.[147] Under Swedish law, the last standard terms prevail; again, the terms choosing Swedish law.[148] Starting from either purported choice ultimately led to Swedish law, and the claimant's standard terms (including their arbitration agreement).[149]

## G. Where Statutory Provisions Require Conflicts Analyses, Irrespective of any Party Choice of Law

In this seventh category, statutory provisions forming part of the governing law may require conflicts analyses, irrespective of any choice of law (leading to those provisions applying in the first place). The Late Payment of Commercial Debts (Interest) Act 1998, s 12 is an example. This '[c]onflict of laws' provision ensures

[142] Hague Principles, Commentary [I.20(b)]; Permanent Bureau of the Hague Conference on Private International Law, 'Choice of Law in International Commercial Contracts: Hague Principles?' (2010) 15 *Uniform Law Review* 883, 884.
[143] Marshall, 'The Hague Choice of Law Principles, CISG, and PICC' (n 141) 211–15.
[144] *SCC Case Code 465 (2008)* in Bergman (ed) (n 10) 223, 223.
[145] ibid 223–24.
[146] ibid 224. An equivalent provision is now contained in Art 10(1) of the Rome I Regulation.
[147] *SCC Case Code 465 (2008)* in Bergman (ed) (n 10) 223, 224–25.
[148] ibid 225.
[149] ibid 224–25.

the Act's (non-)application is based on conflicts analyses, not choice of law. Where UK law is chosen but the governing law would have otherwise been foreign (and no significant UK connection exists), the Act does not apply;[150] and vice versa[151] (though it is the first scenario that is relevant to this chapter's analysis). The Australian Consumer Law, s 67, set out in sch 2 to the Competition and Consumer Act 2010 (Cth), and the Insurance Contracts Act 1984 (Cth) s 8, are similar provisions. All establish that – so far as those Acts are concerned – choice of law is not determinative.

Unlike state courts, arbitrators have no forum,[152] and no *lex fori*.[153] Arbitrators sitting in the UK or in Australia would not automatically apply these provisions (as state court judges do) regardless of the governing law; arbitrators apply these provisions as part of the chosen law. Even so, they may possibly evidence the relevant legislation's mandatory nature, implicating this chapter's ninth and final category of case as well.[154]

## H. Where there is an (Apparent) Choice of Law Clause, but it is Ineffective for Being Unclear, Invalid or Indecisive

In this eighth category, arbitrators' conflicts analyses are required where an (apparent) choice of law is ineffective. This category is grounded in both the interpretation and inherent limits of choices of law. As a matter of law, once interpreted, the choice cannot be given decisive (or perhaps any) effect.

### *i. Uncertain Choices of Law*

Uncertainty is an interpretative issue,[155] described in litigation as '[p]erhaps the greatest practical problem in connection with express choice'.[156] Choice of law clauses can be ineffective for uncertainty, just like any other kind of contractual provision.[157] Where an (apparent) choice of law is sufficiently uncertain, it will have no effect, and arbitrators will themselves identify the governing substantive law.[158]

*SCC Case Code 604 (2011)*[159] is an excellent illustration. In addition to choosing the CISG, as addressed in section A, the parties' agreement stipulated that it was

[150] Late Payment of Commercial Debts (Interest) Act 1998, s 12(1).
[151] ibid, s 12(2).
[152] Poudret and Besson, *Comparative Law of International Arbitration* (n 62) [114].
[153] Greenberg, Kee and Weeramantry (n 5) [3.5].
[154] *Cf* Rome I Regulation, Recital (37); Marshall (n 141) 186, fn 68.
[155] Croft, Kee and Waincymer (n 24) [35.12].
[156] P Stone, *EU Private International Law*, 3rd edn (Cheltenham, Edward Elgar Publishing, 2014) 296.
[157] ibid.
[158] See, eg, *ICC Case No 10422/2001* at Unilex, 'Case' (*UNILEX*, 2001), [6] www.unilex.info/case.cfm?pid=1&do=case&id=957&step=FullText.
[159] *SCC Case Code 604 (2011)* in Bergman (ed) (n 10) 260.

'regulated by the norms of substantive laws of the European Union'.[160] With the applicable interest rate at issue, the tribunal observed:

> The reference to the norms of substantive laws of the European Union is unclear and has not been explained by Claimant. There are no substantive laws of the European Union that are applicable to default interest, not even on debts in Euro and much less in [US Dollars]. The individual member states of the European Union presumably all have domestic legislation on such interest on the currency of each state, but Claimant has not produced any evidence on this and the Arbitrator is not familiar with all such legislation.[161]

This aspect of the choice of law was therefore disregarded. Naturally, a certain magnitude of uncertainty is required before an (apparent) choice of law becomes ineffective. *SCC Case Code 159 (1999)* is an interesting counter-example, with the parties' arbitration agreement providing (in part) that 'the arbiters should take command of the Regulations of Swedish Law of Substance'.[162] Though not as clear as it could have been, this sentence was an effective choice of law, the tribunal finding 'no reason' for it other than as indicating that Swedish substantive law applied.[163]

A clause's uncertainty might be remedied by later agreement, as in *SCC Case Code 428 (2008)*, where the parties' contract was subject to 'international commercial law'.[164] The parties subsequently agreed that this phrase referred to the CISG (excluding national reservations) and the UNIDROIT Principles.[165] There was good reason for this – China (the claimant's state) had an effective CISG written form declaration at the time (since withdrawn),[166] though as the parties had chosen the CISG as 'rules of law', the declaration did not apply.[167]

The *FirstLink* case[168] is a final curiosity within this category; a stay application determined by Singapore's High Court, addressing an arbitration agreement's validity. The parties' purported choice of law, contained in a contract clause headed '[g]eneral', referred to 'the laws of Arbitration Institute of the Stockholm Chamber of Commerce'[169] – that is, procedural arbitration rules.

As noted by the High Court, this was 'undoubtedly an unusual choice', there being 'an obvious curiosity as to how the parties' substantive obligations can be governed by the rules of an arbitral institution'.[170] Nevertheless, the validity of the main contract (and the choice of law clause's effectiveness in that regard) was not in issue.[171] The (separable) arbitration agreement's validity *was* disputed,

[160] ibid 260.
[161] ibid 261.
[162] *SCC Case Code 159 (1999)* in Bergman (ed) (n 10) 110, 111.
[163] ibid.
[164] *SCC Case Code 428 (2008)* in Bergman (ed) (n 10) 213, 213.
[165] ibid 213–14.
[166] See generally CISG, Arts 12 and 96.
[167] *SCC Case Code 428 (2008)* in Bergman (ed) (n 10) 213, 213–14.
[168] *FirstLink Investments Corp Ltd v GT Payment Pte Ltd* [2014] SGHCR 12 (19 June 2014).
[169] ibid [9].
[170] ibid [10].
[171] ibid.

and the clause reinforced an intention for Swedish law to apply (absent express choice).[172] However, the Court also indicated that the *arbitration* agreement (as opposed to the main contract) could feasibly be governed by this clause. As it explained:

> While there should be no excuse for poor drafting, it would be safe to assume that not all commercial men and women (or lawyers for that matter) are avid students of jurisprudence with an acute philosophical understanding of what 'law' is … At least in the realm of international arbitration, it is not entirely inconceivable that a dispute over the validity of an arbitration agreement may be resolved by *rules of law* as opposed to national laws.[173]

## ii. Invalid Choices of Law

As with uncertainty, general contractual principles invalidating terms are also applied to choices of law. A vitiating factor, such as fraud, may render an apparently-valid choice of law clause ineffective.[174] In that case, a choice of law is treated as if never existing, requiring the arbitrators to identify the governing law instead.[175] Where a choice of law is impugned, an anterior conflicts analysis is required to determine the law initially applicable to the choice's material validity.[176]

## iii. Indecisive Choices of Law

The final example for this eighth category involves indecisive choices of law. Where a clause identifies multiple laws as applicable, and they lead to different outcomes, a conflicts analysis is required to identify which of those chosen laws actually governs.

This occurred in *ICC Case No 4145*.[177] The parties' choice of law provided that '[t]he validity and construction of this Agreement shall be governed by the laws of the Canton of Geneva, Switzerland or [Middle Eastern] country X, or both'.[178] The selection was material; country X's law might have invalidated the contract for alleged corruption, while Swiss law validated the agreement.[179] The complexity of the conflicts and choice of law interaction is clearly demonstrated by this case – not only would the two chosen laws have led to different outcomes, but different conflicts rules would have identified different applicable laws. The tribunal

[172] ibid [9] and [17].
[173] ibid [18]. See also ibid [20].
[174] Natov, 'The Autonomy of Arbitrators in Determining the Law Applicable to the Merits of a Case' (n 112) [9.44].
[175] *Cf* ibid.
[176] On the various possible methodologies, see Born (n 2) 2684–89. See also Rome I Regulation, Art 3(5); Rome Convention, Art 3(4).
[177] *ICC Case No 4145* (1987) XII YBCA 97.
[178] *First Interim Award* in *ICC Case No 4145/1983* (1987) XII YBCA 99, [1]. The state's identity is redacted in the published award.
[179] *Second Interim Award* in *ICC Case No 4145/1984* (1987) XII YBCA 100, [10].

ultimately applied Swiss law, adopting the validation principle (ie applying the law that would validate the contract) as a conflicts rule.[180] However, at least according to the defendant's submissions, the closest connection test would have led to country X's law, invalidating the bargain.[181]

Similar circumstances arose in *SCC Case Code 175 (2002)*, involving a contract between Russian and US parties, and the following choice of law:

> This Agreement is governed by the regulations of the International Institute of Arbitration and shall be constructed [*sic*] by the laws of Russian Federation and the State of New York (USA).[182]

At issue was the statute of limitations; the claim was time-barred under Russian law, but timely under New York law.[183] The tribunal applied the conflicts rules of both Russia and New York, finding that both led to New York law.[184]

## I. Where Mandatory Law Lays Claim to Application Irrespective of the Parties' Chosen Law

The ninth and final category of case concerns mandatory law. Even an effective and comprehensive choice of law clause is subject to overriding mandatory law. By its very nature, such law applies irrespective of party choice.[185] The mechanism for mandatory law's application lies in the conflict of laws, and its justification in the inherent limits of party autonomy.[186]

Soviet currency regulations were an example evident in *SCC Case Code 524 (2010)*, where the parties had chosen Swedish law – the tribunal still took those regulations into account.[187] Similarly, in *SCC Case Code 680 (2012)*, the tribunal applied a provision of the French Commercial Code as overriding mandatory law, notwithstanding a choice of Swedish law.[188]

The question of 'when and why' overriding mandatory laws apply is 'vexed'.[189] What is clear is that the conflicts rules used by arbitrators to apply overriding mandatory law differ from those used to identify the *lex contractus*.

Though not compulsorily applicable in arbitration,[190] guidance can be taken from Art 7 of the Rome Convention and Art 9 of the Rome I Regulation.

[180] ibid [15]–[17].
[181] *First Interim Award* in *ICC Case No 4145/1983* (1987) XII YBCA 99, [5].
[182] *SCC Case Code 175 (2002)* in Bergman (ed) (n 10) 138, 138.
[183] ibid.
[184] ibid 139.
[185] Blessing, 'Mandatory Rules of Law' (n 24) 23; Lehmann, 'Liberating the Individual From Battles Between States' (n 77) 429.
[186] *SCC Case Code 680 (2012)* in Bergman (ed) (n 10) 283, 284.
[187] *SCC Case Code 524 (2010)* in Bergman (ed) (n 10) 246, 246–47.
[188] *SCC Case Code 680 (2012)* in Bergman (ed) (n 10) 283, 283–85.
[189] Croft, Kee and Waincymer (n 24) [35.15].
[190] Carducci, 'The Impact of the EU "Rome I" Regulation on International Litigation and Arbitration, A-National Law, Mandatory and Overriding Rules' (n 128) 32–34 and 42.

Both address the application of overriding mandatory law in EU state court proceedings; with the Rome I Regulation now superseding the Rome Convention (except in Denmark).[191] The relevance of these provisions (and the principles upon which they are based) in the arbitral context was explained in *SCC Case Code 680 (2012)*:

> The fact that the Regulation Rome I is not applicable *ratione temporis*, as correctly pointed out by the Respondent, is not pertinent. The principle stated in Article 9(2) of Regulation Rome I that overriding mandatory rules must be applied regardless of the applicable law is the expression of a more general principle that was already present in Article 7(2) of the Convention on the Law Applicable to Contractual Obligations of June 19, 1980 …
>
> In any event, and leaving aside the issue of applicability of those instruments in international arbitration, it is generally acknowledged that arbitrators have a duty to apply the overriding mandatory rules of the laws having a significant connection to the dispute, regardless of the governing law of the relevant relationship.[192]

Notwithstanding use of the word *duty* in this passage, applying overriding mandatory law is 'permissive' (rather than 'obligatory') in arbitration.[193] The issue is delicate, given overriding mandatory law (by definition) is not chosen by the parties, and that arbitral laws and rules tend not to address the application of mandatory law.[194] In practice, the conflicts principles governing mandatory law's application in arbitration are highly discretionary,[195] thus the mere existence of public-law-type regulations does not guarantee their application. In *SCC Case Code 325 (2006)*, an illustrative counter-example, the argument that delivery of nuclear materials under the parties' contract would continue only where furthering the relevant bilateral treaty and complementary Russian legislation was rejected.[196] The tribunal resolved the parties' dispute by reference to Swedish law (the parties' chosen law) only.[197]

## V. Conclusion

Arbitration is an interesting creature of the dispute resolution jungle, in the international context. And though private international law has been described as a

[191] Rome I Regulation, Recital (46) and Art 24(1).

[192] *SCC Case Code 680 (2012)* in Bergman (ed) (n 10) 283, 284.

[193] *SCC Case Code 524 (2010)* in Bergman (ed) (n 10) 246, 247.

[194] *Cf* Hague Principles, Art 11(5), referring to situations where arbitrators are 'required or entitled' to apply overriding mandatory law. On Art 11 of the Hague Principles, see generally A Dickinson, 'Oiling the Machine: Overriding Mandatory Provisions and Public Policy in the Hague Principles on Choice of Law in International Commercial Contracts' (2017) 22 *Uniform Law Review* 402.

[195] Blessing (n 24) 31–33.

[196] *SCC Case Code 325 (2006)* in Bergman (ed) (n 10) 188, 190.

[197] ibid 191–92.

'dismal swamp',[198] its borderline with this jungle is fertile ground for a variety of fascinating arbitral private international law issues. This chapter has focused on how the substantive law governing the merits is identified. While the applicable law's impact should not be overstated, with many cases turning on their facts,[199] the governing law's identification can affect case outcomes.[200]

Rather than being an exercise in technicality for technicality's sake, identifying the governing law is an issue of great practical and commercial interest. As explained by Blessing, in a passage quoted in part in this chapter's introduction:

> These questions may sound academic and may seem to be of interest for professors only, but as a practitioner I can say that they are not. They are questions of crucial practical significance because, depending on their answer, they may sometimes directly determine the outcome of a case. And because this is so, these questions need to be examined and handled very carefully.[201]

Despite this admonition to take care, existing commentary treats choice of law and the conflicts of laws as binary alternatives. The inherent limits of choice of law clauses demonstrate this is untrue; and despite the certainty motivations underpinning choices of law, their drafting also contributes to an interaction between the two. In the spirit of care encouraged by Blessing, this chapter has systematically explored these interactions. The mere existence of an (apparent) choice of law clause is not necessarily definitive as to the law ultimately applied. This chapter has identified nine categories of case where the parties' (apparent) choice will not eliminate the need for arbitrators to themselves resolve conflicts of laws questions.

While parties are rightly encouraged to include choice of law clauses in commercial contracts,[202] it should be understood that absolute certainty is not guaranteed. Party autonomy is a 'guiding principle' of private international law, but like all principles, it has its limits.[203]

Commercial parties would do well to pay careful attention to choice of law clauses, being alert to their inherent limits, and the implications of their drafting. Greater precision in private international lawyers' analyses of these issues might help them to do so, particularly as businesspeople might not understand the legal implications of choice of law clauses even at a more general level.[204] Conflicts of laws may always matter in arbitration, notwithstanding party agreement on the governing law.

[198] Prosser, 'Interstate Publication' (n 3) 971.

[199] Born (n 2) 2617; Blackaby et al (n 5) [6.75].

[200] Hayward (n 9) [1.63]; P Binder, *International Commercial Arbitration and Conciliation in UNCITRAL Model Law Jurisdictions*, 3rd edn (London, Sweet & Maxwell, 2010) [6-011].

[201] Blessing (n 6) 49.

[202] See, eg, J Paulsson, N Rawding and L Reed, *The Freshfields Guide to Arbitration Clauses in International Contracts*, 3rd edn (Alphen aan den Rijn, Kluwer, 2010) 18–19.

[203] Bisping (n 125) 467.

[204] See generally G Cuniberti, 'The International Market for Contracts: The Most Attractive Contract Laws' (2014) 34 *Northwestern Journal of International Law and Business* 455, 515–16.

# 8

# The Conflict of Laws as a Shared Language for the Cross-Border Application of Statutes

MARIA HOOK*

## I. The Problem: Silent Statutes and Foreign Facts

A local resident working for an overseas employer wishes to rely on local employment legislation to bring a personal grievance claim. The legislation does not contain a choice of law rule, neither does it define its own territorial scope. The question arises, then, whether the legislation may still apply to the claim despite its foreign elements; or, put more generally: when will a silent statute be applicable to foreign facts? In a world of cross-border dealings, migration and communication, this question is inevitable. Scholars and courts have been wrestling with it for centuries.[1]

Yet, perhaps now more than ever, disagreement abounds on what is the right way to determine the cross-border application of statutes. At the heart of this disagreement is a conflict of disciplines: a conflict between the conflict of laws, on the one hand, and statutory interpretation, on the other. There are those who say that the territorial scope of statutes is exclusively a matter for Parliament, and so we must turn to principles of statutory interpretation – the statute itself – to determine its reach. They are the statutists. And there are others who say that the question of cross-border application requires us to look outside of the statute, to the traditional rules of the conflict of laws. They are the traditionalists.[2] The implicit assumption uniting the two camps is that their modes of reasoning are incompatible.

* Senior Lecturer, Faculty of Law, University of Otago.

[1] See L Collins (ed), *Dicey, Morris and Collins on the Conflict of Laws*, 15th edn (London, Sweet & Maxwell, 2012) para 1-052.

[2] Based on Adrian Briggs' description of the conflict of laws approach as the 'traditional approach': A Briggs, 'A Note on the Application of the Statute Law of Singapore' [2005] *Singapore Journal of Legal Studies* 189, 194.

## A. Overview of Argument

This chapter argues that it is time to recognise that both forms of reasoning, conflict of laws rules and statutory interpretation, are indispensable tools for determining the cross-border application of statutes. In other words, both approaches are here to stay. So we need to change our focus, from wishing away the conflict, to finding ways of resolving it in the circumstances of a particular case. Instead of fighting the conflict along disciplinary battle lines, we need to shift its locus to within the conflict of laws. It is here, within the conflict of laws, that we can unlock the conflict; and we can do so by analysing and charting the role of statutory interpretation in conflict of laws methodology.

The argument is in three parts. First, I will provide an outline of each of the two competing approaches: the application of traditional conflict of laws rules and the application of statutory interpretation, respectively (section II). Second, I will demonstrate that there is an unresolved conflict between these approaches – a conflict of disciplines – and that this is an undesirable state of affairs (section III). Third, I will make the case for incorporating statutory interpretation in conflict of laws reasoning, which would provide us with a methodology for resolving the conflict (sections IV and V). To illustrate the argument, the chapter will draw mainly on the New Zealand case of *Brown v New Zealand Basing Ltd*.[3]

## B. *Brown v New Zealand Basing Ltd*

The case of *Brown v New Zealand Basing Ltd* involved a dispute whether age discrimination provisions in New Zealand employment legislation applied to Cathay Pacific pilots based in Auckland. The employment contract, expressed to be governed by the law of Hong Kong, provided for a mandatory retirement age of 55. Pursuant to the Employment Relations Act 2000 (NZ) (ERA), however, the pilots could not be required to retire until they had reached the age of 65. Sections 103 and 104 of the Act provide employees with a right to be free from age discrimination in their employment, by reference to s 21 of the Human Rights Act 1991. The pilots brought a personal grievance claim against their employer (NZBL), a Hong Kong based subsidiary of Cathay Pacific, in reliance on the Act. NZBL argued that the Act was inapplicable.

This is not the first time that the cross-border effect of Cathay Pacific's retirement age provisions has been the subject of litigation. In *Lawson v Serco Ltd (Crofts)*,[4]

[3] *Brown v New Zealand Basing* [2017] NZSC 139, [2018] 1 NZLR 245; [2016] NZCA 525, [2017] 2 NZLR 93; [2014] NZEmpC 229, 12 NZELR 419.

[4] *Lawson v Serco Ltd (Crofts)* [2006] UKHL 3, [2006] 1 All ER 823.

the House of Lords held that the right not to be unfairly dismissed under the Employment Rights Act 1996 (UK) applied to UK-based pilots of Cathay Pacific. But the New Zealand Act does not contain an equivalent to s 204(1) of the UK Act, which provides that it is immaterial for the purposes of the Act 'whether the law which (apart from this Act) governs any person's employment is the law of the United Kingdom … or not'. Lord Hoffmann held that it was necessary to imply territorial limits into the Act and that the place where the pilots were based was the appropriate connecting factor. This approach would ensure that international pilots are not 'condemned to fly without any jurisdiction in which they can seek redress'.[5] Following the decision in *Crofts*, Cathay Pacific changed its employment arrangements in the United Kingdom, Canada and Australia by introducing express choices of local law and lifting the age of retirement to 65 years. These changes did not affect the plaintiffs, who turned down new conditions of service providing for the application of New Zealand law and a retirement age of 65 years (but offering a reduced salary).

The Employment Court rejected NZBL's argument and held that the pilots could rely on the Act.[6] NZBL successfully appealed to the Court of Appeal, which applied traditional conflict of laws rules to conclude that the applicable law was the law of Hong Kong, that the Act did not amount to an overriding mandatory rule and that there were no grounds for invoking the public policy exception.[7] The pilots appealed to the Supreme Court. The Supreme Court restored the Employment Court's judgment, holding that the Act had to be construed as affording relief to parties in the pilots' circumstances.[8]

The problem faced by the New Zealand courts in *Brown* is not new. It has been the subject of much debate and analysis.[9] Yet it persists, in New Zealand and other common law jurisdictions. *Brown* is merely an example of a general methodological confusion that may affect many statute-based areas of private law, such as consumer law and family law. More often than not, there are no choice of law rules or express territorial provisions in such statutes, leaving courts to work out whether they apply to a particular set of foreign facts. *Brown* is a timely reminder, then, that there is much work left to do for statutists and traditionalists alike. The problem is not about to disappear. This chapter argues that we should deal with the problem by finding common ground rather than insisting on methodological purity. But before we can look to the future, we need to take a closer look at the two competing approaches, and how they played out in *Brown*.

[5] ibid [31].
[6] *Brown v New Zealand Basing Ltd* [2014] NZEmpC 229, 12 NZELR 419.
[7] *New Zealand Basing Ltd v Brown* [2016] NZCA 525, [2017] 2 NZLR 93.
[8] *Brown v New Zealand Basing Ltd* [2017] NZSC 139, [2018] 1 NZLR 245.
[9] For an overview, see M Keyes, 'Statutes, Choice of Law and the Role of Forum Choice' (2008) 4(1) *Journal of Private International Law* 1.

# II. The Two Approaches

## A. Traditionalism

The traditional conflict of laws approach presumes that silent statutes are subject to the principles and rules of the conflict of laws. The answer is not to be found in the statute. Rather, the court must characterise the issue, which in turn will enable the court to identify the applicable – usually multilateral – choice of law rule and, hence, the law governing the issue. A statute will apply only if it forms part of the applicable law so selected. There are two exceptions to this principle. First, where a statute has overriding mandatory force it will be given effect even if the law governing the issue is foreign law. Second, where the court has excluded a rule of foreign law on the grounds of public policy, the statute may be used to fill the gap left by the public policy exception.

This is the approach proposed in *Dicey on the Conflict of Laws*,[10] and it was also, arguably, the approach adopted by the New Zealand Supreme Court in *Ludgater v Gerling*.[11] The Court of Appeal in *Basing* followed suit and considered that the case was a classic conflict of laws problem, to be resolved by the application of ordinary choice of law rules.[12] The applicable choice of law rule called for identification of the 'proper law' of the contract. The proper law was the law chosen by the parties (provided the choice was bona fide and legal) or, in the absence of choice, the system with the closest and most real connection. Here, the pilots and NZBL had expressly agreed to be bound by the law of Hong Kong, and the agreement was bona fide and legal.[13] So the only remaining questions were whether s 104 of the ERA was a mandatory rule with overriding effect, or whether the application of Hong Kong law would be contrary to public policy to the extent that it did not provide protection against discrimination on grounds of age.

In relation to the first question, the Court concluded that the Employment Court had fallen into error in relying on the House of Lords' decision in *Crofts*.[14] The Court considered that *Crofts* was distinguishable from the present case.[15] Section 204 of the UK Act expressly provided that it was immaterial to the application of the Act whether the proper law of the employment was the law of the United Kingdom. The ERA, however, contained no such provision. The House of Lords proceeded on the assumption that the UK Act had overriding effect; yet this was

[10] *Dicey, Morris and Collins* (n 1) paras 1-037–1-040.

[11] *Ludgater v Gerling* [2010] NZSC 49, [2010] 3 NZLR 713; see D Goddard and C McLachlan *Private International Law – Litigating in the Trans-Tasman Context and Beyond* (Wellington, NZLS, 2012).

[12] *New Zealand Basing Ltd v Brown* [2016] NZCA 525, [2017] 2 NZLR 93, [35]. The following analysis of the Court of Appeal's decision is largely taken from M Hook and J Wass, 'The Employment Relations Act and its Effect on Contracts Governed by Foreign Law' [2017] *New Zealand Law Journal* 80.

[13] ibid [34]–[35].

[14] ibid [40].

[15] ibid [41]–[55].

the very issue that was before the New Zealand court. Moreover, Lord Hoffmann's concern that international pilots may be left without redress was irrelevant in the present case: the parties' choice of law meant that the pilots would have rights of redress in Hong Kong.[16]

Having distinguished *Crofts*, the Court of Appeal then went on to conclude that, without an overriding provision, the parties' choice of Hong Kong law had to prevail,[17] and that the Employment Court erred in construing s 238 as an overriding provision. Section 238 provides that the provisions of the ERA 'have effect despite any provision to the contrary in any contract or agreement'. The purpose of this section was to ensure that employment contracts 'formed in New Zealand and performed here' (ie purely domestic cases) should comply with the standards prescribed by the ERA.[18] It also applied where the parties' choice of foreign law has 'little or no connection to the New Zealand contract'. But in the absence of clear Parliamentary intent, it could not be construed as displacing or overriding settled rules of private international law.[19] The parties' choice was of decisive significance.[20]

In relation to the second question, the Court of Appeal concluded that the application of Hong Kong law would not be contrary to public policy in this case. The parties agreed that the test to be applied was whether enforcement would '"shock the conscience" of a reasonable New Zealander, or be contrary to New Zealand's view of basic morality or a violation of essential principles of justice or moral interests in New Zealand'.[21]

This test, the Court of Appeal emphasised, set a high threshold. A forum's discretion to refuse recognition of an agreed choice of law was 'of an exceptional nature'.[22] To apply the public policy exception was to '[impeach] the contract by condemning the foreign law which would otherwise apply'.[23] Pointing to the case of *Oppenheimer v Cattermole*,[24] where the House of Lords applied the public policy exception to a 1941 decree depriving Jewish émigrés of their German nationality and confiscating their property, the Court of Appeal considered that the infringement had to be 'of a fundamental or *universal* value' (emphasis added). It could not simply be 'the result of a ranking within a spectrum of relative values which are recognised in one legal system but not the other'.[25] Nor is it sufficient that the foreign law be objectionable in the abstract; it is necessary to establish that its application in the particular context is incompatible with public policy.[26]

[16] ibid [55].
[17] ibid [56]–[59].
[18] ibid [56].
[19] ibid [57].
[20] ibid [58].
[21] ibid [62], referring to *Reeves v OneWorld Challenge LLC* [2006] 2 NZLR 184 (CA) [67].
[22] ibid [65].
[23] ibid.
[24] *Oppenheimer v Cattermole* [1976] AC 249 (HL).
[25] *Brown* [68].
[26] ibid [66].

The right to be free from age discrimination was not an absolute value and hence did not meet this threshold. It reflected 'a range of fiscal, social and cultural factors'.[27] This was confirmed by the statutory framework and international human rights law. Moreover, when the contracts were considered as a whole, the choice of Hong Kong law 'provided significant financial benefits to the pilots',[28] so the absence of protection against age discrimination would not infringe New Zealand's public policy on the facts of the particular case. The main such benefit was a favourable income tax rate in Hong Kong of 15 per cent. The pilots' attempt 'to circumvent a bona fide and legal choice of law' was contrary to the fundamentals of private international law, which were to satisfy the 'reasonable and legitimate expectations of the parties'.[29]

## B. Statutism

The alternative approach is to find the answer – whether the statute does or does not apply to foreign facts – within the statute itself, instead of relying on 'external' conflict of laws rules. The question is one of statutory interpretation: whether the Act applies depends on its meaning, which must be ascertained from its text and in light of its purpose. This question requires engagement with the substance of the law. In the absence of evidence to the contrary, Parliament is presumed to have legislated territorially. This was the approach taken by the Supreme Court, which held unanimously that the Act applied to the plaintiffs' claim.[30] There were two judgments. A minority judgment written by William Young J, and a much shorter majority judgment by Ellen France J. The majority 'broadly agree[d] with the approach adopted by William Young J' but wished to express their reasons 'a little differently'.[31]

Both Ellen France J and William Young J considered that the starting point was a question of the interpretation of the Act.[32] In 'that fundamental respect', they 'differ[ed] from the approach taken in the Court of Appeal'. The reason for this, according to Ellen France J, was 'the sui generis nature of employment law'.[33] Starting with the principle that all legislation is territorial in nature, the court's task was to imply territorial limitations into the application of the Act. Her Honour considered that *Crofts* offered support for this approach, and that Lord Hoffmann had taken a statutory interpretation approach to determining the territorial limits of the UK Act because of his 'view of the nature of the employment relationship

[27] ibid [74].
[28] ibid [83].
[29] ibid [79].
[30] *Brown v New Zealand Basing Ltd* [2017] NZSC 139, [2018] 1 NZLR 245.
[31] ibid [75].
[32] ibid [76] and [8].
[33] ibid [77].

in law'.[34] Section 204 of the UK Act was, on this approach, irrelevant (as were the choice of law clause and the Rome Convention).[35]

There was also nothing in the New Zealand Act to suggest that the approach taken in *Crofts* was excluded in relation to its anti-discrimination provisions.[36] On the contrary, Parliament had given consideration to the extent of the territorial application of the Act, in the form of certain exceptions to the right to be free from unlawful discrimination (contained in ss 24 and 26 of the Human Rights Act 1993). These exceptions, which related to crews of ships and aircraft and work performed outside of New Zealand, did not catch the New Zealand-based pilots.[37] Section 238, the no-contracting out provision, reinforced this position.[38] Against this background, the majority considered that 'it would be very odd to construe the 2000 Act to allow discrimination in the employment context in relation to persons in the [pilots'] position, solely on the basis of the parties' choice of law'.[39] In *Crofts*, Lord Hoffmann found that the Act applied to cases involving peripatetic employees who have their home base within the jurisdiction. Here, it was not disputed that the pilots were based in New Zealand. So the Act applied.

The minority also relied on statutory interpretation to reach the same conclusion, but went further than the majority and expressly rejected the conflict of laws approach to statutes proposed in *Dicey on the Conflict of Laws*. In its place, it adopted a 'single step interpretation approach', because 'the territorial reach of legislation [is] best determined on the basis of a purposive interpretation of the statute in question, as required by s 5(1) of the Interpretation Act 1999'.[40] This was not the same as approaching the legislation as an overriding mandatory rule, which would have proceeded from an assumption that it did not apply.[41] Based on the single-step approach, the minority concluded that 'the right not to be discriminated against [was] not confined to conduct which occur[ed] in the context of an employment agreement governed by New Zealand law'.[42]

In particular, the minority pointed to jurisdictional rules in the Employment Court Regulations 2000 – rules relating to overseas service and the court's power to decline jurisdiction – as evidence that the Employment Court was assumed to have jurisdiction in a diverse range of circumstances.[43] This diversity was inconsistent with an approach that sought to read down the definitions of 'employer' and 'employee' so that the Act would apply only to employment relationships with an appropriate level of connection with New Zealand.[44] Their Honours further

[34] ibid [79]–[84].
[35] ibid [84].
[36] ibid [86].
[37] ibid [88]–[89].
[38] ibid [90].
[39] ibid [91].
[40] ibid [8].
[41] ibid [58].
[42] ibid [9].
[43] ibid [45].
[44] ibid [40], [46].

noted that the Act was 'premised on the view that employment involves a relationship (and thus status) and not just contract',[45] and so there was no basis for a 'two-step interpretative exercise' asking whether personal grievance rights were best characterised as contractual.[46] Sitting alongside the rights not to be sexually or racially harassed, which 'are breached by any conduct which occurs within New Zealand', the right to be free from age discrimination had to be interpreted along similar lines,[47] and it applied where the employee works both in and outside New Zealand.[48]

## III. A Conflict of Disciplines?

Now that we have outlined the two approaches, it is necessary to delve a little deeper into the relationship between them. The predominant position, at present, is that they are incompatible (section A). It is conceptually impossible to apply statutory interpretation and conflict of laws rules at once. They are separate disciplines, which may yield different answers. There are also no shared reference points for working out which applies when. Rather, the question comes down to ideology: either you are a statutist or a traditionalist. This is not a desirable state of affairs (section B).

### A. Traditionalism v Statutism

The parties in *Brown* had argued the case as a conflict of laws case. The Court of Appeal, applying traditional conflict of laws reasoning, concluded that the Act did not apply. Yet the Supreme Court simply declared that the matter was one of statutory interpretation. The majority did not even refer to choice of law rules, or overriding mandatory rules, or the public policy exception. It also did not justify its conclusion that the conflict of laws was irrelevant, except to say that employment relations are 'sui generis'.[49] How can this be? Why was there no real attempt to explore the disciplinary boundaries in order to come up with a reasoned choice of statutory interpretation over conflict of laws rules?

The answer lies in the framing of the choice. For the Supreme Court – and also, to some extent, the Court of Appeal – the choice was a choice between disciplines. Disciplines tend to stand on their own, in silos. They lack a shared language to

[45] ibid [56].
[46] ibid [57].
[47] ibid [68].
[48] ibid [72].
[49] ibid [77].

negotiate the spaces between them.[50] There is no common ground, only separate premises that apply on their own terms.[51] The traditionalists' premise is that statutes are subject to (external) principles and rules of the conflict of laws,[52] and hence the Court of Appeal did not bother to look for interpretive clues within the statute. The statutists' premise is that the application of a statute must be determined by reference to its text and purpose,[53] and hence there was no room, on the Supreme Court's analysis, to look to conflict of laws rules outside the statute.

Each premise is inward-focused, or exclusive. The choice starts and ends with the premise. So the only way to justify that the case is one of statutory interpretation is to say that the territorial reach of legislation is a matter for Parliament, that 'there is no reason to suppose that Parliament legislates only within the straitjacket of the rules of the conflict of laws';[54] and vice versa. Notably, the starting point is *not* a shared point of inquiry that is open to movement in either direction. This means that the two approaches are generally seen as incompatible;[55] and that there are self-avowed camps of statutists, on the one hand,[56] and traditionalists, on the other.[57]

The conflict of laws, ironically, has been prone to this type of reasoning based on exclusive premises and siloed categories. I say 'ironically', because the very purpose of the conflict of laws is to negotiate cross-border differences,[58] and reasoning that is designed to exclude appears ill-suited to achieving that purpose. Yet evidence of it can be seen everywhere. There is the heart of the conflict of laws, the multilateral choice of law rule, whose main function is to identify the law with the closest connection, and then there are all the exceptions to, or exclusions from, the rule, which are concerned with matters of substantive policy. The *lex fori* rule, the public policy exception, the exclusion of sovereign claims, the

[50] *Cf* the debate about interdisciplinarity and international law: eg M Koskenniemi, 'Law, Teleology and International Relations: An Essay in Counterdisciplinarity' (2012) 26 *International Relations* 3. On international law as a language, see M Koskenniemi, *From Apology to Utopia: The Structure of International Legal Argument* (Cambridge, Cambridge University Press, 2005) 566.

[51] *Cf* W Gummow, 'The Selection of the Major Premise' (2013) 2 *Cambridge Journal of Comparative and International Law* 47.

[52] FA Mann, 'Statutes and the Conflict of Laws' (1972–73) *British Yearbook of International Law* 117, 123–24; *The Wanganui-Rangitikei Electric Power Board v The Australian Mutual Provident Society* (1934) 50 CLR 581, 601 (Dixon J) ('general words should not be understood as extending to cases which, according to the rules of private international law administered in our Courts, are governed by foreign law').

[53] Briggs, 'A Note on the Application of the Statute Law of Singapore' (n 2); *Brown v New Zealand Basing Ltd* [2017] NZSC 139, [2018] 1 NZLR 245, [8].

[54] Briggs (n 2) 195.

[55] ibid; *Dicey, Morris and Collins* (n 1) paras 1-037–1-040; Keyes, 'Statutes, Choice of Law and the Role of Forum Choice' (n 9); U Grušić, 'The Territorial Scope of Employment Legislation and Choice of Law' (2012) 75 *Modern Law Review* 722, 751.

[56] See the references in Keyes (n 9) fn 110.

[57] See the references in Keyes (n 9) fn 65.

[58] See PS Berman, 'Conflict of Laws and the Legal Negotiation of Difference' in A Sarat et al, *Law and the Stranger* (Stanford, Stanford University Press, 2010) 141; H Muir Watt, 'Hospitality, Tolerance, and Exclusion in Legal Form: Private International Law and the Politics of Difference' (2017) 70 *Current Legal Problems* 111.

role of public law, the (foreign) act of state doctrine are all examples, traditionally, of the defensiveness of the conflict of laws.[59] Either you were in, or you were out; and if you were out, the conflict of laws had a blanket category for you but not much else.

This defensiveness of the conflict of laws has its roots in the subject's fixation on neutrality. If the heart of the subject is the objective allocation of claims to legal systems on the basis of geographical proximity, and the goal is to rise above matters of substantive policy,[60] then unavoidable questions of substantive policy simply do not fit the mould.[61] At the sight of too much policy, the conflict of laws puts up walls, ready simply to exclude.[62] That explains, for example, why *Dicey, Morris and Collins on the Conflict of Laws* dedicates an entire chapter to the (rarely used) common law rules relating to matrimonial property, without explaining how they relate to the (much more common) application of the *lex fori* under the Matrimonial Causes Act 1973.[63] The *lex fori* rule for matrimonial matters barely forms part of the subject because, as a rule of substantive policy, it embodies the limitations of the premise of neutral multilateralism.

The use of statutory interpretation is another example of this dynamic.[64] It often responds to a need to give direct – unilateral – effect to the statute. It is based on substance, not neutrality. So it is not perceived as forming part of the ordinary rules of the conflict of laws. Statutists and traditionalists agree on this in principle: statutes that raise unavoidable issues of policy are excluded because they do not fit the multilateral mould. But they disagree on the extent of the exclusion. A statutist would agree that there are some statutory issues that are properly resolved in accordance with ordinary choice of law rules rather than statutory interpretation: for example, whether a party may avoid a contract on grounds of mistake.[65] A traditionalist would agree that there are some statutes whose scope must be determined in accordance with their substance, and not multilateral conflict of laws rules.[66] But there is no real way of working out where neutrality stops and policy begins. The traditionalist does not speak 'statutory interpretation', and the statutist does not speak 'conflict of laws'.

[59] *Cf* C McLachlan, *Foreign Relations Law* (Cambridge, Cambridge University Press, 2016) para 1.32ff on the exclusionary doctrines applying to foreign states.

[60] FC von Savigny, *System des heutigen Römischen Rechts* (transl Guthrie, 1869) vol VIII, 89, s 360; J Story, *Commentaries on the Conflict of Laws*, 7th edn (Boston, Little, Brown and Company, 1872) ss 17–18; and AV Dicey, *A Digest of the Law of England*, 2nd edn (London, Stevens and Sons, 1908) 'Introduction'.

[61] See O Kahn-Freund, 'Reflections on Public Policy in the English Conflict of Laws' (1953) 39 *Transactions of the Grotius Society* 39, 43.

[62] *Cf* H Muir Watt, 'Private International Law Beyond the Schism' (2011) 2 *Transnational Legal Theory* 347, 375– 81 for a critical account of private international law's 'tunnel-vision'.

[63] *Dicey, Morris and Collins* (n 1) ch 28 (entitled 'The Effect of Marriage on Property') and para 18-180 (on the power to make financial provision and property adjustment orders under the Matrimonial Causes Act 1973).

[64] *cf* Kahn-Freund, 'Reflections on Public Policy in the English Conflict of Laws' (n 61) 59.

[65] The doctrine of mistake is codified in New Zealand: Contract and Commercial Law Act 2017. See Briggs (n 2) 196.

[66] Mann, 'Statutes and the Conflict of Laws' (n 52) 124.

## B. Why the Conflict Matters

The downsides of this state of affairs may be obvious, but they are still worth articulating. If statutists and traditionalists hold on to their distinct, irreconcilable premises, they will each impose their own blanket exclusion. Statutists will err on the side of excluding conflict of laws rules; traditionalists will err on the side of excluding statutory interpretation. This sort of categorical reasoning is unlikely to produce optimal results.

It also creates much uncertainty. The parties in *Brown* had pleaded the case as a conflict of laws case all the way to the Supreme Court, when the Human Rights Commission intervened and persuaded the judges that this was the wrong approach.[67] Yet even now, with the benefit of the Supreme Court's judgment, it is difficult to see how the parties should have known that the conflict of laws was not the right vehicle for resolving the dispute. There is no real basis for predicting whether a court will go with the traditionalist or the statutist premise. In *Brown*, the matter was 'sui generis', and hence outside of the conflict of laws. In *Ludgater v Gerling*, the matter was surely also 'sui generis', in the sense that it did not neatly fit within established categories of choice of law, yet the Supreme Court proceeded to characterise the matter in the ordinary conflict of laws way.[68]

Faced with such uncertainty, how are parties to go about conceptualising and pleading their statutory claims? The status quo could seriously undermine people's faith in the conflict of laws.

# IV. Resolving the Conflict

Clearly, exclusive reasoning does not work, so it is time to try something different. It is time to look for common ground: a basis from which to navigate, rather than exclude, the respective roles of traditional conflict of laws rules and statutory interpretation. In order to do this, we must first accept that there is no need to – and in fact, every reason not to – spread the conflict across disciplines (section A). The two approaches share the same function, which is to determine the application of a domestic statute to a case with foreign elements. The conflict of laws is a discipline dedicated to the resolution of cross-border disputes. So let us think of the question as a question of conflict of laws, without, crucially, closing our minds to the methodology to be used.

This proposition may sound like traditionalism in disguise. But the fact of the matter is that the conflict of laws is capable of true methodological diversity (section B). All we need is a shared starting point of inquiry that allows us to

[67] *Brown v New Zealand Basing Ltd* [2017] NZSC 139, [2018] 1 NZLR 245, [7], [77].
[68] *Ludgater v Gerling* (n 11).

engage in statutory interpretation while taking account of traditionalist concerns, and vice versa. The conflict of laws, despite its dogmatic past, already knows how to do this.

## A. A Conflict of Laws Problem at Heart

The conflict of laws has been defined as that part of the law 'which deals with cases having a foreign element'.[69] The definition points to a specific problem: how to respond to civil claims with foreign elements. The cross-border application of domestic statutes is such a problem. No other discipline is dedicated to solving it; and tellingly, it is conflict of laws scholars who are at odds over what are the best tools for the job. So it would make sense, in the circumstances, to think of the cross-border application of statutes as a conflict of laws problem.

This is not a concession to the traditionalists, because the conflict of laws is more than neutral multilateralism, and it is capable of incorporating statutory interpretation. Despite its, traditionally, defensive reaction against all things 'policy', the conflict of laws has also always been *about* policy. The question whether a matter may be governed by foreign law at all or whether it is subject to the *lex fori* rule; the role of the public policy exception or overriding rules; the admissibility of sovereign claims and the effect of foreign acts of state: they all require reference to substance or policy, in ways that fall outside of the multilateral paradigm. But they are all problems of the conflict of laws.

Indeed, modern conflict of laws is turning away from the mindset of exclusion and beginning to face policy head-on. The premise of neutrality – the source of the multilateralism/policy divide – has been abandoned. Courts no longer buy into the idea that civil relations have a natural seat whose identification is a matter of fact more than judgement.[70] The principle of close connection is neither an end in itself nor a geographical formula.[71] In other words, the normative self-sufficiency of multilateralism is a myth. So when a court needs to work out the law applicable to movable property, it will take account of such policies as security of title,[72] or the integrity of foreign insolvency proceedings;[73] and when it is faced with a

[69] *Dicey, Morris and Collins* (n 1) para 1-001; similarly P Torremans (ed), *Cheshire, North & Fawcett Private International Law*, 15th edn (Oxford, Oxford University Press, 2017) 3 ('Private international law is that part of English law which comes into operation whenever the court is faced with a claim that contains a foreign element').

[70] On the objectives of choice of law, see AJE Jaffey, *Topics in Choice of Law* (London, BIICL, 1996) ch 1.

[71] *Cf* Berman, 'Conflict of Laws and the Legal Negotiation of Difference' (n 58) 141; PS Berman, 'Choice of Law and Jurisdiction on the Internet' (2005) 153 *University of Pennsylvania Law Review* 1819; L Little, 'Conflict of Laws Structure and Vision: Updating a Venerable Discipline' (2015) 31 *Georgia State University Law Review* 231; A Riles, 'Cultural Conflicts' (2008) 71 *Law and Contemporary Problems* 273.

[72] *Winkworth v Christie Manson & Woods Ltd* [1980] Ch 496, 513.

[73] *Ludgater Holdings Ltd v Gerling Australia Insurance Co Pty Ltd* (n 11) [29].

claim for personal injury, it will apply the law of the place where the injury was sustained, prioritising 'the claimant's law' – the victim – over 'the wrong-doer's law'.[74] Multilateralism does not give direct effect to substantive law, but it is no stranger to its policies.

If reliance on the multilateral method requires an engagement with the policies that underlie it, then, in the same vein, the conflict of laws needs to look at policies that militate against the multilateral method. For example, in determining the law applicable to foreign torts, lawmakers cannot start from a premise of multilateralism but also need to inquire whether there are reasons for applying the law of the forum, like the fact that the law of tort touches on important matters of public policy.[75] The modern conflict of laws caters for such inquiries. In particular, it is capable of asking whether the law of the forum must have unilateral effect because of its substance.

This is the ideal environment, therefore, for working out to what extent we should rely on statutory interpretation to determine the cross-border application of a statute. When it comes to the application of statutes to foreign facts, the truth is that the conflict of laws depends on statutory interpretation, and that statutory interpretation depends on the conflict of laws. The conflict of laws cannot be divorced from the laws' substance, and neither can the statute provide all the answers. Indeed, the latter is a common complaint levelled at statutists.[76] Substantive law on its own contains little insight into how it is properly to be delimited, and so statutists fall back on conflict-of-laws-like tools like the presumption of territoriality. There is no need for such parallel inquiries, when the conflict of laws can do it all.

## B. Characterisation as a Vehicle for Methodological Diversity

If the conflict of laws lets go of the exclusive premises of statutism and traditionalism, it is capable of providing a cohesive framework that allows for methodological diversity. The new starting point of inquiry is the process of characterisation. Characterisation has traditionally been associated with the multilateral method, but there is no reason in principle why it should be so confined. The purpose of characterisation is to examine the nature of the contentious issue – the

[74] Private International Law (Choice of Law in Tort) Act 2017, s 8(2)(a); see English and Scottish Law Commissions, 'Private International Law: Choice of Law in Tort and Delict' (Working Paper No 87/Consultative Memorandum No 62) paras 4.78, 4.74, 4.70.

[75] eg *Regie Nationale des Usines Renault SA v Zhang* [2002] HCA 10, 210 CLR 491, [43]-[59] (Gleeson CJ, Gaudron, McHugh, Gummow and Hayne JJ).

[76] eg C Bisping, 'Avoid the Statutist Trap: the International Scope of the Consumer Credit Act 1974' (2012) 8 *Journal of Private International Law* 35, 45.

'true' issue – so as to identify the most appropriate applicable law.[77] This is a broad and open-ended inquiry. Where the issue does not fit within an existing category of choice of law, the court must come up with a new one, all in the spirit of finding 'commonsense solutions based on practical considerations'.[78] So when examining the issue, the court need not be biased in favour of a multilateral solution that gives effect to foreign law.

Crucially, characterisation is undertaken by reference to the functions of the underlying substantive law.[79] When characterising, for example, the question of revocation of a will through subsequent marriage, the court may take into account that the function of the rule (that provides for revocation of the will at the time of marriage) is to reflect the testator's change in status and protect their future family. The court may then identify the most appropriate choice of law rule in light of that function.[80] This means that, if the substantive law in question comes in the form of a statute, the court will have to look at the content of the statute in order to characterise the issue. Examining the content of the statute is, of course, what statutists say we should do. Instead of forcing a hard choice between competing methodologies, characterisation provides statutists and traditionalists with a shared inquiry.

In this shared inquiry, there is room for identifying and balancing considerations that support a unilateral or multilateral approach, respectively. These considerations may come directly from the substantive law in question (ie the statute and, to some extent, its comparative equivalents); or they may be more general in nature, values and concerns that commonly bear on conflict of laws questions. The key distinction is that, in a multilateral scenario, domestic and foreign law will apply on the same terms. This means that multilateralism provides limited scope for connecting factors that are responsive to domestic idiosyncrasies. But an examination of the statute may reveal that such responsiveness would be desirable; for example, because the statute contains socially important rights and processes that ought to be available in a range of different circumstances, involving various constellations of foreign facts;[81] or because comparative foreign sources serve entirely different functions, and so a meaningful two-way connecting factor becomes elusive.[82] It also means that the application of foreign law must

[77] *Schumacher v Summergrove Estates Ltd* [2014] NZCA 412, [2014] 3 NZLR 599, [36], citing *Macmillan Inc v Bishopsgate Investment Trust Plc* [1996] 1 WLR 387; *Raiffeisen Zentralbank Österreich AG v Five Star General Trading LLC* [2001] QB 825 (CA) [27].

[78] *Schumacher* (ibid) [35], citing *MacMillan.*

[79] *Dicey, Morris & Collins* (n 1) para 2-039.

[80] ibid para 2-040.

[81] *Cf Brown v New Zealand Basing Ltd* [2017] NZSC 139, [2018] 1 NZLR 245, [40], [45], [46].

[82] *Cf* English criticism of the then proposed EU Regulation on Matrimonial Property (now Council Regulation (EU) No 2016/1103 of 24 June 2016 implementing enhanced cooperation in the area of jurisdiction, applicable law and the recognition and enforcement of decisions in matters of matrimonial property regimes [2016] OJ L183/1), on the basis that English law (in the form of a judicial discretion under the Matrimonial Causes Act to re-distribute property once a relationship has been dissolved) serves a different function to civil law matrimonial property regimes: Bar Council of England and

be appropriate in principle. This is not necessarily so. In complex areas of law, for example, it may not be practical to put claimants to the trouble of proving foreign law;[83] or the problem may be an inherently local one, requiring limitations on subject-matter jurisdiction.[84]

Thus, depending on its content, the court may or may not engage in a detailed interpretation of the statute.[85] The process of characterisation provides a forum where both statute-specific and 'external' considerations are potentially relevant. In most cases, the two sources will merge and considerations will draw, simultaneously, on the statute and on the general conflict of laws. For example, s 9 of the Law Reform Act 1936 provides a claimant injured by an insolvent insured with a right of direct action against the wrongdoer's insurer. In characterising a claim under s 9, the Supreme Court considered whether application of the section would unduly interfere with Australian insolvency proceedings, because the purpose of the section was to alter the priority of claims against an asset of the insolvent insured.[86] This inquiry drew both on typical conflict of laws concerns (undue interference with foreign proceedings) and the content and history of s 9. But there was no benefit in working out where the general conflict of laws ended and statutory interpretation began. In other words, there is no benefit in maintaining strict methodological boundaries.[87]

The final step in the process is to work out the content of the connecting factor. Whether unilateral or bilateral, the connecting factor ought to reflect the considerations identified as relevant in the course of characterisation. A unilateral connecting factor often goes hand in hand with subject-matter limitations.[88] In other words, the court has subject-matter jurisdiction to the extent that the law of the forum applies, and so the connecting factor defines the extent of the court's jurisdiction. This approach may appear to be inconsistent with statutory interpretation, which relies on a presumption of territoriality to delimit the cross-border application of legislation. But in many ways, territoriality is simply the unilateral version of the principle of close connection.[89] Territoriality has no fixed meaning, leaving courts to evaluate relevant territorial connections, in the same way that they would inquire into the content of a connecting factor. The considerations are

Wales, 'Response of the Bar Council of England and Wales to the Green Paper' (2006) and Resolution, 'Response to Green Paper on Conflict of Laws in Matters Concerning Matrimonial Property Regimes, Including Question of Jurisdiction and Mutual Recognition' (2006).

[83] See eg Ministry of Justice (UK), *European Commission proposed Regulations on matrimonial property regimes and the property consequences of registered partnerships: Response to public consultation* (28 November 2011) [5].

[84] For a more detailed discussion, see M Hook, 'The Statutist Trap and Subject-Matter Jurisdiction' (2017) 13 *Journal of Private International Law* 435, 448–52.

[85] ibid 452.

[86] *Ludgater v Gerling* (n 11).

[87] Although the Supreme Court's reasoning was problematic in other ways, because it mixed statutist and traditionalist premises: Hook, 'The Statutist Trap and Subject-Matter Jurisdiction' (n 84).

[88] ibid.

[89] ibid 450, 444–45.

all considerations that, applying the fiction of Parliamentary intent, Parliament could be said to have deemed relevant.

# V. *Brown*–Take Three

If the Court of Appeal in *Brown* took a doggedly traditionalist approach, and the Supreme Court's approach was so fiercely statutist that it dismissed the relevance of the conflict of laws altogether, what might a more cohesive approach look like? The overall dispute was whether the pilots were entitled to work beyond the age of 55 because the mandatory retirement age amounted to age discrimination. The starting point should be to examine the functions of the underlying substantive law, the ERA, to characterise the 'true' issue in the dispute. Ultimately, this inquiry should determine whether a unilateral or multilateral approach would be more appropriate: whether the ERA should apply on its own terms, or whether it should be subject to a multilateral choice of law rule so that it only applies when New Zealand law has already been determined to be applicable. The inquiry is open-ended and 'practical', so there is a range of considerations that may be relevant.

## A. A Contractual Issue?

The Act deals with relationships that are at least partly contractual. They are, to some extent, relationships created by the parties themselves, acting autonomously and voluntarily, and affecting largely their own interests. One of the functions of the Act is to regulate these contractual relationships: to impose limits on what the parties may, and may not, agree to do, and to provide for additional rights and obligations that will then flow from the contractual relationship. In that sense, the Act is firmly premised on the existence of a contract.[90] The issue in *Brown* might thus be characterised as relating to a breach of contract for unlawful dismissal;[91] or it may be thought to relate to the validity of a contractual term (the term being the compulsory retirement agreement); or perhaps the issue ought to be framed more pointedly, as relating to fundamental rights that are, nevertheless, superimposed on the parties' *contractual* relationship.

A focus on these contractual elements would suggest that we should apply a choice of law rule that is largely facilitative. The rule could point to the law the parties would have expected to be applicable. This expectation would be shaped

[90] See *Coutts Cars Ltd v Baguley* [2002] 2 NZLR 533, [39]–[42]; *cf Grace Team Accounting Ltd v Brake* [2014] NCA 541, [2015] 2 NZLR 494, [55]–[62]; *Brown v New Zealand Basing Ltd* [2017] NZSC 139, [2018] 1 NZLR 245, [51] ('The rights and obligations of employers and employees are dependent upon the existence of an employment agreement').

[91] *New Zealand Basing Ltd v Brown* [2016] NZCA 525, [2017] 2 NZLR 93, [34].

by the terms and the content of the contractual relationship. For example, if Party A and Party B, based in Country A and Country B, agree that Party A should work for Party B in Country A, the parties might expect – and should reasonably anticipate – that the law of Country A would govern their respective rights and obligations. This is, of course, why the choice of law rule for contractual matters designates the law most closely connected to the contract and why, in the first instance, it gives effect to the law chosen by the parties.[92] The Supreme Court relied on s 238 of the ERA, the contracting out provision, to conclude that Parliament would not have intended the parties to be able to choose the applicable law.[93] The better view is that contracting out provisions of this nature do not apply to choice of law agreements (and that Parliament only intended this to be a domestic non-evasion rule).[94]

Nevertheless, as we will see in the following section, the focus on the contractual side of employment relationships does not paint a complete picture. Employment contracts are not like ordinary contracts. They are prone to power imbalances and have significant socio-economic implications, not just for the parties but for society as a whole. A choice of law rule that is concerned only with the parties' expectations, therefore, may not provide the most appropriate choice of law in the circumstances, especially if the expectations are viewed through a false lens of contractual autonomy (pointing to the law most closely connected to the terms of the contract rather than, for example, the socio-economic context within which the contract unfolds).

## B. Or a Question of Status?

So while employment relationships clearly have contractual elements, it is just as important to recognise that the Act confers an additional, non-contractual layer that has been likened to a form of status.[95] The object of the Act is 'to build productive employment relationships through the promotion of good faith in all aspects of the employment environment and of the employment relationship'.[96] This object is achieved 'by recognising that employment relationships must be built not only on the implied mutual obligations of trust and confidence, but also on a legislative requirement for good faith behaviour';[97] and 'by acknowledging and addressing the inherent inequality of power in employment relationships'.[98]

[92] See ibid [35].
[93] See n 38 above.
[94] For a more detailed discussion of this point, see Hook and Wass, 'The Employment Relations Act and its Effect on Contracts Governed by Foreign Law' (n 12).
[95] *Brown v New Zealand Basing Ltd* [2017] NZSC 139, [2018] 1 NZLR 245, [56], [79]; *Lawson v Serco Ltd (Crofts)* [2006] UKHL 3, [2006] 1 All ER 823, [6]; *cf* the exclusion of employment contracts from the *Hague Principles on Choice of Law in International Commercial Contracts* (art 1(1)).
[96] ERA, s 3(a).
[97] ibid, s 3(a)(i).
[98] ibid, s 3(a)(ii).

Thus, the function of the Act could be said to be the creation of rights and obligations that come with being an employee or employer, respectively; and the 'true' issue in *Brown* was whether the pilots, in their capacity as employees, had suffered a personal grievance (or otherwise been treated unlawfully).

### *i. Protecting Employees, Regulating Employers*

If the predominant purpose of this creation of a status-like relationship is to protect employees, then arguably the conflict of laws should ensure that the Act applies to employees who have a close socio-economic connection to New Zealand – or, on a multilateral approach, that the applicable law be the law of the place with the closest socio-economic connection to the employee. Communities have an interest in protecting 'their' employees in the way they see fit; employees are more likely to be familiar with, and identify with, the law of the place where they live and work; and employers can hardly complain about the application of a law that is closely connected to the employee in their capacity as employee.[99]

The Supreme Court's base test comes to mind here. An even clearer (and multilateral) example is the solution adopted in the Rome I Regulation, which provides for the law of the country in which the employee habitually carries out their work.[100] Where the parties have chosen the applicable law, the chosen law applies to the extent that it affords the same, or greater, levels of protection to the employee,[101] underscoring the protective function of the objective choice of law rule.[102]

But what about the flipside of this protective function – the need to regulate employers and hold them to account? If this was the focus, the most appropriate solution would be to apply the Act to employers who operate in New Zealand – over whom New Zealand has control, and for whom it is, therefore, in some ways responsible. On a multilateral approach, the law to be applied might then be the law of the place where the employer is based. This would recognise the base country's interest in regulating 'its own' employers, and it would meet the employer's expectation that its conduct be measured by the laws of its home jurisdiction.

### *ii. Multilateral or Unilateral?*

Assuming the issue is to be characterised as a status-like relationship of employment, would it be more appropriate to apply New Zealand law unilaterally or to rely on a multilateral choice of law rule?

[99] For the point that cross-border relations tend to have multiple 'community affiliations', see Berman (n 58).

[100] Regulation (EC) 593/2008 on the law applicable to contractual obligations [2008] OJ L177/6, art 8(2).

[101] ibid, art 8(1).

[102] ibid, Recitals (23) and (35).

The possible connecting factors that we have identified so far – the employee's or the employer's base – would be capable of 'multilateralisation' as long as one is chosen over the other. The benefit of multilateralism is that it recognises foreign and domestic connections – and the interests associated with these connections – in equal measure. For example, if New Zealand law applies where the employee is based in New Zealand because that provides the overall fairest option to the parties, then the same considerations of fairness will still be given effect if the employee was based overseas (and New Zealand was connected in some other way, perhaps because it is the employer's home jurisdiction). Multilateral choice of law rules are also better at discouraging forum shopping and creating predictable and uniform results.

On the other hand, the employment relationship might be viewed as an inherently local matter that is inextricably linked to New Zealand law and New Zealand's socio-economic policies. Based on this view, an employee or employer carries that status in New Zealand by virtue of New Zealand law.[103] It is not a status that is transplantable from overseas. And so, naturally, it cannot be governed by foreign law; in the same way, for example, that the regulation of health and safety is largely confined to New Zealand workplaces in accordance with New Zealand law.[104] Enforceability, too, might be a relevant consideration,[105] and would be a reason for favouring a unilateral, employer-focused approach. Employment legislation typically contains a range of remedies and powers which, in many cases, would only be enforceable in the employer's home. Why exercise subject-matter jurisdiction over foreign employers (and apply foreign law), if New Zealand lacks the power to make any orders effective?

The extensive infrastructure that supports the regulation and determination of employment matters is further evidence, perhaps, that the New Zealand court's subject-matter jurisdiction over employment disputes should be limited to those governed by New Zealand law. Such infrastructure – like the Employment Relations Authority's power to conduct investigations[106] – is often closely linked to substantive law yet, for obvious reasons, cannot be recreated in the forum.[107]

What if both functions – the protection of employees and the regulation of employers – are integral to the Act? On a multilateral approach, this diversity of purpose would have to be reflected in an open-ended connecting factor that requires courts to weigh all relevant connections on the facts of the case. If the

[103] *Cf* divorce, which has been treated as a question of status/a matter *in rem*: *Salvesen v Administrator of Austrian Property* [1927] AC 641, 662 (Viscount Dunedin).

[104] Health and Safety at Work Act 2015 (but see s 9(1)(b)).

[105] *Société Eram Shipping Co Ltd v Cie Internationale de Navigation* [2003] UKHL 30, [2004] 1 AC 260, [26] (Lord Bingham).

[106] ERA, s 160.

[107] *Cf* the argument by Lord Woolf in *Harding v Wealands* [2006] UKHL 32, [2007] 2 AC 1, [11] that the question of quantum of damages should be characterised as procedural (and hence be governed by the *lex fori*) because the foreign statute was a 'detailed statutory procedural code' that would be 'very difficult, if not impossible, to apply' in an English court.

applicable law was the law 'most closely connected' to the employment relationship, then both the employee's and the employer's base may be relevant factors in determining the closest connection, depending on the facts. If the employee's base is fortuitous – say, because he works remotely from his holiday home in a country where he spends only brief periods of time – then it would not be given much weight, and vice versa. The guiding principle should be to identify meaningful socio-economic connections between communities and 'their' employees and employers.

On a unilateral approach, on the other hand, the court need not pick and choose but may give effect to all relevant connections to New Zealand law. That is the reason, of course, why the unilateral method runs the risk of parochialism. Rather than evaluating all relevant connections to select the law that, on aggregate, is the most appropriate in the circumstances, the forum simply prioritises its own, overall weaker, connection. Indeed, a relatively generous connecting factor would be necessary to avoid cases falling into gaps between inconsistent unilateral laws.[108] So the question that must be asked is: is there something about employment law – its political nature, perhaps – that means we should prioritise New Zealand connections over foreign ones? Is there a justifiable forum bias?

For example, on a broad unilateral approach, the Act might apply to an expatriate Australian employee of an Australian employer who performs most of his work remotely from New Zealand, all on the basis that the employee lives and works in New Zealand. But Australia may have a more meaningful connection to the employment relationship than New Zealand: perhaps Australia is where the employer conducts its business, and the reasons why the employee lives in New Zealand are largely personal. In these circumstances, the relationship would be more closely affiliated with Australia. To give unilateral effect to New Zealand law would be to deny the interests underlying that connection and to prefer local interests (ie New Zealand's wish to protect its own residents). Such forum bias may be justifiable if the relationship raises questions of sensitive policy that mean foreign law should not be 'trusted' (at least in cases where there is some meaningful connection to New Zealand).

Finally, William Young J in the Supreme Court considered that the broad jurisdictional rules in the Employment Regulations indicated the vast range of circumstances in which the Act may be applicable.[109] The argument is difficult to follow. Questions of personal jurisdiction and *forum (non) conveniens* are not to be equated with questions of choice of law. What the rules do indicate, however, is that the legislative scheme is consistent with the potential application of foreign law. Rule 31A(5)(g)(iv), for example, provides for service where the employment agreement 'was expressly or impliedly to be governed by New Zealand law', which

[108] *Cf* Hook (n 84) 441; JHC Morris, 'The Choice of Law Clause in Statutes' (1946) 62 *Law Quarterly Review* 170, 179.
[109] See n 43 above.

must mean that the employment *agreement*, at least, may also be governed by foreign law.[110]

## C. A Human Rights Matter?

A third way of characterising the issue may be to focus on the nature of the right that is alleged to have been breached, the right to be free from age discrimination. In other words, perhaps the 'true' issue is whether the pilots were 'discriminated against in [their] employment'[111] when asked to retire at the age of 55. Age is one of several prohibited grounds of discrimination that are incorporated into the ERA from the Human Rights Act 1993. The right to be free from discrimination is a fundamental human right that is relevant to a number of civil relationships, not just relationships of employment.[112] So arguably the conflict of laws ought to reflect this more general function, of protecting and enforcing human rights.

How is the conflict of laws to do this? The individual is centre-stage of the human rights inquiry, so it would be appropriate to apply New Zealand law where an individual has suffered a human rights breach in New Zealand. But New Zealand law should also arguably be available where the alleged wrongdoer is based in New Zealand, because New Zealand would have an interest in holding New Zealand wrongdoers to account. A helpful example may be that of a New Zealand-based company that moves some of its production overseas to profit from cheap labour. Does New Zealand not have a responsibility to ensure that the company, which is subject to its control, uphold the workers' human rights?[113]

Framed in this way, a unilateral approach may be appropriate to give broad application to New Zealand law. Human rights are of great socio-political importance, so New Zealand could rightfully prioritise its own connections over those of other countries. There is an intuitive appeal in 'exporting' human rights (along the lines of 'the more human rights, the better'). The alternative view is that New Zealand should be wary of engaging in 'rights imperialism', and that we ought to recognise that New Zealand law is not necessarily 'better' – that is, more claimant-friendly – than its foreign counterparts.

[110] *cf* also s 9(1)(b) of the Health and Safety at Work Act 2015, which provides that the Act applies to an aircraft 'operating outside New Zealand, if any workers employed or engaged to work on board the aircraft are employed or engaged under an employment agreement or contract for services governed by New Zealand law'.

[111] ERA, s 103(1)(c).

[112] Human Rights Act 1993, pt 2.

[113] See J Ruggie, 'Protect, Respect and Remedy: A Framework for Business and Human Rights, Report of the Special Representative of the Secretary-General on the Issue of Human Rights and Transnational Corporations and other Business Enterprises' (Human Rights Council, Eighth Session, A/HRC/8/5, 7 April 2008); J Ruggie 'Guiding Principles on Business and Human Rights: Implementing the United Nations "Protect, Respect and Remedy" Framework' (Human Rights Council, Seventh Session, A/HRC/17/31, 21 March 2011) Principle 2.

The territorial provisions in the Human Rights Act, which were relied upon by the Supreme Court, do not offer reliable insight into whether the right to be free from discrimination should apply unilaterally. Section 24 excludes the right to be free from discrimination from employment of 'a person on a ship or aircraft, not being a New Zealand ship or aircraft, if the person employed or seeking employment was engaged or applied for it outside New Zealand'; section 26 excludes the right

> if the duties of the position in respect of which that treatment is accorded (a) are to be performed wholly or mainly outside New Zealand and (b) are such that, because of the laws, customs, or practices of the country in which those duties are to be performed, they are ordinarily carried out only by a person who is of a particular sex or religious or ethical belief, or who is in a particular age group.

It is obvious that Parliament did turn its mind to the cross-border application of the Act in these sections. But sections 24 and 26 on their own are insufficient to delimit the right to be free from discrimination. Clearly New Zealand's anti-discrimination provisions cannot apply in all cases that do not fall within the sections. This approach would be over-inclusive and would lead to potentially absurd results. It would mean, for example, that a person (who is not working on a ship or aircraft) can bring a personal grievance claim for discrimination under the Act even if the relevant duties are duties to be performed wholly or mainly outside New Zealand, as long as the duties are not such that, because of the laws and customs of the country, they are ordinarily carried out only by a person who is in a particular age group.

On one view, these provisions ought to be treated as self-limiting, so that the exclusions take effect once New Zealand law has been determined to be applicable.[114] But self-limiting provisions may create problems when paired with multilateral choice of law rules, because they potentially disapply the legislation in circumstances where New Zealand law has already been identified as applicable, leaving a regulatory hole. On this view, then, a unilateral approach may be more appropriate.

## D. A Little Bit of Everything

The choice between unilateralism and multilateralism is not an easy one. Unilateralism – which would likely result in broad, overlapping employment regimes – does not sit well with an integrated approach to international litigation, and it may fail to recognise important socio-economic ties between the claim, and the parties, and foreign communities. On the other hand, it would be important for New Zealand law to prioritise its own socio-economic ties if

[114] See further Hook (n 84) 439.

employment relationships raised issues requiring substantive regulation, and there is an argument that the court's subject-matter jurisdiction should be confined to local employment matters. Unilateralism would also give employees the option of going forum shopping for the most favourable regime, encouraging a 'race to the top'. Resource constraints may mean that this is not a viable option, and we should not disregard the regulatory burden on employers of being subject to two, or even more, overlapping regimes. Yet if unilateralism has the potential of empowering an otherwise vulnerable group of claimants, it should be given serious thought.

## *i. A Multilateral Choice of Law Rule for Employment*

Leaving aside the question of human rights, my own view is that a multilateral choice of law rule would best cater for the mixed – contractual and status-like – functions of employment law. The Rome I Regulation demonstrates that employment relationships need not be tied to local norms and processes. Whether a claimant is an employee, and what protections they are entitled to as a result, are questions that benefit from co-ordination rather than parallel regimes. Many of the protections are of social, political and economic significance. But they are not necessarily so important that New Zealand's connections ought to be prioritised. The right not to be unfairly dismissed, for example, is unavailable to employees on a fixed-term contract,[115] so it does not appear to be so crucial to the organisation of New Zealand's labour market that New Zealand law should take precedence over laws that, overall, have a more meaningful connection to the claim.

As it happens, the pilots' claim had strong connections to New Zealand.[116] The pilots lived in New Zealand and their tours of duty began and ended in Auckland. In fact, the employment agreement required that the pilots reside in New Zealand, and the salaries took into account their relatively lower cost of living. NZBL, although a Hong Kong company, also carried on business in New Zealand. On the other hand, the pilots paid tax in Hong Kong; their training, administration and management took place in Hong Kong; they were licensed by the Hong Kong Civil Aviation Department; and the majority of their work occurred outside of New Zealand. The parties had also, of course, chosen the law of Hong Kong.

If we accept that rights and obligations attendant on employment relationships are to be characterised as employment matters, involving elements of both contract and status, then these are connections that might well have been relevant to the applicable multilateral connecting factor. Let us assume that the applicable law is

[115] ERA, s 66; *cf* U Grušić, *The European Private International Law of Employment* (Cambridge, Cambridge University Press, 2015) 212; *Dicey, Morris & Collins* (n 1) para 33–282.
[116] *Brown v New Zealand Basing Ltd* [2017] NZSC 139, [2018] 1 NZLR 245, [89].

the law of the place with the closest connection to the employment relationship; that the connection is to reflect the facilitative, protective and regulatory functions of employment law; and that it should take into account the parties' interests as well as those of affected communities. This choice of law rule may be combined with a power to select the applicable law, but the power would have to be limited so as not to undermine the objectives of the rule.[117]

On that approach, New Zealand would have been the place with the closest connection. The pilots lived and performed some of their work here, so they likely felt a personal, social and cultural affiliation with New Zealand. They were based here as part of their employment, so the local community would have had an interest in treating them as 'their own'. NZBL could not complain about the application of New Zealand law, having agreed that the pilots should be based here: New Zealand was hardly a fortuitous place of residence and work, and NZBL could have reasonably expected that its conduct would be subject to New Zealand law.

These considerations would have outweighed a competing interest by Hong Kong to regulate its own employers, in accordance with its own socio-economic and fiscal policies, as well as NZBL's understandable preference to be subject to the law of its home jurisdiction, which would ideally apply to all pilots flying for Cathay Pacific. We should not downplay the importance of the connection to Hong Kong, which was the centre of Cathay Pacific's operations, presumably had greater enforcement jurisdiction over NZBL, and provided a common frame of reference for the plaintiffs, their colleagues and all Cathay-Pacific-related entities. The application of Hong Kong law would not have come as a surprise. But NZBL was set up specifically to employ New Zealand-based pilots, whose day-to-day duties would have had few meaningful links to Hong Kong. In these circumstances, Hong Kong law would have only been applicable if the parties' choice had been given effect. For reasons explored elsewhere, the answer to this question – whether the parties' choice should be given effect – would have been far from obvious.[118]

## *ii. A Unilateral Approach to Discrimination*

A multilateral solution may be appropriate for most employment issues. But some matters, including the question of unlawful discrimination, arguably require a more forum-biased response. It is difficult to escape the conclusion that, insofar as fundamental matters of policy are concerned, control breeds responsibility. If that is correct, we should not shy away from broad connecting factors, which would be ill-suited to multilateralisation.

[117] I have discussed elsewhere how the conflict of laws may rein in party autonomy to ensure consistency with choice of law rules serving protective or regulatory functions: M Hook, *The Choice of Law Contract* (Oxford, Hart, 2016) ch 3.

[118] ibid.

There are a number of ways in which human rights may be accommodated as part of an overall multilateral approach. First, the issue of discrimination could be characterised separately or as an incidental question.[119] So the question whether NZBL had acted unlawfully by discriminating against the pilots would be determined unilaterally by New Zealand law, provided the relevant connecting factors are satisfied. It may be sufficient, for example, that the pilots had close socio-economic ties with New Zealand in their capacity as employees. Depending on the scope of this incidental question, the effect of NZBL's unlawful conduct may then be left to be worked out by the law that governs the relationship more generally. For example, Hong Kong law could apply to determine whether NZBL had an obligation to offer continued employment to the pilots past the age of 55, proceeding on the conclusion that the compulsory retirement on grounds of age would be unlawful.

Alternatively, the right to bring a personal grievance on grounds of discrimination could be treated as an overriding mandatory rule,[120] so it applies not only when the multilateral choice of law rule points to New Zealand law being applicable, but also when New Zealand is connected to the claim in some other way – for example, because the pilots were based in New Zealand. The Court of Appeal should have given serious consideration to the question whether the right to be free from discrimination amounted to a 'crystallised [rule] of public policy' that gives effect to the forum's substantive interests.[121] Overriding rules are not uncommon in the area of employment law.[122] Instead, the Court of Appeal fell back on categorical and exclusive reasoning, thereby avoiding engagement with the underlying substantive issues.

A similar criticism can be made of the Court of Appeal's approach to the public policy exception.[123] The exception would provide an especially flexible tool to accommodate human rights concerns, because it would be invoked only where the foreign law provides less – or much less – protection than would be considered appropriate under New Zealand law. In particular, it would not pre-empt application of a foreign human rights regime that happens to be more protective. But the Court of Appeal viewed the exception in narrow terms, as being engaged by 'absolute' rather than relative values. To get the most out of the exception, we need to recognise that it responds to the same considerations that may have supported a unilateral choice of law rule (or, for that matter, an overriding rule), except that its response may be tailored to the particular circumstances of the case. It is, in that sense, a much less intrusive option.

[119] On incidental questions, see *Dicey, Morris & Collins* (n 1) ch 2.
[120] This question is explored in more detail in Hook and Wass (n 12).
[121] See *Dicey, Morris & Collins* (n 1) para 1-061.
[122] See J Basedow, 'The Law of Open Societies' (2013) 360 *Recueil des Cours* 9, 384–88.
[123] This question is explored in more detail in Hook and Wass (n 12).

# VI. Conclusion

The conflict of laws provides a coherent framework for evaluating and weighing considerations that are commonly perceived as being unique to either the conflict of laws or statutory interpretation. The courts in *Brown* could have relied on this framework to engage in a nuanced, wide-ranging analysis of the cross-border application of the ERA, instead of proceeding from exclusive premises and dismissing a range of potentially relevant considerations off the bat. If they had done so, they likely would have concluded that the pilots could rely on the right to be free from age discrimination, and they could have reached this conclusion in a number of ways, drawing on the ERA, its functions and the many values underlying the principle of connection. It is here, in the methodological diversity of the conflict of laws, that statutists and traditionalists will find a shared language.

# 9

# Choice of Law in the Age of Statutes

## *A Defence of Statutory Interpretation after* Valve

MICHAEL DOUGLAS*

## I. Introduction

The choice of law problems of the twenty-first century arise in an 'age of statutes'.[1] Most cases are determined by law sourced in statute;[2] statutory interpretation has thus become the most important part of judicial work.[3] In Australia, a statutory provision of great importance to the practice of commercial law – or at least, to the resolution of commercial disputes – is the prohibition on misleading or deceptive conduct in s 18(1) of the Australian Consumer Law (ACL).[4] The prohibition promotes informed commercial activity[5] and guards against the social detriment of the unrestrained pursuit of self-interest.[6] The value of these policies can be seen in how regularly the provision is relied upon in civil litigation.[7] The question which underpins this chapter is: to what extent can, or should, Australian courts have regard to those policies in the context of cross-border litigation? The answer

* Part of the research for this chapter was conducted while on PhD exchange at Harvard Law School, which was partly funded by a Walter Reid Scholarship awarded by Sydney Law School, for which I am grateful. Sincere thanks to Professor Mary Keyes for her corrections and kind criticism.

[1] G Calabresi, *A Common Law for the Age of Statutes* (Cambridge, Mass, Harvard University Press, 1982); M Leeming, 'Theories and Principles Underlying the Common Law – The Statutory Elephant in the Room' (2013) 36(3) *University of New South Wales Law Journal* 1002, 1002.

[2] S Gageler, 'Common Law Statutes and Judicial Legislation: Statutory Interpretation as a Common Law Process' (2011) 37(2) *Monash University Law Review* 1, 1.

[3] M Kirby, 'Towards a Grand Theory of Interpretation: The Case of Statutes and Contracts' (2003) 24 *Statute Law Review* 95, 96.

[4] Competition and Consumer Act 2010 (Cth) sch 2 (CCA).

[5] *Bullabidgee Pty Ltd v McLeary* [2011] NSWCA 259, [6] (Allsop P, Basten and Young JJA agreeing) (*Bullabidgee*).

[6] *Peter Bodum A/S v DKSH Aust Pty Ltd* [2011] FCAFC 98, (2011) 280 ALR 639, [201] (Greenwood J; Tracey J agreeing) (*Bodum*), cited in C Lockhart, *The Law of Misleading or Deceptive Conduct*, 4th edn (Chatswood, LexisNexis Butterworths, 2015) 4.

[7] A Asher, 'A "Theory of Everything" for Consumer Protection?' (2006) 14 *Trade Practices Law Journal* 110, 110.

may turn on the broader issue of the proper relationship between choice of law and statutory interpretation in common law legal systems.

Recently, Burrows said that 'it is indisputable that statutes are swallowing up our common law'.[8] Perhaps the same can be said for choice of law principles which were once grounded in the common law.[9] Choice of law statutes are increasingly frequent additions to private international law, both in the common law world and elsewhere.[10] Australia is contemplating enactment of the Hague Principles on Choice of Law in International Commercial Contracts via a proposed 'International Civil Law Act',[11] for example, while in New Zealand, the Private International Law (Choice of Law in Tort) Act 2017 (NZ) recently did away with double actionability.

Apart from these kinds of dedicated choice of law statutes, many other statutes contain provisions expressly dealing with their scope of operation.[12] Some contain multilateral choice of law rules – like s 11(2) of the Defamation Act 2005 (NSW), which provides that, for intra-Australian publications, the law of the place with the closest connection to the harm applies. Others provide that the statute will apply despite a contractual provision to the contrary[13] – like s 8 of the Insurance Contracts Act 1984 (Cth), famously considered in *Akai Pty Ltd v People's Insurance Co Ltd* (*Akai*).[14] But perhaps the most difficult category of statutes, at least for private international lawyers, is so-called 'generally-worded statutes' which do not deal with their scope of operation. There are competing views on the correct approach to such legislation.[15] The leading contemporary Australian authority on this issue, Keyes, favours the view that generally-worded statutes should only be applied by a court if the forum's choice of law rules select the local law as the applicable law.[16] From that perspective, the same can be said for statutes containing

[8] A Burrows, *Thinking About Statutes – Interpretation, Interaction, Improvement* (Cambridge, Cambridge University Press, 2018) 1.

[9] The arrival of European private international law in England provides a stark example; see A Briggs, *Private International Law in English Courts* (Oxford, Oxford University Press, 2014) 18–21.

[10] Choice of law rules have been codified in many parts of the world: SC Symeonides, *Codifying Choice of Law Around the World* (Oxford, Oxford University Press, 2014).

[11] M Douglas and N Loadsman, 'The Impact of the Hague Principles on Choice of Law in International Commercial Contracts' (2018) 19 *Melbourne Journal of International Law* 1. How the following analysis would fit with the carve-out for 'overriding mandatory rules and public policy' in art 11 of the Principles is a subject for detailed consideration elsewhere.

[12] Morris wrote on the subject more than 70 years ago: 'The Choice of Law Clause in Statutes' (1946) 62 *Law Quarterly Review* 170–85. Keyes labels these 'specifically limited statutory provisions': M Keyes, 'Statutes, Choice of Law, and the Role of Forum Statutes' (2008) 4 *Journal of Private International Law* 1, 3–5. On the different academic labels for statutes containing these kinds of provisions, see K Lipstein, 'Inherent Limitations in Statutes and the Conflict of Laws' (1977) 26 *International & Comparative Law Quarterly* 884, 885.

[13] Which might be described as a 'unilateral choice of law rules': see Keyes, ibid 4.

[14] *Akai* [1996] HCA 39, 188 CLR 418 (Toohey, Gaudron and Gummow JJ).

[15] See Hook's account of the debate in ch 8 of this volume. In each case, the relevant question is: what tools should be used to determine the scope of the statute's application in matters with a foreign element?

[16] Keyes, 'Statutes, Choice of Law, and the Role of Forum Statutes' (n 12); see also U Grušić, 'The Territorial Scope of Employment Legislation and Choice of Law' (2012) 75 *Modern Law Review* 72.

so-called 'self-limiting' choice of law provisions.[17] The contrary view is that the potential application of a forum statute may be resolved by statutory interpretation, even in a case with a foreign element.[18] Mann described this method as follows: 'for a court sitting in the legislating State it may frequently be sufficient to ascertain, by interpretation, the scope of a statute and to refrain from investigating the applicability of any general rule of the conflict of laws'.[19] At the risk of alienating colleagues whom I admire, this chapter favours that view. It defends the 'statutory interpretation' approach to putative choice of law problems for international contracts,[20] with primary reference to Australian law. The focus is on the so-called 'mandatory' treatment of forum statutes in cases where there are strong connections to foreign jurisdictions.

The chapter considers a recent Australian case where the Court took a statutory interpretation approach to a choice of law problem for a cross-border contract: *Australian Competition and Consumer Commission v Valve Corporation (No 3)* (*Valve*).[21] Although some have criticised the decision,[22] it was subsequently affirmed by a unanimous Full Court of the Federal Court of Australia,[23] and tacitly, by denial of special leave,[24] also by the High Court of Australia.[25] Edelman J's primary judgment on liability invokes the concept of the 'policy of the law' to justify the mandatory application of a forum statute.[26] Similar language was used by the plurality in *Akai* – another Australian case in which the High Court applied an Australian statute to override an exclusive foreign jurisdiction agreement and a choice of foreign law in a cross-border contract.[27] These cases show that the 'policy of the law' concept can perform a determinative role in cross-border disputes involving commercial contracts. The legislature's policy of the prohibition on misleading or deceptive conduct may apply irrespective of parties' intentions, and despite a chorus of dissent from private international law scholars who prefer the neutrality of so-called 'traditional' choice of law rules.[28]

[17] See Keyes (n 12) 12.

[18] eg *Brown v New Zealand Basing Ltd* [2017] NZSC 139, (2017) 14 NZELR 905, [76] (Ellen France J).

[19] FAP Mann, 'The Doctrine of Justification in International Law' (1954) 111 *Recueil Des Cours* 1, 70, quoted in DStL Kelly, *Localising Rules in the Conflict of Laws* (Adelaide, Woodley Press, 1974) 96.

[20] An approach which might be understood as statutory interpretation *instead of* choice of law.

[21] *Valve* [2016] FCA 196, (2016) 337 ALR 647, [60], [116].

[22] eg L Nottage and J Morrison, 'Accessing and Assessing Australia's International Arbitration Act' (2017) 24 *Journal of International Arbitration* 963, 979–80; *cf* R Garnett, 'Arbitration of Cross-Border Consumer Transactions in Australia: A Way Forward?' (2017) 39 *Sydney Law Review* 569, 580–81.

[23] *Valve Corporation v Australian Competition and Consumer Commission* [2017] FCAFC 224, (2017) 351 ALR 584 (*Valve v ACCC*).

[24] On the significance of special leave decisions, *cf* the treatment of *Western Export Services Inc v Jireh International Pty Ltd* [2011] HCA 45, (2011) 86 ALJR 1 in contract law. See further O Jones, 'Are the High Court's Reasons for Refusing Special Leave Binding?' (2013) 87 *Australian Law Journal* 774.

[25] *Valve Corporation v Australian Competition and Consumer Commission* [2018] HCASL 99 (19 April 2018).

[26] The significance of characterisation of a statute as 'mandatory law' is considered below.

[27] *Akai* [(n 14) 447.

[28] See Hook ch 8, n 2, citing A Briggs, 'A Note on the Application of the Statute Law of Singapore' [2005] *Singapore Journal of Legal Studies* 189, 194.

The argument proceeds as follows. Section II explores the *Valve* litigation. Section III provides an account of the statutory construction principles which can be determinative of choice of law problems for cross-border contracts. Section IV interrogates the 'policy of the law', and considers the consequences of the statutory interpretation approach, good and bad. The goal is to provide an account of what some courts actually do,[29] why they do it, and why I consider this to be acceptable. It is argued that, if the world of common law principle is in retreat,[30] then perhaps, too, are common law approaches to the resolution of choice of law problems.

# II. *Valve*

## A. Background

The subject-matter of the *Valve* litigation is a perfect demonstration of the contemporary significance of private international law. The case concerned videogames downloaded from the internet. The respondent, Valve Corp, is a company based in the State of Washington, USA (Washington), which operates 'Steam', a platform which allows individuals to both download videogames and play them online, and 'Steam Support', an online support service for Steam users.[31] There are more than 2 million Australian Steam accounts, and many millions more Australian gamers.[32]

It may surprise some readers to know that not all videogames are good. In fact, some are disappointing.[33] As with any other product, a consumer of a disappointing videogame may seek a refund. At the heart of this litigation were representations by Valve, to Australian gamers, to the effect that fees paid for videogames via Steam were non-refundable. Those representations were made in the context of the 'Steam Subscriber Agreement' (SSA) to which Steam users were required to agree, as well as in communications via Steam Support.

The Australian regulator, the Australian Competition and Consumer Commission (ACCC), brought proceedings alleging that Valve's representations

[29] See eg *Insight Vacations Pty Ltd v Young* [2011] HCA 15, (2011) 243 CLR 149; *Golden Acres Ltd v Queensland Estates Pty Ltd* [1969] Qd R 378; *Kay's Leasing Corporation Pty Ltd v Fletcher* [1964] HCA 79, (1964) 116 CLR 124 (*Kay's Leasing*); *cf Sweedman v Transport Accident Commission* [2006] HCA 8, (2006) 226 CLR 362.

[30] Kirby, 'Towards a Grand Theory of Interpretation' (n 3) 97.

[31] Valve is perhaps best known for its work on *Half Life 3*, a forthcoming classic.

[32] 97% of Australian households with children have computer games; 67% of Australians play video games; the average Australian gamer is 34 years old: Bond University and Interactive Games & Entertainment Association, 'Digital Australia Report 2018' (2018) 6, www.igea.net/wp-content/uploads/2017/07/Digital-Australia-2018-DA18-Final-1.pdf.

[33] In 2016, Valve offered refunds for the game *No Man's Sky* following the game's near-universal condemnation: M Humphries, 'Steam is issuing No Man's Sky refunds even if you've played for over 70 hours', *Geek.com* (29 August 2016) www.geek.com/tech/steam-is-issuing-no-mans-sky-refunds-even-if-youve-played-for-over-70-hours-1668389/.

contravened the acceptable quality guarantee in the ACL, which could not be modified or excluded under ACL, s 64.[34] It pleaded that, by those representations concerning the existence, exclusion or effect of the ACL's consumer guarantees – ie by representing that no refunds were possible – Valve contravened the prohibition on misleading or deceptive conduct in ACL, s 18(1), and also made false or misleading representations about the existence or effect of the ACL's consumer guarantees in contravention of ACL, s 29(1)(m).[35]

Although the case was pinned on representations to Australian gamers, the facts disclosed a number of connecting factors to foreign places. Valve was incorporated in Washington. Steam depended upon a global network of servers, many of which were based in Washington;[36] data emerged from Washington, and client information was held there, too.[37] In respect of the SSA, the place of the contract was probably Washington,[38] at least according to Australian law[39] giving effect to the relevant UNCITRAL Model Law.[40] Steam Support was provided online and underpinned by a system with servers in Washington.[41] Significantly, the SSA contained the following clause (clause 14):

> 14 APPLICABLE LAW/JURISDICTION
>
> The terms of this section may not apply to European Union consumers.
>
> You agree that this Agreement shall be deemed to have been made and executed in the State of Washington, and any dispute arising hereunder shall be resolved in accordance with the law of Washington. You agree that any claim asserted in any legal proceeding by you against Valve shall be commenced and maintained exclusively in any state or federal court located in King County, Washington, having subject matter jurisdiction with respect to the dispute between the parties and you hereby consent to the exclusive jurisdiction of such courts[42]

However, the ACL has a provision directed to clauses like this. Section 67 of the ACL, which replaced s 67 of the Trade Practices Act 1974 (Cth), provides as follows:

> 67 Conflict of laws
>
> If:
>
> (a) the proper law of a contract for the supply of goods or services to a consumer would be the law of any part of Australia but for a term of the contract that provides otherwise; or

[34] ACL, ss 54, 64.
[35] *Valve* [2016] FCA 196, (2016) 337 ALR 647, [2].
[36] ibid [29].
[37] ibid [82].
[38] ibid [81].
[39] eg Electronic Transactions Act 2011 (WA) s 15.
[40] UNCITRAL Model Law on Electronic Commerce 1996 with additional article 5 bis as adopted in 1998 (adopted 12 June 1996, United Nations).
[41] *Valve* [2016] FCA 196, (2016) 337 ALR 647, [28].
[42] ibid [72].

(b) a contract for the supply of goods or services to a consumer contains a term that purports to substitute, or has the effect of substituting, the following provisions for all or any of the provisions of this Division:

(i) the provisions of the law of a country other than Australia;
(ii) the provisions of the law of a State or a Territory;

the provisions of this Division apply in relation to the supply under the contract despite that term.

The 'Division' is ACL Part 3-2, division 1, which deals with consumer guarantees in the context of consumer transactions. According to the explanatory memorandum, the purpose of this provision is to ensure that the consumer guarantees established in the ACL cannot be excluded by contract.[43]

Davis describes s 67 as 'unnecessary and misdirected'.[44] Certainly, the section is confusing. What is the relationship between subsections (a) and (b)? If a term 'substitutes' Australian law, or part of it, as per subsection (b), would that not be a contract which would be subject to Australian law, or part of it, in the absence of that term, as per subsection (a)? What work is there for subsection (a)? And what if the proper law would *not* be Australian law in the absence of a term? These issues were grappled by Edelman J.

## B. The Private International Law Issues

Edelman J characterised Valve's position in terms of three arguments.[45] First, Valve argued that its conduct did not occur in Australia and that it did not carry on business in Australia. The litigation was conducted on the basis that the question 'of whether Valve carried on business in Australia' only arose if Valve's allegedly misleading conduct was not 'in Australia', apparently on the basis of s 131(1) of the Competition and Consumer Act 2010 (Cth), which provides that the ACL 'applies as a law of the Commonwealth to the conduct of corporations, and in relation to contraventions of Chapter 2, 3 or 4 of Schedule 2 by corporations'.[46] Arguably, Valve's acts were 'bilateral', and occurred in Australia;[47] his Honour held as much, and went on to consider where Valve carried on business in *obiter*.[48]

[43] Explanatory memorandum, Trade Practices Amendment (Australian Consumer Law) Bill (No 2) 2010, 184 [7.17], quoted in JLR Davis, 'Reflections: The Australian Consumer Law and the Conflict of Laws' (2012) 20 *Australian Journal of Competition and Consumer Law* 212, 212; see *Valve* [2016] FCA 196, (2016) 337 ALR 647, [112].
[44] Davis, 'Reflections' (n 43) 212.
[45] *Valve* [2016] FCA 196, (2016) 337 ALR 647, [4]–[6].
[46] See also discussion of CCA s 5(1), below. 'It seems that the assumption of the parties is that the "and" in s 131(1) is not a disjunctive application of two circumstances in which the Australian Consumer Law applies as a law of the Commonwealth': *Valve* [2016] FCA 196, (2016) 337 ALR 647, [159].
[47] See section II.B below.
[48] *Valve* [2016] FCA 196, (2016) 337 ALR 647, [182].

An argument over where a foreign corporation carries on business is familiar to jurisdictional disputes,[49] but here, the matter related to construction of the ACL. The ACL would apply, even if Valve's conduct did not occur in Australia, if Valve carried on business in Australia.[50] Despite the foreign connections listed above, Edelman J held that Valve carried on business in Australia: it had millions of Australian Steam accounts; it generated millions in revenue from Australia; its business depended on servers in Australia, many of which it owned, of significant value; and it paid tens of thousands of dollars per month to Australian businesses for services connected to its business.[51] The mode of his Honour's analysis will surely become more familiar as domestic courts assert their authority over foreign companies whose business depends on services via the internet.[52] As was recently observed in Canadian litigation involving the American Google, 'this analysis would give every state in the world jurisdiction over Google's search services … But if so, it flows as a natural consequence of Google doing business on a global scale, not from a flaw in the territorial competence analysis'.[53]

Second, Valve argued that the SSA was not a contract to which the consumer guarantees in the ACL applied because, in the absence of clause 14 above, the proper law of the contract was the law of Washington. If the consumer guarantees did not apply, then there could not have been misleading or deceptive conduct or misrepresentations in respect of the existence of those guarantees. This argument depended upon construction of the ACL and of s 67 in particular. The parties agreed that, applying ACL, s 67, and following *Akai*, clause 14 of the SSA – comprising a choice of law, an exclusive choice of jurisdiction and a purported deeming of the place of the contract – were to be disregarded.[54] Edelman J noted[55] that s 67 of the ACL brought the language of the predecessor Trade Practices Act 1974 (Cth) s 67 even closer to the language considered in *Akai*, where the High Court determined that the protective aspects of the Insurance Contracts Act 1984 (Cth) would apply, as mandated by s 8(2), even though the contract included a choice of English law and an exclusive choice of English courts.

The key difference between *Akai* and the facts underpinning *Valve*, though, was that in the former case, the 'centre of gravity' of the contract was in New South Wales, Australia, in the absence of the private international law choices in the contract.[56] That is, the parties (really, the insurer) purported to 'contract out' of the

[49] See eg *National Commercial Bank v Wimborne* (1979) 11 NSWLR 156.

[50] Arguably, Valve's acts were 'bilateral', and occurred in Australia; see *Valve* [2016] FCA 196, (2016) 337 ALR 647, [158], [188]; see also Garnett, 'Arbitration of Cross-Border Consumer Transactions in Australia' (n 22) 577.

[51] *Valve* [2016] FCA 196, (2016) 337 ALR 647, [4].

[52] A variant argument is relevant to the business of multinational parent companies generally; see eg *Daimler AG v Bauman*, 134 S Ct 746, 571 US ___ (2014); *Adams v Cape Industries plc* [1990] Ch 433.

[53] *Equustek Solutions Inc v Jack* (2014) 374 DLR (4th) 537, [64] (Fenlon J), quoted in *Equustek Solutions Inc v Google Inc* [2015] BCCA 265, (2015) 386 DLR (4th) 224, [52] (*Equustek*).

[54] *Valve* [2016] FCA 196, (2016) 337 ALR 647, [73]; see ACL, s 64.

[55] ibid [74]; see also [57].

[56] *Akai* (n 14) 437, quoting *Cie Tunisienne de Navigation SA v Cie d'Armement Maritime SA* [1971] AC 672, 590 (Lord Morris of Both-y-Gest).

application of Australian legislation. In the *Valve* case, the situation was different. Although the SSA pulled in different directions, and although contracting parties were based in Australia and playing games in Australia, Edelman J accepted that the law 'with the closest and most real connection'[57] to the SSA was the law of Washington.[58]

Some readers may think that this should be the end of the matter: the applicable law is the law of Washington, and so the ACL does not apply. Indeed, Valve submitted that the acceptable quality guarantee in ACL, s 54 has no application to any 'supply' pursuant to a contract, the proper law of which is not the law of Australia.[59] That position, however, would pay insufficient attention to the detail of s 67.

If s 67(b) of the ACL were satisfied, then the consumer guarantees would apply despite clause 14 of the SSA. The ACCC thus drew attention to the words 'purports to substitute, or has the effect of substituting' in s 67(b). It argued that either limb of this disjunction was satisfied by clause 14 of the SSA; that is, the clause either *purported to substitute* Washington law for ACL, pt 3-2, div 1, or *had the effect of substituting* Washington law for ACL, pt 3-2, div 1.[60] This argument was made in light of evidence of substantive Washington law in true conflict with the substance of ACL, pt 3-2, div 1. In contrast, Valve submitted that s 67(b) only applied if the proper law of the SSA was Australian, in the absence of clause 14.[61] Edelman J held that Valve's submission could only be maintained by making an unacceptable implication into s 67(b); and further, that it would leave the express identification of the proper law in s 67(a) redundant. It was thus held that clause 14 'purported to substitute' Washington law for any or all of the provisions of ACL, pt 3-2, div 1.[62]

That holding was made on the assumption that s 67(b) was not limited to cases where the proper law would be Australian law in the absence of a term – that is, on the assumption that s 67(b) was not limited to cases like *Akai*. In a classic example of contemporary Australian statutory interpretation, his Honour relied upon the text,[63] context,[64] history and purpose,[65] and policy[66] of the ACL in holding that the ACL applied, notwithstanding that the system of law with the closest connection to the contract was not the law of Australia. The basis for that finding is fleshed out in the subsection II.C.

Valve's third argument was that it did not 'supply goods' within the meaning of s 2(1) of the ACL.[67] This point is probably more interesting to consumer lawyers;

[57] *Bonython v Commonwealth* [1950] UKPCHCA 3, (1950) 81 CLR 486, 498 (Lord Simonds).
[58] *Valve* [2016] FCA 196, (2016) 337 ALR 647, [5], [72]–[84].
[59] ibid [56].
[60] ibid [85]–[86].
[61] ibid [87].
[62] ibid [89].
[63] ibid [91].
[64] Ibid [101].
[65] ibid [107].
[66] ibid [116].
[67] ibid [5].

suffice it to say that Edelman J rejected that argument, too.[68] The holding is a neat illustration of a straightforward adaptation of a statute to the needs of contemporary society; an attribution of 'ambulatory meaning'.[69] In section III, below, it is argued that this mode of reasoning could also play a part in the resolution of choice of law questions involving statutes.

## C. The Basis for the Mandatory Application of the ACL

Lawyers schooled in private international law might understand Edelman J's treatment of the ACL in terms of 'mandatory law':[70]

> laws the respect for which is regarded by a country as so crucial for safeguarding public interests (political, social, or economic organization) that they are applicable to any contract falling within their scope, regardless of the law which might otherwise be applied.[71]

But the term and associated jurisprudence[72] were conspicuously absent from Edelman J's judgment in *Valve*. Instead, the question of the statute's scope was resolved by ordinary statutory interpretation techniques.

As explained above, his Honour started with the text.[73] The plain language of s 67 favoured the ACCC. His Honour distinguished s 8(1) of the Insurance Contracts Act 1984 (Cth), as well as s 17(3) of the Contracts Review Act 1980 (NSW), as each provision expressly stated that the Act applied in relation to a contract the proper law of which was (or would have been) the law of part of Australia. There was no express statement in the ACL providing that its words were confined by territorial limitation.[74] Implication may be warranted in statutory construction,[75] but it was not warranted here.

Next, his Honour construed s 67 in its context, as part of a legislative scheme.[76] Among other factors, it was significant that the CCA containing the ACL was framed broadly; it extends, for example, to bodies carrying on business within Australia, even if they are based overseas.[77] Interestingly, Valve conceded, and

[68] ibid [101]–[106].

[69] See consideration of the fact that 'computer software' could be a 'good', even if downloaded and not supplied by a physical medium: ibid [137].

[70] eg Garnett (n 22) 577, fn 29.

[71] A Briggs, *The Conflict of Laws*, 3rd edn (Oxford, Oxford University Press, 2013) 248.

[72] See Lord Collins et al (eds), *Dicey, Morris & Collins – The Conflict of Laws*, 15th edn (London, Sweet & Maxwell, 2012) 1827 [33R-082].

[73] As he should. Where an Act is clear and explicit, courts should give effect to it: *Warburton v Loveland* (1832) 2 D & Cl 480, 489, 6 ER 806; *Momcilovic v R* [2011] HCA 34, 245 CLR 1, [38]–[39] (French CJ).

[74] See *Freehold Land Investments Ltd v Queensland Estates Pty Ltd* (1970) 123 CLR 418, 440 (Walsh J, Barwick CJ agreeing). But see Competition and Consumer Act 2010 (Cth) s 5(1), considered below.

[75] *Commonwealth Bank of Australia v Barker* [2014] HCA 32, (2014) 253 CLR 169, [22]–[25] (French CJ, Bell and Keane JJ).

[76] *Valve* [2016] FCA 196, (2016) 337 ALR 647, [101]–[106].

[77] CCA, s 5(2).

Edelman J accepted, that in the absence of s 67, the consumer guarantees would apply to a contract irrespective of its proper law.[78] In my view, that concession should have been fatal to Valve's case: it was essentially a resignation that the ACL ought to be applied in a mandatory fashion.

As for history and purpose, a key difference between the ACL and its predecessor, the Trade Practices Act 1974 (Cth), was that the new regime was intended to provide consumers with protection without relying on contract law. Ancillary to that intent, s 67 was intended to prevent 'contracting out' of the ACL's consumer protections. 'Purpose' was thus understood as the reason why the legislation was introduced. Different views on purposive statutory interpretation are explored below.

The 'policy of the ACL' was opaquely presented as distinguishable from the 'purpose of the ACL'.[79] The relevant policy was to prevent parties from contracting out of the application of the consumer guarantee. His Honour relied upon *Akai*, where the plurality seemed to frame policy in terms of legislative intent.[80] What is the difference, if any, between the *policy* of the statute, the *purpose* of the statute, and the intention of the legislature? This question goes to the heart of debates on statutory interpretation.[81] In section III, it is argued that Edelman J's use of the 'policy of the law' is practically indistinguishable from a purposive approach to statutory interpretation. For cross-border litigation in Australia, that matters because courts are compelled to take a purposive approach to statutory construction.[82]

## D. On Appeal

As a consequence of Edelman J's construction of the ACL, the consumer guarantees applied, despite Valve's representations to the contrary. Valve was thus held to have contravened both the prohibition on misleading or deceptive conduct (ACL, s 18(1)) and the prohibition on making false or misleading representations concerning the existence, exclusion or effect of consumer guarantees (ACL, s 29(1)(m)). In addition to other relief, Valve was required to pay a 3 million AUD pecuniary penalty and ordered to pay costs.[83]

On appeal, Valve argued that Edelman J erred in relation to: the mandatory application of the ACL's consumer guarantees despite Washington law having the

[78] *Valve* [2016] FCA 196, (2016) 337 ALR 647, [102], applying *Francis Travel Marketing Pty Ltd v Virgin Atlantic Airways Ltd* (1996) 39 NSWLR 160, 164 (Gleeson CJ, Meagher and Sheller JJA agreeing). The concession runs contrary to the argument advanced by Keyes (n 12).

[79] *Valve* [2016] FCA 196, (2016) 337 ALR 647, [116]–[124].

[80] *Akai* (n 14) 433.

[81] See eg M Radin, 'Statutory Interpretation' (1930) 43 *Harvard Law Review* 863, 875; Burrows, *Thinking About Statutes* (n 8) 13–21.

[82] For federal statutes: Acts Interpretation Act 1901 (Cth) s 15AA.

[83] See *Australian Competition and Consumer Commission v Valve Corporation (No 7)* [2016] FCA 1553.

closest and most real connection to the underlying contract; the holding that Valve made representations in Australia; and the holding that Valve carried on business in Australia, among other things.[84]

The unanimous Full Court dismissed all of Valve's grounds of appeal. Importantly, it affirmed Edelman J's interpretation of s 67. It emphasised the context of the provision: a legislative scheme designed to specifically prevent 'contracting out', and to provide guarantees which do not depend on an underlying contract.[85] It recognised that some provisions of the ACL overlapped, but maintained that each subsection of s 67 performed a distinct function. While s 67(a) would cover *Akai*-style situations where the contract's centre of gravity was in Australia, s 67(b) would apply to a contract which purported to replace the ACL's consumer guarantees with some other place's guarantees, whatever the contract's centre of gravity.[86] The purpose of s 67 was not to specify the scope of the consumer guarantees, but to prevent contracting out.[87]

The *Valve* appeal is significant not just for what was held, but for *how* it was held. The mode of analysis was traditional statutory interpretation. Statutory interpretation may determine both the territorial scope of a statute and whether it applies in a mandatory fashion.[88]

# III. Statutory Interpretation in Cross-Border Litigation

## A. Statutory Interpretation v Characterisation as Mandatory Law

For private international lawyers, the issue of whether a forum statute applies in cross-border litigation – the key issue in *Valve* – may turn on whether statutory rules should be characterised as 'mandatory'. Mandatory rules 'purport to exist over and above the domain of private international law'.[89] The concept is entrenched in continental European private international law[90] but it is also invoked, occasionally, by common law courts.[91] Despite my own use of the term

[84] *Valve v ACCC* (n 23) [11].

[85] ibid [108].

[86] ibid [108]–[109].

[87] ibid [112].

[88] The difference between these dimensions is explored in Keyes (n 12). This view is not particularly novel; see S Dutson, 'The Territorial Application of Statutes' (1996) 22 *Monash University Law Review* 59, 79–81.

[89] M Whincop and M Keyes, 'Putting the "Private" Back into Private International Law: Default Rules and the Proper Law of the Contract' (1997) 21 *Melbourne University Law Review* 515, 521.

[90] eg Regulation (EC) 593/2008 on the law applicable to contractual obligations [2008] OJ L177/6 (Rome I) art 9; Case C-184/12 *Unamar v Navigation Maritime Bulgare* ECLI:EU:C:2013:663, [2014] 1 All ER (Comm) 625 [49]; see B Lindsay, 'The Exclusion of Foreign Law in International Private Law' (PhD thesis, University of Glasgow 2017) §1.B.4.4.

[91] For a recent interstate example, see *Huntingdale Village Pty Ltd v Corrs Chambers Westgarth* [2018] WASCA 90, (2018) 128 ACSR 168.

throughout, perhaps that occasional invocation is unfortunate. The 'mandatory law' concept was once unknown to the common law.[92] The concept distracts attention from the fact that, at least in Australia, all local statutes are mandatory. The English dogma of parliamentary sovereignty[93] should be transposed to Australia's unique constitutional context,[94] but even so, the truth remains that the legislature makes law, and the courts' primary function is to apply the law. All of this should be trite, but reading a textbook on the subject, it might be forgotten that the conflict of laws is still just law. We should remember that statutes are of a higher order than common law rules, including common law choice of law rules.[95]

The primacy of forum statutes vis-à-vis orthodox (common law) choice of law techniques is illustrated, at least indirectly, by their respective treatment in civil procedure. The orthodox treatment of choice of law problems in common law legal systems is the product of domestic principles.[96] As the majority said in *McKain v RW Miller & Co (South Australia) Pty Ltd*, it is 'axiomatic' that 'conflict of laws rules' are furnished by the law of the forum.[97] The invocation of those rules is voluntary: a party wishing to rely on foreign law in civil litigation must raise the issue on the pleadings, then prove the content of the foreign law by way of evidence.[98] With forum statutes, however, things are different. A party must plead material facts sufficient to found a cause of action or to make out a defence, but there is no obligation to plead law;[99] it is not even necessary to specify a cause of action on the pleadings.[100] Once pleaded, the content of forum law need not be proved.[101] Parties may rely upon any of the legal consequences of the pleaded facts.[102] Except where a statutory cause of action is involved,[103] it is probably

[92] See TC Hartley, 'Mandatory Rules in International Contracts: The Common Law Approach' (1997) 266 *Recueil Des Cours* 1, 346, fn 4, cited in Keyes (n 12) 6 n 29.

[93] See D Greenberg (ed), *Craies on Legislation*, 11th edn (London, Sweet & Maxwell, 2017) [2.1.1].

[94] *Attorney-General for Western Australia v Marquet* [2003] HCA 67, (2003) 217 CLR 545, [66] (Gleeson CJ, Gummow, Hayne and Heydon JJ); see also *Lange v Australian Broadcasting Corporation* [1997] HCA 25, (1997) 189 CLR 520, 563–64 (Brennan CJ, Dawson, Toohey, Gaudron, McHugh, Gummow and Kirby JJ).

[95] Briggs, 'A Note on the Application of the Statute Law of Singapore' (n 28) 195.

[96] *Cf* academic views that private international law is truly international, eg, A Mills, 'The Private History of International Law' (2006) 55 *International & Comparative Law Quarterly* 1.

[97] *McKain v RW Miller & Co (South Australia) Pty Ltd* (1991) 174 CLR 1, 34 (Brennan, Dawson, Toohey and McHugh JJ), cited in *John Pfeiffer Pty Ltd v Rogerson* [2000] HCA 36, (2000) 203 CLR 503, [42] (Gleeson CJ, Gaudron, McHugh, Gummow and Hayne JJ).

[98] *Neilson v Overseas Projects Corporation of Victoria* [2005] HCA 54, (2005) 223 CLR 331, [115]–[116] (Gummow and Hayne JJ).

[99] But a party may plead a conclusion of law, provided that the conclusion is supported by pleaded material facts; see eg Supreme Court (General Civil Procedure) Rules 2015 (Vic) r 13.02(2); *cf* the view that law should not be pleaded at all: *Williamson v L & NW Railway Co* (1879) 12 Ch D 787, 793.

[100] *Agar v Hyde* (2000) 201 CLR 552, 577–78 (Gaudron, McHugh, Gummow and Hayne JJ); see also *Philip Morris Inc v Adam P Brown Male Fashions Pty Ltd* (1981) 148 CLR 457, 472.

[101] Evidence Act 1995 (Cth) s 143.

[102] *Lever Brothers Ltd v Bell* [1931] 1 KB 557, 583.

[103] *Jeans West Corp Pty Ltd v Archer* [2004] WASCA 132; see also Federal Court Rules 2011 (Cth) r 16.02(1)(e).

bad practice to plead principles of law. Relevant statutes will be revealed in submissions – advocates have a duty to inform the court of authority which bears upon matters under debate.[104] But a court could apply a forum statute not even mentioned in the pleadings. Indeed, if the facts engage the statute, it *must* do so.[105] In the words of Lord Wilberforce, '[j]udges are more than mere selectors between rival views – they are entitled to and do think for themselves'.[106] As Heydon J wrote in *PGA v The Queen*, '[t]he courts are masters of the common law, but servants of statutes'.[107] In the common law tradition, parties are masters of common law choice of law rules but slaves of forum statutes.

This does not mean that courts should never apply foreign law. But where the facts of a matter come within the scope of a forum statute, the court should apply the forum statute. The scope of the statute is key. Putative conflicts of laws may be identified and resolved by ordinary statutory interpretation.[108]

## B. Tools of the Statute-First Approach Relevant to Modern Cross-Border Litigation

That statutory interpretation could provide the solution to what are otherwise considered choice of law problems is nothing new.[109] This subsection considers three fundamental interpretive principles which could determine the application of forum statutes in contemporary cross-border litigation.

### *i. Territorial Presumption*

In *Wanganui-Rangitikei Electric Power Board v The Australian Mutual Provident Society* (*Wanganui*), Dixon J held that:

> an enactment describing acts, matters or things in general words, so that, if restrained by no consideration lying outside its expressed meaning, its intended application would be universal, is to be read as confined to what, according to the rules of international law administered or recognized in our Courts, it is within the province of our law to affect or control.[110]

[104] *D'Orta-Ekenaike v Victoria Legal Aid* (2005) 223 CLR 1, 41 [112] (McHugh J).

[105] The attribution of meaning *in the context of a matter* has been described as the court's 'duty': *Brown v Tasmania* [2017] HCA 43, (2017) 91 ALJR 1089, [452] (Edelman J).

[106] *Saif Ali v Sydney Mitchell & Co* [1980] AC 198, 212, quoted in *Project Blue Sky Inc v Australian Broadcasting Authority* [1998] HCA 28, (1998) 194 CLR 355, [13] (Brennan J).

[107] *PGA v The Queen* [2012] HCA 21, (2012) 245 CLR 355, [133].

[108] An approach which might be associated with interest analysis: see B Currie, 'Married Women's Contracts: A Study in Conflict-of-Laws Method', *Selected Essays on the Conflict of Laws* (Durham, NC, Duke University Press, 1963) 77.

[109] The approach was favoured by the medieval statutists: C Bisping, 'Avoid the Statutist Trap: The International Scope of the Consumer Credit Act 1974' (2012) 8 *Journal of Private International Law* 35, 44; see also B Currie, 'Notes on Methods and Objectives in the Conflict of Laws', *Selected Essays on the Conflict of Laws* (Durham NC, Duke University Press, 1963) 177, 183–84.

[110] *Wanganui* (1934) 50 CLR 581, 601.

This dictum is cited as authority for the presumption of statutory interpretation that legislation does not have extraterritorial effect.[111] A variant principle is enshrined in s 21(1)(b) of the Acts Interpretation Act 1901 (Cth): 'references to localities jurisdictions and other matters and things shall be construed as references to such localities jurisdictions and other matters and things in and of the Commonwealth'.[112] These principles of interpretation obviously have a role to play in cross-border litigation, where 'acts, matters or things' are located outside of the court's territorial jurisdiction.

In the very next sentence following the dictum above, Dixon J clarified that the principle against extraterritorial application of legislation is a presumption only, which may have little or no place 'where some other restriction is supplied by context or subject matter'.[113] Similarly, the presumption will have little or no place if the clear words of the statute *extend* its operation to acts, matters or things with strong connections to foreign places. Parliaments in the common law tradition are not averse to legislating for events occurring abroad.[114] In Australia, where the words of an Act clearly extend its operation to foreign subject-matter, the only territorial worry will be in respect of jurisdiction *in personam*,[115] provided that the statute meets the constitutional criterion of some 'general' territorial nexus.[116] See, for example, s 5(1) of the CCA:

> (1) Each of the following provisions:
>
> (a) Part IV;
> (b) Part XI;
> (c) the Australian Consumer Law (other than Part 5-3);
> (f) the remaining provisions of this Act (to the extent to which they relate to any of the provisions covered by paragraph (a), (b) or (c));

[111] See eg M Sanson, *Statutory Interpretation* 2nd edn (Melbourne, Oxford University Press, 2016) 229–30; M Hook, 'The "Statutist Trap" and Subject Matter Jurisdiction' (2017) 13 *Journal of Private International Law* 435, 436.

[112] *cf* s 15AA, considered below.

[113] *Wanganui* (n 110) 601.

[114] eg Railways and Transport Safety Act 2003, s 91, quoted in Greenberg, *Craies on Legislation* (n 93) [11.2.3] n 46.

[115] Apart from foreign jurisdiction agreements, *forum non conveniens* is not likely to prevent an Australian court from exercising jurisdiction, given the low threshold of the Australian 'clearly inappropriate forum' test. *cf* the position on anti-suit injunctions issued in courts' inherent jurisdiction to control the administration of justice, where the *forum non conveniens* doctrine is not invoked at all because the forum court is the only court with any interest in the matter: *CSR Ltd v Cigna Insurance Australia Ltd* [1997] HCA 33, (1997) 189 CLR 345, 398 (Dawson, Toohey, Gaudron, McHugh, Gummow and Kirby JJ). Australian courts are likely to take a similar view where an Australian statute is in play; there is a 'legitimate juridical advantage' in proceeding locally: see *Puttick v Tennon Ltd* [2008] HCA 54, (2008) 238 CLR 265, [43] (Heydon and Crennan JJ).

[116] *Union Steamship Co of Australia Pty Ltd v King* [1988] HCA 55, (1988) 166 CLR 1, 13–14, quoted in *Lavender v Director of Fisheries Compliance, Department of Industry Skills and Regional Development* [2018] NSWCA 174, [156] (Basten JA).

*extends to the engaging in conduct outside Australia by*:

(g) bodies corporate incorporated or carrying on business within Australia; or
(h) Australian citizens; or
(i) persons ordinarily resident within Australia…. (emphasis added.)

The tension between the homing factors in CCA, s 5(1)(g)–(i), and the identification of conduct occurring outside Australia as per the emphasised phrase, shows that defining the 'territoriality' of a statute may not always be straightforward. When does an Act have an 'extraterritorial' effect? According to Lord Hoffmann in *Office of Fair Trading v Lloyds TSB Bank plc*, in respect of the presumption against extraterritorial effect, 'extraterritorial effect means seeking to regulate conduct or affect the liabilities of people over whom the United Kingdom has no jurisdiction'.[117] In that case, the House of Lords considered a provision analogous to CCA, s 5(1),[118] which provided that the statute applied:

> only to agreements with a creditor carrying on business in the United Kingdom … If the supplier is a foreigner, the Act does not purport to regulate his conduct or impose liabilities upon him. It is only the UK creditor who is affected. To construe it as applying to such cases does not therefore conflict with the presumption against extraterritoriality.[119]

Applying this view, the CCA does not really operate extraterritorially, even in respect of an entity incorporated overseas, provided that the entity carries on business in Australia, applying ACL, s 5(1), above.[120] As was subsequently held – by no less than Lawrence Collins LJ – in *Masri v Consolidated Contractors International UK Ltd (No 2)*:

> it used to be said that there was a presumption that Parliament did not design its statutes to operate beyond the territorial limits of the United Kingdom. But nowadays the presumption has little force and it is simply a matter of construction.[121]

The territorial presumption is just one tool for the work of statutory construction.[122] The facts of *Valve* illustrate that the changing nature of globalisation has made that work more complicated. Where the relevant conduct involves the internet, it may be very difficult, and even arbitrary, to determine where an action occurred, causing problems for construction of provisions which turn on the location of the action.[123] The Full Court grappled with this in *Valve*.[124]

[117] *Office of Fair Trading v Lloyds TSB Bank plc* [2007] UKHL 48, [2008] AC 316, [4] (*OFT v Lloyds*).
[118] Consumer Credit Act 1974, s 75(1).
[119] *OFT v Lloyds* (n 117) [4].
[120] *Cf* Bisping, 'Avoid the Statutist Trap' (n 109).
[121] *Masri v Consolidated Contractors International UK Ltd and Others (No 2)* [2008] EWCA Civ 625, [2009] QB 503, [31].
[122] It must be considered together with, and subject to, the mandated purposive approach to statutory interpretation: see section III.C, below.
[123] Greenberg (n 93) [11.2.1]; see also R Sullivan, *Sullivan on the Construction of Statutes*, 6th edn (Markham, LexisNexis Canada, 2014) [26.7].
[124] *Valve v ACCC* (n 23) [120]–[125].

It considered the decisions on localisation of torts in *Voth v Manildra Flour Mills Pty Ltd*,[125] and in respect of online defamation in *Dow Jones v Co Inc v Gutnick*, where the majority characterised publication as a 'bilateral act'.[126] In relation to misleading or deceptive conduct under ACL, s 18, and the false or misleading representations under ACL, s 29, the Full Court held:

> If the respondent is based overseas and has a relationship with customers in Australia, it is likely that representations addressed to those customers will be taken to have been made in Australia, being the place where the customer accesses and reads the representations on his or her computer. This is likely to be the case even if the representations are available to be accessed by consumers in other countries around the world. A distinction is to be drawn between the conduct proscribed by ss 18 and 29 and the causation of loss or damage. It is not necessary, for the purposes of these provisions, to establish loss or damage. It follows that, for the purposes of determining the place where the representations were made, it is not necessary to determine whether any loss or damage was suffered and, if so, the place of that loss or damage. The approach we have outlined is both consistent with the general principles discussed in the cases and reflective of the consumer protection purpose of the statutory provisions ... In circumstances where Valve had a direct relationship with a large number of Australian consumers, and Valve required consumers to agree to the SSA before they could open an account and purchase a game, the [representations] were made in Australia when consumers in Australia accessed and read the SSA on their computers. This is where, in substance, for the purposes of ss 18 and 29(1)(m), the representations were made.[127]

Notwithstanding all of the foreign connecting factors, the CCA was not operating truly extraterritorially. The broader takeaway is that where human activity straddles multiple jurisdictions, including the forum jurisdiction, a forum statute regulating that activity may not be 'extraterritorial' at all, and the territorial presumption will be inapplicable. This was considered in the *Morrison* litigation before the US Supreme Court, a case which had such strong connections to Australia that Justice Ginsburg said that it had '"Australia" written all over it'.[128] Justice Scalia opined that:

> it is a rare case of prohibited extraterritorial application that lacks *all* contact with the territory of the United States. But the presumption against extraterritorial application would be a craven watchdog, indeed, it if retreated to its kennel whenever *some* domestic activity is involved in the case[129]

To keep running with Scalia's ugly metaphor: in the twenty-first century, the dog is losing its bite. It is sometimes said that Parliament gave no consideration to the

[125] *Voth v Manildra Flour Mills Pty Ltd* (1990) 171 CLR 538.

[126] *Dow Jones v Co Inc v Gutnick* [2002] HCA 56, (2002) 210 CLR 575, [26]–[27] (Gleeson CJ, McHugh, Gummow and Hayne JJ).

[127] *Valve v ACCC* (n 23) [134]–[135].

[128] Transcript of Oral Argument, 7–8, quoted in TA Dubbs, '*Morrison v National Australia Bank*: The US Supreme Court Limits Collective Redress for Securities Fraud' in D Fairgrieve and E Lein (eds), *Extraterritoriality and Collective Redress* (Oxford, Oxford University Press 2012) 335, 335.

[129] *Morrison* 561 US__, 130 S Ct 2869, 2884, quoted in Dubbs, '*Morrison v National Australia Bank*' (n 128) 352.

territorial scope of application of a given statute.[130] That may have been true in the time of Dixon J, but these days, in an increasingly interconnected world, it would be negligent for a draftsperson to fail to consider the matter. Over time, the extraterritorial presumption will continue to come under strain. Eventually, as old statutes are patched over, it will fade away altogether.

## ii. *Ambulatory Meaning*

In contrast, a principle of construction which will be of increasing contemporary importance is that a statute is 'always speaking'; ie a statute is to be attributed an 'ambulatory meaning'.[131] The principle is that words of a statute may be adapted to circumstances unforeseen at the time of the enactment.[132] The idea is illustrated by the judgment of Lady Hale in *Yemshaw v Hounslow Lonson BC*:

> [I]t is not for government and official bodies to interpret the meaning of the words which Parliament has used. That role lies with the courts. And the courts recognise that, where Parliament uses a word such as 'violence', the factual circumstances to which it applies can develop and change over the years … The essential question … is whether an updated meaning is consistent with the statutory purpose[133]

Like the territorial presumption, this principle has also been described as a presumption. But in *Forsyth*, the majority warned that:

> [t]he terminology of rebuttable presumption is apt to mislead. What it bespeaks is an exercise in statutory interpretation which seeks to discern what is called the intention of the legislature in enacting the specific provision, having regard to its context, scope and purpose.[134]

This principle of construction is just another gloss on the orthodox method of interpretation applied by Edelman J in *Valve*.

The relevance of the ambulatory presumption is this: as the world changes; as globalisation continues; as globalisation *itself* changes; our understanding of the territorial scope of regulation ought to change with it. The statute should move with its context. Increasingly, general words in statutes should be adapted to capture subject-matter with connections to foreign places – indeed, that is

[130] *Barcelo v Electrolytic Zinc Co of Australasia Ltd* [1932] HCA 52, (1932) 48 CLR 391, 423 (Dixon J); Dutson, 'The Territorial Application of Statutes' (n 88) 59; Currie, 'Married Women's Contracts' (n 108) 82.

[131] See Burrows (n 8) 21–34.

[132] *Forsyth v Deputy Commissioner of Taxation* [2007] HCA 8, (2007) 231 CLR 531, [3] (Gleeson CJ, Gummow, Hayne, Callinan, Heydon and Crennan JJ) (*Forsyth*); see also Acts Interpretation Act 1915 (SA) s 21; Interpretation Act 1984 (WA) s 8: 'A written law shall be considered as always speaking and whenever a matter or thing is expressed in the present tense, it shall be applied to the circumstances as they arise, so that effect may be given to every part of the law according to its true spirit, intent, and meaning'.

[133] *Yemshaw v Hounslow Lonson BC* [2011] UKSC, [2011] 1 WLR 433, [24], quoted in Burrows (n 8) 26.

[134] *Forsyth* (n 132) [3] (Gleeson CJ, Gummow, Hayne, Callinan, Heydon and Crennan JJ).

exactly what happened in *Valve*. As consumers participate in cross-border transactions with increasing frequency, it would defy the uniformity-logic so valued by the traditionalists for businesses to escape the application of the law by structuring their affairs via corporate groups with overseas parents.[135] The waning of the extraterritorial presumption ought to accompany the waxing of the ambulatory presumption. The mediator between these opposing forces is the purpose of the statute.

It is not just societal changes which should affect an ambulatory construction. Changes in the common law may do the same. Leeming once wrote that 'the legal meaning of the same statutory language can and will change depending upon the contextual change in the judge-made law in which the statute operates'.[136] Changing attitudes to the scope of courts' personal jurisdiction can thus inform, and *should* inform, the meaning those courts attribute to legislation. Compare the historical understanding of 'exorbitant jurisdiction' as a dirty word,[137] to the modern approach of Lord Sumption:

> Longmore LJ described the service of the English Court's process out of the jurisdiction as an 'exorbitant' jurisdiction ... This characterisation of the jurisdiction to allow service out is traditional, and was originally based on the notion that the service of proceedings abroad was an assertion of sovereign power over the Defendant and a corresponding interference with the sovereignty of the state in which process was served. This is no longer a realistic view of the situation. ... Litigation between residents of different states is a routine incident of modern commercial life ... It should no longer be necessary to resort to the kind of muscular presumptions against service out which are implicit in adjectives like 'exorbitant'. The decision is generally a pragmatic one in the interests of the efficient conduct of litigation in an appropriate forum.[138]

As courts are increasingly comfortable with asserting their authority over players in a global game, they should also be increasingly comfortable with adapting forum laws to activity touching upon their spheres of authority. As the Canadian courts suggested in *Equustek*: if this impacts global businesses, well, that is the price of doing business globally.[139] In *Valve*, Edelman J quoted the following passage,[140] which is apposite:

> When it entered a foreign jurisdiction Lloyd's was required to deal with the legal system it found. In my view, names in markets without effective consumer protection laws have no legitimate complaint about the operation of laws in other jurisdictions simply because they may produce different results. It is one thing to require claims to

[135] See *Kay's Leasing* (n 29) 143 (Kitto J). Moreover, arguably, it would defy the principle of legality: see *Tabcorp Holdings Ltd v Victoria* [2016] HCA 4, (2016) 90 ALJR 276, [68] (French CJ, Kiefel, Bell, Keane and Gordon JJ).

[136] Leeming, 'Theories and Principles Underlying the Common Law' (n 1) 1025.

[137] *Amin Rasheed Shipping Corporation v Kuwait Insurance Co* [1984] AC 50, 65 (Lord Diplock). See also L Collins, 'Sovereignty and Exorbitant Jurisdiction' (2014) 130(Oct) *Law Quarterly Review* 555.

[138] *Abela v Baadarani* [2013] UKSC 44, [2013] 1 WLR 2043, 2062–63 [53] (Lord Sumption).

[139] *Equustek* (n 53) [52].

[140] *Valve* [2016] FCA 196, (2016) 337 ALR 647, [125].

be determined by the courts of one country; it is another to require all claims to be determined by the same laws whether or not they are the appropriate laws to govern the transaction giving rise to a claim.[141]

In the same year, Edelman J joined with Allsop CJ in expressing a similar idea in a maritime dispute: 'to choose the lex fori for a task is not necessarily a choice that is parochial and provincial – it is the forum's approach to the expression of the law that governs or regulates inherently international activity'.[142]

### *iii. Purposive Approach*

The purposive approach to statutory interpretation is the sharpest tool with which a court can cut through a case with a foreign element via a forum statute.

The common law world has moved on from 'an old literal to a modern contextual and purposive approach',[143] embodied in the poetry of Judge Learned Hand, quoted by Gageler:

> [while the words used] are the primary, and ordinarily the most reliable, source of interpreting the meaning of any writing … it is one of the surest indexes of a mature and developed jurisprudence not to make a fortress out of the dictionary; but to remember that statutes always have some purpose or object to accomplish, whose sympathetic and imaginative discovery is the surest guide to their meaning.[144]

This purposive approach dominates in the common law world, but in Australia, the approach is mandated by provisions like s 15AA of the Acts Interpretation Act 1901 (Cth):

> In interpreting a provision of an Act, the interpretation that would best achieve the purpose or object of the Act (whether or not that purpose or object is expressly stated in the Act) is to be preferred to each other interpretation.

Private international law scholars tend to revile the use of the purposive approach to determine the application of forum statutes in matters with a foreign element. The editors of *Dicey* call this an 'artificial' and 'perhaps … dangerous' method.[145] Their position depended on the proposition that 'the legislature gave no thought to the matter [of the statute's territorial scope]'.[146] Similarly, in his Hague Academy course on mandatory law, Hartley said that generally-worded forum statutes:

> cause problems in practice because it may not be clear whether the legislature intended the statute to override the normal choice-of-law rules; consequently, a court may

[141] *Society of Lloyd's v White* [2004] VSCA 101, [19] (Buchanan JA).

[142] *Sam Hawk v Reiter Petroleum Inc* [2016] FCAFC 26, (2016) 246 FCR 337, [85].

[143] Burrows (n 8) 5.

[144] *Cabell v Markham*, 148 F 2d 737, 739 (2d Cir, 1945), quoted in Gageler, 'Common Law Statutes and Judicial Legislation' (n 2) 2; *Thiess v Collector of Customs* [2014] HCA 12, (2014) 250 CLR 664, [23] (French CJ, Hayne, Kiefel, Gageler and Keane JJ).

[145] Lord Collins et al, *Dicey, Morris & Collins – The Conflict of Laws* (n 72) [1-040].

[146] ibid.

> not know whether a statute is intended to be applicable only when the proper law is that of the forum, or whether it contains an implied unilateral choice-of-law rule of its own.[147]

Like the editors of *Dicey*, Hartley seemingly assumes that the court's goal is to identify the legislature's subjective intent. That is not quite right.

Although some scholars (and conservative Americans)[148] maintain the idea that the object of interpretation is to give effect to statutory intent,[149] that is not the orthodox view[150] – at least not in Australia.[151] Kirby described the term 'Parliamentary intention' as 'potentially misleading' and 'unhelpful'.[152] The High Court has called legislative intent a 'fiction'[153] and a 'metaphor'.[154] In *Plaintiff M47/2012 v Director General of Security*, Gummow J explained as follows:

> Care is required in resolving the issue of statutory construction that is presented here by the invocation of legislative 'intention'. It has become better understood than it was when McHugh J, in *Al-Kateb*, used the term 'intention' and cognate expressions, that they are indicative of the constitutional relationship between the arms of government respecting the making, interpretation and application of laws.[155]

An over-reliance on intention may give credibility to the fear of the likes of Scalia that judges will use the concept as cover to 'pursue their own objectives and desires'.[156] This view is that 'the gravest sins are perpetrated in the name of the intent of the legislature'.[157] In Australia, the use of subjective intention as a guide to interpretation has been explicitly rejected.[158] The modern view is that reference to 'intention' is a placeholder for the *telos* of contextual, purposive statutory interpretation, and a reminder of the separation of powers by which lawmaking is the province of the legislature.[159]

[147] Hartley, 'Mandatory Rules in International Contracts' (n 92) 354–55.

[148] As representative, see A Scalia, *A Matter of Interpretation* (Princeton, Princeton University Press, 1997) 17.

[149] R Ekins, *The Nature of Legislative Intent* (Oxford, Oxford University Press 2012); R Ekins and J Goldsworthy, 'The Reality and Indispensability of Legislative Intentions' (2014) 36 *Sydney Law Review* 39.

[150] See Burrows (n 8) 15–21.

[151] See J Dharmananda, 'Using Parliamentary Materials in Interpretation: Insights from Parliamentary Process' (2018) 41 *University of New South Wales Law Journal* 4, 8.

[152] Kirby (n 3) 98.

[153] *Zheng v Cai* [2009] HCA 52, (2009) 239 CLR 446, [28] (French CJ, Gummow, Crennan, Kiefel and Bell JJ).

[154] *Momcilovic v R* [2011] HCA 34, (2011) 245 CLR 1, [38] (French CJ); see Ekins and Goldsworthy, 'The Reality and Indispensability of Legislative Intentions' (n 149) 41, fn 10.

[155] *Plaintiff M47/2012 v Director General of Security* [2012] HCA 46, (2012) 251 CLR 1, [118] (citation omitted).

[156] Scalia, *A Matter of Interpretation* (n 148) 17–18; Burrows (n 8) 18–19.

[157] Scalia (n 148) 18, quoting JM Landis, 'A Note on "Statutory Interpretation"' (1930) 43 *Harvard Law Review* 886, 891.

[158] *Queensland v Congoo* [2015] HCA 17, (2015) 256 CLR 239, [36] (Gageler J).

[159] *Lacey v Attorney-General for Queensland* [2011] HCA 10, (2011) 242 CLR 573, [44] (French CJ, Gummow, Hayne, Crennan, Kiefel and Bell JJ).

For Burrows, whose view seems to align to that of the High Court, the modern purposive approach may be understood as follows:

> When we talk of 'purpose', we are looking for the policy behind the statute of statutory provision. Identifying the policy is not dependent on identifying any person's intentions. It may be said to be analogous to identifying the principle behind a common law precedent and that, too, is not dependent on trying to identify any person's (i.e. judge's) intention … [I]t may be helpful to focus on the statute, rather than the legislator, and say that we are concerned with the meaning of the statute, ascertained by considering *the statute's* words, context and purpose.[160]

Burrows' understanding of purposive construction connects to the concept of the 'policy of the law'. The term has arisen in High Court judgments with increasing frequency.[161] It is used in deliberate contradistinction to the more fluid concept of 'public policy'; judges opine on the 'policy of the law', not 'public policy' or 'legal policy'.[162] For McHugh and Gummow JJ, the 'policy of the law' is internal to the statute, while 'legal policy', a distinguishable concept, consists of judges' own normative views.[163] Reliance on the former in judicial reasoning is consistent with modern legalism, while reliance on the latter is probably not.[164] For Cane, the difference between the policy of the law and the principle in the statute is one of degree: 'policies "of the law" are abstract legal propositions that explain or rationalize relatively less abstract legal propositions'.[165]

The 'policy of the law' has been used to determine the application of forum statutes in cross-border litigation. In *Akai*, the plurality referred to 'the policy of the law that the parties who have made a contract should be kept to it', and held that

> courts may disregard or refuse effect to contractual obligations which, whilst not directly contrary to any express or implied statutory prohibition, nevertheless contravene 'the policy of the law' as discerned from a consideration of the scope and purpose of the particular statute.

They identified that the policy of the Insurance Contracts Act 1984 (Cth), as 'evinced by s 8, is against the use of private engagements to circumvent its remedial provisions'.[166] In *Valve*, Edelman J described the 'policy of the ACL' as follows:

> the legislative intent underlying ss 64, 67, and 276 was to comprise a 'legislative regime' to ensure that the operation of the provisions in Div 1, Pt 3–2 (Ch 3) are within the

[160] Burrows (n 8) 19–20.

[161] See eg *Alley v Gillespie* [2018] HCA 11, (2018) 82 ALJR 373, [89]; *Equuscorp Pty Ltd v Haxton* [2012] HCA 7, (2012) 246 CLR 498, [25], [33] (French CJ, Crennan and Kiefel JJ); *Nelson v Nelson* (1995) 184 CLR 538, 552 (Deane and Gummow JJ), 611 (McHugh J).

[162] *Cattanach v Melchior* [2003] HCA 38, (2003) 215 CLR 1, [70]–[75] (McHugh and Gummow JJ), considering *Egerton v Brownlow* (1853) 4 HL Cas 1, (1853) 10 ER 359, 394–95 (Creswell J).

[163] *Cattanach v Melchior* (n 162) [70]–[75].

[164] See W Gummow, 'The 2017 Winterton Lecture – Sir Owen Dixon Today' (2018) 43 *University of Western Australia Law Review* 30, 51.

[165] P Cane, 'Taking Disagreement Seriously: Courts, Legislatures and the Reform of Tort Law' (2005) 25 *Oxford Journal of Legal Studies* 393, 398.

[166] *Akai* (n 14) 447.

> reach of the Australian Consumer Law. It was a scheme introduced for reasons including simplicity and clarity. Section 67 is not a redundant part of this regime … [T]he section does exactly what it says. It ensures that there can be no possibility of varying the operation of the Division by contractual terms. If there is such a term, s 67 requires that the provisions in the Division 'apply in relation to the supply under the contract despite that term'.[167]

His Honour then quoted Kitto J in *Kay's Leasing*, who held that a forum statute rendering a provision void to effect 'a specific policy directed against practices which the legislature has deemed oppressive or unjust' could justify the mandatory application of the statute.[168]

Reading these authorities together, Cane's view seems right: the 'policy of the law' is the label given by judges to a kind of principle that explains the narrower principles in a statute. Policy is identified by reading a particular provision,[169] or provisions, in its or their broader context. The context includes the structure of the statute, why it was enacted,[170] how it operates, and even how courts have subsequently considered it.[171] Characterisation of how the statute operates in determining the statute's policy entails an inevitable degree of circularity; but nonetheless, from an accumulation of counterfactuals and examples, a judge can reasonably derive the slightly-broader policy – or, to borrow from a great Australian legal mind, the 'vibe' – of the statute.[172] Indeed, in *Valve*, Edelman J considered counterfactuals of what would happen if Valve's submissions were accepted, under the heading of the 'Policy of the ACL'.[173] A mosaic of possible applications of an Act can approximate a principle which underlies that Act. That principle is the policy of the law.

The next section fleshes out how the policy of the law of a forum statute can determine putative choice of law problems.

# IV. The Policy of the Law in Cross-Border Litigation

## A. The Policy of the Law Explains both How and Why the Forum Statute Applies

This chapter was introduced, like Hook's, in terms of the tension between the 'statutory interpretation' approach and the 'traditional choice of law' approach to

[167] *Valve* [2016] FCA 196, (2016) 337 ALR 647, [60], [119].
[168] *Kay's Leasing* (n 29) 143.
[169] eg Edelman J's reference to 'the policy of s 67': [90].
[170] Including the 'mischief' it was directed to: *Heydon's case* (1584) 3 Co Rep 7, 76 ER 637.
[171] See Gageler (n 2); Leeming (n 1).
[172] J Campbell and R Campbell, 'Why Statutory Interpretation is Done as it is Done' (2014) 39 *Australian Bar Review* 1, 32.
[173] *Valve* [2016] FCA 196, (2016) 337 ALR 647, [122]–[124].

forum statutes in cross-border litigation. It has used the *Valve* litigation as a frame for a discussion of the principles justifying the statutory interpretation approach. For the most part, the chapter explains how the approach works in terms of principle, and hence why it is justified in common law systems. Here, it is argued that the 'policy of the law', as the end-state of purposive statutory interpretation, will not only determine *how* the statutory interpretation approach works in matters with a foreign element; it will also explain *why* the method ought to be preferred in cases where others would prefer a traditional choice of law analysis.

## *i. How the Forum Statute Applies*

Private international lawyers often see the issue of a statute's territorial scope as distinct from the issue of whether it has overriding mandatory effect.[174] A statute may be mandatory – ie, it may override a 'traditional' choice of law analysis – in certain cases, but in other cases, the facts may fall outside of its territorial scope.[175]

The purposive approach to statutory interpretation may require courts to treat these two dimensions as one and the same. The only question is whether the statute applies to the facts;[176] that question is to be answered with primary reference to the policy of the law, as revealed by the required purposive approach to interpretation. Where the policy of the law is silent on the facts in issue, *this* is the kind of case which is naturally determined by foreign law applying the forum's choice of law rules. But if the policy of the law mandates an extraterritorial interpretation, so be it: in Australia, that interpretation must be preferred to any other interpretation. So for example, if the policy of a certain statute is to guard against the evils of the pursuit of unrestrained self-interest in commercial contracts, then the court should have regard to that policy in deciding whether the terms of the statute extend to a factual matrix with foreign connections; and further, the court should have regard to that policy in deciding whether any express choices in the contract ought to be upheld. That was the approach of both the majority in *Akai*[177] and of Edelman J in *Valve*;[178] it is the necessary result of the strongest contemporary authority on the fundamental mechanics of the Australian legal system.

## *ii. Why the Forum Statute Applies*

Although the 'policy of the law' is framed at a greater level of abstraction than specific principles in a statute, its value may be understood with examples. In *Valve*, Edelman J explained the policy of the ACL in its effect, with reference

[174] eg Keyes (n 12).
[175] Grušić, 'The Territorial Scope of Employment Legislation and Choice of Law' (n 16) 743.
[176] The common law tradition is adversarial; Australian courts do not provide advisory opinions.
[177] *Akai* (n 14) 447.
[178] *Valve* [2016] FCA 196, (2016) 337 ALR 647, [122]–[124].

to counterfactuals.[179] Implicitly, that effect normatively justifies the ACL, teleologically. The forum statute is thus an instrument of value,[180] and a representation of political morality.[181] Primary reliance on statutory interpretation in cross-border cases is normatively justified by that underlying morality.

If one prefers a more procedural kind of morality, then the statutory interpretation is justified from that perspective, too. Reliance on the policy of the law in construing the territorial and mandatory qualities of a statute is to give effect to a policy created by the legislature with the mandate of the Australian people. The statutory interpretation approach to forum statutes is thus normatively justified by our constitutional democracy. As the High Court said in *Durham Holdings Pty Ltd v New South Wales*, judges owe a 'duty of obedience to a law made by a Parliament of a State [which] derives from the observance of parliamentary procedures and the conformity of the resulting law with the State and federal Constitutions'; the duty does not derive from the judge's own notions of fundamental rights.[182] The policy of the law is at the heart of the rule of law: the judge applies the law's policy, not her own. To prefer judge-made common law choice of law rules, or the choices made by contracting parties, to the policy of the legislature, is to undermine the very premise from which the court derives its authority to decide.

## B. Negative Consequences of the Statutory Interpretation Approach

The statutory interpretation approach has several negative consequences, which one could spend a lifetime interrogating.[183] This subsection attempts to briefly respond to the two most pressing problems for this approach: forum shopping and uncertainty.

### *i. Forum Shopping*

It must be accepted that the statutory interpretation approach to forum statutes incentivises forum shopping, the 'cardinal sin in private international law'.[184] Accordingly, this approach is a barrier to uniformity of outcome.[185]

[179] See his Honour's discussion of counterfactuals: of what would happen if Valve's submissions were accepted: ibid [119].

[180] RCA Higgins, 'Contingency, Law and the Practice of Value' in JT Gleeson and RCA Higgins (eds), *Constituting Law – Legal Argument and Social Values* (Sydney, Federation Press 2011) 33, 37.

[181] See generally R Dworkin, *Justice for Hedgehogs* (Cambridge, Harvard University Press, 2011).

[182] *Durham Holdings Pty Ltd v New South Wales* [2001] HCA 7, (2001) 205 CLR 39, [61] (Gaudron, McHugh, Gummow, Kirby, Hayne and Callinan JJ).

[183] For an overview, see Keyes (n 12) 13–25.

[184] R Garnett, 'The Dominance of Uniformity of Outcome in Australian Choice of *Law*: Is It Time to Relax the Grip?' (2013) 37 *Australian Bar Review* 192, 193.

[185] Which, admittedly, the High Court has expressed support for, in respect of cross-border torts; see eg *John Pfeiffer Pty Ltd v Rogerson* [2000] HCA 36, (2000) 203 CLR 503.

As the Australian Law Reform Commission said in the 1990s, 'it seems unacceptable that the result of a particular case would depend on venue, rather than on the application of a relevant law chosen on rational criteria'.[186] The retort: lack of decisional uniformity is lamentable, but ignoring the policy of the law, its normative foundation and its democratic mandate, is worse. The court's role is not to effect the purposes of some Platonic plane of private international law, which favours uniformity and international harmony. Its role is to apply domestic law, as per its constitutional framework, to provide justice in the matter before it. If the result is more forum shopping in Australia, perhaps that is because the products on offer are desirable to shoppers.

### *ii. Uncertainty*

While one must admit that the statutory interpretation approach will breed forum shopping, the same does not hold for the objection that this approach necessarily creates uncertainty. Nygh foreshadowed the response to this objection in his monograph on autonomy:

> The essential point is that a law is mandatory when the State enacting the same evinces the wish that it apply unilaterally, despite an earlier presumption that its ambit be defined by a bilateral rule, *or when the court reads into the legislation such a desire.* (Emphasis added.)[187]

The highlighted passage does not indicate some unusual or nefarious judicial activity. In Australia, courts have the 'conclusive authority to determine the meaning of a statutory text'.[188] The purposive approach *requires* the court to 'read into the legislation' mandatory operation, if that is what the policy of the law dictates. The exercise of determining the policy of the law is not some arbitrary exercise; the result is not the length of the Chancellor's foot. As Gageler wrote before his judicial appointment, *stare decisis*:

> creates an impetus for courts to proceed cautiously and incrementally in the attribution of meaning to a statutory text. That is, courts will tend to expound that text no further than is necessary for the application of the law to the facts in the case at hand, conscious that whatever meaning is attributed to the text in that case will have a bearing on the disposition of other cases in the future and draw, in each case, on the accumulated experience of courts in earlier cases in the application of the law to the varied facts of those cases.[189]

The validity of his analysis is seen in the High Court's repeated emphasis that 'intermediate appellate courts are bound to follow the decisions of other Australian

[186] Australian Law Reform Commission, *Choice of Law*, Report No 58 (Sydney, Commonwealth of Australia 1992) 21 [3.14].
[187] P Nygh, *Autonomy in International Contracts* (Oxford, Oxford University Press 1999) 204.
[188] Gageler (n 2) 2.
[189] ibid 4.

intermediate appellate courts' in matters of statutory interpretation 'unless persuaded that those decisions are plainly wrong'.[190]

If this leaves readers dissatisfied, and if it is felt that the ideal of uniformity is too precious to leave to statutory interpretation, then by way of reply: consider the circumstances which caused the Americans to choose revolution instead of the traditional approach to choice of law.[191] If statutory interpretation is malleable, well, so is characterisation of issues; characterisation of procedure; exclusionary doctrines; *renvoi*; and the presumption of similarity. These common law escape devices depend on 'the same inherently dynamic legal process' as statutory interpretation.[192] In each of these cases, there is 'leeway for judicial selection of the field upon which [the] issues will be determined'.[193] But not all hope is lost: through judicial interpretation, rules and principles emerge to navigate the 'penumbra of uncertainty'.[194] The statutory interpretation approach is just as certain, or just as uncertain, as the traditional method of choice of law.

## C. What this Means for the Prohibition on Misleading or Deceptive Conduct

At the risk of riling up the reader without catharsis, this subsection is very brief. It sets the scene for an argument to be fleshed out elsewhere.

It is notable that *Valve* concerned the rights of consumers. The policy of the law being considered was that directed towards consumer protection. It is uncontroversial that consumer protection is a key area for the operation of mandatory law.[195] Would the Court have taken a similarly mandatory approach to the prohibition on misleading or deceptive conduct in the absence of that consumer dimension? Perhaps not.

But it could have, and perhaps it *should* have. The statute is generally-worded;[196] there is room to manoeuvre. The promotion of informed commercial activity[197] and protection against the social detriment of the unrestrained pursuit of self-interest[198] will be served if s 18 is applied to contracts with strong connections to foreign places – provided they come within the scope of s 5(1) – even if the parties

[190] *The Queen v Falzon* [2018] HCA 29, (2018) 92 ALJR 701, [49] (Kiefel CJ, Bell, Keane, Nettle and Gordon JJ).

[191] See Currie (n 108) 77.

[192] Gageler (n 2) 2.

[193] W Gummow, 'The Selection of the Major Premise' (2013) 2 *Cambridge Journal of International and Comparative Law* 47, 59.

[194] L Zines, *The High Court and the Constitution*, 4th edn (Sydney, Federation Press, 1997) 195.

[195] See G Rühl, 'The Protection of Weaker Parties in the Private International Law of the European Union: A Portrait of Inconsistency and Conceptual Truancy' (2015) 10(3) *Journal of Private International Law* 335, 352.

[196] See CCA, s 5(1).

[197] *Bullabidgee* (n 5) [6] (Allsop P, Basten and Young JJA agreeing).

[198] *Bodum* (n 6) [201] (Greenwood J; Tracey J agreeing).

have agreed otherwise. On the other hand, s 67 does not apply where the contract is not a consumer contract; *expressio unius* suggests a policy that ACL, s 18 *may* be contracted out of. But the matter is not explicit.

If the statutory interpretation approach dominates, contracting parties may seek to sideline the Australian justice system, favouring selection of foreign law, foreign courts and arbitration.[199] That may be so, but the policy of the law would not stand in vain. Australian courts would be warranted in issuing an anti-suit injunction to stop such litigation or arbitration, in equity's auxiliary jurisdiction, in aid of the legal rights in the statute which the parties sought to avoid.[200] In typical Australian fashion, a court could force the parties to be fair: it could enforce the prohibition on misleading or deceptive conduct in mandatory fashion, with the aid of injunctive relief.[201]

A few years ago, Spigelman described the prospect of the Trade Practices Act 1974 (Cth) applying as mandatory law 'uncertain', and called for this to be 'fixed'.[202] If the problem is uncertainty, then courts could fix the situation by applying s 18 in a mandatory manner in every case. This would run contrary to the global trend towards party autonomy[203] – but just because everyone else is moving in that direction does not make it right. Further, this would be a parochial, almost imperial solution. I, for one, am comfortable with such liberal interventionism. 'Don't mislead; don't deceive; don't be dodgy': we should be comfortable with imposing these categorical imperatives on the world.

## V. Conclusion

A few years ago, Briggs considered that there was some merit to the view that 'the pedagogic convenience which segregated private international law from the rest of the law now does more harm than good'.[204] This chapter was written with that view in mind.

The exaltation of continental legal philosophy from centuries ago as a pseudo-source of positive law in a common law system is lamentable.[205] Savigny's policy of neutrality is nothing in comparison to the policy of the law enacted by mandate of the people of Australia. Mandatory law has a limited role to play in the EU, but

[199] JJ Spigelman, 'Between the Parochial and the Cosmopolitan' in JT Gleeson and RCA Higgins (eds), *Constituting Law – Legal Argument and Social Values* (Sydney, Federation Press 2011) 234, 239.

[200] See M Douglas, 'Anti-Suit Injunctions in Australia' (2017) 41 *Melbourne University Law Review* 66.

[201] Autonomy may have primacy in private international law, but domestic legal systems contain innumerable examples of anti-autonomy measures, eg Australia's compulsory voting system.

[202] Spigelman, 'Between the Parochial and the Cosmopolitan' (n 199) 234, 239, citing W Jo-Mei Ma, 'What's my Choice: Deciphering the Provisions on Conflict of Laws in the Trade Practices Act' (2001) 11 *Trade Practices Law Journal* 149.

[203] See Yeo, ch 11 of this volume.

[204] Briggs, *The Conflict of Laws* (n 71) 5.

[205] Written with utmost respect for my *de facto* mentors: R Mortensen, M Keyes and R Garnett, *Private International Law in Australia*, 3rd edn (Sydney, LexisNexis Butterworths, 2015) 24–25.

Australia is not a part of the EU.[206] Common law private international law may be different from that applicable in other parts of the world. Even within the common law world, diversity is to be expected. If you were to ask a Queenslander, a Western Australian, an Englishman and an American, 'what is football?', you would get four different answers. Naturally, I prefer my indigenous answer.

It must be conceded that the position advanced in this chapter would result in forum shopping. It would grate against the international politeness and civility of comity. But we do not live in an age of international civility. We live in an age of statutes.

[206] And by the time this is published, it may be that neither is the United Kingdom.

# PART IV

# The Developing Legal Landscape

# 10

# New and Alternative Approaches to Proof of Foreign Law

## *A Practitioners' Perspective*

JUSTIN HOGAN-DORAN AND DOMINIQUE HOGAN-DORAN

## I. Introduction

Globalisation is a cultural, social and political phenomenon which encompasses an increased interaction and integration between people, companies and governments worldwide. As globalisation has evolved, propelled by advances in transportation and communication technology, so too have the interconnections between legal systems and jurisdictions. One manifestation of this is an increase in foreign law issues arising in litigation in Australian courts.[1]

Proof of the content of foreign law lies at both the beginning and end of the choice of law process in any given case. Each case comprises a set of juridical facts which, when arranged in some order, interacts with law to produce a bundle of rights: a chose in action or cause of action. Where one or more juridical facts take place in another foreign law area, the possibility arises for some foreign law to have some application so as to enhance, negate, or otherwise adjust the legal rights of the parties.

Proof of foreign law arises at inception of a case because the orthodox approach of the common law courts is to leave to parties the choice of whether to plead the 'foreignness' of any relevant juridical facts – as well as the foreign law acting upon those facts – to produce a particular chose in action. By pleading some foreign element that connects the case with another particular system of foreign law, the choice of law rules of the forum will be engaged. Proof of foreign law also arises during (either at, or near, the conclusion of) the case because a court, once seized

[1] See JJ Spigelman, 'Cross Border Issues for Commercial Courts: An Overview' (Address to the Second Judicial Seminar on Commercial Litigation, Hong Kong, 13 January 2010); JJ Spigelman, 'Conflict of Laws in Australia' (speech delivered in Sydney, 16 April 2010) 5.

of the issue, having selected the appropriate choice of law rule, must then determine what is the content of the relevant foreign law and how it is to be applied to the facts of the case, based on material put before it or of which it can take judicial notice.

Once the choice of law rule points to some foreign law, the question arises whether it is the burden of the parties or of the court to determine the content and application of the foreign law. However, proof of foreign law is rarely the subject of detailed consideration and analysis within academia or the profession.[2] This is so, despite it becoming increasingly important to international ligation, for both factual reasons – like the growth of international trade and movement of peoples – and legal reasons – like increasingly divergent statutory regimes, the abandonment of the double actionability rule for choice of law in tort in favour of the *lex loci delicti* rule,[3] and the narrowing of the scope of legal rules characterised as procedural and as such governed solely by the law of the forum. The 'foreign law' includes foreign substantive law and, with the growth of *renvoi*, the choice of law rules of the foreign legal system.[4] The mere fact that questions of foreign law arise in proceedings does not of itself warrant the transfer of proceedings to the foreign court,[5] nor does it warrant a stay on the basis of *forum non conveniens*.[6]

Issues of foreign law inevitably raise two research problems for parties, practitioners and judges: the search for content, and the search for meaning. Orthodox rules of English common law require parties to formally plead and prove, by expert evidence, the content of foreign law.[7] The procedure is inefficient, time-consuming and expensive[8] as well as being fraught with risk of error. For the practitioner, the search for content is aimed at determining whether foreign law is at least likely to be different in some way that it may (materially) affect the outcome of the litigation. Traditionally, even this stage has required the assistance of foreign lawyers.

Writing in 1945, Kuhn observed that oral or written testimony of witnesses learned in the existing law of the foreign country 'is often difficult to procure'.[9]

[2] But see J McComish, 'Pleading and Proving Foreign Law in Australia' (2007) 31(2) *Melbourne University Law Review* 400; R Fentiman, *Foreign Law in English Courts – Pleasing, Proof and Choice of Law* (Oxford, Oxford University Press, 1998); TC Hartley, 'Pleading and Proof of Foreign Law: The Major European Systems Compared' (1996) 45(2) *International and Comparative Law Quarterly* 271; see also EE Þorláksson, 'Proof of Foreign Law before Icelandic Courts: a Change of Course?' (2016) 12(2) *Journal of Private International Law* 301.

[3] See *Regie Nationale des Usines Renault SA v Zhang* [2002] HCA 10, 210 CLR 491 (*Renault v Zhang*).

[4] *Neilson v Overseas Projects Corporation of Victoria Ltd* [2005] HCA 54, (2005) 223 CLR 331 (*Neilson*).

[5] At least where the choice is made between Australia and New Zealand. See *Puttick v Tenon* [2008] HCA 54, (2008) 238 CLR 264 (*Puttick*). *Quaere* whether the same outcome would subsist with the entry into force of the *Trans-Tasman Proceedings Act 2010* (Cth) ss 19, 21.

[6] *Renault v Zhang* (n 3).

[7] See ibid [70] (Gleeson CJ, Gaudron, McHugh, Gummow and Hayne JJ).

[8] See generally A Nussbaum, 'Proving the Law of Foreign Countries' (1954) 3 *American Journal of Comparative Law* 60.

[9] A Kuhn, 'Judicial Notice of Foreign Law' (1945) 39 *American Journal of International Law* 86, 87.

With the advent of the internet and even the ready accessibility offered by automatic translation software, the practitioner need not travel far to find what they seek. The World Legal Information Institute (WorldLII) is perhaps the most well-known example, if perhaps not the best source, of the aggregation on the internet of primary law resources.[10] The rise of English as the new *lingua franca* has promoted the publication online (as unofficial texts) in English of statutes and ordinances in countries where English is not the national language by state agencies,[11] public institutes and private experts. Google and other search engines, as well as subscription services translating and republishing foreign law sources, have made it easier to find foreign laws or at least the means of accessing foreign law sources. In turn, private subscription providers and university law libraries have undertaken the task of aggregating such sources.[12]

More difficult is the search for meaning. Local practitioners perhaps ought to be, but rarely are, educated in comparative law, at least at an undergraduate level.[13] Professional concern for clients may make lawyers reticent to give a firm opinion on foreign law; while such opinions would likely still attract legal professional privilege,[14] the expertise of the lawyer would be in question. Language barriers compound the difficulty. Foreign laws are often translated by linguistic experts who are less astute on legal meanings or the culture in which the foreign law was created that shapes the meaning of words.[15] Thus, 'identical provision of the law of two countries may have wholly different moral backgrounds, may have been brought about by the interplay of wholly different forces, and hence the similarity may be due to the purest coincidence'.[16] De Boer encapsulated the problem:

> Like a language, foreign law is difficult to learn by anyone who has not been born and bred in the social environment in which it is used… Most judges dealing with foreign law in a conflicts case are unaccustomed to its vernacular, unaware of its various layers of meaning, insensitive to its subtleties, ignorant of its usage, oblivious to its context. Small wonder that they are apt to make mistakes that their colleagues abroad would avoid instinctively.[17]

[10] World Legal Information Institute (2018) www.worldlii.org.

[11] eg Legifrance is the French Government entity responsible for publishing legal texts online and publishes translations of key statutes and codes into English (which have no legal force): see Legifrance (2018), www.legifrance.gouv.fr/Traductions/en-English.

[12] See eg the following guide to foreign law sources: Georgetown University Law Library, 'Foreign and Comparative law Research Guide' (2018), guides.ll.georgetown.edu/c.php?g=362128&p=2446014.

[13] See S Blay, 'The Function of International And Comparative Law in Australian Legal Education' (1996) *Australian International Law Journal* 80; T Hutchinson, 'Developing Legal Research Skills: Expanding the Paradigm' (2008) 32(3) *Melbourne University Law Review* 1065. For a recent illustration of the relevance of comparative legal analysis to civil litigation in Australia, see S Spottiswood, 'The Use of Foreign Law by the High Court of Australia' (2018) 46 *Federal Law Review* 161.

[14] See D Butler, 'In-house Counsel Advising on Foreign Law: Is it Privileged?' (2018) *Hearsay: The Journal of the Bar Association of Queensland*. For a recent illustration of the dangers of assuming knowledge of the laws of a 'foreign' jurisdiction, see *Waldron v Joondalup Hospital Pty Ltd* [2018] NSWSCA 182.

[15] See L Lessig, 'Fidelity in Translation' (1993) 71 *Texas Law Review* 1165, 1194–96.

[16] P Lepaulle, 'Function of Comparative Law' (1922) 35 *Harvard Law Review* 838, 853.

[17] ThM De Boer, 'Facultative Choice of Law: The Procedural Status of Choice-of-Law, Rules and Foreign Law' (1996) 257 *Recueil des cours de l'Academie de droit international de La Haye* 222, 305.

The potential burden for the parties and the courts has meant that the need to prove foreign law, and the potential for cost, delay, error and the like, makes it a factor in an application for a stay of proceedings based on *forum non conveniens* grounds.[18] Where the applicant for a stay contends that there is some relevant advantage to it of proceedings under the foreign law, it must prove the foreign law and the aspects of it that are said to provide an advantage.[19]

Against that backdrop, this chapter considers first the orthodox approach to determining the content and meaning of foreign law, and then considers means of shortcutting this approach in search of a more just, cheap and quick solution. The limited steps taken on the international plane to enhance discovery of foreign law and cooperation between national courts will be considered. A brief consideration is then given to the general approach in international commercial arbitration and one of the recently emerged international financial courts. Finally, the authors argue that common law courts should have a broad, discretionary power to choose amongst the various methods that have been tried and found reliable in other legal of systems. In each case, the judge hearing the case should be empowered to choose the most just, cheap and quick procedure for resolving foreign law issues in any given case, depending on the degree of familiarity with and confidence in applying the foreign law in question, the willingness of the parties and the value of the claims involved.

## II. Orthodox Approach

The approach to foreign law in common law courts in England and the dominions and territories[20] is heavily influenced by the historical development of the common law courts.[21] Early common law courts applied English law to English disputes, and juries were locals with local knowledge of the facts, not a tribunal of fact for determining factual disputes based on the evidence presented. Disputes between merchants and traders were heard in the courts of piepowder and staples, which determined disputes according to the law merchant (*lex mercatoria*). From the fourteenth century, the court of Admiralty came into existence, and over time came to determine all foreign causes according to the law of nations. While the law merchant found its way into English common law through the Admiralty courts, foreign laws, which had never been administered by English courts, remained 'unknown'.[22]

[18] Though not sufficient in and of itself: *Puttick v Tenon* [2008] HCA 54, (2008) 238 CLR 264, 277–78 (French CJ, Gummow, Hayne and Kiefel JJ); see also *Voth v Manildra Flour Mills* [1990] HCA 55, (1990) 171 CLR 538, 566 (Mason CJ, Deane, Dawson and Gaudron JJ).

[19] *Renault v Zhang* (n 3) [72] (Gleeson CJ, Gaudron, McHugh, Gummow and Hayne JJ).

[20] Including South Africa; see *Standard Bank of Ltd v Ocean Commodities Incorporated* 1983 1 SA 276 (A) (Supreme Court of Appeal). See generally BSC Martin, 'Judicial Notice of Foreign Law' (1998) 31 *Comparative and International Law Journal of Southern Africa* 61.

[21] See generally SL Sass, 'Foreign Law in Civil Litigation: A Comparative Survey' (1968) 16 *American Journal of Comparative Law* 332, 335–37.

[22] ibid 335.

The means of determining the content of foreign law appears to have first been considered by Lord Mansfield in a case involving the unlawful detention and torture of a Maltese man by the English Governor in *Mostyn v Fabrigas*.[23] Lord Mansfield considered that foreign laws must be proved by facts, with the judge assisting the jury (by jury direction) in discovering them from the evidence presented. The soundest doctrinal basis for this view of foreign law as fact is to be found in Dicey's 'acquired [ie vested] rights theory'. On this view, foreign laws, on certain facts, give rise to rights between the parties when the facts of the cause are applied to those laws. The common law court gives effect to these rights as with any other right; by proving its existence as a matter of fact.[24]

By at least Story's time, it had come to be recognised that foreign law was to be proved not for the jury but for the court, and this principle has been widely accepted in the jurisprudence of America and also by the Administration of Justice Act 1920 and the Supreme Court of Judicature Act of 1925.[25] That tradition continues in the orthodox principles which govern proof of foreign law in Australian courts.

A number of interwoven principles[26] govern the treatment of foreign law in an English or Australian court. That foreign laws are treated as facts,[27] not law, in a common law court, acts as a qualifier that moulds each of the principles.[28]

First, no judicial notice is taken of foreign laws.[29] They are unknown and unknowable to the judge, unless notorious. The historical explanation for this is set out above.

Second, as a corollary of this, foreign law must be formally proved. Foreign laws must be pleaded as facts, and as such are subject to the rules of pleading. If they are not pleaded and proved, the court will apply local law instead, for knowing only local law the court presumes foreign law to be the same.[30]

Third, unlike ordinary facts, however, an expert ordinarily is required to prove the content of foreign law.[31] As an exception to this, ss 174–175 of certain Australian States' 'Uniform Evidence Acts'[32] provide short cuts to proving the contents of foreign statutes, proclamations, treaties or acts of state, and case law, without expert evidence but instead through the admission into evidence of apparently

[23] *Mostyn v Fabrigas* (1774) 1 Cowp 161, 174, 98 ER 1021, 1028.

[24] See AV Dicey, *Conflict of Laws*, 1st edn (Stevens & Sons, 1896) 23–26.

[25] See Kuhn, 'Judicial Notice of Foreign Law' (n 9) 86.

[26] Fentiman, Foreign Law in English Courts (n 2) 3–4.

[27] Albeit facts of a peculiar kind: *Parkasho v Singh* [1968] P 233, 250 (Cairns J).

[28] The following orthodox principles were considered by the High Court in *Neilson* (n 4); see [115] (Gummow and Hayne JJ).

[29] *Cf* Evidence Act 1995 (Cth) s 143.

[30] But see *Damberg v Damberg* [2001] NSWCA 87, (2001) 52 NSWLR 492.

[31] *Sussex Peerage Case* (1844) 11 Cl & F 85, 115, 8 ER 1034, 1046.

[32] Which have so far only been adopted in NSW, Victoria, Tasmania, the ACT and the Northern Territory. To similar effect to s 174 in Queensland, see s 68 Evidence Act 1977 (as to any statute, proclamation, treaty or act of state only).

reliable sources.[33] In South Australia and Western Australia, official and unofficial publications of foreign written laws may be tendered to prove foreign law, although the court is not bound to accept them.[34] In Western Australia, official publications are *prima facie* evidence of foreign law as printed.[35] At times, judicial notice is taken of well-known sources of foreign case law, which is at least indicative of the cosmopolitan education of the modern lawyer.[36] To this is applied a presumption of continuance, namely that legislation once made will continue in force and in the same terms unless proven otherwise.[37]

Fourth, a judge and not a jury must determine the existence of the content of foreign law.[38] A common law court can substitute its own interpretation of a foreign law if the expert evidence is absurd, untenable or contradictory. Even short of this, where there is doubt or conflict between the experts, judges may prefer to look at the foreign sources and draw conclusions based on them (informed by the expert evidence where appropriate).[39]

Fifth, if the content of the foreign law is pleaded, proved and determined by the court as a matter of fact, the court will then 'apply' those facts to other facts, as it would any legal rule. This is the first way in which foreign law is a 'fact' of a peculiar kind. However, there is no 'doctrine of precedent' such that a decision by a judge as to the content and meaning of a certain foreign law is binding in any way on a subsequent judge considering the same question between different parties or on different causes.

The principle then is that the application of foreign law is for the judge, not the expert. This is oft-repeated,[40] but it is of dubious correctness at least in those jurisdictions which have done away with the ultimate issue rule of evidence.[41] Further,

[33] See eg s 176 of the (almost) Uniform Evidence Act of the Commonwealth (1995), NSW (1995), Victoria (2008), Tasmania (2001), the ACT (2011) and the Northern Territory (Evidence (National Uniform Legislation) Act 2011). These Acts are based on the Model Uniform Evidence Bill, as endorsed by the then Standing Committee of Attorneys-General in 2007. It has been considered that the websites of the Legislative Assembly of the State of Georgia and that of the State of Minnesota are reliable sources of information with respect to the relevant laws in those jurisdictions as to service of documents: *Rasmussen v Eltrax Systems Pty Ltd (No 4)* [2006] NSWIRComm 225, [40] (Marks J), citing *MindShare Communications Ltd v Orleans Investments Pty Ltd* [2000] FCA 521 (Katz J).

[34] Evidence Act 1929 (SA) s 63; Evidence Act 1906 (WA) s 71.

[35] Evidence Act 1906 (WA) s 70.

[36] *Optus Networks Pty. Limited v Gilsan (International) Limited* [2006] NSWCA 171, [87] (Hodgson JA, Beazley and McColl JJA agreeing).

[37] ibid [89]. This at least can be done where the legislation is not obviously directed only at one year such as annual tax legislation.

[38] See above n 34.

[39] *A/S Tallinna Laevauhisus v Estonian State Steamship Line* (1947) 80 Lloyds LR 99, 107.

[40] See J McComish, 'Pleading and Proving Foreign Law in Australia' (2007) 31(2) *Melbourne University Law Review* 400, 418 and the texts and cases cited at nn 122 and 124 on that page.

[41] See *Allstate Life Insurance Co v Australia and New Zealand Banking Group Ltd (No 6)* (1996) 64 FCR 79, 82–83 (Federal Court of Australia, Lindgren J); *Noza Holdings Pty Ltd (ACN 098 410 881) v Commissioner of Taxation* [2010] FCA 990, but see *Idoport Pty Ltd v National Australia Bank* [2000] NSWSC 1077, (2000) 50 NSWLR 640; *John Edward Platts v The Nominal Defendant* [1996] ACTSC 87; *Walton v Corporate Venture Pty Ltd* [1996] ACTSC 55: suggesting that s 80 has entirely displaced the common law relating to evidence on an ultimate issue.

wherever some discretion is to be exercised by a court under the foreign law, evidence may be received as to how a foreign court would exercise that discretion. The lack of that evidence calls into question the extent to which the local court, having identified that a foreign law rule applies, can then apply its own notions of the proper exercise of discretion.[42]

Sixth, the application of foreign law to fact is a question of law. Thus, while the application of the law to fact is a function for the judge – and not the expert – an appellate court may give little deference to the trial judge's appreciation of foreign laws as 'facts' unless a review on the factual findings is entirely excluded. Thus, appellate review of factual findings of foreign law is less constrained.

Seventh, where foreign law that is pleaded is not proved, the court ordinarily resorts to the 'presumption of similarity'; that the *lex causae* is the same as the *lex fori*.[43] That approach is not without energetic criticism. Briggs described it as a 'truly grotesque proposition'.[44] In *Neilson v Overseas Projects Corporation of Victoria Ltd*, in dissent, Kirby J suggested it 'stretched credulity' to assume that the approach to statutory interpretation in China would be akin to Australia: '[w]e do not advance the orderly development of private international law by encouraging the defective presentation of cases and by adopting incredible fictions to cure such defects'.[45]

# III. Addressing the Limitations of the Orthodox Approach

It is not readily apparent what solution should present where the parties are unwilling or unable to incur the costs of foreign law experts but are content to proceed on the basis that foreign law is the same in whole or in part as local law for the purposes of resolving their disputes. Not every litigant is able to engage experts of such eminence as retired judges of foreign appellate courts, and not every case where discrete issues of foreign law can be applied to a narrow range of facts.[46]

[42] Evidence Act 1995 (Cth) s 80(a); Evidence Act 1995 (NSW) s 80(a); Evidence Act 2001 (Tas) s 80(a). See *Neilson* (n 4) [119] (Gummow & Hayne JJ); *Sheahan v ANZ Bank NZ Ltd* [2013] NZHC 888, [2013] NZHC 888.

[43] *Lloyd v Gilbert* (1865) LR 1 WB 115; *Wright Heaton & Co Ltd v Barrett* (1892) 9 WN (NSW) 13, 15; *United States Surgical Corporation v Hospital Products International Pty Ltd* [1982] 2 NSWLR 766, 799 (McLelland J) (*Hospital Products*); Neilson (n 4) (Gleeson CJ), [45] (McHugh J), [116], [125] (Gummow and Hayne JJ), [249], [261] (Callinan J), [267] (Heydon J).

[44] A Briggs, 'The Meaning and Proof of Foreign Law' [2006] *Lloyd's Maritime and Commercial Law Quarterly* 1, 4.

[45] *Neilson* (n 4) [208] (Kirby J).

[46] As occurred in *Babcock & Brown DIF III Global Co-Investment Fund, LP v Babcock & Brown International Pty Limited* [2016] VSC 623. The applicability of exceptions to the privity of contract rule was an important factual issue, because the plaintiffs relied on three clauses which they contended demonstrated a clear contrary intent, with the effect that some of the defendants were unable to enforce a forum selection clause, with the consequence that their stay application under s 30 of the Supreme Court Act 1986 (Vic) was dismissed: at [84]. An appeal against the decision was dismissed: *Royal Bank of Scotland PLC v Babcock & Brown DIF III Global Co-Investment Fund LP* [2017] VSCA 138.

In many cases, there may be gaps in the evidence, or the foreign law is unsettled, ambiguous or complex, and expert evidence proffers conflicting conclusions as to its content. This may not be apparent until trial. What, then, is the court to do?

Where the parties do raise issues of foreign law, and appear to be committed to incurring both private and public expense of engaging experts and asking a judge to resolve foreign law issues, a number of procedures are available to facilitate a determination that is just, cheap and quick. These include:

A. relaxation of the restrictions on judicial notice;
B. relaxation of rights of appearance and representation;
C. referral to referees;
D. commencement of foreign court proceedings;
E. engagement of international judicial co-operation.

These are addressed in turn.

## A. Judicial Notice of Foreign Laws and the Relaxation of the Orthodox Approach

The absence of judicial notice of all but the most notorious foreign laws[47] places on the parties the whole burden of proving the content of foreign law. At best, the judge must search between inconsistent or unclear sources, but will not stray beyond the evidence, even expert evidence.

Some of the civilian jurisdictions take the opposite view. In countries heavily influenced by the German legal tradition (Germany, Italy, Austria, The Netherlands, Denmark, Finland, Norway and Sweden), courts take judicial notice of foreign laws.[48] The origin of this approach is the work of German Roman law scholars such as Von Savigny, who advocated an internationalist approach to the development of a Roman common law for all civilian countries.[49] This approach was embodied in the first German Federal Code of Civil Procedure of 1877, in art 293 (originally, 265):

> Laws in force in another country, customary law, and municipal ordinances require proof only insofar as they are unknown to the court. In ascertaining these legal norms, the court is not confined to the evidence adduced by the parties; it is authorized to avail itself of other sources of information and to make such orders as may be necessary for the purpose.

[47] Such as that gaming is legal in Monte Carlo: *Saxby v Fulton* [1909] 2 KB 208, 211.

[48] Sass, 'Foreign Law in Civil Litigation' (n 21); see also Hartley, 'Pleading and Proof of Foreign Law' (n 2).

[49] F von Savigny, *Private International Law, and the Retrospective Operation of Statutes – A Treatise on the Conflict of Laws, and the Limits of their Operation in Respect of Place and Time* (London, William Guthrie (translator), T&T Clark/Stevens & Sons, 1840) §186.

Most commonly, the court will choose a German professor of comparative law, or seek the assistance of the Max Planck Institute for Comparative and International Private Law.[50]

Historically, French courts followed the practice of treating foreign law as a matter of fact.[51] This has been repeatedly affirmed by the Cour de cassation by announcing that interpretation of such law falls within the sovereign authority of the trial judge, and therefore escapes the control of the highest court. In 2005 the Cour de cassation held that courts could also determine foreign law of their own initiative.[52] Other civilian countries maintain the 'foreign law as fact' tradition.[53]

The United States inherited the English rules of proof of foreign law, and applied it both to non-US and interstate laws.[54] The obvious impracticality of this has meant that the National Conference of Commissioners on Uniform State Laws (NCCUSL) in 1936 proposed uniform legislation – the Uniform Judicial Notice of Foreign Law Act – that many States have since passed,[55] to permit courts to take judicial notice of the laws of other US States, with varying requirements of notice (whether pleading or otherwise) and proof (or 'information') of its content.[56]

Some US States, such as Massachusetts,[57] made mandatory the taking of judicial notice of both sister-state and foreign laws (Maryland extended the obligation only to common law States).[58] The courts heavily circumscribed these rules with notice and evidence requirements that pared the laws back close to the orthodox English view. New York permitted such notice to be taken, with the court having the power to consider material provided by counsel or researched by itself.[59] It has since adopted the Uniform Law.[60] The court is given a wide power as to the form of proof it shall admit. Rule 4511(d) of the current New York rules provides a hybrid

[50] P Rogerson and J Collier, *Collier's Conflict of Laws*, 4th edn (Cambridge, Cambridge University Press, 2013) 51.

[51] *Lautour* case, Cour de cassation, 1ère Chambre civile, 37.414, 25 May 1948.

[52] *Itraco* case, Cour de cassation, Chambre commercial, 02-14686, 28 June 2005: 'It falls to the French judge who deems a foreign law to be applicable to establish, either *sua sponte* or upon the request of the party invoking the foreign law, the content of such a law, with the help of the parties or personally if necessary, and to decide the disputed question in conformity with the foreign law'.

[53] Such as Spain and the Latin American states, Greece, Turkey. See Sass (n 21) 351–54.

[54] See JH Beale, *A Treatise on the Conflict of Laws* (Boston, Harvard University Press, 1935) 1663. The 'full faith and credit clause' of the US Constitution (art IV, s 1) did not extend to judicial notice of the laws of sister-states that State courts were bound to give effect to.

[55] By 1966, it had been adopted in 26 States; see Federal Rules of Civil Procedure r 44.1, 'Notes of Advisory Committee Rules – 1966'. See eg Colorado (Colo. Rev. Stat. §13-25-106); Maine (Me. Rev. Stat. tit. 16, §401); Illinois (735 ILCS 5/8-1001); Maryland (Md. Code, Cts. & Jud. Proc. art., §10-501); Minnesota (Minn. Stat. § 599.04); Missouri (Mo. Rev. Stat. §490.070); Nebraska (Neb. Rev. Stat. § 25-12,101.; South Carolina: S.C. Code § 19-3-110; Washington (Wash. Rev. Code §5.24.010); Wisconsin (Wis. Stats. §902.02).

[56] See eg the Californian Evidence Code, §450-460 (enacted in 1965).

[57] Massachusetts (Mass. Gen Laws, Ch 233, §70, Supp 1956)).

[58] Maryland (Md. Ann. Code, art 35, §47 (1957)).

[59] New York Civil Practice Act 1943, §344-A.

[60] New York Civil Practice Law and Rules (Ch 8, Consolidated Laws of New York) R4511 (2016).

of a wide discretion with rules of evidence similar to ss 174–175 of Australia's uniform Evidence Acts:

> In considering whether a matter of law should be judicially noticed and in determining the matter of law to be judicially noticed, the court may consider any testimony, document, information or argument on the subject, whether offered by a party or discovered through its own research. Whether or not judicial notice is taken, a printed copy of a statute or other written law or a proclamation, edict, decree or ordinance by an executive contained in a book or publication, purporting to have been published by a government or commonly admitted as evidence of the existing law in the judicial tribunals of the jurisdiction where it is in force, is prima facie evidence of such law and the unwritten or common law of a jurisdiction may be proved by witnesses or printed reports of cases of the courts of the jurisdiction.

Other States followed the approach adopted by NCCUSL and the ABA in 1953; the Uniform Rules of Evidence, r 9(2), (3). These statutes allow the court to take judicial notice of foreign (non-US) laws while mandating certain notice and proof requirements. They typically provide that (1) judicial notice *may* be taken of foreign law without request by a party; and (2) judicial notice *shall* be taken of such law if a party requests it and then gives the judge sufficient information (evidence) properly to comply with the request and gives the adverse party such notice as the judge may require to meet that case.

For example, the California Evidence Code allows judicial notice to be taken of 'the law of an organization of nations and of foreign nations and public entities in foreign nations' (§452(f)) if a party requests it and gives notice and sufficient information to enable the court to do so (§453). However, the court would do so after considering the source of that information, including the expertise of any author (of a book or report etc), and where experts are used they may give evidence orally or in writing (§454). Where the foreign law would have 'substantial consequence on the action', then, after giving the parties time to provide evidence as to whether it should do so, and considering the material provided, it may make its own enquiries. However (§455):

> If the trial court resorts to any source of information not received in open court, including the advice of persons learned in the subject matter, such information and its source shall be made a part of the record in the action and the court shall afford each party reasonable opportunity to meet such information before judicial notice of the matter may be taken.

Generally, the interpretation of foreign laws is treated as a matter for the judge, but some States and deeper historical cases supported leaving any conflict of expert evidence on foreign law as a matter for the jury to resolve.[61] A less structured approach is taken in Federal Rule of Civil Procedure 44.1, which provides:

> A party who intends to raise an issue about a foreign country's law must give notice by a pleading or other writing. In determining foreign law, the court may consider any

[61] See *Hite v Keane*, 149 Wis 207, 215 (1912), criticised in *Fitzpatrick v International Railway*, 252 NY 127, 169 NE 112 (1929).

> relevant material or source, including testimony, whether or not submitted by a party or admissible under the Federal Rules of Evidence. The court's determination must be treated as a ruling on a question of law.

According to the 1966 Notes to FRCP 44.1:

> [The Court] may engage in its own research and consider any relevant material thus found. The court may have at its disposal better foreign law materials than counsel have presented, or may wish to re-examine and amplify material that has been presented by counsel in partisan fashion or in insufficient detail…

The spectrum of approaches to this rule is found in *Bodum USA v La Cafetiere*.[62] This involved a contract dispute between the distributor of certain French press coffee-makers (cafetieres a piston) and a US rival (Bodum), as to whether the contract permitted the distributor's similar product being sold in the same US market subject to not using certain trade marks. French law governed the contract. Article 1156 of the French Code Civil provided that: '[o]ne must in agreements seek what the common intention of the contracting parties was, rather than pay attention to the literal meaning of the terms'.

Bodum advanced the proposition, on which the parties' respective French law experts disagreed, that evidence of subjective intention could be admitted such that the trial court might find that such subjective intention was shared and should be applied, irrespective of the words used. The trial court rejected this argument and gave summary judgment for the distributor.

The Circuit Court's principal opinion, authored by Chief Judge Easterbrook, constrained the permissive approach of the rule such that 'Judges should use the best of the available sources', and that the 'court may have at its disposal better foreign law materials than counsel have presented'.[63] The opinion reflected a certain cynical realism, pointing out that expert evidence was not only expensive but 'adds an adversary's spin, which the court then must discount'.[64] The Court preferred the published treatises about French law (published in English) without such a slant and their ready availability meant that 'we prefer them to the parties' declarations'. The Circuit Court found that the above quoted article of the French Civil Code means that the court must seek the parties' 'common intention', and not merely the unilateral claimed intent of one party. The Court cited a 2007 United States law review article for this proposition, along with a number of French judicial decisions and other statutes.[65]

Judge Posner, a learned comparative law and economics scholar, and French linguist, concurred, writing a separate opinion as he said 'to express emphatic

[62] *Bodum USA v La Cafetiere*, 621 F.3d 624 (7th Cir 2010) (*Bodum*).
[63] ibid 628.
[64] ibid 629.
[65] *Bodum* (n 62) 629, citing AL Zuppi, 'The Parol Evidence Rule: A Comparative Study of the Common Law, the Civil Law Tradition, and Lex Mercatoria' (2007) 35 *Georgia Journal of International and Comparative Law* 233, 258–60.

support for, and modestly to amplify, the court's criticism of a common and authorized but unsound judicial practice'.[66] He remarked that as the rule permits, but does not mandate, affidavit evidence, 'the court doesn't have to rely on testimony; and in only a few cases, I believe, is it justified in doing so. This case is not one of them'.[67] Much of the support cited by Judge Posner for his conclusions were American scholarly publications about French law or translations into English.[68]

However, Judge Wood, though concurring in the result, demonstrated far less enthusiasm. He said that:

> [r]ule 44.1 itself establishes no hierarchy for sources of foreign law, and I am unpersuaded by my colleagues' assertion that expert testimony is categorically inferior to published, English language materials. Exercises in comparative law are notoriously difficult, because the U.S. reader is likely to miss nuances in the foreign law, to fail to appreciate the way in which one branch of the other country's law interacts with another, or to assume erroneously that the foreign law mirrors U.S. law when it does not.[69]

As a matter of practice, the rule permits both expert evidence and primary and secondary materials without expert testimony. As the type of proof that the trial court will accept as well as its preference between sources is up to the trial judge's discretion, parties are best armed with both.

Relaxation of judicial notice has not formally been adopted in Australia. In *United States Surgical Corp v Hospital Products Int'l Pty Ltd*, the parties agreed to a direction to the effect of FRCP 44.1 in respect of argument about the content and application of the *Sherman* and *Clayton Acts*.[70] However, McLelland J declined to go beyond evidence.[71] Otherwise, Australian courts only take judicial notice of conventional and customary international law.[72]

Informally, the rule is often relaxed where foreign laws inform legal argument on the meaning and application of local laws. Practitioners regularly cite foreign legal authority, especially the laws of England and other common law countries to discover the common law rule applicable to their case, to illustrate comparative law points made in argument, or in cases under international treaties where consistency of interpretation between states parties is mandated.[73]

The South African *Law of Evidence Amendment*, Act 45 of 1988, which overcomes the fear of lack of authoritativeness by permitting judicial notice where the

[66] *Bodum* (n 62) 631.

[67] ibid 632.

[68] ibid 633.

[69] ibid 638–39.

[70] *United States Surgical Corporation v Hospital Products International Pty Ltd* [1982] 2 NSWLR 766.

[71] ibid 801.

[72] See *Australian Competition and Consumer Commission v PT Garuda Indonesia (No 9)* [2013] FCA 323, [29]–[48].

[73] See *TCL Air Conditioner (Zhongshan) Co Ltd v Castel Electronics Pty Ltd* [2014] FCAFC 83, (2014) 232 FCR 361, [75].

foreign law is 'readily ascertainable' and with 'sufficient certainty', such as the law of England & Wales.[74]

The Canadian approach is more explicit. The Evidence Acts of five provinces[75] require that judicial notice be taken of the laws of other provinces and the public Acts and regulations or ordinances of the nations of the British Commonwealth. The common law, and cases interpreting such legislation, or the relationship between the legislation and other principles of law, are not however included.

## B. Relaxation of Rules of Admission and Representation by Foreign Lawyers

Another potential means of determining foreign law is to grant to foreign lawyers of suitable standing a right of appearance in local courts, in order to make competing submissions as to the content of foreign laws, as any local lawyers may do in providing case law and academic commentary in support of one or another interpretation or application of local common law or of statutes.[76] The foreign lawyer is then available for questions from and arguments before the bench, and the judge can deploy their own research in the course of argument.

At least in the United States, many States permit foreign and interstate lawyers to be admitted '*pro hac vice*' (for this occasion) to practise in a specific case despite not being licensed by the regional bar, working alongside a locally admitted lawyer,[77] sometimes limited to one or a few cases each year.[78] The practice is widespread for disputes involving interstate law matters. International lawyers are permitted *pro hac vice* admission in at least 15 States[79] and before the US Supreme Court.[80] The practice is not very common, but has occurred in a

[74] See Martin, 'Judicial Notice of Foreign Law' (n 20).

[75] See also Manitoba (Revised Statutes of Manitoba 1970, c E-150, ss 31–32), New Brunswick (Revised Statutes of New Brunswick 1973, c E-11, s 70); Prince Edward Island (Revised Statutes of Prince Edward Island 1974, c E-10, s 21); and Saskatchewan (Revised Statutes of Saskatchewan 1953, c 73, s 3). eg s 24 of the Evidence Act of British Columbia (Revised Statutes of British Columbia 1996, Ch 124) provides: '(2) Judicial notice must be taken of all of the following: … (e) Acts and ordinances of the Legislature of, or other legislative body or authority competent to make laws for, any dominion, empire, commonwealth, state, province, colony, territory, possession or protectorate of Her Majesty;… (3) This section applies to: (a) all dominions, empires, commonwealths, states, provinces, colonies, territories, possessions and protectorates now existing and those constituted at some time in the future'.

[76] See proposal by R Clem, 'Proof of Foreign Law in Federal Court: One Case, Three Approaches', *Richard P. Clem: Minnesota Attorney and CLE Provider* (2014) richardclem.com/casesummaries/Bodum.html.

[77] See eg Arizona (Arizona Revised Statutes Annotated, Supreme Court Rules, Rule 39, comment 'b'); Michigan (Michigan Court Rules 8.126, para A). See www.michbar.org/professional/prohacvice.

[78] An example of the number of cases restriction is in the rules of the Supreme Court of the Virgin Islands, r 201(a)(4).

[79] See ABA Center for Professional Responsibility, *Comparison Chart of ABA Model Rule for Pro Hac Vice Admission With State Versions and Amendments Since 2002* (2012), www.americanbar.org/content/dam/aba/administrative/professional_responsibility/prohac_admin_comp.authcheckdam.pdf.

[80] Supreme Court Rules (US) r 6(2). See *Ohio v Wyandotte Chemicals Corp*, 401 US 493 (1971).

range of cases.[81] The broadening of this practice for international cases was expressly supported by the ABA Commission on Ethics 20/20 to 'meet the needs of 21st century clients'.[82] It has since become part of r 5.5(d) of the ABA Model Rules of Professional Conduct.[83]

The value of this liberalisation is perhaps understated. Unlike a foreign lawyer as expert witness, the foreign lawyer as an admitted lawyer *pro hac vice* is subject to the disciplinary regime of the forum, as with any locally admitted lawyer. Further, the court is able to determine both content and application of law in the same manner in which local law is argued, including in areas of law where the judge has only some limited experience. The judge can question the lawyers and invite submission and counter-submission, in a free exchange largely uninterrupted by inexpert local counsel. This model does not require the question and answer format of oral testimony. The foreign lawyer's contribution may be ongoing; it would not be limited by assumptions that may change through the course of the case.

There is no provision for such admission in Australia, where practitioners are entitled to appear in all State and Territory courts as well as the federal courts. Appearance by foreign counsel as counsel is restricted to stay applications under s 18(4) of the Trans-Tasman Proceedings Act 2010 (Cth), where New Zealand counsel may appear by video-link to argue the application. A similar temporary privilege is afforded Australian counsel before a New Zealand court in like circumstances under s 23(4) of the New Zealand Act.[84]

## C. Facilitation of Determination Outside of the Court

Where a discrete issue, such as a question of foreign law, arises in proceedings, various procedural devices may be available to litigants and the court seeking to manage the proceedings, to ensure the 'just, cheap and quick' resolution of the issues.

Service of process outside Australia or New Zealand may be confined to superior courts in some States and Territories.[85] However, issues of foreign law can

[81] *DataTreasury Corp v Wells Fargo & Co*, Slip Copy, 2010 WL 3912498 (E D Tex, 2010) (Canadian lawyer – patent infringement); *Rudich v Metro Goldwyn Studio, Inc*, No 08-cv-389-bbc, Opinion and Order (28 Aug 2008) (Wisconsin Western District Court) (Israeli lawyer – copyright); *US v Black*, No 05 CR 00727 (ND Ill, Dec 1, 2005) (Canadian lawyer – criminal case).

[82] See American Bar Association, ABA Commission on Ethics 20/20 Proposal, '*Pro Hac Vice* and Foreign Lawyers' September 19, 2011, 6, www.americanbar.org/content/dam/aba/administrative/ethics_2020/20110919_ethics_20_20_foreign_lawyers_and_pro_hac_vice_resolution_report_posting.authcheckdam.pdf.

[83] See www.americanbar.org/groups/professional_responsibility/publications/model_rules_of_professional_conduct/rule_5_5_unauthorized_practice_of_law_multijurisdictional_practice_of_law.html.

[84] Trans-Tasman Proceedings Act 2010 (NZ).

[85] In NSW, it is restricted to the Supreme Court – see Uniform Civil Procedure Rules 2005 (NSW) pt 11, r 11.1 9. However, in Queensland, it is permitted for the District Court: Uniform Civil Procedure Rules 1999 (Qld) r 124 read with r 3. In Victoria, County Court process may be served outside Australia

arise at all levels of the court hierarchy.[86] In the Supreme Court of New South Wales,[87] any issue of foreign law must be raised in a 'foreign law' notice filed within six weeks of filing of the originating process or cross-claim. The notice must set out 'the relevant principles of foreign law and their application to the issue'. The party disputing the notice must file a corresponding notice of dispute within eight weeks of service of the foreign law notice.

Where an issue of foreign law is identified, whether in the formal notice process or any pleading, a NSW court may:

1. appoint a referee to report on the content and application of foreign law. This may be done in the Supreme Court by the court of its own motion,[88] and in the inferior courts,[89] with the court reserving the right to adopt or reject the referee's report in whole or in part;
2. in the Supreme Court, at least with the parties' consent, 'order that proceedings be commenced in a foreign court in order to answer a question as to the principles of foreign law or as to their application';[90] and
3. make an order for separate determination of any question, whether before, at or after a trial is concluded.[91] Such an order formalises the issue that is to be hived off to the foreign proceedings or referee.

## *i. Appointment of a Referee*

In the United Kingdom and parts of Australia, over a long period of time, references have been adopted by commercial courts as a way of ensuring that discrete issues in litigation are determined with maximum efficiency.[92] Referral of a question of foreign law to a referee permits, in particular, complex factual questions to be determined efficiently (without the necessity for resolution by a judge evaluating contested and contrary expert evidence) by a person with the appropriate expertise. As the Chief Justice of the Federal Court of Australia recently remarked, 'in an

or New Zealand: ord 7, pt 2 (for service in countries not party to the Hague Service Convention), ord 80 (for service under the Hague Service Convention).

[86] The view expressed by Gibson DCJ in *Park v Lee* [2016] NSWDC 75 that r 6.43 has the effect that issues of foreign law can only be determined in the Supreme Court of NSW is plainly wrong. The mechanism in r 6.44 may, however, be a factor supporting a transfer of proceedings to the Supreme Court.

[87] Uniform Civil Procedure Rules 2005 (NSW) r 6.44(1).

[88] Uniform Civil Procedure Rules 2005 (NSW) r 6.44(2), together with r 20.14. In *Marshall v Fleming* [2013] NSWSC 566, Harrison J determined that the direction to commence foreign proceedings and the ordering of a reference, on issues of foreign law, were alternatives available to the parties and the court and the former rule did not circumscribe or limit the other.

[89] Uniform Civil Procedure Rules 2005 (NSW) r 20.14.

[90] ibid, r 6.44.

[91] ibid, r 28.2.

[92] Reference type procedures are not a recent invention: for a very early example, see *Gyles v Wilcox*[1740] EngR 76, (1740) 2 Atk 141, 26 ER 489. In a helpful discussion in *Kadam v MiiResorts Group 1 Pty Ltd (No 4)* [2017] FCA 1139, [35]–[63], Lee J summarised the history and use of referees in Australia.

appropriate case it reflects an approach of long standing which has a flexibility and a feature of focused skill that can see cases resolved expeditiously'.[93]

The findings of a referee are treated as if they are the verdict of a special jury,[94] although court rules provide that the court may deal with the report as it thinks fit – ie adopt, vary, reject it or make such orders as the court thinks fit.[95] There are rules to similar effect in each of the superior courts of the Australian States and Territories.[96]

Court rules commonly provide for an application by one or more parties, or at the court's own motion.[97] Traditionally, the usual practice has been to only refer with the parties' consent,[98] although Australian courts have been reluctant to accept that, absent consent, a reference should only be made in exceptional or special circumstances.[99] Where the rule does not expressly require consent, such a constraint is not to be implied.[100]

Even so, in *Kadam v MiiResorts Group 1 Pty Ltd (No 4)*, Lee J, a newly appointed Federal Court judge, pragmatically referred a question of Indian domestic law to a referee despite the opposition of one party to the reference, where the appointment of a referee was consistent with the overarching purpose pursuant to s 37M of the Federal Court of Australia Act 1976 (Cth).[101]

In that matter, two proceedings by two sets of plaintiffs were conjoined. The first was a representative action by various investors in an alleged Ponzi scheme. The second was commenced, somewhat belatedly, by the Securities and Exchange Board of India (SEBI), a body charged under the laws of India with vindicating the rights of investors who contributed funds to the scheme operator. The antagonism between the parties included an allegation by the group members that SEBI had no

[93] *Sheehan v Lloyds Names Munich Re Syndicate Ltd* [2017] FCA 1340, [13] (Allsop CJ).

[94] *Super Pty Ltd v SJP Formwork (Aust) Pty Ltd* (1992) 29 NSWLR 549, 563 (Gleeson CJ) (New South Wales Court of Appeal).

[95] See s 54A(3) of the Federal Court of Australia Act 1976 (Cth). This provision is supplemented by r 28.67 of the Federal Court Rules 2011 (Cth), which allows a party to ask the court to do various things in relation to a referee's report.

[96] See eg Court Procedure Rules 2006, Div 2.15.14 (ACT); Supreme Court (General Civil Procedure) Rules 2015, ord 50.01–50.04 (Vic)).

[97] Thus, see s 54A of the Federal Court of Australia Act 1976 (Cth). Div 28.6 of the Federal Court Rules 2011 (Cth) as a whole provides rules for the conduct of a referral to a referee more broadly. A referee must conduct an inquiry in accordance with any directions made by the court but, in the absence of such directions, may conduct the inquiry in any way the referee think fits, is not bound by the rules of evidence but may be informed in any way the referee thinks fit and can fix a time for each party to provide him or her with a brief statement of the findings of fact and law contended for by the party.

[98] See *Fleming v Marshall* [2011] NSWCA 86, (2011) 279 ALR 737 [9] (Spigelman J).

[99] Even in superior courts where there has been traditionally more reluctance to order references: see eg *Talacko v Talacko* [2009] VSC 98, [27] (Kyrou J); *Bill Express Ltd (In Liq) v Pitcher Partners (A Firm)* [2014] VSC 482, [28] (Macaulay J).

[100] *Super Pty Ltd v SJP Framework (Aust) Pty Ltd* (1992) 29 NSWLR 649, 556 and 558 (Gleeson CJ) (New South Wales Court of Appeal). Mahoney JA pointed out (at 568) that the construction which should be placed on provisions, if possible, should be one to provide for powers appropriate to the effective, efficient, timely and just disposal of the proceedings.

[101] *Kadam v MiiResorts Group 1 Pty Ltd (No 4)* [2017] FCA 1139, (2017) 252 FCR 298, [7]–[16].

standing to seek the relief it sought in its proceedings. Each party filed an expert report by a retired judge of the High Court of India. The reports, which passed as ships in the night, did not directly engage with the real issue of standing: one considered whether SEBI was a trustee of any rights, and the other did not refer at all to the former. Lee J appeared to have lost some patience with the parties. His Honour later observed:

> An essentially straightforward case, primarily over funds held in trust, has been made overly complex by the creation of a fog of irrelevancies and collateral disputation. Groping steadily through the brume of false issues to reach the real questions requiring determination, has presented considerable case management challenges.

The parties also could not agree on the appointment of an Indian referee. The referee appointed by Lee J was the Hon Ian Callinan, former judge of the High Court of Australia. Ultimately, his report was adopted by the Court, with the consent of the parties.[102]

### *ii. Arrangements for a Foreign Court to Decide Issues of Foreign Law*

There are two means of arranging for a foreign court to determine the foreign law issue in question. Each involves the determination of the issue of foreign law by a person able to take judicial notice of that law, thus absolving the parties of the burden of formal proof.

The first, now envisaged by r 6.44(1) UCPR, allows for the proceedings to be stayed to permit proceedings to be brought in a foreign court for the determination of an issue arising under the law of that foreign state. The referral of the question of foreign law to a foreign court is not without legal precedent in Australia. The British Law Ascertainment Act 1859 (22 & 23 Vict c 63) authorised the courts of one of the dominions to refer a case stated to the courts of another dominion 'to ascertain the law applicable to the facts of the case' wherever it was necessary or expedient to do so. That law is no longer in force in Australia in light of s 8 of the Imperial Acts Application Act 1969 (NSW) and its equivalent in other States and Territories.[103]

It is trite to observe that the best court to adjudge the law of a particular forum is a court of that forum.[104] At least in this region, the procedure was only first adopted in 2008 by the Supreme Court of Singapore in *Westacre Investments Inc v The State-Owned Company Yugoimport SDPR (also known as Jugoimport-SDPR)*.[105]

[102] See *Kadam v MiiResorts Group 1 Pty Ltd* [No 5] [2018] FCA 1086, [33].

[103] eg Imperial Acts Application Act 1980 (Vic), Imperial Acts Application Ordinance 1986 (ACT); Imperial Acts Application Act 1984 (Qld) s 7. See Official Trustee in *Bankruptcy v Udowenko* [2004] NSWSC 890.

[104] *McGregor v Potts* [2005] NSWSC 1098, [54] (Brereton J).

[105] *Westacre Investments Inc v The State-Owned Company Yugoimport* [2009] 2 SLR(R) 166 (Supreme Court of Singapore).

In that case, Westacre had obtained in 1998 a judgment of the High Court of Justice in England after suing at common law on an English award. On 5 October 2004, Westacre discovered a bank account in Singapore holding funds said to be those of Yugoimport.

In 2005, Westacre commenced proceedings in Singapore seeking recognition and enforcement of the 1998 judgment under the Reciprocal Enforcement of Commonwealth Judgments Act (Cap 264, 1985 Rev Ed).[106] Under that Act, a foreign judgment could only be registered more than one year after it was rendered if the Singapore, or such longer period as the court might allow.

While an Assistant Registrar was prepared to register the 1998 judgment, a judge sitting on appeal from the Registrar did not think it 'just and convenient to do so' in the absence of an adequate explanation for the delay in seeking registration. One issue that arose between the parties was whether the English judgment was enforceable anyway; it being six years after the judgment, leave was required to issue a writ of enforcement which would only be granted in circumstances that took the case out of the ordinary (under then ord 46, r 2(1)(a) of the RSC). Westacre countered, saying that no leave was required for third party garnishment, so the judgment was at least in part enforceable (under pt 72 of the Civil Procedure Rules). Their respective experts were diametrically opposed.

During the course of the further appeal to the Singapore Court of Appeal, that court directed the judgment creditor to apply to an English court for declaratory relief for an authoritative statement of the relevant English law on the question:

> On the assumption that there was a third party within the jurisdiction of the English court who owed or held money to the credit of the [Respondent], whether an English court in the exercise of its discretion would have given leave [to the Appellant] to enforce the English Judgment dated 13 March 1998 if the [Appellant] had applied for a third party debt order on 5 October 2004.[107]

In the subsequent decision of *Westacre Investments Inc v Yugoimport SDPR*, Tomlinson J held that and English judgment was 'conceptually … enforceable without limit of time' and in any event had leave been sought its grounds would have been 'virtually axiomatic' and as such the English court 'would unhesitatingly have permitted enforcement' of the judgment.[108] There was no appeal from that decision. The resolution of the issue before Tomlinson J meant that the issue before the Court of Appeal was 'fairly uncomplicated', turning as it did on the proper exercise of the discretion to permit registration, which the Court of Appeal determined should be permitted.

[106] The Singapore Act is the local equivalent of the Foreign Judgments Act 1991 (Cth).

[107] *Westacre Investments Inc v The State-Owned Company Yugoimport SDPR (also known as Jugoimport-SDPR)* [2008] SGCA 48 [11].

[108] *Westacre Investments Inc v Yugoimport SDPR* [2008] EWHC 801 (Comm) [3], [23].

A favourable view of this approach was formed by the then Chief Justice of NSW, James Spigelman.[109] First, s 125 of the Supreme Court Act 1970 (NSW) was inserted by sch 17 of the Courts and Crimes Legislation Further Amendment Act 2010 (NSW). That section provides for arrangements to be made between the Supreme Court of New South Wales and foreign courts where a court can refer a matter of foreign law to a court of another jurisdiction 'for information, advice or assistance (with or without the consent of parties to proceedings)'.[110] Second, in late 2010, the Uniform Rules committee introduced r 6.44, which covered both the *Westacre* procedure and a reference procedure peculiar to foreign law claims.

In parallel with these legislative changes, Spigelman CJ caused the Supreme Court to enter into memoranda of understanding with two jurisdictions to that effect, providing an effective and inexpensive method by which questions of foreign law can be determined. This is the second method, and involves either an addition to, or a hybrid of, the reference on a case stated and the appointment of a referee.

The Supreme Court of Singapore and the Supreme Court of New South Wales Memorandum of Understanding on References of Questions of Law of September 2010[111] provides that if proceedings are instituted for an answer to questions of foreign law, then the court will undertake to provide such an answer as expeditiously as its procedures allow.

The Memorandum of Understanding entered into between the Chief Justice of New South Wales and the Chief Judge of the State of New York[112] and proposed Administrative Order by Chief Judge Lippman[113] similarly contemplates the institution of proceedings for an answer to the relevant question of foreign law in the jurisdiction whose governing law is that 'foreign law'. In the language of art 1, the relevant question is to be referred to the court of governing law 'for an answer to be provided in accordance with the procedures of the requested jurisdiction'.

The New York MOU involves the co-operation of the parties both in identifying the questions of law arising on particular facts and assumptions (and possibly alternative sets of facts and assumptions) and agreeing to be bound by the result.[114] This overcomes the constitutional prohibition on the Court of Appeals of New York giving what are effectively 'advisory opinions' on the law of New York.

[109] J Spigelman, 'Proof of Foreign Law by Reference to the Foreign Court' (2011) 127 *Law Quarterly Review* 208.

[110] See Uniform Civil Procedure Rules 2005 (NSW) pt 6, div 9. s 125(1)(b) of the Supreme Court Act 1970 (NSW) facilitates a reciprocal arrangement, namely the making of rules for the provision by the court, to a foreign court, of information, advice or assistance on a question as to the principles of Australian law, or their application.

[111] See www.lawlink.nsw.gov.au/practice_notes/nswsc_pc.nsf/pages/529.

[112] See www.lawlink.nsw.gov.au/practice_notes/nswsc_pc.nsf/6a64691105a54031ca256880000c25d7/7480f2fa23a0ae8dca2577ff00127763?OpenDocument.

[113] See 'Practice – MOU between New York and New South Wales', 2010 *Bar News – Journal of the NSW Bar Association* (Summer 2010–11) 69, 71.

[114] Art 4 also provides for 'other less formal forms of communication and consultation between the Parties regarding questions of law'.

The New York MOU contemplates that a Panel of Referees will be available to respond to questions of law which are the subject of a letter of referral from the Chief Justice of this court to the Chief Judge of the State of New York.

Despite the utility of these arrangements, a primary judge, quite properly endeavouring to make orders to dispose of the matter as inexpensively and expeditiously as possible, risks appellate intervention if the parties' notices and the form of order do not identify adequately the foreign law issues involved.

Thus, in *Marshall v Fleming*, the moving party neglected to identify the cause of action under the foreign law on which they relied, the elements of that cause of action, and the facts which they said made out those elements.[115] The New South Wales Court of Appeal (Bathurst CJ, Beazley P, Meagher JA) explained that the respondents then should be in a position to indicate whether they dispute the existence of the cause of action, its elements as articulated by the applicants and what facts they dispute. This would demonstrate whether there was any dispute as to principles of foreign law and the extent of the factual dispute between the parties. The effect of this may be that parties seeking to rely on foreign law must in effect plead the case twice.

The proceedings involved a damages claim by a mother and son against their former attorneys, a law firm based in New York. The proceedings had a lengthy and unhappy history. At the final hearing before Payne JA in 2017, no reference having been successfully made, the plaintiffs tendered four expert reports of a partner at a New York Law firm and the defendants tendered three expert reports on the New York law of indemnification. Both experts were cross-examined, the trial judge ultimately preferring the evidence of the defendants' expert who, on the critical issues which divided the experts, was able to give references to authority and principles derived from cases decided by the Court of Appeal of New York to support the views he was expressing.[116] The plaintiffs suffered a humiliating costs order, the trial judge holding that based on the defendants' expert's final report, the case that was opened in the trial was 'hopeless, and, acting properly, should have been known to be hopeless by the Marshalls' Australian representatives'.[117]

## D. Co-operation on the International Plane

There are few efforts to develop any broad international convention to facilitate the referral of questions of foreign law to the courts of the country in question. Two examples of at least co-operation in ascertaining the content of foreign law may be mentioned.

[115] *Marshall v Fleming* [2014] NSWCA 64.
[116] *Marshall v Fleming* [2017] NSWSC 1107, [174].
[117] *Marshall v Fleming [No 2]* [2017] NSWSC 1679, [28].

The first is the 1968 European Convention on Information on Foreign Law: the 'London Convention'[118] and its Additional Protocol.[119] This convention was prepared within the framework of the Council of Europe, by a Committee of Governmental Experts set up by the European Committee on Legal Co-operation (CCJ). The term 'information' rather than 'proof' reflects the fact that judicial notice is taken of foreign laws in many civilian countries, provided information about that law is put before the court. States agree to provide 'information on their law and procedure in civil and commercial fields as well as on their judicial organisation' (art 1) when sought by judicial authorities (art 3). Such requests are handled through ministerial or other state 'transmitting agencies' and 'receiving agencies' in answer to requests, and to establishing 'transmitting agencies' to handle requests form their own courts (art 2). These bodies serve a similar function to the 'central authority' role within Hague Conference conventions.

The requests for information must 'specify exactly as possible the questions on which information concerning the law of the requested State is desired' and it must 'state the facts necessary both for its proper understanding and for the formulation of an exact and precise reply' (art 4). Responses are to be given 'as rapidly as possible' (art 10). The responses are not, however, binding (art 8). The receiving agency may answer the request, or forward it on to another body. In Germany, for example, the Max-Planck-Institute is often used.[120]

Ultimately, the Convention does nothing to eliminate the need for expert evidence in a common law court, nor the costs of doing so. It also separates the parties from control over who is selected to answer the question, slows the process of iteration of reports, and does not make the expert giving the answer amenable to questioning in the court to whom the report is returned.

Since 2002,[121] the European Commission's European Justice Network has extended its services from criminal law to civil and commercial matters. It can facilitate finding points of contacts for judicial officers seeking information on other EU State domestic laws. While a 2014 evaluation of the EJN indicated it enhanced judicial co-operation in cross-border cases, there was no evaluation of its utility in enhancing the process of access to and proof of foreign law.[122]

[118] ETS No 62. UK-ETS No 117 (Cmnd 4229, 1969). For greater detail on the individual provisions of the Convention, see Council of Europe. *Explanatory Report on the Convention on Information on Foreign Law* (1978). The Convention has been ratified by the UK, but not implemented through domestic legislation.

[119] Additional Protocol to the European Convention on Information on Foreign Law, Cmnd.8431, TS No 88 (1981), ETS No 97, signed in Strasbourg, 15 March 1978. This entered into force in the UK on 3 December 1981. Costa Rica, Iceland, Liechtenstein, Malta and Turkey have not signed the Protocol. The Additional Protocol expands the categories of information that must be provided to encompass 'substantive and procedural law and judicial organisation in the criminal field, including prosecuting authorities, as well as on the law concerning the enforcement of penal measures'.

[120] See n 50.

[121] Pursuant to the Council Decision of 28 May 2001 establishing a European Judicial Network in civil and commercial matters (2001/470/EC).

[122] European Commission, 'Evaluation of the activities of the European Judicial Network in civil and commercial matters' Final Report, June 10, 2014 (JUST/2014/JCIV/FW/01013/A4).

The second example is Inter-American Convention of 8 May 1979 on Proof and Information on Foreign Law.[123] The Convention uses the 'central authority' process of Hague Conventions to facilitate the transmission of requests on questions of foreign law sent to another state party. The answers to be given can include 'the elements of proof of and reports on the text, validity, meaning, and legal scope of their law' (art 2). Answers are to be given by any 'suitable means' which may include (art 4):

1. documentary proof consisting of certified copies of legal texts together with an indication of their validity, or judicial precedents;
2. expert testimony, consisting of opinions of attorneys or experts on the matter; and
3. the reports of the state of destination on the text, validity, meaning and scope of its law on specific points.

As with the London Convention, requests emanate from judicial authorities (art 4) and the answers are not binding on the providing state or the receiving state (or its courts) (art 6).

## E. Arbitral Bodies and International Commercial Courts

An arbitrator appointed to a dispute does not sit as a judge required to take judicial notice of the laws of any particular legal system. Instead, the arbitrator sits as adjudicator of the issues of whatever law is determined to be applicable to the dispute or issue at hand. The relevant law might be agreed by the parties, or it may be for the arbitrator to choose the appropriate law to apply. National arbitration law (including the UNCITRAL Model Law on International Commercial Arbitration) and the rules of arbitral institutions are entirely agnostic on the question of how tribunals are to determine the applicable law. Moreover, there is no 'domestic law' to fall back on as a matter of presumption. Thus, to the arbitrator, all laws are just laws[124] and are matters of law, not fact.

At least in theory, the parties can make submissions as to the content of the law and its application without requiring expert evidence of that law. Thus, the question of law is briefed and argued as would any question of domestic law before a court.

In practice, however, where a particular issue within a case is a matter of foreign law in which the parties and the adjudicators are not experts, expert evidence

[123] 1986 UNTS 110. For the text in English, see www.un.org/ruleoflaw/files/volume-1439-I-24393-English.pdf.

[124] P Karrer, 'Legal Experts' Report – When Academic Theory Meets Arbitral Practice' in W Ebke et al, *Festschrift für Siegfried H. Elsing zum 65 Geburtstag* (Frankfurt am Main, Deutscher Fachverlag, 2015) 211, 212.

will be called, with perhaps some legal argument thrown in for good measure. Alternatively, counsel learned in that law may be briefed to argue the foreign law directly.

A more liberal approach to arguing foreign law was taken by the Dubai International Financial Centre Court (DIFC). The DIFC is not constrained as to how it procedurally deals with issues of non-UAE law.[125] In *Fidel v Felecia & Faraz*,[126] the Chief Justice of the DIFC Court of Appeal (himself an experienced international arbitrator) adopted what he called the 'the international approach'[127] of not formally excluding the possibility of using expert opinions, but finding that the primary form should be through legal submissions. The Court said that the historic preference for expert evidence even in international arbitration was changing, and that the use of cross-examination as a means of determining the content and application of foreign law was both 'doctrinally unnecessary' and 'forensically inefficient'.[128] Thenceforth, the presumptive rule is that lawyers should write briefs and make oral submissions applying the legal principles to the facts as alleged by the parties, and so argue for a particular outcome.

## IV. Conclusion

Despite the range of international approaches to the challenges of discovering and applying foreign law, each is directed to determining the content of that law that will permit the forum to determine the legal issue before it, and to do so in a reliable way that is fair to the parties. Whether foreign law is a matter of fact to be proved, or a matter of law to be learned, the strangeness of that law to the forum requires some means of determining and interpreting that law which is reliable. That is, it is accurate as to content and sufficiently comprehensive and explicable as to be capable of application with a degree of confidence that would approach arguing the matter in the courts of the country whose law is to be applied. It must also be fair, in that some process of notice to another party must be given of the meaning and effect of that law on the issues at hand. Finally, it should be quick and cheap, at least as far as the case permits.

'Outsourcing' of the problem – be it to a referee of sufficient standing, a foreign agency or central authority of sufficient expertise, or even requiring parties to litigate a particular question of foreign law in a relevant foreign court – can be a prudent response to a forum's legitimate apprehension that it may misinterpret or misapply foreign law to the issues in dispute. It also reflects a justifiable lack of

[125] Art 50 of the DIFC Court Law empowered the court, on this matter of procedure, to apply the rules it 'consider[ed] appropriate to be applied in the circumstances'.
[126] [2015] DIFC CA 002, Claim No CA 002/2015 (Nov 23, 2015).
[127] ibid [67].
[128] ibid [72].

confidence in the assured reliability of using expert 'evidence' to prove the content and effect of foreign law. However, each of these steps adds burdens and inefficiencies that can be inimical to the just, cheap and quick resolution of issues in dispute. Multiple layers of lawyers, multiplicity of proceedings, and the time and financial cost, may make the outsourcing approach unattractive, save in cases where the amount in dispute is very substantial.

In the authors' opinion, a clash of opinions between legal experts is unlikely to be best resolved by the cross-examination of those experts by inexpert local counsel, fed questions and lines of attack by their party's expert or some other 'expert' behind the scenes. Even the process of identifying and formulating the relevant evidence risks double and triple handling between lawyers in different jurisdictions.

Ultimately, a court hearing expert evidence is not substituting an expert's opinion for its own. It must decide between competing contentions so as to, as Donovan puts it, 'adopt that iteration of the law that [is] most compelling, most persuasive, in light of the available legal authorities that stand independent of the case being presented'.[129] That is so, whether the content and potential application of foreign law is derived in accordance with the rules of evidence, or more informally through the foreign and comparative law research of counsel, or with the assistance of a foreign lawyer appearing *pro hac vice*.

If there is a lesson in all this, it is that courts can and should be given a broad power to determine the procedure by which foreign law issues will be best resolved in the local court, provided only that proper notice should be given by the party raising the matter to the court and other parties. Where a common law court is determining an issue of law from another common law jurisdiction, even if statutory law intrudes, local counsel (with dual admission, or experience in that foreign law, or instructed by a foreign lawyer not required to act as an expert) should suffice. The techniques of case law analysis, reasoning by analogy, and statutory interpretation should be sufficiently similar that the forum court can arrive at a result with a sufficiently high degree of confidence that it has done so correctly.

Where the legal system or area of law is far removed from the experience and expertise of local laws, lawyers and judges, a more traditional approach may be warranted, especially out of fairness to the other parties. Alternatively, a mechanism for admission *pro hac vice* should be considered so that the issues can suitably be argued before the forum without the unnecessary and costly barriers of treating law first as evidence then asking the local court to apply it as an exercise of the judicial function.

[129] D Donovan, 'Reexamining the Legal Expert in International Arbitration' (Kaplan Lecture, Hong Kong, 15 November 2017).

Wherever the amount in dispute is relatively low value, or where the means or circumstances of the parties do not permit the less efficient, and more expensive, path of contested expert evidence, the 'cheap and quick' resolution of the dispute is as important as its correctness to the requirement that the decision be 'just'. Similarly, where the amount in dispute is far greater, the time and means of the parties extensive, and the importance of getting a 'more correct' result far outweighs a more 'cheap and quick' approach, orders for reference, for seeking international judicial assistance, or requiring the parties to approach a foreign court are more likely to be warranted.

# 11

# The Rise of Party Autonomy in Commercial Conflict of Laws

YEO TIONG MIN*

## I. Introduction

### A. Internationalisation of Private International Law and Commercial Courts

There are two related important current trends in international commercial litigation. First, the trend towards internationalisation of private international law is gaining momentum. At a formal level, international instruments are gaining significance across the world. Two important recent ones are the Hague Convention on Choice of Court Agreements 2005 (Choice of Court Convention) and the Hague Principles of Choice of Law in International Commercial Contracts 2015 (Hague Principles). At a practical level, lawyers working on international business deals increasingly have to concern themselves not only with foreign law but also foreign private international law. From the common law perspective, private international law is really domestic law about how to deal with foreign elements arising in the domestic court. But increasingly, transnational lawyers must take a bigger view, and contemplate outcomes based on the private international law of foreign countries.

Harmonisation through unification instruments is one way of dealing with transnational differences in private international law, and experience of the European Union provides valuable lessons. The Hague Conference on Private International Law is doing very valuable work on international harmonisation. Convergence, which is the organic process where national laws fall into alignment because of common interests and goals, is perhaps a slower and more arduous

* I am grateful for the comments of participants at the Conference on Commercial Issues in Private International Law on the paper presented at that conference, on which this chapter is based.

process, but it remains a very real option in Australasia where there are substantially more obstacles to harmonisation than in regional groupings like the EU.[1]

The second trend is the creation of international commercial courts, which are essentially domestic courts specialising in transnational business disputes. The London Commercial Court is the leading one in all but name. Others that have sprung up in recent years include the Dubai International Financial Court and the Singapore International Commercial Court. Similar commercial courts or divisions have sprung up in Europe, including in France and the Netherlands, and Germany and Brussels have similar plans.[2] Shortly after signing the Choice of Court Convention, China announced that it was setting up three international commercial courts to deal with Belt and Road Initiative (BRI) disputes,[3] and two were launched in June 2018.[4] Kazakhstan has joined the game.[5] There has been expression of interest in Australia[6] as well.

These developments emphasise the importance of lawyers' familiarity with private international law on a global scale in order to function effectively as transnational lawyers. An important theme that runs through both trends is the increasing effect given to party autonomy in international commercial law and litigation.

## B. Party Autonomy

Apart from philosophical justifications, party autonomy is an important driver for international trade. From the perspective of harmonisation and convergence, there is no greater common interest for Asian nations than the promotion of cross-border trade. The success of commercial arbitration on an international scale attests to the value of party autonomy. It is foreseeable that international commercial courts will pay comparable regard to party autonomy. Party autonomy has clearly driven some of the very important recent developments in private international law globally, including in Asia. It is recognised as a simple and convenient way of creating certainty and predictability in international business transactions.

[1] Australia and Singapore are, together with others, partners in a joint venture started in 2016, the Asian Business Law Institute in Singapore, which will promote research with a view to reducing or mitigating legal obstacles to cross-border business in Asia (for which purpose includes Australia), and to promote convergence of commercial laws. Australians are playing very important roles in this effort, sitting on its Board of Governors, its Advisory Board, and working on research projects.

[2] See conflictoflaws.net/2018/the-domino-effect-of-international-commercial-courts-in-europe-whos-next.

[3] www.straitstimes.com/asia/east-asia/chinas-courts-for-bri-disputes-a-logical-step.

[4] cicc.court.gov.cn/html/1/219/208/209/814.html.

[5] aifc-court.kz.

[6] The Honourable Chief Justice Marilyn Warren AC and The Honourable Justice Clyde Croft, 'An International Commercial Court for Australia: Looking Beyond the New York Convention', assets.justice.vic.gov.au/supreme/resources/2a7ead53-9ae9-4e26-9bad-56ef25d7d34c/aninternationalcommercialcourtforaustralialookingbeyondthenewyorkconvention.pdf.

One relevant dimension is the growing international competition to offer legal dispute resolution services for transnational commercial transactions, as can be seen in the tide of international commercial courts. Choice of court agreements are growing in significance. A choice of court agreement is effectively a choice of the private international law to be applied by that court. To the extent that choice of court agreements are given effect to, parties are effectively selecting the private international law as applied by the chosen court. Everything else being equal, commercial parties are more likely to prefer a system that will give the greater effect to party autonomy.[7]

But party autonomy is not an unqualified good, and the limitations to party autonomy are as important as the central principle itself. The limitations can appear at different levels: domestic rules, mandatory rules and public policy of the *lex causae*, choice of law, mandatory rules and public policy of the *lex fori*, and sometimes intermediate positions as well.[8] We also need to recognise that the degree to which a country accepts party autonomy in its choice of law rules depends on its own values. At a practical level, while the growing acceptance of the role of party autonomy across nations will lessen the conflict of laws, it will also create fresh litigation opportunities at the edges of the principle.

## II. The Hague Convention on Choice of Court Agreements

### A. Objectives and Scope

After failing to reach a conclusion after a massive project on jurisdiction and foreign judgments, the Hague Conference finally concluded a more modest Convention on Choice of Court Agreements in 2005. The objective of the Convention is to give effect to party autonomy in the selection of the forum for litigation, and the promotion of the international circulation of the resulting judgment, in order to facilitate cross-border trade.[9] The Convention is effective in the European Union,[10]

[7] This consideration appears prominently in Singapore case law: see, eg, *Ong Ghee Soon Kevin v Ho Yong Chong* [2017] 3 SLR 711, [108].

[8] For a survey of the techniques, see S Symeonides, 'Party Autonomy in International Contracts and the Multiple Ways of Slicing the Apple' (2014) 39 *Brooklyn Journal of International Law* 1123.

[9] Choice of Court Convention, Preamble.

[10] Denmark acceded to the Convention in May 2018: www.hcch.net/en/news-archive/details/?varevent=611. While the UK prepares to leave the EU, its government has declared its intention to continue applying the Convention: HM Government, 'Providing a Cross-Border Civil Judicial Cooperation Framework: a Future Partnership Paper', [21]-[22] available at: assets.publishing.service.gov.uk/government/uploads/system.uploads/attachment_data/file/639271/Providing_a_cross-border_civil_judicial_cooperation_framework.pdf.

Mexico, Montenegro and Singapore. Signatories which have not implemented the Convention are the United States, China and Ukraine.[11]

Because party autonomy raises greater concerns in employment and consumer contracts, these are excluded from the scope of the Convention.[12] There are a number of subject-matter exclusions as well.[13]

The Convention only applies to 'international' cases,[14] which for this purpose only excludes localised transactions. A transaction is localised where the choice of court agreement is the only element in the case that connects it to another country.

## B. Functions

The Convention performs three fundamental functions where the parties have made an exclusive choice of the court of a Contracting State to resolve their dispute:

1. The chosen court of a Contracting State will assume jurisdiction to hear the case unless the choice of court agreement is null and void.[15]
2. A non-chosen court in another Contracting State will not assume jurisdiction to hear the case, unless the choice of court agreement is null and void, or where the chosen court has declined jurisdiction, or for highly exceptional reasons.[16]
3. A resulting judgment from the chosen court of a Contracting State will be recognised or enforced in another Contracting State,[17] subject to limited defences.[18]

## C. Comparison with the Common Law

The common law generally gives strong effect to party autonomy in this context. This is often expressed as requiring a party to demonstrate strong cause or reasons why it should be allowed to resile from the exclusive choice of court agreement. The trend of giving strong effect to the jurisdiction agreement is evident in a number of jurisdictions. It has been said that under English law, after *Donohue v Armco Inc*,[19] where there is an exclusive choice of foreign court clause, 'the orthodox view is that the court leans in favour of stay unless exceptional reasons

[11] Status table of the Convention of 30 June 2005 on Choice of Court Agreements, at www.hcch.net/en/instruments/conventions/status-table/?cid=98.

[12] Choice of Court Convention, Art 2(1).

[13] ibid, Art 2(2).

[14] ibid, Art 1.

[15] ibid, Art 5.

[16] ibid, Art 6.

[17] ibid, Art 8.

[18] ibid, Art 9.

[19] [2001] 1 All ER 749 (HL).

dictate otherwise, and the management of multipartite litigation may be the only real exception'.[20] Similarly, Australian case law has played down the significance of forensic inconvenience to the contracting parties and highlighted the importance of factors like inconvenience to third parties, effects on the due administration of justice, and any appropriate public policy considerations.[21] The Supreme Court of the United States in *Atlantic Marine Construction Co Inc v United States District Court for the Western District of Texas*[22] has re-affirmed and indeed strengthened the proposition in *Bremen v Zapata*[23] on the enforcement of exclusive jurisdiction agreements, directing all US courts to disregard private interest factors and only consider public interest factors in deciding whether to give effect to the parties' choice of venue. Though the US Supreme Court was dealing with an intra-state case, it had no doubt that the same principles applied to an exclusive foreign (non-US) jurisdiction clause.[24] The Supreme Court of Canada had resisted an earlier attempt by lower courts to dilute the strong cause test for denying stay of proceedings in the face of an exclusive choice of foreign court clause,[25] and has recently affirmed that the stricter strong cause test applies to the exclusion of *forum non conveniens* analysis when there is an exclusive jurisdiction agreement.[26]

The Choice of Court Convention gives very strong effect to party autonomy. The Convention affirms a trend in the common law to treat the choice of court agreement as separate from the main contract so that a challenge to the main contract does not for that reason alone impugn the choice of court agreement.[27] However, unlike the situation in the common law, the chosen court of a Contracting State under the Convention has no discretion not to hear the case; either there is a valid choice of court agreement or not.[28] Second, a non-chosen court of a Contracting State has a narrowly defined discretion to disregard a valid choice of foreign court agreement, which is arguably stricter than the common law.[29]

There are a few other important practical differences between the Convention and the common law which are notable. First, the Convention has a narrower meaning of 'choice of court agreement' than the common law. It does not include asymmetric choice of court agreements which frequently appear in common law contracts. They are regarded as non-exclusive for the somewhat dogmatic reason that they bind only one party;[30] from the common law perspective this

[20] A Briggs, *Civil Jurisdiction and Judgments*, 6th edn (London, Informa Law, 2015) [4.52].
[21] *Incitec Limited v Akimos Shipping Corp* (2004) 206 ALR 558, [49].
[22] 134 S Ct 568 (2013).
[23] 407 US 1 (1972).
[24] ibid, fn 8.
[25] *ZI Pompey Industrie v ECU-Line NV* 2003 SCC 27, [2003] 1 SCR 450.
[26] *Douez v Facebook Inc* 2017 SCC 33, [2017] 1 SCR 751. However, the decision has created uncertainty as to the relevance of public policy factors in the strong cause analysis.
[27] Choice of Court Convention, Art 3(a).
[28] ibid, Art 5(1).
[29] ibid, Art 6.
[30] T Hartley and M Dogauchi, *Convention of 30 June 2005 on Choice of Court Agreements, Explanatory Report* (Explanatory Report) [32], [105], [249].

is a limitation to party autonomy.[31] Second, the choice of a court of a Contracting State is deemed to be exclusive unless the parties have expressly provided otherwise;[32] under the common law it is always a question of contractual interpretation in each case. Third, there is a formal requirement for writing under the Convention, though it is easily satisfied with a retrievable record,[33] while under the common law a choice of court agreement may be purely oral or even arise by estoppel. Fourth, in the context of recognition or enforcement of a foreign judgment, a determination by the chosen court of a Contracting State on the validity of the choice of court agreement is binding in all other Contracting States.[34] Under the common law, a foreign judgment cannot be recognised until the forum has, under its own private international law, determined the existence of the juridical reason[35] for such recognition.

## D. Existence of Party Autonomy within the Convention

Much case law has developed in the field of international commercial arbitration on the scope and extent of party autonomy in the context of the UNCITRAL Model Law on International Commercial Arbitration and the New York Convention. It is anticipated that, similarly, the scope and extent of party autonomy will also be the subject of much litigation. One aspect, alluded to above, will be the scale of exceptional reasons needed by a non-chosen court to disregard a choice of court agreement.

A focal point is likely to be whether parties have actually agreed to the choice of the court. The Choice of Court Convention refers this question to the law of the Contracting State of the chosen court, including its private international law.[36] Some countries may view this issue as a procedural one governed by their own domestic laws. As a matter of common law, the existence of a choice of court agreement raises a substantive question which may be characterised as an issue of incorporation of terms or formation of a contract. In theory, if the main contract

[31] In contrast, common law countries, which tend to be highly influenced by contractual thinking, and will enforce an asymmetric jurisdiction clause against the promisor in equal measure as in a two-way exclusive clause. The English High Court in *Commerzbank AG v Liquimar Tankers Management Inc* [2017] 1 WLR 3497 suggested in *obiter* that asymmetric clauses do fall within the Choice of Court Convention, but it is doubtful that this is the correct interpretation of the Convention: see this author's paper, 'Scope and Limits of Party Autonomy under the Hague Convention on Choice of Court Agreements', 11th Yong Pung How Professorship of Law Lecture, 16 May 2018, available at cebcla.smu.edu.sg/sites/cebcla.smu.edu.sg/files/Paper2018.pdf.

[32] Choice of Court Convention, Art 3(b).

[33] ibid, Art 6(c).

[34] ibid, Art 9(a).

[35] ie that the foreign court had international jurisdiction over the defendant, either through the presence (or residence in some common law countries) of the defendant at the time of commencement of the foreign proceedings, or the voluntary submission of the defendant to the foreign court.

[36] Explanatory Report (n 30) [94].

is not challenged, the issue is one of incorporation governed by the applicable law of the contract. In reality, because the choice of court agreement is the strongest indicator of an implied choice of law in the absence of an express choice of law (or where the choice of court agreement is inextricably linked to a choice of law clause), the analysis often treads the path of formation. The Convention forces a formation characterisation in directing that the choice of court agreement shall be treated as an independent agreement.[37]

Many common law countries do not have a clear view on the law governing the issue of formation. The debate is generally between the *lex fori* and the law applicable to the putative agreement. On one view, consent is inextricably tied to validity, and this is the view under the Rome I Regulation on the law applicable to contractual obligations.[38] It is a view that is gaining support under Singapore common law.[39] On the other hand, the Australian High Court has expressed support for the application of the *lex fori*.[40] Civil law countries may not see a choice of law issue at all, as the tendency is to view choice of court as a procedural matter. In the EU, the revised Brussels I Regulation now refers the question to the law of the Member State of the chosen court, aligned with the approach in the Choice of Court Convention.[41]

The justification for applying this approach is pragmatic, assuming that parties negotiate contracts with reference to such putative clauses. After all, the forensic analysis behind the drafting of substantive clauses must assume a framework of private international law and resulting applicable domestic laws, as applied by the chosen court. It may be argued that these clauses are often thrown into contracts at the last minute ('midnight clauses'). However, it is also arguable that the law should not be constrained by actual practice, and should be framed on the basis of how rational parties should behave. Applying this approach to choice of court agreements is workable for the most part. However, it fails to provide a solution when two or more competing courts assume jurisdiction on the basis that they are respectively *the* chosen court.[42] The Convention provides

[37] Choice of Court Convention, Art 3(d). This appears to go further than the arbitration context, where the clause may be treated as separable only for the purpose of preventing it from being tainted by a challenge to the existence or validity of the main contract: see Yeo, 'Scope and Limits of Party Autonomy under the Hague Convention on Choice of Court Agreements' (n 31) [27]–[34].

[38] Regulation (EC) No 593/2008 of the European Parliament and of the Council of 17 June 2008 on the law applicable to contractual obligations (Rome I) OJ 177/6 of 4.7.2008 (Rome I Regulation) Art 3(5). It does not apply to jurisdiction agreements (Art 1(2)(c)), so the issue is left to national private international law.

[39] *CIMB Bank Bhd v Dresdner Kleinwort Ltd* [2008] 4 SLR 543, [30]; and *PT First Media TBK v Astro Nusantara International BV* [2014] 1 SLR 372, [157]–[158].

[40] *Oceanic Sun Line Inc v Fay* (1988) 165 CLR 197, 225 (Gaudron J), 261 (Brennan J). *Cf* Deane J at 255. The factual matrix would take the case outside the scope of the Choice of Court Convention for two independent reasons: (1) one party contracted as a consumer; and (2) the jurisdiction clause was asymmetric.

[41] Regulation (EU) No 1215/2012 of the European Parliament and of the Council of 12 December 2012 on jurisdiction and the recognition and enforcement of judgments in civil and commercial matters (recast) OJC L 351/1 of 20.12.2012, Art 25(1).

[42] This situation could arise from ambiguous drafting or competing rules of incorporation of terms.

no solution to the competition for jurisdiction,[43] though at the recognition and enforcement stage, the earlier judgment will prevail if both can be recognised in the requested state.[44]

There may be another avenue to challenge the existence of consent. It is possible for a court (whether at the jurisdiction or judgment[45] stage) to take the view that a case falls outside the Convention because there is no 'agreement' to begin with,[46] if the rules applied by the foreign chosen court are contrary to fundamental principles of what amounts to consent.[47] This is not a licence to apply the *lex fori* principles of *consensus ad idem*. It is intended to be applied only in very exceptional situations. The example given in the Explanatory Report is where the foreign court applies the rule of acceptance by silence.[48] There is some uncertainty and scope for litigation. It is hoped that shared understanding will develop among Contracting States, moving towards a harmonised approach.

The legal capacity of natural persons is excluded as substantive subject-matter of the Convention.[49] This is a common exclusion in international conventions because of fundamental differences of views between civil law and common law jurisdictions. Civil law countries tend to view it as an issue of personal status for choice of law purposes, while common law countries tend to look at it, at least outside family and succession contexts, as an issue of formation (with debate whether it is the subjective or objective proper law that applies, and whether the domicile of the party may be an alternative connecting factor to validate the contract).

The concept of the preliminary question is important in this context. It is a technique used in the Convention to prevent parties from dragging cases out of the Convention by raising excluded subject-matter issues. Thus, a case does not fall outside the Convention if an excluded subject-matter like capacity arises as a preliminary issue and is not the object of the proceedings.[50] If a party seeks a declaration that she has or lacks capacity to enter into the substantive contract, the case will fall outside the Convention altogether. However, if the party raises her own incapacity as a defence for breach of contract, the incapacity is only a preliminary question and the case is not taken out of the scope of the Convention. However, the ruling on capacity will not be recognised by other Contracting States under the Convention.[51] The requested court has discretion to refuse to recognise the judgment to the extent that it is based on the ruling on the excluded matter.[52]

[43] English common law reverts to the *lex fori* in such cases: *The Heidberg* [1994] 2 Lloyd's Rep 351; *Dornoch Ltd v Mauritius Union Assurance Co Ltd* [2006] 2 Lloyd's Rep 475 (CA). It does not resolve any competition for jurisdiction since other courts may reach a different conclusion anyway.

[44] Choice of Court Convention, Art 9(g).

[45] ibid, Art 9(a) prevents the requested court from questioning a determination of the chosen court that the choice of court agreement is valid, but this argument outflanks the Convention altogether.

[46] ibid, Art 3(a).

[47] Explanatory Report (n 30) [95].

[48] ibid [96].

[49] Choice of Court Convention, Art 2(2)(a).

[50] ibid, Art 2(3).

[51] ibid, Art 10(1).

[52] ibid, Art 10(4).

The Explanatory Report mentions that this discretion should be exercised against non-recognition only if the requested court would have determined the preliminary question the other way.[53] It does not, however, say that it should always be invoked when the requested court would have decided another way. In comparison, under the common law, a foreign ruling on capacity in a case where the common law court would have decided differently, is not by itself a reason for non-recognition, unless the fundamental public policy of the forum is otherwise engaged.

If a party has no capacity to enter into the main contract, it is likely that the same incapacity will also infect the choice of court agreement, notwithstanding the separability principle under the Convention. Under the common law, whether the party had capacity to agree to the choice of court agreement is a relevant inquiry at the jurisdictional stage, and it also affects the existence of international jurisdiction of the foreign court for the purpose of recognition and enforcement (unless another independent ground of international jurisdiction exists). In both contexts, it is answered by the court's own private international law.

The issue of capacity to consent to a choice of court agreement is addressed to a limited extent under the Convention. This capacity may be challenged at either the jurisdiction or the recognition and enforcement of judgment stage. At the jurisdiction stage, capacity may be challenged on the basis that the choice of court agreement is null and void under the law of the Contracting State of the chosen court.[54] If the challenge is made in the chosen court of a Contracting State, the court applies its own choice of law rule to determine the question of capacity.[55] If the challenge is made before a non-chosen court of a Contracting State, the court is required to apply the choice of law rule of the Contracting State of the chosen court.[56] At this stage, there is no scope[57] for the application of the non-chosen court's own choice of law rules for capacity.[58]

At the recognition and enforcement stage, capacity may be challenged under two grounds under the Convention. In addition to the challenge based on the private international law of the Contracting State of the chosen court, which is qualified by the exception that a ruling by the chosen court that the agreement is valid is binding,[59] there is an independent ground of challenge based on incapacity under the law of the Contracting State requested to recognise or enforce the

[53] Explanatory Report (n 30) [197].
[54] Choice of Court Convention, Art 5(1).
[55] ibid.
[56] ibid, Art 6(a).
[57] But there may be scope for the argument that the capacity rule applied by the chosen court fails to meet certain fundamental principles of agreement (see above, text to n 47).
[58] One possible argument is that legal capacity of natural persons is excluded from the scope of the Convention so there is nothing to prevent the non-chosen court from applying its own capacity rules to the choice of court agreement. However, the better view is that the exclusion only relates to the substantive contract since capacity to enter into a choice of court agreement is expressly dealt with under the Convention and is therefore clearly intended to be within its scope.
[59] Choice of Court Convention, Art 9(a).

judgment, which is not qualified.[60] Since a challenge can be made to the capacity of either the judgment creditor or the judgment debtor, the judgment debtor may have up to four challenges: (1) incapacity of the judgment creditor under the private international law of the Contracting State of the chosen court; (2) incapacity of the judgment debtor under the private international law of the Contracting State of the chosen court; (3) incapacity of the judgment creditor under the private international law of the Contracting State of the requested court; or (4) incapacity of the judgment debtor under the private international law of the Contracting State of the requested court. In addition, there is a potential issue of double incapacity rules under the domestic law ultimately applicable under one of the choice of law rules above. For example, a domestic law that says that the age of majority is 20 may mean only that a party has no capacity to contract if he is under 20, or it could also mean that additionally, a party of any age has no capacity to contract with anyone under 20. Moreover, apart from age of majority, there could be controversy as to what other types of laws would fall within the category of 'legal capacity' of natural persons.

## III. The Hague Principles on Choice of Law for International Commercial Contracts

### A. Objectives and Scope

In a break from tradition, the Hague Conference on Private International Law did not position the Hague Principles as a convention, but as a model law. This instrument has three main objectives.[61] First, it sends a strong signal to affirm party autonomy with limited exceptions in the choice of law for contracts. An effective exclusive choice of court agreement under the Choice of Court Convention gets the contracting parties to the point where they can decide and predict with certainty which court will adjudicate upon their disputes. The Hague Principles goes a further step to apply party autonomy to the question of which law the chosen court will apply to the substantive contract in dispute. Second, it provides a model for 'national, regional, supranational or international' law reform. Third, it may be used to 'interpret, supplement and develop rules of private international law' of individual countries.

The instrument applies only to international commercial contracts; it does not apply to employment or consumer contracts. It applies only where each contracting party is exercising a trade or profession.[62] Purely domestic contracts are excluded from its scope, ie where all the connections (apart from the choice of

[60] ibid, Art 9(b).
[61] Hague Principles, Preamble.
[62] ibid, Art 1(1).

law) are with one state only.[63] It does not apply to choice of court or arbitration agreements. There are subject-matter exclusions, including capacity of natural persons.[64] Because it is scoped to focus on commercial transactions, it pushes party autonomy very far.

## B. Function

The Hague Principles applies party autonomy to a wide range of issues:

1. It affirms that the choice of law agreement is separable from the main contract and a challenge to the main contract will not for that reason alone attack the choice of law agreement.[65] This has not been as evident a development in the common law for choice of law clauses as it has been for choice of court agreements. To the extent that they both perform the function of providing a mechanism for dispute resolution, this consistency of treatment is welcome.
2. It affirms the principle of party autonomy for the express and tacit choice of law by the parties.[66] Unlike the common law, there is no restriction based on a choice that is bona fide, legal and not against public policy. The control will lie in the traditional exceptions of public policy and mandatory rules of the forum instead.
3. It affirms that party autonomy extends to *dépeçage* (ie allowing different parts of the contract to be governed by different laws).[67]
4. It affirms that parties may change the applicable law of the contract, provided that the change does not prejudice the formal validity of the contract or the rights of third parties.[68] There are few common law authorities on this issue, and they sometimes conflate the situation where the parties have changed the proper law of the contract from an objective to an express choice, with the situation where the parties intended no law to govern their contract until a decision made after the conclusion of the contract.[69]
5. It affirms that contracting parties can choose a law to govern a contract that is unconnected to themselves or the transaction.[70] This is consistent with the common law. However, the US Second Restatement on the Conflict of Laws requires that the chosen law should bear a reasonable relation to the transaction,[71] a requirement that has been controversial within the US itself.[72]

[63] ibid, Art 1(2).
[64] ibid, Art 1(3).
[65] ibid, Art 7.
[66] ibid, Art 4.
[67] ibid, Art 2(2).
[68] ibid, Art 2(3).
[69] eg *The Iran Vojdan* [1984] 2 Lloyd's Rep 380.
[70] Hague Principles, Art 2(4).
[71] Restatement (Second) of Conflict of Laws (1971) §187(2)(a).
[72] Some States have legislatively done away with the requirement totally (Louisiana Civil Code, Art 3540; Oregon Revised Statutes §81.120) or for transactions above a certain amount (Texas Business &

6. It allows the parties to choose non-state rules of law that are 'generally accepted on an international, supranational or regional level as a balanced set of rules', unless prohibited by the forum.[73] This is possibly the hardest push made in the instrument for party autonomy. This is not possible under the Rome I Regulation on the law applicable to contractual obligations,[74] and English case law[75] suggests that it is not possible under the common law. The provision for the *lex fori* was probably made because there was not the level of international consensus required for an unqualified proposition.

The Hague Principles takes inspiration from the Rome I Regulation[76] in requiring the existence of a tacit choice of law to be clear from the provisions of the contract or the circumstances.[77] This is in contrast to the common law where the court may undertake a free-ranging exercise to infer an implied selection of law. It is intended to create greater certainty in the process of determining the chosen law.[78] The instrument does not deal with the situation where the parties have not made a choice (express or tacit) of law, principally because the objective of the instrument is to deal with party autonomy, and probably also because it is difficult to get consensus on what law should govern in the absence of choice.

The Hague Principles draws further inspiration from the Rome I Regulation[79] on the vexed question of formation of contracts: the question of the existence of a choice of law agreement is resolved by applying the law purportedly agreed to, with a proviso that the law of the party's establishment would apply to the issue of consent if it would not be reasonable to apply the purportedly governing law in the circumstances.[80] The application of the law purportedly agreed to has been the subject of much criticism in the common law world, not least from the High Court of Australia in *Oceanic Sun Line Special Shipping Co Inc v Fay*.[81] The main criticism is the circularity of reasoning that puts party autonomy

Commerce Code §35.51 (c); New York General Obligations Law § 5-1401; 735 Illinois Compiled Statute 105/5-5; California Civil Code §1646.5). See generally G Rühl, 'Party Autonomy in the Private International Law of Contracts: Transatlantic Convergence and Economic Efficiency' in E Gottschalk, R Michaels, G Rühl and J von Hein (eds), *Conflict of Laws in a Globalized World* (Cambridge, Cambridge University Press, 2007).

[73] Hague Principles, Art 3.

[74] See, eg, *Shamil Bank of Bahrain EC v Beximco Pharmaceuticals Ltd* [2004] EWCA Civ 19, [2004] 1 WLR 1784 (CA); and *Halpern v Halpern* [2007] EWCA Civ 291, [2008] 1 QB 105 (CA).

[75] *Musawi v RE International (UK) Ltd* [2007] EWHC 2981 (Ch).

[76] Rome I Regulation, Art 3(1).

[77] Hague Principles, Art 3.

[78] The effectiveness of tacit choice is taken for granted in many countries, but may not be recognised in some (eg its status is unclear in China: ZS Tang, Y Xiao and Z Huo, *Conflict of Laws in the People's Republic of China* (Cheltenham, Edward Elgar, 2016) [8.07]). Thus, this article is also intended to encourage the expansion of party autonomy in such countries.

[79] Rome I Regulation, Arts 3(5) and 10.

[80] Hague Principles, Art 6. Rome I Regulation, Art 11, which restricts the application of capacity rules, is not imported into the Hague Principles because of the total exclusion of capacity from its scope.

[81] Above n 40.

on its head: we should not test whether the parties have agreed by assuming that they have agreed. However, this may be overcome if we understand the connecting factor as the choice of a legal system that is most likely to produce a fair result because that is likely to be the law by reference to which the parties had conducted their negotiations. However, the reality is that in many cases the choice of law (and choice of court) agreements tend to be midnight clauses. But there is nothing wrong with a rule that is formulated with reference to how reasonable commercial parties ought to behave. In addition, the proviso prevents the abuse of the rule by one of the parties.

It has been seen above that a choice of court agreement may be argued to be non-existent and therefore not attract the application of the Choice of Court Convention, if the forum court takes the view that the foreign law purporting to validate the agreement did not comply with fundamental standards of contract formation.[82] It is not clear whether there is scope for this type of argument in respect of a choice of law agreement under the Hague Principles. It is unlikely that this avenue was contemplated by the drafters, because provision had already been made to counter unfair results created by the application of the law purportedly agreed to.

Another way in which the Hague Principles stretches party autonomy is to direct that they apply to pre-contractual obligations.[83] These may arise in domestic law variously classified as torts, restitution (or unjust enrichment), estoppel, equity, *culpa in contrahendo* etc. This provision avoids the difficulty of classifying these obligations for choice of law purposes, by bringing them (howsoever called in domestic law) within the scope of the applicable law. This probably accords with the commercial intentions of contracting parties, but it may be challenging to align with the private international law of national systems. For example, the Australian courts have taken a hardline position on the application of the *lex loci delicti* without exception for torts,[84] and have also been reluctant to subject equitable doctrines to choice of law.[85]

One interesting effect of the provision on pre-contractual liability, read with the separability of the choice of law clause, is that it is possible for the parties to choose a law to govern pre-contractual obligations at the start of the negotiations (rather than at the conclusion of the contract). Read with the provision on *dépeçage*, this law need not even be the same law eventually chosen to govern the substantive contract. The commentary to the Hague Principles suggests that this choice of law could be effective even if no contract is eventually concluded,[86] presumably on the basis that matters leading up to the formation of a contract fall within the

[82] Above, text to n 47.
[83] Hague Principles, Art 9(g).
[84] *Regie National des Usines Renault SA v Zhang* (2002) 210 CLR 491, [2002] HCA 10.
[85] See discussion below on 'Choice of Law for Fiduciary Duties', text to nn 109–117.
[86] *Principles on Choice of Law in International Commercial Contracts* (The Hague, HCCH, 2015) [9.12].

scope of the Hague Principles even if a contract does not legally materialise. This pushes party autonomy very far, and may well create a pathway for a new species of dispute resolution agreement centred on the law governing liabilities arising from the process of negotiations.

## IV. Choice of Law for Torts

National choice of law rules for torts are highly diverse. There is generally great significance placed on the *lex loci delicti* (but with differences of emphases on the place of the act and place of injury). The major role played historically by the *lex fori* has diminished in the modern world, and has been abolished in many civil law and common law countries, the latter including England,[87] Canada,[88] Australia[89] and most recently New Zealand.[90] Hong Kong SAR[91] and Singapore,[92] which continue to apply double actionability, have both developed significant flexibility into the exception.

The Rome II Regulation on the law applicable to non-contractual obligations[93] introduced the idea of party autonomy into the realm of choice of law for torts. It allows parties to choose the law to govern most torts. There is no restriction on the ability of the parties to choose a law to govern a tort which has already occurred.[94] A choice of law made before the occurrence of the tort is effective only if the contracting parties were pursuing commercial activities and the agreement was freely negotiated.[95] There had obviously been concerns about inequality of bargaining power.

In principle, party autonomy may be relevant in the realm of choice of law for torts through five, perhaps six, possible choice of law techniques:

1. A direct choice of law rule permitting parties to select the governing law, as in the case of contracts. This is the technique adopted in the Rome II Regulation.[96]
2. Characterisation: where particular issues, which may be 'tortious' in domestic law, are characterised as contractual for choice of law purposes because of their close connection to the contract. This technique is used in the Hague Principles, but is restricted to pre-contractual obligations.

[87] Private International Law (Miscellaneous Provisions) Act 1995, largely superseded by the Rome II Regulation.

[88] *Tolofsen v Jensen* [1994] 3 SCR 1022.

[89] *Regie National des Usines Renault SA v Zhang* (n 84).

[90] Private International Law (Choice of Law in Tort) Act 2017.

[91] *Red Sea Insurance Co Ltd v Bouygues SA* [1995] 1 AC 190.

[92] *Rickshaw Investments Ltd v Nicolai Baron von Uexkull* [2007] 1 SLR(R) 377.

[93] Regulation (EC) No 864/2007 of the European parliament and of the Council of 11 July 2007 on the law applicable to non-contractual obligations (Rome II) OJ L199/40 of 31.7.2007 (Rome II Regulation).

[94] Rome II Regulation, Art 14(1)(a).

[95] ibid, Art 14(1)(b).

[96] ibid, Art 14.

3. Indirect choice of law: by means of a connecting factor that is defined in a way that is broad enough to include the choice of the parties. In countries which apply a flexible exception to double actionability, a court may be able to apply the parties' choice of law as the law with the closest connection to the tort. This technique could apply even if the choice of law agreement does not purport to include tort issues. The argument here is that the tort is most closely connected with the underlying contractual relationship. This technique is also incorporated in the Rome II Regulation.[97]
4. Accessory choice of law: where one category of issues (in this case tort arising from a contractual relationship) is made subject to the connecting factor of another category (contract) because of the close connections. This can produce very similar results as the previous technique, but it uses a more direct route. However, there is judicial resistance to this technique in the common law.[98]
5. Procedure can play an important role. Courts of common law countries will generally apply their own law in default of proof of foreign law, and litigants can effectively choose to apply the *lex fori* by agreeing not to raise foreign law in a common law court. Some civil law countries allow procedural agreements of this nature as well,[99] after the tort has occurred. Hence, post-tort choice of the *lex fori* is already a reality in many countries.
6. Party autonomy may also become relevant through *renvoi*. This may well be peculiar to Australian choice of law because its reference to the *lex loci delicti* includes its private international law. Insofar as party autonomy is part of the private international law of the *lex loci delicti*, it will be applied in an Australian court (subject to its own public policy and mandatory rules).

The thinking on party autonomy in the Rome II Regulation has had some influence in Asia. South Korea (which has done away with the application of the *lex fori*) adopted the indirect route in using a system of tiered connecting factors, but which allows for the application of the law governing the underlying legal relationship of the parties to a tort which violates that relationship.[100] Japan had accepted the notion of parties' choice of (foreign) law to govern a tort but only after the tort has occurred.[101] However, Japan has retained the double actionability rule, and the *lex fori* cannot be derogated from,[102] so the *lex fori* will apply irrespective of the parties' choice.

[97] ibid, Art 4(3), for torts.

[98] In *Coupland v Arabian Gulf Oil Co* [1983] 1 WLR 1136, the English Court of Appeal refused to apply the law governing the contract to a connected tort.

[99] YL Tan, 'Post-dispute Agreements on Choice of Law' (2017) 13 *Journal of Private International Law* 35.

[100] Private International Law Act (Law No 6465 of 7 April 2001) Art 32. See generally Kwang Hyun Suk, 'The New Conflict of Laws Act of the Republic of Korea' (2003) 5 *Yearbook of Private International Law* 99.

[101] Act on General Rules for Application of Laws (Act No 78 of 21 June 2006) Art 21.

[102] ibid, Art 22.

The private international law of the People's Republic of China allows parties to choose the *lex fori* or foreign law to govern torts, though only after the tort has occurred.[103] Certain torts are excluded from party autonomy, and for intellectual property infringements, parties can only choose the *lex fori*. More recently, the new Civil Code 2015[104] in Vietnam allows contracting parties to choose a law to govern non-contractual obligations, whether before or after the dispute has arisen. The only qualification is that the application of foreign law is subject to the fundamental principles of Vietnamese law.[105]

What Aikens J said in the English High Court probably reflects the mindset of many commercially-minded common law judges: 'it would seem bizarre for all those parties' contractual relations to be governed by one applicable law, yet hold that the law of another country is to determine non-contractual rights and obligations'.[106] This was stated in the context of statutory choice of law rules for torts,[107] but applies equally to the common law. Another commercial judge, in Asia, had remarked extra-judicially: 'A strong argument can be made that, when the relationship between the parties is primarily contractual, causes of action relating to the contract should also be governed by the proper law of the contract'.[108]

There are difficult issues involved in balancing party autonomy with other demands of justice. Doctrine aside, relevant policy considerations will include:

1. the strength of desire to give effect to party autonomy in the interest of commercial certainty;
2. the type of tort in question: whether it is primarily concerned with market-regulation or loss distribution;
3. whether the choice is made before or after the tort has occurred;
4. whether the choice is made in the context of a 'commercial' arrangement;
5. whether the choice is the result of free negotiation;
6. whether the choice is of the *lex fori* or of foreign law; and
7. the degree of connection between the tort and the underlying legal relationship between the parties.

[103] Statute on the Application of Laws to Civil Relationships Involving Foreign Elements of the People's Republic of China (2010), Arts 44, 45, 46, and 50. See generally Chen Weizuo and Kevin M Moore, 'Statute on the Application of Laws to Civil Relationships Involving Foreign Elements of the People's Republic of China' (2010) 12 *Yearbook of Private International Law* 669.

[104] It took legal effect from 1 January 2017. A translation of the Code can be found at wipo.int/edocs/lexdocs/laws/en/vn/vn079en.pdf.

[105] Civil Code 2015, Art 670(1)(a). This could be broader than public policy as generally understood elsewhere. Localised transactions (where the only foreign connection is the choice of law) do not attract the application of the private international law provisions.

[106] *Trafigura Beheer BV v Kookmin Bank Co* [2006] 2 Lloyd's Rep 455, [118].

[107] Private International Law (Miscellaneous Provisions) Act 1995 (now largely superseded by the Rome II Regulation), laying down the general rule in favour of the law of the place where elements constituting the tort had occurred subject to an exception of a law that is substantially more closely connected to the tort.

[108] VK Rajah, 'International Trade in Hong Kong and Singapore – An Indivisible Link' (2010) 40 *Hong Kong Law Journal* 815, 822. See *Ong Ghee Soon Kevin v Ho Yong Chong* [2017] 3 SLR 711 discussing but not deciding the matter; TM Yeo, 'The Effective Reach of Choice of Law Agreements' (2008) 20 *Singapore Academy of Law Journal* 723.

## V. Choice of Law for Fiduciary Duties

When confronted with a question which invokes its equitable jurisdiction under domestic law, should the court apply its own equity with some flexibility to mould it according to the foreign circumstances of the case, or are its doctrines of equity applicable as part of the law applicable according to the relevant choice of law rules or to the extent that they constitute fundamental public policy or international mandatory rules of the forum? I have elsewhere argued for the latter view.[109]

In relation to fiduciary duties, I have argued elsewhere that for the purposes of choice of law, they are not a unitary concept, and that they may be characterised as contract, wrong, restitution, trust, corporations, etc, depending on the context in which they appear. Fiduciary obligations arising between contracting parties is the most significant fiduciary context for commercial dealings. Today, England, New Zealand and Singapore will apply the law of the underlying contractual relationship, though perhaps for different reasons. In England, the issue will be governed by the Rome I Regulation: fiduciary obligations will be regarded as part of the package of obligations voluntarily assumed by one party towards another, and therefore 'contractual' under European law.[110] There is also judicial support for contractual characterisation under English common law.[111] Both New Zealand[112] and Singapore[113] will take the approach that equitable principles are relevant only as part of the applicable law as determined by its choice of law rule (or as public policy or international forum mandatory rules of the forum).

There is some judicial authority in Australia supporting the application of the law of the underlying contractual relationship to the issue of fiduciary duties arising between the parties as a result of that relationship;[114] but there are at least two pathways to that conclusion. One is that the choice of law rule developed in the equitable jurisdiction points to the law of the underlying contract as the applicable law.[115] The significance of this approach is that the development of choice of law principles ought to be governed by the same considerations whether common

[109] TM Yeo, *Choice of Law for Equitable Doctrines* (Oxford, Oxford University Press, 2004).

[110] A Briggs, *The Conflict of Laws*, 3rd edn (Oxford, Clarendon 2013) 223.

[111] *Twin Benefits Ltd v Barker* [2017] EWHC 1412 (Ch).

[112] *Attorney-General for England and Wales v R* [2002] 2 NZLR91 (CA), affd [2003] UKPC 22.

[113] *Rickshaw Investments Ltd v Nicolai Baron von Uexkull* (n 92); *Guy Neale v Nine Squares Pty Ltd* [2013] SGHC 249, [145], reversed on other grounds while approving the choice of law approach in [2015] 1 SLR 1097, [133].

[114] *Murakami v Wiryadi* [2010] NSWCA 7, (2010) 268 ALR 377; *Fleming v Marshall* [2011] NSWCA 86.

[115] This is supported by the language in the cases, ibid particularly in the detailed reasoning of Spigelman CJ in *Murkami v Wiryadi*. See also J Edelman, 'Four Fiduciary Puzzles' in E Bant and M Harding (eds), *Exploring Private Law* (Melbourne, Cambridge University Press, 2010) 298, 309–10; J Edelman, 'When Do Fiduciary Duties Arise?' (2010) 126 *Law Quarterly Review* 302, 303; J Edelman, 'The Importance of the Fiduciary Undertaking', paper presented at the Conference on Fiduciary Law, University of New South Wales, 22 March 2013, supremecourt.wa.gov.au/_files/UNSW Conference of Fiduciary Law 22 Mar 2013 Edelman J.pdf.

law or equitable principles are at stake. Another route is that the equitable principles of the forum apply as mandatory rules or public policy, and are moulded in the court's discretion to fit the foreign circumstances of the case (in this case, the foreign law applicable to the contractual relationship).[116] There remains a strong judicial thread supporting the general application of *lex fori* equity, with the scope of exceptions remaining unclear.[117] The methodology remains controversial in Australia.

One question that could arise if Australia were to adopt the Hague Principles is whether fiduciary obligations arising from a contractual relationship will be 'contractual' for the purpose of the principles. Of course, through the lens of domestic doctrinal law, fiduciary obligations are clearly not contractual. However, international instruments, especially in private international law and dealing with characterisation, are not necessarily to be interpreted according to domestic legal notions.

## VI. Recognition and Enforcement of Foreign Judgments

Party autonomy can also be relevant at the stage of recognition and enforcement of foreign judgments. Its significance as a basis for the recognition or enforcement has been covered in the discussion above on the Choice of Court Convention. Outside the Convention, submission by agreement is a very common and important basis of international jurisdiction in the common law.

The Choice of Court Convention only deals with judgments from a chosen court. It leaves it to national laws to deal with judgments obtained in breach of choice of court agreements. The current draft convention of the broader Judgments Convention from the Hague Conference on Private International Law provides that a Convention judgment may be refused recognition or enforcement if the foreign proceedings had been commenced in contravention of a choice of court agreement.[118]

[116] B Chen, 'Historical Foundations of Choice of Law for Fiduciary Obligations' (2014) 10 *Journal of Private International Law* 171.

[117] *National Commercial Bank v Wimborne* (1978) 5 BPR 97,423; *Paramasivam v Flynn* (1998) 90 FCR 489; *Nicholls v Michael Wilson & Partners* [2010] NSWCA 222, (2010) 243 FLR 177; *Spirits International BV v Federal Treasury Enterprise (FKP) Sojuzplodoimport* [2011] FCAFC 69, (2011) 91 IPR 438.

[118] Art 7(1)(d) of the 2018 Draft Convention (May 2018 draft) provides for a defence where 'the proceedings in the court of origin were contrary to an agreement, or a designation in a trust instrument, under which the dispute in question was to be determined in a court other than the court of origin': assets.hcch.net/docs/23b6dac3-7900-49f3-9a94-aa0ffbe0d0dd.pdf. This could encompass not only exclusive choice of court agreements, but some varieties of non-exclusive choice of court agreements as well, eg, where parties have agreed to courts in State A or State B and no other courts, and proceedings are then started in a court in State C.

Outside the Brussels I Regulation context, the UK has legislatively provided for the non-recognition (and enforcement) of judgments given by a court other than that chosen by the parties as having exclusive jurisdiction.[119] Both Australia[120] and Singapore[121] have provisions in reciprocal enforcement statutes which prevent the enforcement of such foreign judgments, but the position at common law remains unclear. The consequences of a breach of agreement at common law is determined by the governing law of the agreement. If we accept that there is a substantive contractual obligation in the choice of court agreement, prior to the fusion of administration of common law and equity, an injunction to restrain the recognition and enforcement of the foreign judgment may have been an appropriate remedy to undo the consequences of the breach of contract, which would be translated into a defence in a court with fused administration.

There are other means for the consequences of contractual agreement to reach the recognition and enforcement stage, and these could gain importance in the future. An obvious one is the non-exclusive choice of court agreement which is a basis of international jurisdiction under the common law, and which is a ground of indirect jurisdiction under the current draft Judgments Convention.[122] Another is the use of an anti-suit injunction restraining the breach of a choice of court agreement as a (public policy) defence to the recognition or enforcement of a judgment obtained in breach of the injunction.[123] Another example is the model clause which is implied (rebuttable only by express provision to the contrary) under Singapore law to a choice of the Singapore International Commercial Court agreement, under which the parties promise to carry out any order of the court, and to waive any recourse to any court or tribunal outside Singapore against the enforcement of such order, insofar as such recourse can be validly waived.[124] What defences can be validly waived: (1) under the Choice of Court Convention in a case falling within it; or (2) under national private international law outside it? Issues of domestic law would also arise: What defences can be validly waived at the execution stage under national procedural law? What types of damages would be recoverable for breach of promise to carry out a judgment?

[119] Civil Jurisdiction and Judgments Act 1982, s 32.

[120] Foreign Judgments Act 1991 (Cth) s 7(4)(b).

[121] Reciprocal Enforcement of Foreign Judgments Act (Cap 256, 2001 Rev Ed) s 5(3)(b). Only Hong Kong SAR has been gazetted under this statute. There is no such provision in the Reciprocal Enforcement of Commonwealth Judgments Act (Cap 264, 1985 Rev Ed), but the court has discretion to disallow registration where it is not 'just and convenient' to do so, which could be used to deal with breaches of agreement.

[122] 2018 Draft Convention, Art 5(1)(e); see above n 118.

[123] See, eg, *WSG Nimbus Pte Ltd v Board of Control for Cricket in Sri Lanka* [2002] 1 SLR(R) 1088.

[124] Supreme Court of Judicature Act (Cap 322, 2007 Rev Ed) s 18F. This is similar to terms implied under the common law to arbitration agreements, so there is scope for common law development in this direction as well.

## VII. Conclusion

The internationalisation of private international law and internationalisation of commercial courts have made it more important to look at the private international laws of countries beyond one's own. Party autonomy is recognised to be an important driver of international trade and as a useful point for harmonisation or convergence of private international law at least as far as international commercial law is concerned. As greater effect is given internationally to party autonomy in the choice of litigation forum, the issue of choosing private international law becomes very real, especially as the number of international commercial courts increases. This could result in competitive pressure to enlarge the role of party autonomy in national rules of private international law (whether through domestic law reform or adoption of international instruments) as a result.

Party autonomy must of course be balanced against other considerations of conflicts justice.[125] There are concerns about appropriateness of subject-matter for party autonomy as well as potential imbalance of bargaining power which must be addressed, and which can be addressed within domestic laws and conflict of laws. The Hague Principles pushes party autonomy farther in the context of choice of law than the Choice of Court Convention in the context of jurisdiction and judgments, at least from the perspective of the common law. One important difference is that the Choice of Court Convention applies to civil and commercial matters while the Hague Principles applies to commercial contracts only. Within the sphere of commercial law, there is greater scope for pushing party autonomy. Ultimately, however, every country must find its own balance.

[125] *Douez v Facebook Inc* (n 26) is a timely reminder that private international law rules in the common law, which are usually of general application, must be flexible enough to deal with commercial as well as non-commercial situations.

# 12

# Developing Australian Private International Law

## *The Hague Choice of Court Convention & The Hague Principles of Choice of Law in International Commercial Contracts*

MARY KEYES

## I. Introduction

The structure and fundamental concepts of Australian private international law remain founded on the nineteenth-century English common law which Australia inherited from England because of its former colonial relationship to Great Britain. For most of the twentieth century, Australian private international law was dependent for its development on English law, partly because fewer international cases were litigated in Australia than in England, and partly because Australia only achieved full formal legal independence from the United Kingdom in the late 1980s. In the last 30 years, many modifications and refinements have been made to the Australian law. While some of these changes, particularly in the areas of jurisdiction and intra-national litigation, have been developed locally, Hague Conventions have been a crucial source of change to Australian private international law since 1985, often bringing about radical reforms to the law.

Australia has been a member of the Hague Conference on Private International Law since 1973, and is a Contracting State to 11 Hague Conventions in a range of areas, including service, the taking of evidence, trusts, wills, marriage validity, child abduction, child protection and intercountry adoption.[1] Hague Conventions

[1] As at June 2018, Australia was a Contracting State to the following Conventions: Form of Wills 1961; Apostille 1961; Service Abroad 1965; Divorce Recognition 1970; Taking of Evidence 1970; Maintenance Enforcement 1973; Marriage 1978; Abduction 1980; Trusts 1985; Inter-country Adoption 1993; and Child Protection 1996. These entered into force between 1985 (Divorce and Marriage) and 2010 (Service). For full details, see the Status Table on the Hague Conference on Private International Law website, www.hcch.net/en/instruments/status-charts.

have, therefore, already made a substantial contribution to the development of Australian private international law.

With the exception of choice of law for tort, most of the changes that have been made in recent years to Australian choice of law rules have emanated from Hague Conventions. This looks set to continue in the short term: in 2016, the Australian Federal Parliament's Joint Standing Committee on Treaties accepted a proposal that Australia accede to the Hague Convention on Choice of Court Agreements.[2] The proposal to accede to this Convention is generally regarded as likely to improve the Australian law.[3]

In 2016, the Australian Joint Standing Committee on Treaties also recommended that the legislation which will give effect to the Choice of Court Agreements Convention should enact the Hague Principles on Choice of Law in International Commercial Contracts.[4] This aspect of the proposal has so far attracted little attention in Australia.[5] Modifying aspects of the law, including international commercial law, by way of adopting model laws is not unknown in Australia. Australia has adopted the United Nations Commission on International Trade Law (UNCITRAL) Model Laws on Electronic Commerce,[6] International Commercial Arbitration[7] and on Cross-border Insolvency.[8] The main gist of the Hague Principles on Choice of Law in International Commercial Contracts is to uphold the parties' actual choices of law. The Principles also address other issues relevant to contract choice of law.

This chapter considers the impact that adopting the Hague Choice of Court Convention and the Hague Principles on Choice of Law in International

[2] Hague Convention on Choice of Court Agreements (the Hague Choice of Court Convention), entered into force on 1 October 2015. See Joint Standing Committee on Treaties, Report No 166, [3.22] available at www.aph.gov.au/Parliamentary_Business/Committees/Joint/Treaties/ChoiceofCourts/Report_166/section?id=committees%2freportjnt%2f024013%2f24043. At the time of writing in August 2018, the proposal to develop an International Civil Law Bill, in order to give effect to the recommendation of the Joint Standing Committee on Treaties, appears to have stalled. This Bill was listed in the public list of legislation proposed for introduction in the 2017 autumn sittings of the Federal Parliament, but does not appear in the public list of legislation proposed for introduction in the 2018 spring sittings (the spring session covers from 13 August to 31 December 2018).

[3] M Douglas, 'Will Australia Accede to the Hague Convention on Choice of Court Agreements?' (2017) 17 *Macquarie Law Journal* 148; BA Marshall and M Keyes, 'Australia's Accession to the Hague Convention on Choice of Court Agreements' (2017) 41 *Melbourne University Law Review* 246; A Mills, 'The Hague Choice of Court Convention and Cross-border Commercial Dispute Resolution in Australia and the Asia-Pacific' (2017) 18 *Melbourne Journal of International* 1, 14.

[4] Joint Standing Committee on Treaties (n 2) [3.5].

[5] But see M Douglas and N Loadsman, 'The Impact of the *Hague Principles on Choice of Law in International Commercial Contracts*' (2018) 19 *Melbourne Journal of International Law* 1 and BA Marshall, 'The Hague Choice of Law Principles, CISG, and PICC: A Hard Look at a Choice of Soft Law' (2018) 66 *American Journal of Comparative Law* 175 (referring to Australian law in particular at 179, 185, 186, 194). In 'Reconsidering the Proper Law of the Contract' (2012) 13 *Melbourne Journal of International Law* 1, Marshall refers to the Draft Hague Principles, which were, at the time that article was published, still a work in progress.

[6] This Model Law is incorporated in legislation of the same name at the national, State and Territory levels: eg Electronic Transactions Act 1999 (Cth).

[7] This Model Law is incorporated in the International Arbitration Act 1974 (Cth) pt III and sch 2.

[8] This Model Law is enacted in the Cross-border Insolvency Act 2008 (Cth).

Commercial Contracts would have on Australian law. It is structured as follows: section II describes the current Australian law in terms of the effect of choice of court agreements; considers how that law will be changed by acceding to the Hague Choice of Court Convention; and identifies some issues which will not be affected or resolved by acceding to the Convention. Section III describes the existing Australian contract choice of law rules, considers how these rules would be affected by adopting the Hague Principles and identifies aspects of the contract choice of law rule which will not be addressed by adoption of the Hague Principles. Section IV concludes that Australian law is in need of reform both in relation to the effect of choice of court agreements, and choice of law for contractual matters, and that the proposal to adopt the Convention and the Principles provides an important opportunity to reflect on the suitability of the existing Australian law.

## II. Choice of Court Agreements

This section first describes the current Australian law dealing with the effect of choice of court agreements, and then explains how the Hague Choice of Court Convention will modify the Australian law. It concludes by identifying some issues which will not be resolved simply by acceding to this Convention.

### A. Choice of Court Agreements in Australian law

There are currently four different schemes in Australian law which regulate choice of court agreements, which are generally called jurisdiction clauses. Two of these schemes apply only to intra-national cases.[9] As the Hague Convention only applies to international contracts,[10] the existing schemes for intra-Australian cases will not be directly affected by acceding to the Convention. For the purposes of this chapter, it is sufficient to note that the schemes applicable to intra-national cases are very different from the scheme of the Hague Convention, because they do not explicitly, and have not been interpreted to, require the enforcement of exclusive choice of court agreements in the same way that exclusive choice of court agreements are enforced in international cases. Instead, choice of court agreements – whether exclusive or non-exclusive – are merely one factor to be taken

[9] There are different schemes depending on whether proceedings are commenced in the superior courts or the lower courts. In the superior courts (the Federal Court, the Family Court and the State and Territory Supreme Courts), a court is required to transfer proceedings to another Australian superior court in particular circumstances: eg Jurisdiction of Courts (Cross-vesting) Act 1987 (Cth) s 5. In the lower courts (the intermediate courts, called District and County Courts; and the inferior courts, called Magistrates or Local Courts), Australian courts are required to stay proceedings in favour of litigation in other lower courts if the other court is 'the appropriate court': Service and Execution of Process Act 1992 (Cth) s 20.

[10] Hague Convention, art 1.

into account in deciding whether to stay proceedings, or transfer proceedings to another Australian court.[11]

The focus of this chapter, like the Convention, is on the effect of choice of court agreements in international disputes. In that context, the Australian law is composed of two quite different schemes: the first applies only to the allocation of jurisdiction between the courts of Australia and New Zealand; the second applies in all other cases.

### i. *Choice of Court Agreements in Australia-New Zealand Disputes*

The allocation of jurisdiction in Trans-Tasman disputes is regulated by a bilateral treaty,[12] which has been given effect in Australian and New Zealand by national legislation. In Australia, the legislation is the Trans-Tasman Proceedings Act 2010.[13] Although the treaty itself contains no reference to choice of court agreements, the legislation provides for the effect of choice of court agreements. The relevant provisions of the Act were strongly influenced by the Hague Choice of Court Convention,[14] although the legislation differs in some ways from the Convention.

Like the Convention, the Trans-Tasman Proceedings Act requires the strict enforcement of exclusive choice of court agreements which nominate the courts of Australia or New Zealand, and the provisions dealing with exclusive choice of court agreements exclude the effect of such agreements in consumer and employee contracts.[15] The definition of exclusive choice of court agreements in the Trans-Tasman Proceedings Act is similar to the definition in the Convention,[16] but unlike the Convention, the Act does not deem choice of court agreements to be exclusive.[17]

In accordance with the Convention, the Act requires an Australian court which is exclusively chosen by the parties to exercise jurisdiction,[18] unless the choice of

[11] In the context of litigation in the superior courts, see *River Gum Homes Pty Ltd v Meridian Pty Ltd* [2010] QCA 293, [20]; *World Firefighters Games Brisbane v World Firefighters Games Western Australia Inc* (2001) 161 FLR 355, 364–65. In the context of litigation in the lower courts, see Service and Execution of Process Act 1992 (Cth) s 20(4)(d) (referring to 'any agreement between the parties about the court or place in which the proceeding should be instituted'). See M Keyes, 'Improving Australian Private International Law' in A Dickinson, M Keyes and T John (eds), *Australian Private International Law for the 21st Century: Facing Outwards* (Oxford, Hart Publishing, 2014) 23–24.

[12] Agreement between the Government of Australia and the Government of New Zealand on Trans-Tasman Court Proceedings and Regulatory Enforcement [2013] Australian Treaty Series 32.

[13] In New Zealand, the legislation is the Trans-Tasman Proceedings Act 2010 (NZ).

[14] Trans-Tasman Working Group, Report on Trans-Tasman Court Proceedings and Regulatory Enforcement (December 2006) 20.

[15] Hague Convention, art 2.1; Trans-Tasman Proceedings Act 2010 (Cth) s 20(3)(b). The effect of exclusive choice of court agreements in consumer and employee contracts under the legislation is discussed below, text to nn 27–28.

[16] Hague Convention, art 3(a); Trans-Tasman Proceedings Act 2010 (Cth) s 20(3)(a).

[17] Hague Convention, art 3(b).

[18] ibid, art 5(2); Trans-Tasman Proceedings Act 2010 (Cth) s 20(1)(b).

court agreement is null and void under Australian law as the law of the country of the chosen court. The Act differs from the Convention in that the Act explicitly states that this reference to Australian law includes the Australian rules 'of private international law'.[19] This raises two interesting issues. The first is what law governs the issue of whether an exclusive choice of court agreement is null and void under Australian law. It is now well-established in Australia that the *lex fori* per se applies to whether the parties have validly concluded a choice of court agreement;[20] this might also apply to whether a choice of court agreement is null and void. The alternative would be the governing law of the choice of court agreement; this is likely to be Australian law, because choice of court and choice of law clauses typically nominate the courts and law of the same legal systems. Even if there is no express choice of law agreement, the Australian jurisdiction clause is likely to be regarded as inferring a choice of Australian law as the governing law.[21]

The second issue only arises if the Australian choice of law rule indicates foreign law as the governing law to determine whether the choice of court agreement is null and void. In that case it is possible that the Australian court will refer to the choice of law rules of the foreign legal system. This is because the High Court of Australia has stated that a reference to foreign law as the governing law of the tort requires Australian courts to apply the choice of law rules of the foreign law.[22] As explained in further detail below, the implications of this decision for contract choice of law are uncertain;[23] the extension of *renvoi* to the context of choice of court agreements would be a novelty in Australian law.

Like the Convention, the Trans-Tasman Proceedings Act requires that Australian courts enforce exclusive choice of court agreements in favour of New Zealand courts by staying proceedings, subject to very limited exceptions which are nearly the same as those that apply under the Convention.[24] Again, the exception to enforcement which applies if the choice of court agreement is null and void under New Zealand law as the law of the chosen court is, explicitly in the Act although not in the Convention, stated to require reference to New Zealand's 'rules of private international law'.[25]

[19] Trans-Tasman Proceedings Act 2010 (Cth) s 20(2A). As discussed further below at text to n 75, in the Explanatory Report to the Convention, Hartley and Dogauchi assert that the reference to the law of the state of the chosen court in the text of the Convention 'includes the choice-of-law rules' of that state: T Hartley and M Dogauchi, *Explanatory Report*, Proceedings of the Twentieth Session, Tome III, Choice of Court Agreements (The Hague, Hague Conference on Private International Law, 2013) 815, 821.

[20] *Oceanic Sun Line Special Shipping Co Inc v Fay* (1988) 165 CLR 197, 225, 260–61; *Venter v Ilona MY Ltd* [2012] NSWSC 1029, [25]–[27]; *Hargood v OHTL Public Company* [2015] NSWSC 446, [23]; *Central Petroleum Ltd v Geoscience Recovery LLC* [2017] QSC 223, [49]. The Full Court of the Federal Court recently applied the same reasoning to arbitration clauses: *Trina Solar (US), Inc v Jasmin Solar Pty Ltd* (2017) 247 FCR 1; [2017] FCAFC 6, [38], [43], [46], [128], [133].

[21] See below, text to n 99.

[22] *Neilson v Overseas Projects Corporation of Victoria Ltd* [2005] HCA 54, (2005) 223 CLR 331.

[23] See below, text accompanying nn 127–33.

[24] Hague Convention, art 6; Trans-Tasman Proceedings Act 2010 (Cth) s 20(1)(a), (2). See further below, text to nn 71–77.

[25] Trans-Tasman Proceedings Act 2010 (Cth) s 20(2)(a).

The aforementioned provisions of the Trans-Tasman Proceedings Act do not apply to exclusive choice of court agreements to which consumers and employees are party,[26] or to non-exclusive choice of court agreements. Choice of court agreements which are non-exclusive on their proper construction, and those to which consumers and employees are party, are regulated according to another provision of the Trans-Tasman Proceedings Act. This requires the Australian court to stay proceedings in favour of the New Zealand court if the latter court is the 'more appropriate court'.[27] In deciding whether it is 'more appropriate', 'any agreement between the parties', other than an exclusive choice of court agreement, 'about the court or place in which [the matters in dispute] should be determined or the proceeding should be commenced' is one of several factors that the court must take into account.[28] The legislation does not give such agreements any priority, nor does it indicate what weight should be given to such a provision. In the case of consumer contracts, the legislation does not differentiate exclusive from non-exclusive choice of court clauses.

The Trans-Tasman Proceedings Act came into effect in October 2013. There have been few published cases in which the provisions of the Act dealing with exclusive choice of court agreements have been considered by Australian courts.[29]

### *ii. Choice of Court Agreements in International Disputes not Involving New Zealand*

In all other international cases, common law principles determine the effect of choice of court agreements. If the choice of court nominates an Australian court, this is regarded as a submission to the jurisdiction of that court, and on that basis the Australian court will be jurisdictionally competent.[30] In Australia, as in other common law jurisdictions, the fact that the court is competent does not preclude the court from declining to exercise jurisdiction. If the defendant objects to the Australian courts' jurisdiction, notwithstanding an express choice of

[26] ibid, s 20(3)(b) and (c).

[27] ibid, s 17(1), 19(1).

[28] ibid, s 19(2)(d).

[29] *Australian Gourmet Pastes Pty Ltd v IAG New Zealand Ltd* [2017] VSCA 155 (choice of New Zealand court not enforced because it was not an agreement between the parties to the Australian litigation); *Re Douglas Webber Events Pty Ltd* [2014] NSWSC 1544, (2014) 291 FLR 173 (choice of New Zealand court not enforced because it was not an agreement between the parties to the Australian litigation); *Z487 Ltd v Skelton* [2014] QSC 309 (choice of Australian court enforced).

[30] The rules of court of three of the Australian superior courts authorise service out of the jurisdiction where the proceedings are based on a contract which includes a jurisdiction clause nominating the relevant court: Uniform Civil Procedure Rules 1999 (Qld); Supreme Court Rules 1987 (NT) r 7.01(1)(h); Rules of the Supreme Court 1971 (WA) ord 10, r 2. The rules of court of all Australian superior courts permit service of initiating process outside the jurisdiction if the defendant has submitted to the jurisdiction, see eg Federal Court Rules 2011 (Cth) r 10.42(19); Uniform Civil Procedure Rules 2005 (NSW) sch 6(k). Dickinson notes that, by contrast with the former rules, the latter provisions do not explicitly apply to agreements to submit to the court of the forum: '*In Absentia*: The Evolution and Reform of Australian Rules of Adjudicatory Jurisdiction', ch 2 in this collection, n 136.

Australian courts, the character of the express choice becomes relevant: exclusive and non-exclusive choice of court agreements have different effects.

Whether a choice of court agreement is exclusive or not is determined by common law principles. The issue is whether the parties are obliged to litigate, if at all, only in the nominated court.[31] This is a question of interpretation of the clause,[32] which in practice is generally done according to Australian law although in principle it should be determined by the proper law of the choice of court agreement.[33] The courts refer to a number of factors which are intended to assist in ascertaining the parties' presumed intentions. These include whether the words 'exclusive' or 'non-exclusive' are used in the jurisdiction clause;[34] whether the selected court would have been jurisdictionally competent without the contractual nomination of that court;[35] the use of mandatory language such as 'shall' or 'must' and the comprehensive reference to 'all' or 'any' disputes;[36] and whether the parties submitted themselves, or their disputes, to the jurisdiction of the nominated court.[37]

If the jurisdiction clause nominating Australian courts is exclusive, the Australian court will enforce it in relation to claims within its subject-matter or material scope, absent 'strong reasons' for non-enforcement,[38] and assuming that there is no mandatory Australian law directing a court to decline jurisdiction. In commercial cases, the Australian courts generally interpret the material scope of jurisdiction clauses broadly, on the assumption that rational commercial parties would not intend to engage in litigation in multiple legal systems.[39] It is unlikely that an Australian court would refuse to enforce an express exclusive choice of Australian courts, but it has the discretion to do so at common law.[40]

If the jurisdiction clause obliges the parties to litigate exclusively in a foreign court, the Australian courts will enforce that agreement unless Australian legislation directs the court not to do so, or there are strong grounds for non-enforcement.[41]

[31] *Akai Pty Ltd v The People's Insurance Company* (1996) 188 CLR 418, 425.

[32] *FAI General Insurance Co Ltd v Ocean Marine Mutual Protection and Indemnity Association* (1997) 41 NSWLR 117, 126.

[33] *Faxtech Pty Ltd v ITL Optronics Ltd* [2011] FCA 1320, [5].

[34] *FAI General Insurance Co Ltd v Ocean Marine Mutual Protection and Indemnity Association* (n 32) 126; *ACE Insurance Ltd v Moose Enterprise Pty Ltd* [2009] NSWSC 724, [33].

[35] If it was, this is a factor in favour of exclusivity, because otherwise the choice of choice clause would be redundant: *FAI General Insurance Co Ltd v Ocean Marine Mutual Protection and Indemnity Association* (n 32) 127; *ACE Insurance Ltd v Moose Enterprise Pty Ltd* (n 34) [33].

[36] *ACE Insurance Ltd v Moose Enterprise Pty Ltd* (n 34) [33].

[37] *FAI General Insurance Co Ltd v Ocean Marine Mutual Protection and Indemnity Association* (n 32) 126, 127. The former is likely to be interpreted as a submission to the jurisdiction, relevant to the question of whether the court is competent, in the sense of having personal jurisdiction over the defendant: see n 30 above. The latter is likely to be interpreted as relevant to establishing that the parties intended to litigate only in the nominated courts.

[38] *ACE Insurance Ltd v Moose Enterprise Pty Ltd* (n 34) [33].

[39] *Global Partners Fund Ltd v Babcock & Brown Ltd (in liq)* [2010] NSWCA 196, (2010) ACSR 383, [60].

[40] *Donohue v Armco Inc* [2002] 1 All ER 749, 759, 760.

[41] *Akai Pty Ltd v The People's Insurance Company* (n 31) 427–28, 444–45.

There are very few Australian statutes which in terms direct Australian courts not to stay proceedings in favour of an exclusive choice of foreign court clause.[42] Constitutionally, the courts are obliged to apply any such statutory direction.[43] In some cases, Australian courts have refused to enforce foreign jurisdiction clauses if the nominated foreign court would not have had subject-matter jurisdiction to deal with claims under Australian legislation.[44] This is rather controversial and there are conflicting authorities on this point.[45]

The term 'strong grounds' justifying non-enforcement of an exclusive foreign choice of court agreement has not been definitively explained in the Australian cases, and there is a lack of clarity as to what constitutes strong grounds. This makes the determination of the effect of an exclusive foreign jurisdiction clause difficult. There are at least two situations which may constitute strong grounds; each involves the application of a discretion.

The first situation is where enforcement of the foreign choice of court agreement 'offends the public policy of the forum'.[46] This includes legislation which explicitly prohibits 'contracting out' of its application,[47] which is taken to have the effect of invalidating exclusive choices of foreign court.[48] In addition, exclusive foreign choice of court agreements may not be enforced if 'whilst not directly contrary to any express or implied statutory prohibition [they] nevertheless contravene "the policy of the law" as discerned from a consideration of the scope and purpose of the particular statute'.[49] This is more likely if the particular legislation is regarded as 'protective', for example, of Australian insureds,[50] investors[51] or consumers.[52] There is no simple test to ascertain whether the choice of court agreement contravenes the policy of Australian law.

The second situation which might amount to 'strong grounds' justifying non-enforcement of an exclusive choice of foreign court is where litigation in Australia involves third parties to the choice of court agreement,[53] or claims outside the material scope of the choice of court agreement. In such a case, the public policies in favour of avoiding 'parallel proceedings and the risk of inconsistent findings'

[42] Carriage of Goods by Sea Act 1991 (Cth) s 11(2) provides that the Australian courts have jurisdiction to deal with disputes arising from contracts for the carriage of goods by sea from an Australian port to a foreign port, notwithstanding any agreement by the parties to the contrary.

[43] *Compagnie des Messageries Maritimes v Wilson* (1954) 94 CLR 577.

[44] *Faxtech Pty Ltd v ITL Optronics Ltd* (n 33) [18]; *Re Douglas Webber Events Pty Ltd* (n 29) [33].

[45] eg *Nicola v Ideal Image Development Corporation Inc* [2009] FCA 1177, (2009) 215 FCR 76, [72]–[73], [75].

[46] *Akai Pty Ltd v The People's Insurance Company* (n 31) 445.

[47] See eg Insurance Contracts Act 1984 (Cth) s 52(1).

[48] *Akai Pty Ltd v The People's Insurance Company* (n 31) 447–48; *Proactive Building Services Pty Ltd v Mackenzie Keck* [2014] NSWSC 1500.

[49] *Akai Pty Ltd v The People's Insurance Company* (n 31) 447.

[50] ibid.

[51] *Commonwealth Bank of Australia v White* [1999] 2 VR 681.

[52] *Quinlan v Safe International Försäkrings AB* [2005] FCA 1362, (2006) 14 ANZ Ins Cas 61-693.

[53] *Royal Bank of Scotland plc v Babcock & Brown DIF III Global Co-investment Fund LP* [2017] VSCA 138.

and 'inconvenience to third parties'[54] might be taken to outweigh the parties' private interests in the enforcement of their agreement.

Although the Australian courts had previously been somewhat reluctant to enforce foreign exclusive choice of court agreements, Garnett suggested that since 1996, they have become more likely to do so.[55] However, there remain inconsistencies in the treatment of exclusive jurisdiction clauses by Australian courts.[56] The status of an exclusive jurisdiction clause in contracts involving consumers and employees is particularly unclear. In most of the Australian cases in which consumers have challenged foreign jurisdiction clauses, the courts have not enforced those clauses.[57] In *Quinlan v Safe International Försäkrings AB*, Nicholson J noted that the applicant consumer had to 'take or leave' the exclusive jurisdiction clause, and stated that there was

> authority to suggest that in a consumer situation the Court should not place as much weight on an exclusive jurisdiction clause in determining a stay application as would be placed on such a clause where there was negotiation between business people.[58]

However, in a 2017 decision of the New South Wales Supreme Court, *Gonzalez v Agoda*, a foreign exclusive jurisdiction clause was enforced against an Australian consumer.[59] In this case, Button J but did not accept 'that there is anything unfair about an international corporation seeking to protect itself from claims being litigated in the courts of countless countries applying countless different substantive and procedural laws'.[60]

Foreign non-exclusive choice of court agreements have a completely different effect to foreign exclusive agreements.[61] They are said to be merely a factor to be considered in the normal *forum non conveniens* analysis.[62] The weighting they

[54] *Incitec Ltd v Alkimos Shipping Corporation* [2004] FCA 698, (2004) 138 FCR 496, [47]. See also *Vautin v BY Winddown, Inc* [2016] FCA 1235, [53].

[55] R Garnett, 'Jurisdiction Clauses Since *Akai*' (2013) 87 *Australian Law Journal* 134.

[56] eg in *Benson v Rational Entertainment Enterprises Ltd*, Robb J placed 'little weight' on the exclusive jurisdiction clause because there was 'no real connection' between the chosen forum and either the parties or the facts of the dispute: [2015] NSWSC 906, [132]. A lack of connection is often explained on the basis that the parties prefer a neutral forum, and is not generally regarded as a reason for not enforcing choice of court agreements in Australia.

[57] Usually, the reason is that the jurisdiction clause is held not to form part of the contract: see eg *Knight v Adventure Associates Pty Ltd* [1999] NSWSC 861; *Hargood v OHTL Public Company Ltd* (n 20).

[58] (2006) 14 ANZ Ins Cas 61-693, [46]. The authorities to which Nicholson J referred were *Sohio Supply Co v Gatoil (USA) Inc* [1989] 1 Lloyd's Rep 588, 591–92 and *Incitec Ltd v Alkimos Shipping Corporation* (n 54) [50]. This passage of *Quinlan* was cited by three members of the majority of the Supreme Court of Canada in *Douez v Facebook Inc* [2017] 1 SCR 751, [34].

[59] *Gonzalez v Agoda Company Pte Ltd* [2017] NSWSC 1133.

[60] ibid [126].

[61] *Incitec Ltd v Alkimos Shipping Corporation* (n 54) [42]; *Eurogold Ltd v Oxus Holdings (Malta) Ltd* [2007] FCA 811. See BA Marshall, 'Australia: Inconsistencies in the Treatment of Choice of Court Agreements' in M Keyes (ed), *Optional Choice of Court Agreements in Private International Law* (Springer, forthcoming).

[62] *Global Partners Fund Ltd v Babcock & Brown Ltd (in liq)* (n 39) [118].

should be given, relative to the other factors which are taken into account,[63] is not discussed in the relatively few cases in which the effect of a foreign non-exclusive clause has been addressed.[64]

## B. Effect of the Hague Choice of Court Convention on Australian Law

As already noted, the Trans-Tasman Proceedings Act is based on the Convention, and so aspects of the Convention already form part of Australian law, as far as international litigation involving New Zealand is concerned. Acceding to the Convention would therefore not be a radical change to the law, in the sense that it will merely extend one of the schemes currently in force, although the Trans-Tasman Proceedings Act is not identical in scope or detail to the Convention.

Aside from the fact that the Convention contains a much more detailed treatment of choice of court agreements than the Act,[65] the main point of difference between the Convention and the Trans-Tasman Proceedings Act is that the Act does not deem choice of court agreements to be exclusive unless the parties have expressly provided otherwise. This inconsistency will be resolved only if both Australia and New Zealand accede to the Hague Convention because the Convention would prevail over inconsistent national legislation.[66] Unless and until New Zealand accedes to the Convention, the treatment of exclusive choice of court agreements in favour of New Zealand will not be entirely consistent with the Convention.

The Convention will significantly change the Australian law applicable in other international cases, so far as exclusive choices of the courts of Contracting States

[63] These include factors of cost and convenience, the parties' places of residence or business, the governing law, and the existence of any legitimate juridical or personal advantage to the plaintiff of litigating in the forum: *Spiliada Maritime Corporation v Cansulex Ltd* [1987] 1 AC 460, approved in *Voth v Manildra Flour Mills Pty Ltd* (1990) 171 CLR 538.

[64] In *Bagsfirst Global v Global Brands (Football)*, the contract contained a non-exclusive choice of Singapore courts. McDougall J stated that it was legitimate to infer from that clause 'that the parties in fact accepted the possibility, as a real possibility, that litigation might occur elsewhere', and that he did not think that 'the terms of the contract accorded any strong indication in favour of one jurisdiction rather than the other' [2010] NSWSC 988, [24], [27]. He did not explicitly give the non-exclusive jurisdiction clause any particular weight in his analysis, and ultimately concluded that the NSW Supreme Court had not been shown to be clearly inappropriate.

[65] The sole section of the Trans-Tasman Proceedings Act 2010 (Cth) dealing with exclusive choice of court provisions contains provisions which are the same as or similar to arts 2(1), 3(a), 5(2) and 6. The Act does not address many of the other issues addressed in the Convention, although its very liberal rules in relation to the recognition of New Zealand judgments have a similar overall effect.

[66] Although the Trans-Tasman Proceedings Act 2010 (Cth) gives effect to a bilateral treaty, the treaty itself does not address the effect of choice of court agreements, so there would be no direct inconsistency between the treaty and the Convention.

are concerned.[67] This will have the effect of complicating the Australian law on choice of court agreements by creating an additional scheme which is inconsistent in various ways with the other Australian schemes.

Like the current Australian law, the Convention distinguishes exclusive from non-exclusive choice of court agreements. The definition of exclusivity in the Convention is not dissimilar to the Australian common law definition, although the Convention deems choice of court agreements to be exclusive 'unless the parties have expressly provided otherwise'.[68] There is no such presumption in the common law; this aspect of the Convention should simplify the Australian law.

The Convention would require Australian courts, if exclusively chosen by the parties, to exercise jurisdiction, unless the choice of court agreement is null and void under Australian law, as the law of the chosen court.[69] This will change the current law in that, although they are unlikely to exercise it, Australian courts currently have a discretion to decline to exercise jurisdiction even though the parties have expressly nominated Australian courts as having exclusive jurisdiction.[70]

The Convention will have an even greater impact on the treatment of exclusive choice of court agreements in favour of the courts of other Contracting States. The Australian courts would no longer have any discretion not to enforce a foreign choice of court agreement; instead, the courts will be required to enforce such agreements, with five exceptions.[71] Only two of these five seem likely to arise in practice:[72] these are the first, and the third, exceptions in the order they are listed in the Convention. The first exception states that the choice of court agreement is not enforceable if it is null and void according to the law of the state of the chosen court.[73] This is a significant change to the current law, under which Australian courts apply forum law to determine whether the parties validly concluded a foreign choice of court agreement.[74] In the Explanatory Report to the Convention, Hartley and Dogauchi assert that the reference to the law of the state of the chosen court in the text of the Convention 'includes the choice-of-law rules' of that state.[75]

[67] The Convention only applies to exclusive choice of court agreements in favour of Contracting States: art 3(a), subject to art 19. There has been no indication that Australia intends to make a declaration under art 19.

[68] Hague Convention, art 3(b).

[69] ibid, art 5(1).

[70] The Hague Convention explicitly states that the chosen court has no discretion to decline to exercise jurisdiction: art 5(2).

[71] ibid, art 6.

[72] The other exceptions refer to the situation that one party to the contract lacked capacity (art 6(b)); where 'for exceptional reasons beyond the control of the parties, the agreement cannot reasonably be performed' (art 6(d)); and where the chosen court has refused to hear the case (art 6(e)). For detailed discussion of all the exceptions, see M Keyes, 'Jurisdiction Under the Hague Choice of Courts Convention: Its Likely Effect on Australian Practice' (2009) 5 *Journal of Private International Law* 181, 207–09; Marshall and Keyes, 'Australia's Accession to the *Hague Convention on Choice of Court Agreements*' (n 3) 258–66.

[73] Hague Convention, art 6(a).

[74] n 20 above.

[75] Hartley and Dogauchi, *Explanatory Report* (n 19) 815 (reasoning that '[i]f this had not been the intention, the text would have used the phrase "internal law of the State"': fn 158). See also ibid 821, fn 184.

Insofar as Australian courts refer to foreign law to determine the ongoing effectiveness of choice of court agreements, they do not treat the foreign choice of law rules as relevant, so this would be a change to the law.

The third exception states that the choice of court agreement is not enforceable if 'giving effect to the agreement would lead to a manifest injustice or would be manifestly contrary to the public policy of the State of the court seised'.[76] This is intended to be narrowly construed,[77] but even so, commentators are unsure whether it would modify the current Australian law, according to which the courts may refuse to enforce foreign jurisdiction clauses if enforcement of the clause would contravene Australian public policy.[78]

The Convention also requires courts of Contracting States to recognise judgments given by courts of other Contracting States nominated in exclusive choice of court agreements,[79] subject to limited exceptions.[80] This would not substantially change the existing law, according to which the Australian courts are likely, other things being equal, to recognise foreign judgments given by courts to which the parties submitted, whether by exclusive jurisdiction clause or otherwise.[81]

## C. Remaining Issues

A number of important issues concerning the effect of jurisdiction clauses fall outside the scope of, and are otherwise unresolved by, the Hague Choice of Court Convention, leaving considerable scope for the application of the existing Australian law. The Convention only applies to exclusive choice of court agreements in international cases, and then only those which nominate the courts of Contracting States.[82] It also only applies to choice of court agreements which nominate

[76] Hague Convention, art 6(c).

[77] In their Explanatory Report on the Convention, Hartley and Dogauchi stated that this provision 'is intended to set a high threshold. It refers to basic norms or principles of that state; it does not permit the court seised to hear the case simply because the chosen court might violate, in some technical way, a mandatory rule of the State of the court seised … the standard is intended to be high: the provision does not permit a court to disregard a choice of court agreement simply because it would not be binding under domestic law': (n 19) [153] (footnote omitted).

[78] Garnett suggests that 'an Australian court may well be tempted to conclude, in line with the existing law' that possible loss of rights under Australian legislation (by enforcing the foreign jurisdiction clause) 'would violate the "basic norms or principles" of the forum state and so not enforce the clause': (n 55) 146.

[79] Hague Convention, art 8.

[80] ibid, art 9.

[81] For detailed discussion of this issue, see Marshall and Keyes (n 3) 270.

[82] Hague Convention, art 3(a). It is possible that the Australian legislation will extend the application of the Convention's scheme to cover exclusive choice of court agreements that nominate the courts of non-Contracting States: Joint Standing Committee on Treaties (n 2) [3.17] (referring to the evidence of Mr Andrew Walter, of the Australian Attorney-General's Department, to the Committee). As at October 2018, the Contracting States to the Convention are Mexico, Montenegro, Singapore and the Member States of the European Union, including Denmark.

the courts of a single country as having exclusive jurisdiction. It does not apply to choice of court agreements purporting to nominate the courts of multiple countries as having exclusive jurisdiction, or asymmetric choice of court agreements, which are only exclusive so far as one party is concerned.[83]

The Convention excludes choice of court agreements in a wide range of situations, including those in consumer and employment contracts.[84] The Convention does not directly address the effect of non-exclusive choice of court agreements.[85] It is also ambiguous on the crucial question of how to determine whether the parties actually concluded a choice of court agreement. Commentators have expressed conflicting views as to whether the Convention should be interpreted as addressing this point.[86]

Therefore, Australian national law will continue to play a significant role after accession to the Convention. It will continue to determine the effect of exclusive choice of court agreements in favour of non-Contracting States; exclusive choice of court agreements in intra-national cases; exclusive choice of court agreements in employment, consumer, and a variety of other contracts; non-exclusive jurisdiction clauses; and asymmetric choice of court agreements. It is possible that national law will continue to be applied to determine whether the parties concluded a choice of court agreement. The Australian law dealing with many of these issues is either unclear or unsatisfactory, so any improvements achieved by acceding to the Convention, welcome though they may be, will only achieve a partial improvement of the law.

Finally, it remains to be seen what effect the Convention will have on the other means by which exclusive jurisdiction clauses might be enforced. In addition to their effect on the courts' decision whether to stay or dismiss proceedings, an exclusive jurisdiction clause in favour of the forum courts can currently also be enforced by the grant of an anti-suit injunction,[87] and damages can be awarded

[83] Hartley and Dogauchi (n 19) 811. A contrary view is expressed by Cranston J in dicta in the English High Court decision *Commerzbank AG v Liquimar Tankers Management Inc*, where he said that 'there are good arguments in my view that the words of the definition in art 3(a) of the Hague Convention cover asymmetric jurisdiction clauses': [2017] EWHC 161 (Comm), [2017] 1 WLR 3497, [74]. Yeo suggests that 'it is doubtful that this is the correct interpretation of the Convention': 'The Rise of Party Autonomy in Commercial Conflict of Laws', ch 11 in this collection, fn 31. The effect of asymmetric jurisdiction agreements is discussed in M Keyes and BA Marshall, 'Jurisdiction Agreements: Exclusive, Optional and Asymmetrical' (2015) 11 *Journal of Private International Law* 345.

[84] Choice of court agreements in consumer and employment contracts are specifically excluded in art 2(1). There is an extensive list of other exclusions in art 2(2).

[85] A Contracting State may declare under art 22 that it will recognise and enforce judgments of the courts of other Contracting States which were nominated in non-exclusive choice of court agreements and which have also made a declaration under art 22. As at June 2018, none of the Contracting States to the Convention had made a declaration under art 22, and there is no indication that Australia intends to make such a declaration. See BA Marshall, 'Recognition of Judgments Based on Non-exclusive Jurisdiction Agreements', ch 5 in this collection.

[86] See Marshall and Keyes (n 3) 260–61.

[87] *ACE Insurance Ltd v Moose Enterprise Pty Ltd* (n 34).

for breach of an exclusive jurisdiction agreement.[88] The Convention does not explicitly refer to either of these means of enforcing exclusive choice of court agreements.[89]

Accession to the Hague Choice of Court Convention risks creating greater complexity in the Australian law, by adding a further scheme to this already crowded and confusing area of law, and leaving many aspects of the regulation of choice of court agreements untouched. Unfortunately, the scheme of the Convention is not entirely consistent with the other, mutually inconsistent, schemes that exist. For example, the current regimes relating to choice of court agreements in intra-Australian litigation are entirely incompatible with the Convention. The possibility of extending the scheme of the Convention to intra-national cases, with appropriate modifications, raises issues of policy about the allocation of jurisdiction within Australia[90] that go beyond the scope of this chapter.

Many of the issues that fall outside the scope of the Convention require reform, including the effect of choice of court agreements in intra-Australian cases, and in cases involving weaker parties, including consumers. Hopefully, the process of accession will highlight the need, and create the opportunity, for the evaluation and review of other aspects of choice of court agreements in Australian law.

## III. Choice of Law Agreements

This section begins with a description of the current Australian contract choice of law rule. It then explains how the Hague Principles would modify the law, and then identifies some issues in contract choice of law which will not be affected by enacting the Hague Principles.

### A. The Current Australian Contract Choice of Law Rules

In comparison to the complexity of the rules on choice of court agreements, the rules on choice of law agreements are, at least at first blush, delightfully simple. There is only one set of contract choice of law rules which applies in all

[88] Although there is no published case in which an Australian court has awarded damages, Australian judges have said that damages should be available for breach of an exclusive choice of court agreement: *Commonwealth Bank v White (No 2)* [2004] VSC 268, [5]; *Compagnie des Messageries Maritime v Wilson* (n 43) 587.

[89] See M Ahmed and P Beaumont, 'Exclusive Choice of Court Agreements: Some Issues on the Hague Convention on Choice of Court Agreements and Its Relationship with the Brussels I Recast Especially Anti-suit Injunctions, Concurrent Proceedings and the Implications of BREXIT' (2017) 13 *Journal of Private International Law* 386.

[90] In *World Firefighters Games Brisbane v World Firefighters Games Western Australia Inc* [2001] QSC 164, (2001) 161 FLR 355, Philippides J took the view that the effect of the cross-vesting legislation was entirely to supersede the common law rules relating to staying proceedings. It would be inconsistent with that view to extend the application of the Convention to intra-national cases.

international and intra-national cases. However, the contract choice of law rules are derived from case law, and for that reason can be difficult for non-experts, including laypeople and foreign lawyers, to access, interpret and apply. Contract choice of law is seldom litigated in Australia;[91] therefore the body of case law is limited. There are a number of secondary issues relating to contract choice of law on which there is no Australian authority, and others on which the authorities are divided.

### i. *The Primary Contract Choice of Law Rule*

The primary Australian contract choice of law rule requires the court to give effect to the parties' actual choices of law to govern their contract,[92] subject to limitations which are not clearly stated and can be difficult to identify.[93] The parties' actual choice of law, whether expressed or inferred from the terms of the contract and surrounding circumstances, should be enforced.[94] There are no formal requirements that must be satisfied. The parties can choose a law which has no objective connection to the contract,[95] but they are not at liberty to choose non-state law as the applicable law.[96]

If the parties have not expressed their intention in the form of a choice of law clause, then the question is 'whether, upon the true construction of the contract…, the court may properly infer that the parties intend their contract to be governed by reference to a particular system of law'.[97] This is done by considering the terms and nature of the contract and the surrounding circumstances.[98] Precisely how that formula should be applied is not entirely clear, mainly because there are so few Australian cases in which the court has inferred a choice of law. A foreign exclusive jurisdiction or arbitration clause is a strong indication of the parties' intentions.[99]

[91] In the recent Australian cases, the choice of law issue has arisen in jurisdictional disputes. eg the most recent authority of the High Court of Australia on contract choice of law, *Akai Pty Ltd v The People's Insurance Company* (n 31), was a jurisdictional dispute.

[92] *Merwin Pastoral Co Pty Ltd v Moolpa Pastoral Co Pty Ltd* (1933) 48 CLR 565, 573–74; *Mynott v Barnard* (1939) 62 CLR 68.

[93] These are discussed further below, text to nn 104–123.

[94] *Merwin Pastoral Co Pty Ltd v Moolpa Pastoral Co Pty Ltd* (n 92), 574; *Akai Pty Ltd v The People's Insurance Company Ltd* (1996) 188 CLR 418, 440–41.

[95] *BHP Petroleum Pty Ltd v Oil Basins Ltd* [1985] VR 725; *Re Bulong Nickel Pty Ltd* [2002] WASC 126, (2002) 42 ACSR 52.

[96] M Davies, AS Bell and PLG Brereton, *Nygh's Conflict of Laws in Australia*, 9th edn (Sydney, LexisNexis, 2014) 442. If the contract is governed by Australian law, the parties 'can incorporate into the contract, as terms of the contract, provisions of another system of law' including religious law: *Re South Head & District Synagogue (Sydney) (administrators appointed)* [2017] NSWSC 823, [29]. See also [32], where Brereton J stated that 'there is no difficulty in relying on orthodox Jewish law as part of the contractual framework'. See also *Engel v Adelaide Hebrew Congregation Inc* (2007) 98 SASR 402.

[97] *Akai Pty Ltd v The People's Insurance Company* (n 31) 441. See also *Merwin Pastoral Co Pty Ltd v Moolpa Pastoral Co Pty Ltd* (n 92), where Rich and Dixon JJ referred to an 'actual intention' which 'appears by implication or as a matter of necessary intendment': at 574.

[98] *Akai Pty Ltd v The People's Insurance Company* (n 31) 441.

[99] ibid 442; *Oceanic Sun Line Special Shipping Co Inc v Fay* (n 20) 224–25 (Brennan J).

In *John Kaldor Fabricmaker Pty Ltd v Mitchell Cotts Freight (Australia) Pty Ltd*, one of the very few Australian cases in which it was found that there was an actual although unexpressed choice of law, Brownie J held that, on the strength of an arbitration clause alone, it could 'be inferred that the actual intention of the parties was that the contract would be governed by the provisions of English law'.[100]

It is difficult to prove that the parties shared an intention as to the governing law, in the absence of an expressed choice of law, and the parties rarely attempt it.[101] If no actual expressed or inferred choice of law can be proven, the governing law of the contract is the law of the legal system with the closest and most real connection to the contract, referred to as the objective proper law of the contract.[102] This test is considered further below.[103]

The parties' freedom to select the governing law is not unconstrained, but determining the limitations is difficult. Commentators often refer to the constraints mentioned by Lord Wright in *Vita Food Products v UNUS Shipping*, where his Lordship stated that it was 'difficult to see' what limitations applied to the parties' expressed choice of law, as long as the choice was 'bona fide, legal and not contrary to public policy'.[104] Individual Australian judges have referred to this formula;[105] while commentators assume that it remains relevant to Australian law, it has never been explicitly adopted by a majority of the High Court, which had, before the Privy Council had decided *Vita Food Products*, already established a complete contract choice of law principle. In a series of cases decided between 1932 and 1939 (the year *Vita Food Products* was decided),[106] the High Court had established that the parties' actual – whether express or inferred – choices of law should be applied, and that this freedom was not unconstrained. In *Mynott v Barnard*, Latham CJ noted that '[p]arties cannot by agreeing that their contract should be governed by the law of a foreign country exclude the operation of a "peremptory rule" otherwise applicable to their transaction'.[107] Nevertheless, later Australian cases are generally concerned with the effect of local mandatory rules, rather than those of foreign states. Foreign laws, including foreign mandatory rules, are only applied if they form part of the *lex causae*.[108]

[100] (1989) 19 NSWLR 172, 187.

[101] Suggestions that the search for the parties' inferred choice of law and the objective proper law are really the same were rejected by the High Court in *Akai v The People's Insurance Company* (n 31) 440 (the majority rejecting a suggestion that inferred choice 'is really no choice at all').

[102] *Akai Pty Ltd v The People's Insurance Company Ltd* (n 31) 440–41.

[103] Text to nn 200–03 below.

[104] [1939] AC 277, 290. This is referred to by Davies et al, *Nygh's Conflict of Laws in Australia* (n 96) 450. The Australian Law Reform Commission criticised this formula as being unclear: Report No 58: *Choice of Law* (Commonwealth of Australia, 1992) para 8.11.

[105] eg *Golden Acres Ltd v Queensland Estates Pty Ltd* [1969] Qd R 378; *Augustus v Permanent Trustee Co (Canberra) Ltd* (1971) 124 CLR 245, 260; *ACE Insurance Ltd v Moose Enterprise Pty Ltd* (n 34) [52].

[106] *Barcelo v Electrolytic Zinc Co of Australasia Ltd* (1932) 48 CLR 391; *Wanganui-Rangitikei Electric Power Board v Australian Mutual Provident Society* (1934) 50 CLR 581; *Mynott v Barnard* (1939) 62 CLR 68.

[107] (1939) 62 CLR 68, 80.

[108] *Akai Pty Ltd v The People's Insurance Company Ltd* (n 31) 442.

Identifying which Australian legislation will be treated as having a 'peremptory' (in the modern terminology, mandatory) effect in international cases can be challenging. This requires the ability to identify and interpret potentially applicable Australian statutes; a task which is rendered all the more difficult because most Australian legislation does not indicate its intended scope of application, particularly, whether it is applicable in international cases.

A small number of Australian statutes stipulate their scope of application in international cases. The Carriage of Goods by Sea Act 1991 contains an unusual type of statutory choice of law rule. It states that the parties to a contract for the carriage of goods by sea from an Australian port to a foreign port 'are taken to have intended to contract according to the laws in force at the place of shipment',[109] and that any actual agreement to the contrary is ineffective.[110] Some Australian legislation only invalidates the parties' actual choice of law to the extent that the chosen law is inconsistent with the application of the relevant legislation. This is usually done by stating that the legislation in question applies to transactions which have a particular connection to Australia. For example, the Insurance Contracts Act 1984 applies to insurance contracts, the proper law of which is that of an Australian State or Territory,[111] notwithstanding an expressed choice of foreign law.[112] An even more limited example is contained in the Australian Consumer Law, which states that the 'consumer guarantees' established in that law apply to consumer contracts, 'the proper law' of which 'would be the law of any part of Australia but for a term of the contract that provides otherwise';[113] that is, the contract has its closest and most real connection to an Australian State or Territory.[114] The Australian courts are constitutionally required to give effect to such provisions,[115] irrespective of the parties' express choices of law.

If the Australian statute in issue does not explicitly limit its scope of application, there are two inconsistent methods that Australian courts use to determine whether the statute should be applied. The first is to apply the normal choice of law rule and then apply the statute if Australian law is the law applicable to the claim.[116] This method gives no priority to forum legislation. The second method assumes that the court should refer to the Australian statute prior to any choice of

[109] Carriage of Goods by Sea Act 1991 (Cth) s 11(1).

[110] ibid, s 11(2).

[111] Insurance Contracts Act 1984 (Cth) s 8(1).

[112] ibid, s 8(2).

[113] Australian Consumer Law 2010, s 67(a). This provision is misconceived. Presumably it was intended to protect Australian consumers by preserving the application of the consumer guarantees; in fact, it is likely that the objective proper law of a contract for the provision of goods and services by a foreign supplier to an Australian consumer will be the law of the place where the foreign supplier operates. See eg *ACCC v Valve Corp (No 3)* [2016] FCA 196, (2016) 337 ALR 647, 663–65; *Gonzalez v Agoda Company Pte Ltd* (n 59) [134].

[114] *ACCC v Valve Corp (No 3)* (n 113) 662–63.

[115] *Akai Pty Ltd v The People's Insurance Co Ltd* (n 31) 443 fn 63.

[116] ibid 443, citing the older case of *Wanganui-Rangitikei Electric Power Board v Australian Mutual Provident Society* (n 106) 601. See also *KA & C Smith Pty Ltd v Ward* (1998) 45 NSWLR 702.

law analysis, and interpret the statute to see if there are any implied limits to its application in the particular case. There are High Court authorities in favour of both methods; most recently, the Court has recently endorsed the second method, stating that where the legislation contains 'no expressed connecting factor, the issue becomes whether there is to be implied any restraint upon the apparently universal application of the law'.[117] Some restraint is always implied,[118] but the result is usually that the legislation is applied, and is therefore given priority over the parties' express choice of foreign law.

The second method is obviously likely to interfere with the effect of the choice of law rule. The fact that Australian courts might use this method is not at all evident from the choice of law rule, which does not clearly indicate that forum legislation may be given an overriding effect, even if the legislation does not say so specifically.

The Australian contract choice of law rule established in the 1930s is not necessarily inconsistent with the limitations mentioned by Lord Wright in *Vita Food Products v UNUS Shipping*, although the High Court did not independently impose requirements of bona fides or legality of the express choice. The first of these has always been a controversial element of the exception referred to in *Vita Food Products*; the only reported application of the limitation of bona fides is found in a first instance decision of the Supreme Court of Queensland, *Golden Acres Ltd v Queensland Estates Pty Ltd*.[119] The issue in this case was whether Queensland legislation applied to a case in which the contract stipulated that it was deemed to have been made in Hong Kong. Justice Hoare treated that stipulation as an express choice of Hong Kong law, and held that it was not enforceable because the selection of foreign law was not bona fide. His Honour held that the objective proper law of the contract was Queensland law, that the selection of foreign law was intended to avoid the application of Queensland law, and that this was contrary to public policy.[120] On appeal, the High Court determined that the Queensland legislation should be interpreted as applying to contracts for the sale of Queensland land, and that the governing law of the contract was irrelevant in determining whether the legislation applied.[121]

[117] *Akai Pty Ltd v The People's Insurance Company Ltd* (n 31) 443. Their endorsement of this method seems clear from their earlier statement that 'A situation conceptually distinct from that in this case arises where the statute in question before an Australian court is a foreign law. Then the question will be whether, subject to any local law which qualified what otherwise would be the applicable common law principles of choice of law, the common law rules in the Australian forum pick up the foreign statute as part of the *lex causae* by the application of which the dispute is to be resolved by the Australian court': ibid 442–43. In support of the second method, see M Douglas, 'Choice of Law in the Age of Statutes: A Defence of Statutory Interpretation after *Valve*', ch 9 in this collection.

[118] eg the statutory prohibition on misleading conduct is interpreted as being applicable only to conduct which occurred in Australia: *Bray v Hoffman-La Roche Ltd* (2002) 118 FCR 1, [50]; *Valve Corporation v Australian Competition and Consumer Commission* [2017] FCAFC 224, (2017) 351 ALR 584, [105].

[119] [1969] Qd R 378.

[120] ibid 384–85.

[121] *Freehold Land Investments Ltd v Queensland Estates Pty Ltd* (1970) 123 CLR 418.

Australian commentators generally prefer the High Court's analysis of the problem that arose in *Golden Acres v Queensland Estates* to Hoare J's reference to the requirement that a choice of law be bona fide.[122] There is no other Australian case in which it has been held that a choice of law was not bona fide.

There is no Australian authority on the second limitation mentioned by Lord Wright in *Vita Food Products*, that the parties' choice of law must be legal. Clearly, his Lordship anticipated that the legality of the choice should be assessed by reference to forum law. This is probably redundant because legality can be considered to be an aspect of public policy.

To the extent that the three limitations to the effect of an express choice of law articulated by Lord Wright in *Vita Food Products* were ever part of the Australian contract choice of law rule, the only one of the limitations which is clearly still good law is the requirement that the choice is not contrary to public policy.[123] This limitation is broadly consistent with the way that Australian courts deal with the effect of Australian legislation in international cases, which is in practice the most important limitation to the effect of an actual choice of foreign law. In all events, determining the limits to the effectiveness of an express choice of law is a complicated undertaking.

### *ii. Secondary Aspects of the Contract Choice of Law Rule*

Some, albeit infrequently litigated, aspects of the contract choice of law rule are unclear because Australian cases take different positions. For example, some cases assume that a contract can have multiple governing laws,[124] but others suggest not.[125]

The contract choice of law rule is further complicated by the possibility that, if foreign law is the governing law of the contract, this might be treated as a reference to the foreign law's choice of law rule. In *Neilson v Overseas Projects Corporation of Victoria Ltd*, the High Court of Australia held that where the Australian tort choice of law rule indicated foreign law as the governing law, Australian courts

[122] Davies et al (n 96) [119]–[120]; M Tilbury, G Davis and B Opeskin, *Conflict of Laws in Australia* (Oxford, Oxford University Press, 2002) 746. Mortensen et al suggest that this limitation 'should no longer be regarded as good law': R Mortensen, R Garnett and M Keyes, *Private International Law in Australia*, 4th edn (Sydney, LexisNexis Butterworths, 2019) [17.11].

[123] In *Augustus v Permanent Trustee Co (Canberra) Ltd*, Walsh J, with whom the other members of the Court agreed, referred to the limitation that 'there must be no reason for avoiding the choice on the ground of public policy', citing *Vita Food Products*, but did not refer to the other two limitations (which were not in issue in that case): (1971) 124 CLR 245, 260.

[124] *Olex Focas Pty Ltd v Skodaexport Co Ltd* [1998] 3 VR 380, 395; and *Rataplan Pty Ltd v Federal Commissioner of Taxation* (2004) ATC 4,801, 4,807–4,809.

[125] In *Wanganui-Rangitikei Electric Power Board v Australian Mutual Provident Society*, Evatt J expressed the view that 'the law of one country, and one country alone, can be the proper or governing law of the contract', but that the law of another country might be applied to a particular issue if the governing law 'requires or concedes' that consequence: (1934) 50 CLR 581 at 604. See also *Busst v Lotsirb Nominees Pty Ltd* [2003] 1 Qd R 477, 480.

should apply the foreign choice of law rule.[126] The implications of that decision for other areas of law were not made clear by the High Court.[127] It has been described as 'an open question' as to whether it applies to contract.[128] Prior to *Neilson*, it was assumed in Australia that if the contract choice of law rule indicated foreign law, that reference should be taken to be a reference to the foreign legal system's internal law, rather than its choice of law rule.[129] The authorities as to the effect of *Neilson* on contract choice of law are divided and this creates confusion. In *O'Driscoll v J Ray McDermott SA*,[130] it was assumed for the purposes of the appeal to the Western Australian Court of Appeal that *renvoi* applied to contract choice of law, but in *Proactive Building Solutions v Mackenzie Keck*, McDougall J held that the traditional view, that *renvoi* had no application to contract, had not been modified by *Neilson*.[131] Some commentators take the view that the operation of *renvoi* to contract is open, on the authority of *Neilson*;[132] but it has been suggested that this should be so only where the contract is not expressly chosen by the parties.[133] Although the issue of *renvoi* is usually ignored in practice, the lack of clarity on this issue is undesirable.

Other issues which are currently undeveloped in the Australian law have possible analogues in the context of choice of court agreements.[134] One such issue is whether the parties have concluded an agreement as to choice of law. In the related context of choice of court and arbitration agreements, the law of the forum determines whether the parties had reached an agreement.[135] Another issue which is undeveloped is what law determines the construction of the choice of law agreement. In principle, this ought to be the proper law of the contract, but in the context of jurisdiction clauses, the Australian courts often apply forum law without justifying doing so. For example, in *Akai*, the majority of the High Court referred to domestic Australian law in their discussion of whether it could be inferred that the parties had reached an agreement as to the governing law,[136] which they said was an issue of the construction of the contract. They did not address the choice of law issue in doing so.

[126] *Neilson v Overseas Projects Corporation of Victoria Ltd* (n 22).

[127] For discussion, see M Keyes, 'Foreign Law in Australian Courts' (2007) 15 *Torts Law Journal* 9, 30–32.

[128] Davies et al (n 96) 443.

[129] *Barcelo v Electrolytic Zinc Co of Australasia Ltd* (n 106) 437–38; PE Nygh and M Davies, *Conflict of Laws in Australia*, 7th edn (Sydney, LexisNexis 2002) 296–97.

[130] [2006] WASCA 25.

[131] [2013] NSWSC 1500, [27]–[28].

[132] Keyes, 'Foreign Law in Australian Courts' (n 127) 31–32; Davies et al (n 96) 443.

[133] ibid. See likewise *Proactive Building Solutions v Mackenzie Keck* [2013] NSWSC 1500, [27]–[28].

[134] Edelman J noted that similar issues arise in the related contexts of the enforcement of exclusive choice of foreign court agreements and of choice of law agreements: *Australian Competition and Consumer Commission v Valve Corp (No 3)* (n 113) 672–73.

[135] n 20 above.

[136] *Akai Pty Ltd v The People's Insurance Company Ltd* (n 31) 441 (citing *Codelfa Construction Pty Ltd v State Rail Authority of NSW* (1982) 149 CLR 337, 347–53, and *Thompson & Morgan (United Kingdom) Ltd v Erica Vale Australia Pty Ltd* (1995) 31 IPR 335, 344–46).

The relationship between choice of law in contract and tort has already been mentioned in the context of the application of *renvoi*. A more general issue is the extent to which the governing law of the contract determines related non-contractual issues. In Australia, accumulation of actions is possible. In the situation of a concurrence of liability, the governing law of the contract and of the tort are determined separately, using different choice of law rules,[137] which may well identify different laws for what is effectively the same claim. In *John Pfeiffer Pty Ltd v Rogerson*, the plurality noted in *obiter dicta* the possibility that some tortious claims could alternatively be framed in contract or under statute.[138] They acknowledged that '[c]haracterising such actions may be difficult and may raise questions whether the private international law rules about tort or some other rules are to be applied'.[139] Earlier in their judgment, the plurality noted that '[t]he action was framed in tort and the present matter must be decided on that basis notwithstanding that, in this Court, the respondent sought also to frame the case in contract'.[140] In *Busst v Lotsirb Nominees*, which involved a workplace injury and a concurrence of liability, the Queensland Court of Appeal held that the objective proper law of the contract had to be determined without reference to the nature of the breach of contract, which was negligence in failing to provide a safe system of work.[141] Whereas the governing law of the tort was New South Wales, in accordance with the *lex loci delicti* principle, the Court held that the contract was governed by Queensland law, as the law with the closest and most real connection to the contract.

In *Busst v Lotsirb Nominees*, there was no actual choice of law, and the proper law of the contract was determined objectively. Two issues remain open: whether in principle, the parties can choose the law to determine their tortious rights and liabilities; and if so, how the choice of law agreement should be interpreted to determine if they have effectively done so. Neither issue has been the subject of close analysis in Australia.

There is no direct Australian authority as to whether an express choice of law applies to tort claims: or, to put it another way, whether tort choice of law is

[137] The tort choice of law rule is very different from the contract choice of law rule. Cross-border torts are governed by the law of the place where the tort occurred: *John Pfeiffer Pty Ltd v Rogerson* [2000] HCA 36, (2000) 203 CLR 503; *Regie des Nationale Usines Renault SA v Zhang* (2002) 210 CLR 491. If that is a foreign law, then this requires reference to the foreign choice of law rule: *Neilson v Overseas Projects Corporation of Victoria Ltd* (n 22).

[138] [2000] HCA 36, (2000) 203 CLR 503, [81].

[139] ibid [81].

[140] ibid [5]. It is not clear why the claim was not framed in contract. In the lower courts it appears that the only issue was whether the New South Wales law was procedural or substantive: *John Pfeiffer Pty Ltd v David Rogerson* [1998] FCA 815 (decision of the Full Court of the Federal Court); *John Pfeiffer Pty Ltd v David Rogerson* (Unreported, Full Court of the Supreme Court of the Australian Capital Territory, No SCA 34 of 1997, 3 December 1997). It is also unclear whether the reason that the plurality held that the matter 'must' be determined on the basis that the claim was tortious was that that was how the plaintiff had framed the claim (and therefore could not subsequently complain about it) or whether changing the basis of the claim on the final (in this case, the third) appeal was impermissible because of the prejudice to the defendant.

[141] [2003] 1 Qd R 477, [10].

contractible. To some extent,[142] the parties can implicitly agree that forum law should be applied even if the tort occurred outside the forum, by invoking (in the case of the plaintiff) and not challenging (in the case of the defendant) the so-called presumption of similarity between foreign and forum law. It is unclear whether, otherwise, a choice of law agreement is effective to displace the general tort choice of law rule.

Assuming for the sake of the argument that it were possible for the parties to choose the law to determine their tortious rights and liabilities, the next issue is one of construction: whether a particular choice of law agreement applies to non-contractual claims. There is no direct authority on this point either. In the context of the material scope of arbitration and jurisdiction clauses, this issue has been developed in detail. Australian courts generally take a liberal approach to the construction of the material scope of arbitration and jurisdiction clauses.[143] The consequence is that jurisdiction clauses are usually treated as applying to non-contractual as well as contractual claims, if that is consistent with the wording of the clause. Tort and statutory claims may be comprehended by arbitration or exclusive jurisdiction clauses which refer to claims 'in connection with',[144] and 'arising out of'[145] the contract. The main justification for applying a liberal construction is that it is said to be consistent with the presumed intentions of commercial parties that they would not intend the inconvenience and expense of engaging in dispute resolution of the same underlying dispute in multiple venues.[146] This justification is inapplicable in the context of choice of law; if different claims were governed by different laws, this would not require the parties to litigate in different forums. A liberal approach to the interpretation of the material scope of choice of law agreements would require a different justification to that which is used in the context of choice of court agreements.[147]

[142] Australian courts will not apply the presumption of similarity if the foreign law is evidently substantively dissimilar to Australian law: *Damberg v Damberg* [2001] NSWCA 87, (2001) 52 NSWLR 492 (in which case the New South Wales Court of Appeal rejected the parties' actual agreement that the German law of capital gains tax was the same as the Australian law). However, a majority of the High Court applied the presumption in *Neilson v Overseas Projects Corporation of Victoria*, holding that it could be presumed that the Chinese law of statutory interpretation was the same as the Australian law: [2005] HCA 54, (2005) 223 CLR 331. For discussion, see M Keyes, 'Foreign Law in Australian International Litigation: Developing the Common Law' in Y Nishitani (ed), *Treatment of Foreign Law: Dynamics Towards Convergence* (Cham, Springer, 2017) 516–18.

[143] Text to n 39 above.

[144] *Global Partners Fund Ltd v Babcock & Brown Ltd (in liq)* (n 39) [56].

[145] *Comandate Marine Corporation v Pan Australia Shipping Pty Ltd* [2006] FCAFC 192, (2006) 157 FCR 45.

[146] *Francis Travel Marketing Pty Ltd v Virgin Atlantic Airways Ltd* (1996) 39 NSWLR 160, 165; *Comandate Marine Corporation v Pan Australia Shipping Pty Ltd* (n 145) [165]; *Global Partners Fund Ltd v Babcock & Brown Ltd (in liq)* (n 39) [60]–[67].

[147] In *Trafigura Beheer BV v Kookmin Bank Co*, Aikens J suggest that 'when the law governing all the contractual relationships between relevant parties concerned with the sale contract and its financing is English law, it would seem bizarre to hold that the applicable law to determine issues arising in relation to Kookmin's tort claim against Trafigura should be the law of another country, *viz* Singapore': [2006] 2 Lloyd's Rep 455, [113]; he repeats the point at [118]. Briggs argues that the parties' express choice of law should be applied 'as part of their agreement for the resolution of disputes, without noticing whether

In addition to tort claims, both commercial and non-commercial parties often raise statutory claims in cross-border litigation, particularly for breach of the statutory prohibition of misleading or deceptive conduct under Australian legislation.[148] At the choice of law stage, such claims are usually treated as having a *sui generis* character; they are usually not subjected to either the contract or tort choice of law rules.[149] As noted above, Australian courts tend to apply forum legislation, if it is applicable according to its terms (explicitly or by implication), without reference to choice of law.[150]

The common law approach, which prevails in Australia, is not to differentiate consumer from commercial contracts, whether in the domestic or international context. Whether choice of law agreements contained in suppliers' standard form terms should be enforced with the same vigour as those in commercial contracts is a question that has received very little attention in Australia. It is rare for consumers and employees to litigate international disputes, but when they do, Australian courts are likely to apply protective Australian legislation without reference to the normal choice of law analysis.[151] In most Australian cases involving jurisdiction clauses in consumer contracts, the Australian courts have explicitly or implicitly taken the view that such clauses should not be as strictly enforced as in the commercial context.[152] The effect of any choice of law clauses, the efficacy of which does not depend on the exercise of discretion, is rarely addressed. Some statutes, including the Insurance Contracts Act, make it clear that any express choice of law is ineffective in excluding the application of that legislation.[153] Similarly, the consumer guarantees in the Australian Consumer Law cannot be excluded by an express choice of foreign law.[154] However, the cases are inconsistent, and in

the claim is contractual, tortious, based on unjust enrichment, or something else': *Agreements on Jurisdiction and Choice of Law* (Oxford, Oxford University Press 2008) 387. For a contrary view, see J Harris, 'Agreements on Jurisdiction and Choice of Law: Where Next?' [2009] *Lloyd's Maritime and Commercial Law Quarterly* 537, 551–52.

[148] Section 18(1) of the Australian Consumer Law prohibits 'a person, in trade or commerce' from engaging in conduct which is misleading or deceptive, or is likely to mislead or deceive. Claims under s 18(1) are a common feature of international commercial litigation in Australia. Consumers might claim for breaches of the statutory consumer guarantees contained in the Australian consumer law, which, inter alia, include guarantees that use the negligence standard. eg s 60 creates a guarantee that the provider of services to consumer will render those services with due care and skill. This raises the prospect of a three-way concurrence of liability between contract, tort and statute. In *Insight Vacations Pty Ltd v Young* [2011] HCA 16, (2011) 243 CLR 149, an Australian consumer who was injured in a road accident in Slovakia claimed against a tour provider for breach of s 74(1) of the Trade Practices Act 1974 (Cth), the predecessor provision to s 60 of the Australian Consumer Law 2010. The fact that the plaintiff had identical claims in contract and tort was not raised or addressed.

[149] Although some Australian legislation uses the default contract choice of law rule as the criterion of application of the legislation, eg Insurance Contracts Act 1984 (Cth) s 8(1).

[150] See text to nn 117–18 above.

[151] *Insight Vacations Pty Ltd v Young* (n 148); *Quinlan v Safe International Försäkrings AB* (n 52); *Old UGC, Inc v Industrial Relations Commission of NSW* (2006) 225 CLR 274.

[152] See in particular *Quinlan v Safe International Försäkrings AB* (n 52) [46]. *Cf Gonzalez v Agoda Company Pte Ltd* (n 59).

[153] Insurance Contracts Act 1984 (Cth) s 8.

[154] *Valve Corporation v Australian Competition and Consumer Commission* [2017] FCAFC 224, (2017) 351 ALR 584.

*Gonzalez v Agoda Company Pte Ltd*, Button J stated that he accepted 'that the law of the contract is that of Singapore, whether one arrives at that destination by way of the exclusive jurisdiction clause',[155] or by application of the default choice of law rule.[156] In justifying his conclusion that the objective proper law of the contract was Singapore, one of the factors to which Button J referred was that the terms of Agoda's contract with Ms Gonzalez 'were a standard form intended to apply to contracts which may be formed with individuals in a multiplicity of jurisdictions, given Agoda's business'.[157] Given that standard form terms used by foreign suppliers of goods and services in their dealings with Australian consumers almost invariably include express choices of foreign law, the effect of such choices seems only likely to become more important in practice.

## B. Using the Hague Principles to Reform Australian Law?

The Preamble to the Hague Principles on Choice of Law in International Commercial Contracts (the Hague Principles) states that they may be used for three purposes: first, 'as a model for national, regional, supranational or international instruments', second, 'to interpret, supplement and develop rules of private international law', and third, by courts.[158] The official Commentary elaborates that 'The Principles can be seen both as an illustration of how a comprehensive choice of law regime for giving effect to party autonomy may be constructed and as a guide to "best practices" in establishing and refining such a regime'.[159] The Commentary states that the instrument is not 'a model law that States are encouraged to enact';[160] instead, the Hague Conference encourages states to 'incorporate' the Principles 'into their domestic choice of law regimes in a manner appropriate for the circumstances of each State'.[161] It is envisaged that the Principles might be enacted either in whole or in part, by way of reform to national law.[162] While using the Principles in part only seems the most sensible approach from an Australian perspective, it is not completely compatible with the idea that the Principles will advance international harmonisation.[163]

[155] His reference to the exclusive jurisdiction clause was presumably intended as a reference also to the express choice of Singaporean law.

[156] [2017] NSWSC 1133, [128].

[157] ibid.

[158] It also states that they may be applied by arbitral tribunals, but arbitration is beyond the scope of this chapter.

[159] Hague Conference on Private International Law, *Commentary on the Principles on Choice of Law in International Commercial Contracts* (The Hague, 2013) para 1.5 (Hague Conference, *Commentary*).

[160] See likewise D Girsberger and N Cohen, 'Key Features of the Hague Principles on Choice of Law in International Commercial Contracts' (2017) 22 *Uniform Law Review* 316, 318.

[161] Hague Conference, *Commentary* (n 159) [1.8].

[162] ibid [1.20].

[163] Girsberger and Cohen, 'Key Features' (n 160) suggest (at 318) that the adoption of the Principles may achieve 'substantive harmonization' among the states that adopt them.

The Principles at a general level are similar to the current Australian contract choice of law rule relating to the subjective governing law. In addition, the Principles deal explicitly with some issues that are uncertain or not determined in the current Australian law; some of the relevant provisions either improve on the Australian law in some way, or would at least not be objectionable, in the sense that they are consistent with current principles and their underlying policies. However, some of the Principles are incompatible with Australian choice of law theory, principle, or policy, and should not be adopted in Australia without a thorough consideration of whether their adoption is necessary or desirable, and the broader consequences of adopting them. Moreover, the Principles are not comprehensive; they apply only to international commercial contracts, and they contain several references to the law of the forum.[164] Adopting them without careful consideration risks creating inconsistency between the Australian choice of law rule for international commercial contracts on the one hand, and the choice of law rule for all other cross-border contracts (international non-commercial, and all intranational contracts) on the other.

There would be some clear benefits in adopting the Principles, not least of which is that the effect of doing so would make the law more accessible to non-experts, including laypeople, foreign lawyers, and Australian lawyers who are not specialist in private international law. As noted above, identifying the common law choice of law rule, and particularly the limits to its application, can be challenging.

Like the current Australian law, the Principles recognise the parties' freedom to choose the governing law of the contract,[165] and their ability to vary the governing law.[166] The Principles, like the Australian law, do not require that the chosen law be connected to the parties or the contract,[167] and do not impose any formal requirements.[168]

If the parties' choice is not expressed, the Hague Principles state that the choice must 'appear clearly from the provisions of the contract or the circumstances'.[169] There is no such explicit requirement under the current Australian law. In 1992, the Australian Law Reform Commission recommended that a similar limitation should be adopted in Australian law.[170] Because the issue of an actual, unexpressed, choice of law is rarely litigated, there is no pressing case for such a change to the choice of law rule, although it is not objectionable.

The Principles bluntly state that an express choice of court or arbitration 'is not in itself equivalent to a choice of law'.[171] This is not dissimilar to the Australian

[164] Hague Principles, arts 3, 11(1), 11(2), 11(3), 11(4).
[165] ibid, art 2(1).
[166] ibid, art 2(3); *Busst v Lotsirb Nominees Pty Ltd* (n 125) 479.
[167] ibid, art 2(4).
[168] ibid, art 5.
[169] Hague Principles, art 4.
[170] The Australian Law Reform Commission recommended that there should be a requirement that any choice should be 'clearly inferred from the circumstances': (n 104) [8.9].
[171] Hague Principles, art 4.

law, but in Australian law, it is clear that a choice of court or arbitration may be a significant factor in establishing an actual, unexpressed, choice of law.[172] In comparison, the Principles give no guidance as to the weight to be attributed to this factor.[173]

As noted above, there are conflicting Australian authorities on some aspects of contract choice of law. In parts, the Principles are more definitive than the Australian law, and their adoption would improve the certainty of the law. For example, the Principles provide that 'A choice of law does not refer to rules of private international law of the law chosen by the parties unless the parties expressly provide otherwise'.[174] Assuming that this is not inconsistent with the policy of Australian choice of law,[175] making it clear that a choice of foreign law should be interpreted as a choice of the foreign internal law would be a welcome clarification to the Australian law. The Principles recognise that the parties can select different laws to apply to different parts of the contract;[176] an issue on which there is conflicting Australian authority.[177] There seems no strong reason in principle why the parties should not be permitted to do so expressly.[178]

The Principles address some issues on which there is no Australian authority, and the solutions provided by the Principles are unobjectionable. For example, the Principles state that 'A choice of law cannot be contested solely on the ground that the contract to which it applies is not valid'.[179] The doctrine of severability applies in Australia in the context of choice of court agreements;[180] it would be consistent to adopt this doctrine in the context of choice of law,[181] particularly because choice of court and choice of law clauses are usually set out in the same contractual provision.

[172] As noted above at n 100, in *John Kaldor Fabricmaker*, a choice of law was inferred on the basis of an arbitration agreement alone: (1989) 19 NSWLR 172.

[173] Girsberger and Cohen (n 160) assert (at 323) that 'a choice of the law of a state as the governing law of the contract will not be inferred solely from an agreement between the parties agreeing to confer jurisdiction on a court or arbitral tribunal in that State'.

[174] The Principles provide that 'A choice of law does not refer to rules of private international law of the law chosen by the parties unless the parties expressly provide otherwise': art 8.

[175] The justifications given by members of the majority in *Neilson v Overseas Projects Corporation of Victoria Ltd* (n 22) in favour of applying the foreign choice of law rule are not confined to tort choice of law, suggesting that they may have broader application: see Keyes (n 127) 30–32.

[176] Hague Principles, art 2.2(b).

[177] Above, text to nn 124–25.

[178] See likewise Douglas and Loadsman, 'The Impact of the *Hague Principles on Choice of Law in International Commercial Contracts*' (n 5) 8–9.

[179] Hague Principles, art 7.

[180] *FAI General Insurance Co Ltd v Ocean Marine Mutual Protection and Indemnity Association* (1997) 41 NSWLR 559, 567.

[181] The doctrine of severability is not universally admired. Symeonides describes it as 'bad policy', both in the context of arbitration and choice of law: SC Symeonides 'The Hague Principles on Choice of Law for International Contracts: Some Preliminary Comments' (2013) 61 *American Journal of Comparative Law* 873, 891. Douglas and Loadsman suggest that, because choice of law agreements are not promissory in nature (according to the analysis of Brereton J in *ACE Insurance Ltd v Moose Enterprise Pty Ltd* (n 34) [51]), they are not severable agreements in the same way that jurisdiction agreements are: (n 5) text to nn 97–99.

On the other hand, some aspects of the Principles are inconsistent with the current Australian law, and do not clearly improve on the current law. Most prominently art 6, which addresses the applicable law for the issue of whether 'the parties have agreed to a choice of law', is not consistent with the current Australian law. Article 6(1)(a) provides that 'whether the parties have agreed to a choice of law is determined by the law that was purportedly agreed to'.[182] In Australia, the related issue of whether the parties have agreed to a choice of court or arbitration is determined by the law of the forum.[183] As Beach J noted:

> it is counter-intuitive to suggest that the choice of law to assess consensus ad idem should be that set out in an agreement that an entity says it is not a party to because there was no consensus ad idem. That would be to assume what was to be proved.[184]

Whether the solution proposed by the Hague Principles is superior to this view is a matter that should be debated;[185] art 6(1)(a) is one of several provisions which requires careful consideration before adoption in Australia.

The simplicity of art 6(1)(a) of the Principles is undermined by the two remaining provisions of art 6. Article 6(1)(b) addresses the battle of the forms. This provision is even less readily reconciled with the current Australian law than art 6(1)(a). Article 6(1)(b) awkwardly stipulates that

> if the parties have used standard terms designating two different laws and under both of these laws the same standard terms prevail, the law designated in the prevailing terms applies; if under these laws different standard terms prevail, or if under one or both of these laws no standard terms prevail, there is no choice of law.

This provision is not only complicated in expression, but its assumption that the parties could somehow be putatively bound by two potentially conflicting choice of law terms (and indeed by two different sets of standard terms) is incompatible with Australian law (assuming, as noted above, that the law of the forum applies to determine whether there is a consensus), under which the transaction must be analysed to identify which of the two sets of standard terms, or the relevant provisions thereof, represented the parties' final consensus;[186] an approach which seems no less consistent with the Principles' underlying commitment to autonomy than the complicated solution contained in art 6(1)(b). Rather ironically, the result of application of this provision may well be that 'there is no choice of law', leaving the

[182] Hague Principles, art 6(1)(a). This seems potentially inconsistent with art 5, stipulating that 'A choice of law is not subject to any requirement as to form unless otherwise agreed by the parties'.

[183] n 20 above.

[184] *Trina Solar v Jasmin Solar* (n 20) [130]. See likewise TM Yeo, 'Choice of Law for Contracts: The Hague Principles from a Singaporean and Asian Perspective', 10th Yong Pung How Professorship of Law Lecture, 18 May 2017, [25].

[185] See Douglas and Loadsman (n 5) text to fn 92. The popularity of the solution in the Hague Principles is reflected in, or perhaps in part due to, its acceptance in the European Union: see Regulation (EC) No 593/2008 of the European Parliament and of the Council of 17 June 2008 on the law applicable to contractual obligations OJ L 177/6 (Rome I Regulation) arts 3(5) and 10(1).

[186] *Maxitherm Boilers Pty Ltd v Pacific Dunlop Insurances Pte Ltd* [1998] 4 VR 559.

parties to the vagaries of the potentially applicable default contract choice of law rules, which are not addressed in the Principles and therefore must be supplied by forum law.[187] This solution seems extraordinary, given that the motivation for the provision is to ameliorate the inconsistency in national laws regarding the battle of the forms, 'to promote party autonomy...and...to enhance legal certainty and foreseeability'.[188] This provision achieves none of these things and does not recommend itself for adoption in Australia. It is inconsistent with both the Principles' and the Australian law's commitment to identifying and upholding the parties' actual agreement.[189] This also appears to be a non-problem in practice;[190] there are no Australian cases raising this issue.

Article 6(2) provides an exception to the operation of the two subsections of art 6(1), stating that

> The law of the State in which a party has its establishment determines whether that party has consented to the choice of law if, under the circumstances, it would not be reasonable to make that determination under the law specified in paragraph 1.

The provision is clearly based, like many others in the Principles, on the European Union's Rome I Regulation. Article 10(2) of the Rome I Regulation provides, far more clearly than art 6(2) of the Principles, that a party can invoke the law of the state of its habitual residence to establish a lack of consent 'if it appears from the circumstances that it would not be reasonable to determine the effect of his conduct in accordance with' the general principle established in art 10(1) of the Rome I Regulation, which is that the existence and validity of a contract is determined according to the putative proper law. Whatever the merits of that provision in the European Union context, it is difficult to see in the Australian context why the law of the habitual residence of either party (or both, for that matter), should have a role in determining the existence or validity of a contract between commercial parties.

The scope of the chosen law, dealt with in art 9, is generally similar to the current Australian law, although the statement that the chosen law applies to 'pre-contractual obligations' is inconsistent with Australian law, because it would apply to tortious misrepresentation and the statutory claim for misleading conduct. Neither of these types of claim is currently subjected to the proper law of the contract, and it is not clearly consistent with the policy of the current Australian choice of law to subject such claims to the proper law of the contract. This is certainly something that requires consideration, especially for commercial contracts.

[187] See further below, text to nn 200–03.

[188] TK Graziano, 'Solving the Riddle of Conflicting Choice of Law Clauses in Battle of Forms Situations: The Hague Solution' (2012–13) 14 *Yearbook of Private International Law* 71, 100.

[189] *Cf* Yeo, 'Choice of Law for Contracts' (n 184) [34] (suggesting that 'the practical way in which [art 6(1)(b)] cuts through the morass of competing choice of law clauses in the battle of forms situation provides a pragmatic approach that is worth considering for the common law').

[190] The author of this provision acknowledges that cases on the battle of the forms in the context of choice of law terms are 'rare': Graziano, 'Solving the Riddle' (n 188) 87 and 99.

Article 11 of the Principles deals with the circumstances in which the parties' chosen law might not be applied, in favour of 'overriding mandatory rules and public policy', whether of the forum or of a foreign state. Two of the subsections address the operation of mandatory rules,[191] and two deal with public policy.[192] Article 11(1) states that 'The Principles shall not prevent a court from applying overriding mandatory provisions of the law of the forum which apply irrespective of the law chosen by the parties'. The thrust of this provision is not dissimilar to the current Australian law, but its interpretation will not be straightforward, because Australian laws tend not to be expressed by reference to whether they are applicable notwithstanding an express choice of foreign law.[193]

Article 11(2) addresses foreign mandatory laws, and states that 'The law of the forum determines when a court may or must apply or take into account overriding mandatory provisions of another law'. Currently, under Australian law, foreign law is only ever applied if it is the governing law;[194] in which case foreign mandatory provisions are not given any special consideration. Enacting this provision therefore would be potentially confusing, unless it is separately intended that Australian law should be developed so as to give separate effect to overriding mandatory provisions of foreign law in some situations.

Article 11(3) stipulates that

> A court may exclude application of a provision of the law chosen by the parties only if and to the extent that the result of such application would be manifestly incompatible with fundamental notions of public policy (*ordre public*) of the forum.

This restates the general exception available under Australian choice of law rules to exclude application of foreign law on the basis of its incompatibility with Australian public policy.

Article 11(4) states that forum law 'determines when a court may or must apply or take into account the public policy (*ordre public*) of a State the law of which would be applicable in the absence of a choice of law'. Australian legislation and cases sometimes justify giving the public policy of the forum an overriding effect on the basis that forum law has the closest connection to the contract,[195] but it would modify Australian law to extend this to safeguard the public policy of

[191] Hague Principles, art 11(1) and (2).

[192] ibid, art 11(3) and (4). A fifth subsection (art 11(5)) deals with the operation of mandatory rules and public policy in arbitration, which is beyond the scope of this chapter.

[193] But see the Carriage of Goods by Sea Act 1991 (Cth) s 11(2), and Insurance Contracts Act 1984 (Cth) s 8(2).

[194] *Akai Pty Ltd v The People's Insurance Company Ltd* (n 31) 442. The Australian Law Reform Commission's recommendation in 1992 that mandatory rules of the objective proper law should be applied has not been acted upon: (n 104) 93.

[195] In *Golden Acres Ltd v Queensland Estates Pty Ltd*, Hoare J considered that forum law was the objective proper law of the contract, and for that reason investigated the bona fides of the parties' choice of foreign law: [1969] Qd R 378. The objective proper law is also used as a criterion of application of some Australian legislation: eg Insurance Contracts Act 1984 (Cth) s 8; Australian Consumer Law 2010, s 67(a).

another country which is currently only ever applied if it is the law of the cause.[196] Again, enacting art 11(4) would be potentially confusing without modifying the Australian law.

Article 3 of the Principles has attracted significant controversy.[197] It permits the parties to choose 'rules of law that are generally accepted on an international, supranational or regional level as a neutral and balanced set of rules'.[198] Enacting such a principle is less controversial than it might first appear for countries like Australia which do not allow the choice of non-state law, because art 3 also states that the parties' ability to choose non-state law is subject to whether this is permitted under forum law.[199] However, given that Australian law does not permit such a choice, it would not make sense to enact art 3; it would be confusing to do so unless it is separately proposed that Australian law should be changed to enable a choice of non-state law.

## C. Issues not Addressed by the Hague Principles

The major problem that has been identified with the Australian contract choice of law rule lies not in the primary rule, giving effect to the parties' agreement, but in the default rule, requiring the identification of the legal system with which the contract has its closest and most real connection. This rule has been widely criticised.[200] In *Australian Competition and Consumer Commission v Valve (No 3)*, Edelman J observed that 'Whilst the language of "closest and most real connection" trips off the tongue, the underlying concept is far from clear'.[201]

Factors that are considered in identifying the objective proper law include the places where the contract was made and performed, the parties' places of residence or business and the 'nature and subject-matter of the contract'.[202] As Justice Edelman noted in *Australian Competition and Consumer Commission v Valve (No 3)*, a difficulty with this rule

> is that different factors will often point in different directions. Some of those factors are said to be of little weight. Some are said to be of substantial weight. But without a governing principle it is difficult to determine why some matters are more important for a close connection than others.[203]

[196] This would be consistent with a recommendation of the Australian Law Reform Commission in its *Choice of Law Report*: (n 104) 93.

[197] Symeonides, 'The Hague Principles on Choice of Law for International Contracts' (n 181) 892–94.

[198] Hague Principles, art 3.

[199] ibid, art 3.

[200] Australian Law Reform Commission (n 104) 94; Davies et al (n 96) 453–56; EI Sykes and MC Pryles, *Australian Private International Law*, 3rd edn (Sydney, Law Book, 1991) 611.

[201] *Australian Competition and Consumer Commission v Valve (No 3)* (n 113) 661.

[202] *Akai Pty Ltd v The People's Insurance Company Ltd* (n 31) 437.

[203] *Australian Competition and Consumer Commission v Valve (No 3)* (n 113) [65].

It is especially interesting that the High Court has repeatedly rejected the objective proper law in the context of reforms to tort choice of law, in which context it is often referred to as the flexible exception, on the basis that it is too uncertain and unpredictable.[204] The same concerns are even more salient in the context of contract choice of law.

The Hague Principles briefly refer to,[205] but do not address,[206] the default contract choice of law rule.[207] They provide no explicit guidance in terms of how the problems with the Australian default choice of law rule for contract could be addressed, to ensure compatibility of the default rule with the primary rule established in the Principles. Given the influence of the European Union's Rome I Regulation on the Hague Principles, it would make sense to at least consider the default rules in the Rome I Regulation in any reform to the common law rule.[208] It would certainly seem odd to reform only that part of the choice of law rule which is relatively functional, and to ignore that part which has attracted fairly universal criticism.

Like the Choice of Court Convention, the Principles only apply to international contracts,[209] and do not apply to consumer or employment contracts.[210] The exclusion of intra-national and consumer and employment contracts creates an inference that the Principles are inappropriate to those types of agreements, but implies nothing further about why they are inappropriate, and therefore, what factors are relevant in developing an appropriate choice of law rule for contracts of those kinds. Again, the European Union's influence is clear; in the Rome I Regulation, explicit provision is made for contract choice of law for consumer and employment contracts, which differs from the choice of law rules otherwise

[204] *John Pfeiffer Pty Ltd v Rogerson* (n 137); *Regie Nationale des Usines Renault SA v Zhang* (2002) 210 CLR 491, 520; *Neilson v Overseas Projects Corporation of Victoria Ltd* (n 22) [34], [64], [91], [93].

[205] The reference to the default choice of law rule is found in the Hague Principles, art 11(4), stating that the 'law of the forum determines when a court may or must apply or take into account the public policy (ordre public) of a State *the law of which would be applicable in the absence of a choice of law*' (emphasis added).

[206] The Commentary states that there are two reasons for this: first, because 'the goal of the Principles is to further party autonomy rather than provide a comprehensive body of principles for determining the law applicable to international commercial contracts', and secondly, because of a lack of consensus on the default rule: (n 159) 25.

[207] The reference to the default choice of law rule is found in the Hague Principles, art 11(4), stating that the 'law of the forum determines when a court may or must apply or take into account the public policy (ordre public) of a State *the law of which would be applicable in the absence of a choice of law*' (emphasis added).

[208] In 1992, the Australian Law Reform Commission (n 104) recommended that the Australian Government should enact choice of law legislation, including choice of law rules for contract, which were based on the Rome Convention, the predecessor to the Rome I Regulation. In particular, it recommended (ibid [8.48]) adoption of the characteristic performance presumption.

[209] Hague Principles, art 1(1).

[210] ibid, art 1(1). The definition of 'international' is found in art 1(2). Like the Hague Convention, the Principles contain a list of exclusions from its scope in addition to the exclusion of consumer and employment contracts.

applicable.[211] Given the frequency with which Australian consumers now acquire goods and services from foreign suppliers, according to standard terms that typically choose foreign law as the governing law, reform to the Australian law making clear the status of express choice of law, as well as of court, agreements in international consumer contracts should be regarded as a priority.

Rather inconsistently with the Principles' emphasis that they apply to international cases only, the Commentary to the Principles asserts their suitability for intra-national contracts.[212] The concerns with the operation of the Principles mentioned above would apply also in the intra-national context. But if contract choice of law for international contracts is to be reformed, then choice of law for intra-national contracts should also be reviewed. If the proposed International Civil Law Act only dealt with contract choice of law in international cases, the result would be to create another, non-identical, scheme of contract choice of law. This would be a regrettable outcome.

## IV. Conclusion

There have been many calls for reform to the Australian laws relating to the effect of choice of court and choice of law agreements, from academics,[213] judges[214] and the Australian Law Reform Commission.[215] Since the 1970s, instruments developed under the auspices of the Hague Conference on Private International Law have been a primary source of the development of Australian private international law, although so far these have had limited impact in the area of commercial private international law.

Australia's proposed accession to the Hague Choice of Courts Convention is unremarkable for three reasons. First, the treatment of choice of court agreements under existing laws is at least generally consistent with their treatment under the Convention. Second, the Trans-Tasman Proceedings Act has already given effect to key provisions of the Convention. Third, Australia has since 1975 been a party to the United Nations Convention on the Recognition and Enforcement of Foreign Arbitral Awards 1958 (the New York Convention), which inspired the Choice of Court Convention.[216] In Australia, arbitration and foreign exclusive choice of

[211] Rome I Regulation, art 6 (consumer contracts), art 8 (individual employment contracts). The Rome I Regulation also includes protective provisions for insurance contracts.

[212] Hague Conference, *Commentary* (n 159) [1.22].

[213] eg A Dickinson, 'The Future of Private International Law in Australia' (2012) 19 *Australian International Law Journal* 1, 5 ('The common law rules governing the law applicable to contractual obligations seem…in the character of a pre-fabricated bungalow, full of character but ripe for renovation or rebuilding').

[214] eg *Australian Competition and Consumer Commission v Valve (No 3)* (n 113) [65] (Edelman J).

[215] Australian Law Reform Commission (n 104) ch 8. The Commission recommended implementation of the Choice of Law Report again in 2001, in *The Judicial Power of the Commonwealth: A Review of the* Judiciary Act 1903 *and Related Legislation*, Report No 92 (Commonwealth of Australia, 2001) 39.

[216] Hartley and Dogauchi (n 19) 791.

court agreements are already treated as legally cognate;[217] extending the strong protection of arbitration agreements to commercial choice of court agreements makes good sense. The most significant concern with acceding to this Convention is that it risks further complicating an already complex area, by adding yet another, inconsistent, scheme to the mix.

Adopting the Hague Principles on Choice of Law in International Commercial Contracts would not necessarily be the best solution to the problems that have been identified with the Australian contract choice of law rule. Australian law already admits a large role for party autonomy in choice of law for contract, although there remain aspects of the choice of law rule that are unclear or undetermined. This, however, only highlights that contract choice of law is rarely litigated in Australia, which suggests that there is no pressing need for reform to the rules relating to the subjective proper law of the contract. While some provisions of the Principles are compatible with the Australian law, and some would certainly improve on aspects of it, other provisions of the Principles are incompatible with the current Australian law, which have not been influenced by the European Union legislation on which the Principles are based. If the Principles are to be used to reform the Australian law, I have suggested that this should only be done in part,[218] and that adopting some of the Principles may require modification of the underlying law.

Nonetheless, the proposal to adopt the Hague Choice of Court Convention and the Hague Principles on Choice of Law in International Commercial Contracts presents a welcome opportunity to reflect on Australian private international law, particularly those rules of greatest relevance to international commercial parties, and especially, to do so by reference to instruments reflecting current international consensus. This process of evaluating the current law also calls attention to problems with the Australian law that will not be rectified by acceding to the Convention or adoption of the Principles. An important change that can be achieved by the enactment of legislation based on the Convention and the Principles is that the relevant law will be expressed in legislation, which will improve its accessibility and certainty.

[217] *Global Partners Fund Ltd v Babcock & Brown Ltd (in liq)* (n 39) [60].

[218] The Preamble to the Principles states that the Principles may be used to 'supplement and develop rules of private international law', and the Commentary notes that the Hague Conference encourages states to incorporate the principles 'in a manner appropriate for the circumstances of each State', as noted above at text to nn 161–62.

# PART V

# Concluding Remarks

# 13

# Conclusion

JUSTICE PAUL LE GAY BRERETON, AM, RFD

## I. Introduction

In these closing observations, I propose to address a number of issues which have been touched on in earlier chapters, and in particular:

- in connection with jurisdiction, the new harmonised rules for service out of the jurisdiction;
- in connection with concurrent proceedings, the test for declining jurisdiction, the state of the law of *lis alibi pendens* in Australia, and the Australian approach to 'case management' stays; and
- in connection with evidence and procedure, some observations relating to the use of subpoenas, and the proof of foreign law.

## II. The New Harmonised Rules for Service *Ex Juris*

Professor Dickinson, in his challenging and entertaining chapter, has raised a number of issues, philosophical, substantive and procedural, with the new harmonised 'long-arm' service rules, and I will address some of them.[1] Like Professor Dickinson I will use the NSW rules as the vehicle for the discussion. However, I am not aware of any opposition to their adoption in any other jurisdiction, least of all the Federal Court, and I expect that it is only a matter of time and priority until they will be more or less universally adopted.[2]

[1] In doing so I should disclose that I am a member of the Harmonisation of Rules Committee, and of its working group which drafted the new rules.

[2] The harmonised rules have been implemented in the Australian Capital Territory (pt 5.8, div 6.8.9 of the Court Procedure Rules 2006 (ACT), with effect from 8 July 2017, by r 27 of the Court Procedures Amendment Rules 2017 (No 3) (ACT)); New South Wales (pt 11, div 1A of the Uniform Civil Procedure Rules 2005 (NSW), with effect from 9 December 2016, by sch 1 [2] of the Uniform Civil Procedure (Amendment No 83) Rule 2016 (NSW)); South Australia (ch 3, pt 4, div 2 of the Supreme Court Civil Rules 2006 (SA), with effect from 1 September 2016, by the Supreme Court Civil Rules 2006 (Amendment No 32), as subsequently amended with effect from 1 October 2016 by the Supreme Court

As Professor Dickinson has observed, the harmonised rules provide for service *ex juris* without leave in defined categories of case,[3] and service with prior leave in other cases.[4] The defined categories in which prior leave is not required, though they include some novelties, are broadly consistent with the traditional categories in which service *ex juris* has been permitted, though somewhat enlarged. Notably, each of them requires a nexus with Australia beyond a mere personal connecting factor for the plaintiff.

The provision for service with leave in cases outside the traditional and defined categories provides flexibility, to address cases of a kind which have not yet been contemplated. However, the rules[5] stipulate that the court may grant leave only if satisfied that (a) the claim has a real and substantial connection with Australia; (b) Australia is an appropriate forum for the trial, and (c) in all the circumstances the court should assume jurisdiction – that is, that it is appropriate to assert jurisdiction in relation to the claim. It may be anticipated that the content of the concept of 'real and substantial connection with Australia' will develop by analogy with the established categories, and that something more than a plaintiff's personal connecting factor with Australia will be required to satisfy it.

The philosophical point was that delegated legislation in the form of judge-made rules is an inappropriate instrument for the definition of the jurisdiction of a court. Philosophically, there may be much to be said for that position, and although there is attraction in Rares J's observation, in the course of his intervention, that arguably, absent such rules, there would be no constraint on the service of process abroad, and that the effect of the rules is to impose limitations on service of process out of the territorial jurisdiction which do not apply to service within it, I doubt it: the conventional position is that the writ of the court runs only within its territorial jurisdiction, and that to be amenable to the command of the writ, the defendant must be present within the jurisdiction.[6] However, the practice of service *ex juris* being authorised and regulated by rules of court is, as Professor Dickinson's chapter shows, well-established and entrenched, in England and Wales as well as in Australia, and there is no indication of this being a cause of mischief. The validity of such rules has been upheld.[7] So while there may be a philosophical objection, I doubt that there is any legal or practical problem.

Civil Rules 2006 (Amendment No 33)); and Victoria (ord 7, pt 1 of the Supreme Court (General Civil Procedure) Rules 2015 (Vic), with effect from 1 October 2016, by r 5 of the Supreme Court (Service Out of Australia Amendment) Rules 2016 (Vic)). It is understood that it is intended that the harmonised rules will be implemented in the Federal Court of Australia when the Federal Court Rules 2011 (Cth) are next amended. The harmonised rules have not yet been implemented in ord 7, pt 1 of the Supreme Court Rules (NT); ch 4, pt 7, div 1 of the Uniform Civil Procedure Rules 1999 (Qld); ord 10 of the Rules of the Supreme Court 1971 (WA); or pt 7, div 10 of the Supreme Court Rules 2000 (Tas).

[3] Uniform Civil Procedure Rules 2005 (NSW) (UCPR) sch 6.

[4] UCPR, r 11.5.

[5] UCPR, r 11.5(5).

[6] *Laurie v Carroll* (1958) 98 CLR 310, 323.

[7] *Ashbury v Ellis* [1893] AC 339 (NZ rule authorising service *ex juris* in an action founded on a contract made or to be performed in New Zealand upheld); *Flaherty v Girgis* (1985) 4 NSWLR 248 (NSWCA) (NSW rule allowing service *ex juris* in respect of a claim in tort in respect of damage suffered in NSW upheld); see also *Mobil Oil Australia Pty Ltd v State of Victoria* (2002) 211 CLR 1.

In terms of procedure, it may be accepted that the harmonised rules were the initiative of the Council of Chief Justices and its Harmonisation of Rules Committee, which are not statutory bodies. However, in New South Wales the rule-making authority was – as will be the case in every jurisdiction – the legally empowered rules committee. I do not see how the circumstance that the formal acts of a duly constituted rule-making authority may be informed by advice or recommendations from what may strictly be an informal source is any objection to the validity or propriety of the process.

It can also be accepted that there was no such extensive public consultation as might be undertaken by a Law Reform Commission. But the creation and amendment of rules of court are rarely subject to public consultation. There was widespread consultation between the courts. The members of the Harmonisation Committee consult their own courts and typically convey a corporate view on behalf of their court to the Committee. Consensus was reached on these rules after such consultation, and not without some compromise – more on matters of drafting than of principle, though there was a debate about *Agar v Hyde*,[8] to which we shall come.

Professor Dickinson raised two substantive matters. The first concerned the evidentiary basis for jurisdiction, where leave to proceed is sought against a foreign defendant who has not entered an appearance.[9] To obtain leave to proceed, the plaintiff must establish (1) proper service of the originating process on the defendant;[10] and (2) that service was authorised – either by prior leave, or under UCPR, sch 6.[11] The requirement is the same, whether service is authorised by prior leave, or without prior leave. The decision not to stipulate that it was necessary, on an application for leave to proceed, to show a 'good arguable case' was a deliberate (and at one stage contentious) one. The committee decided to leave alone *Agar v Hyde*[12] – which holds that the appropriate test is that applicable on a summary disposal application – rather than to seek to reverse it. Thus while there is no express requirement that the court be 'satisfied' that the qualifying conditions for external service have been made out, consistently with *Agar v Hyde* some measure of satisfaction is inherent in the requirement to obtain leave, and the appropriate standard of satisfaction is the same as that required to survive an ordinary application for summary judgment, which requires only demonstration that there is a real

[8] [2000] HCA 41, (2000) 201 CLR 552.

[9] UCPR, r 11.8AA.

[10] *Castagna v Conceria Pell Mec Spa* (NSWCA, Mahoney P, Handley JA and Waddell AJA, 15 March 1996, unreported, BC9601018); *Bulldogs Rugby League Club Ltd v Williams* [2008] NSWSC 822, [30]ff (personal service effected); *Australian Securities and Investments Commission v Sweeney (No 2)* [2001] NSWSC 477, (2001) 38 ASCR 743, [40] (proper service effected by substituted service); *Building Insurers' Guarantee Corporation v Eddie* [2008] NSWSC 195 (proper service effected by substituted service).

[11] *Bank of America v Bank of New York* (1995) ATPR 41-390; *News Corp Ltd v Lenfest Communications Inc* (1996) 21 ACSR 553; *Bulldogs Rugby League Club Ltd v Williams* [2008] NSWSC 822, [31]ff (sufficient evidence of submission to the jurisdiction).

[12] *Agar v Hyde* [2000] HCA 41, (2000) 201 CLR 552 (overruling *Bank of America v Bank of New York* (n 11), in so far as it suggested a requirement that the plaintiff have a 'good arguable case').

issue to be determined. This is entirely appropriate, given the extant authority of the High Court, and also that at the early stage of proceedings at which this question arises, it is desirable that whether or not jurisdiction has been invoked should depend *prima facie* on the record – namely what is asserted in the pleading, rather than on evidence. It remains open to a foreign defendant to challenge jurisdiction under r 11.6, on grounds including that service of the originating process is not authorised by the rules, or that the court is an inappropriate forum, or that the claim has insufficient prospects of success to warrant putting the person served outside Australia to the time, expense and trouble of defending the claim. Such an application may be made without filing an appearance.[13] One feature of modern methods of communication is that this is substantially less onerous an undertaking than it once was.

The second substantive matter concerned the description in the harmonised rules of the relevant nexus as one with Australia, rather than New South Wales. As Professor Dickinson said, this was deliberate – and carefully considered. That is because the Supreme Court of New South Wales – like the Supreme Court of every other State – may, by operation of s 4(3) of the Cross-vesting Acts of every other State, exercise all the civil jurisdiction of each other State Supreme Court.[14] Even if the Cross-vesting Acts deal only with subject-matter and not adjudicatory (or personal) jurisdiction,[15] they do not stand on their own. Service and Execution of Process Act 1992 (Cth) (SEPA), which by s 15 permits the service anywhere in Australia of process issued in any State or Territory, and by s 12 gives such service the same effect as if service were effected in the place of issue – has the effect that the personal jurisdiction of each State Supreme Court also extends throughout territorial Australia. Thus it is the combined effect of the Cross-vesting Acts and SEPA that each State Supreme Court now has nationwide jurisdiction, which is not dependent on any nexus with the State of the particular court – although a party may apply for a transfer of the proceedings to a more appropriate Australian superior court. The rationale of the approach adopted in the harmonised rules is not that the jurisdiction of the other State Supreme Courts to allow service *ex juris* has been cross-vested, but that given that the jurisdiction of each Supreme Court is now Australia-wide (like that of the Federal Court and the Family Court), a connection with Australia is sufficient to enliven that Court's own power to permit service outside Australia. The new harmonised rules therefore reflect a uniform national approach to service *ex juris*, in the light of the national jurisdiction now enjoyed by each State Supreme Court.

[13] UCPR, r 12.11(3).

[14] Jurisdiction of Courts (Cross-vesting) Act 1987 (NSW); Jurisdiction of Courts (Cross-vesting) Act 1987 (Qld); Jurisdiction of Courts (Cross-vesting) Act 1987 (SA); Jurisdiction of Courts (Cross-vesting) Act 1987 (Tas); Jurisdiction of Courts (Cross-vesting) Act 1987 (Vic); Jurisdiction of Courts (Cross-vesting) Act 1987 (WA).

[15] As suggested by *David Syme & Co Ltd v Grey* (1992) 38 FCR 303; *Scott v Northern Territory* (2005) 147 NTR 6, [145]; and *BHP Billiton Ltd v Schultz* (2004) 221 CLR 400, [45]

As the 'long-arm' rules apply only to the Supreme Courts, the circumstance that cross-vesting does not apply to inferior courts is beside the point.

# III. Concurrent Proceedings

Professor Mortenson has addressed the European position in respect of concurrent proceedings, *forum non conveniens* and managerial stays. My comments are directed to the Australian position.

## A. *Forum Non Conveniens*: The Test for Declining Jurisdiction

The harmonised rules provide that the court may (on the defendant's application) decline jurisdiction if inter alia it is an 'inappropriate forum'.[16] This criterion is somewhat less emphatic than the 'clearly inappropriate forum' criterion of the common law *Voth* test.[17] However, the *Voth* principles will continue to inform the approach under the rules, though in a somewhat mitigated form having regard to the difference in emphasis.[18]

This now leaves us with three – and perhaps four – tests: (1) the general law 'clearly inappropriate forum' test in *Voth*; (2) the 'inappropriate forum' test under the harmonised rules; (3) that another court is 'the appropriate court' test in SEPA, s 20(3); which is not necessarily identical to (4) the 'more appropriate forum' test contained in the Cross-vesting legislation, and in the Trans-Tasman Proceedings Act 2010 (Cth).

Is this a problem? In principle, courts should not be able to pick and choose which cases they hear. If the jurisdiction of a court is regularly invoked, then it is the duty of the court to exercise it. Only where its process is abused should that jurisdiction be declined, and the 'clearly inappropriate forum' test reflects that.

On the other hand, in the context of a federal system, or reciprocal arrangements between closely related systems of law, there is something to be said, as a matter of comity, for the 'more appropriate forum' test. That test directs attention to the more *appropriate,* not the more *convenient*, court, and while convenience is undoubtedly an important consideration, it is not determinative; notions of the 'natural forum' often inform what is the 'more appropriate forum'.[19] Thus, in the corporations context, the concept of the 'centre of main interest' used in cross-border insolvency law may assist in identifying a natural forum.

[16] UCPR, r 11.6.

[17] *Voth v Manildra Flour Mills Pty Ltd* (1990) 171 CLR 538, 562–64; *Oceanic Sun Line Special Shipping Co Inc v Fay* (1988) 165 CLR 197, 247; *Hyde v Agar* (1998) 45 NSWLR 487; *Regie National des Usines Renault SA v Zhang* [2002] HCA 10, (2002) 210 CLR 491, [23]–[25].

[18] See *Studorp Ltd v Robinson* [2012] NSWCA 382, [5], [62].

[19] See *BioAg Pty Ltd v Hickey* [2007] NSWSC 296, [7].

## B. *Lis Alibi Pendens*

In *Henry v Henry*,[20] Dawson, Gaudron, McHugh and Gummow JJ said:[21]

> It is prima facie vexatious and oppressive, in the strict sense of those terms, to commence a second or subsequent action in the court of this country if an action is already pending with respect to the matter in issue (66). And although there are cases in which it has been held that it is not prima facie vexatious, in the strict sense of that word, to bring proceedings in different countries (67), the problems which arise if the identical issue or the same controversy is to be litigated in different countries which have jurisdiction with respect to the matter are such, in our view, that prima facie, the continuation of one or the other should be seen as vexatious or oppressive within the *Voth* sense of those words.

In that passage, the High Court referred (in note 67) to cases that had held that it was not *prima facie* vexatious to bring proceedings in different countries.[22] The Court did not refer to *Societe Nationale Industrielle Aerospatiale v Lee Kui Jak*,[23] in which the Privy Council, in a Brunei appeal, had applied *McHenry v Lewis* and *Peruvian Guano.*[24] If, in the second sentence of the passage to which I have referred, the High Court intended to overrule that long line of authority, we would have the curious position that in closely related areas of private international law, the law of Australia departed from that of England in two respects, in different directions: on the one hand, Australia applies the *Voth* 'clearly inappropriate forum' rather than the *Spiliada*[25] 'more appropriate forum' test, so that an Australian court is less likely to decline jurisdiction on *forum non conveniens* grounds; yet on the other, Australia presumes parallel proceedings in different jurisdictions to be vexatious when England does not, so that an Australian court is more likely to stay (or restrain) proceedings on *lis alibi pendens* grounds.

Subsequent to *Henry v Henry*, however, in *CSR Ltd v Cigna Insurance Australia Ltd*,[26] the High Court referred with evident approval to the English authorities, including *Societe Nationale*, which their Honours said emphasised the continuing significance of, inter alia, *Peruvian Guano*:[27]

> In *Societe Aerospatiale*, the Privy Council emphasised that the various cases decided in the nineteenth century with respect of vexation and oppression, including *Peruvian Guano Co v Bockwoldt* (119), have continuing significance for the grant of anti-suit

[20] *Henry v Henry* (1996) 185 CLR 571.

[21] (1996) 185 CLR 571, 591 (citations omitted).

[22] *McHenry v Lewis* (1882) 22 Ch D 397 (CA); *Peruvian Guano Co v Bockwoldt* (1883) 23 Ch D 225 (CA); *Hyman v Helm* (1883) 24 Ch D 531 (CA); *Cohen v Rothfield* [1919] 1 KB 410 (CA); *Ionian Bank Ltd v Couvreur* [1969] 1 WLR 781, [1969] 2 All ER 651 (CA); to which was contrasted *Australian Commercial Research & Development Ltd v ANZ McCaughan Merchant Bank Ltd* [1989] 3 All ER 65.

[23] *Societe Nationale Industrielle Aerospatiale v Lee Kui Jak* [1987] AC 871.

[24] [1987] AC 871, 893–94.

[25] *Spiliada Maritime Corp v Cansulex Ltd* [1987] AC 460.

[26] *CSR Ltd v Cigna Insurance Australia Ltd* [1997] HCA 33, (1997) 189 CLR 345.

[27] [1997] HCA 33, (1997) 189 CLR 345, 393 (citations omitted).

> injunctions (120). Those cases establish that the mere co-existence of proceedings in different countries does not constitute vexation or oppression (121). In particular, *Peruvian Guano* establishes that "double litigation [which] has no other element of oppression than this, that an action is going on simultaneously abroad, which will give other or additional remedies beyond those attainable in [the domestic forum]" (122) does not amount to vexation or oppression.

The cases referred to in note (121) were *McHenry v Lewis*, *Peruvian Guano*, *Hyman v Helm*, *Cohen v Rothfield* and *Ionian Bank Ltd v Couvreur* – the very same authorities that had arguably been overruled in *Henry v Henry*. Their Honours continued:[28]

> More recently, in *Bank of Tokyo Ltd v Karoon* (123), Robert Goff LJ pointed out, correctly, in our view, although without specific reference to underlying equitable principle, that foreign proceedings are to be viewed as vexatious or oppressive only if there is nothing which can be gained by them over and above what may be gained in the local proceedings. On the other hand, they are vexatious or oppressive if there is a complete correspondence between the proceedings or, in terms used in *Carron Iron Co*, if "complete relief" (124) is available in the local proceedings.

In this context, there was no reference to what had been said in *Henry v Henry*, which was in any event *obiter*. Accordingly, to the extent that doubt was cast upon the English line of authority by *Henry*, those authorities have been rehabilitated by *CSR v Cigna*, and in Australia, as in England, it is not *prima facie* vexatious to bring parallel proceedings with respect to the same matter in different countries.

But even if it be assumed that, as *Henry v Henry* might suggest, the Australian position were that where proceedings are brought in two jurisdictions with respect to 'the same matter' or 'the identical issue' or 'the same controversy', the continuation of one or the other is *prima facie* vexatious or oppressive in the *Voth* sense, it would be necessary to note the following matters. First, the High Court used several terms to describe the requisite degree of connection between the proceedings to attract the proposition: the proceedings must involve 'the same matter', 'the identical issue' or 'the same controversy'. Although there is of course a well-established jurisprudence as to what constitutes 'the same matter' or 'a single justiciable controversy' for the purposes of constitutional law – namely a common substratum of fact – it is not clear that it was intended to import that relatively broad concept into this field of discourse. Use of the term 'identical issue' describes a narrower concept. The paragraph from *Henry v Henry* quoted above suggests that it was not considered that a common substratum of fact alone would warrant a permanent stay of proceedings.

This accords with the basis on which the courts would require a plaintiff to elect between two parallel proceedings in different jurisdictions. In *The Mali Ivo*,[29]

[28] ibid, (citations omitted).
[29] *The Mali Ivo* (1869) LR 2 A&E 356.

where actions had been instituted in both the High Court of Admiralty and the Austrian consular court of Constantinople, Phillimore J said that if he were satisfied 'that there was a *lis alibi pendens* before a tribunal which could afford the plaintiff a complete remedy', then he would be under a 'duty either to suspend proceedings in this Court, or to put the parties to their election as to which court they would have recourse to'.[30] Where there is pending in the local forum a litigation in which complete relief may be had, and a party to the suit instituted proceedings abroad, the foreign suit will generally be regarded as vexatious, and an anti-suit injunction may be granted.[31] Thus a plaintiff who initiates proceedings against the same defendant in two separate jurisdictions in respect of the same subject-matter is required to elect which set of proceedings it wishes to pursue and, if it elects to pursue the foreign proceedings, to submit to dismissal of the local proceedings.[32] In articulating that proposition in *Australian Commercial Research and Development Ltd*,[33] Browne-Wilkinson V-C cited the following passage from *Dicey & Morris*:[34]

> The court may be asked to stay an action in England, or to enjoin an action abroad, in two distinct situations: first, where the same plaintiff sues the same defendant in England and abroad; and secondly, where the plaintiff in England is defendant abroad, or vice versa. In the first situation it is not likely that the court would allow, except in very unusual circumstances, the continuation of proceedings by the same plaintiff against the same defendant for a similar cause of action in two different jurisdictions. The court would put the plaintiff to his election, and stay the English proceedings or enjoin the foreign proceedings.

Of this, the Vice-Chancellor said:

> In my judgment that reflects the position, save that in my view it is not a question simply of a plaintiff applying for a stay of its own action: the action must go.

The second observation is that the proposition that proceedings are *prima facie* vexatious or oppressive does not mean that they are in fact vexatious and should be stayed. The effect of the dictum in *Henry v Henry* is at the highest only that whereas under the English authorities parallel proceedings in different jurisdictions (unlike parallel proceedings within the same jurisdiction) were not *prima facie* vexatious, so that a party alleging that parallel proceedings in different jurisdictions were vexatious bore the onus of proving that to be so (or, in the words of Jessel MR in *McHenry v Lewis*, to make out 'a special case for vexation'), *Henry v Henry* may have shifted the onus to a party who disputes the *prima facie* position

[30] (1869) LR 2 A&E 356, 359. See also *The Delta* (1876) 1 PD 393, 404; *McHenry v Lewis* (n 22) 400; *Peruvian Guano Co* (n 22); *The Christianborg* (1885) 10 PD 141, 153.

[31] *Carron Iron Co* (1855) 5 HL Cas 416, 437, 10 ER 961, 970; *Wedderburn v Wedderburn* (1840) 4 My & Cr 585, 41 ER 225; *McHenry v Lewis* (n 22).

[32] *Australian Commercial Research & Development Ltd v ANZ McCaughan Merchant Bank Ltd* [1989] 3 All ER 65, 69–73.

[33] [1989] 3 All ER 65, 70.

[34] Dicey & Morris, *Conflict of Laws*, 11th edn (London, Sweet & Maxwell, 1987) 395.

to establish that the parallel proceedings were not vexatious. As was emphasised in *CSR v Cigna*, it is well-established that the maintenance of parallel litigation in a foreign jurisdiction is not vexatious or oppressive if it offers remedies or advantages not available in the domestic forum.[35] And a court will not readily conclude that the foreign proceedings offer no such advantage.[36]

Accordingly, the law in Australia is now that it is not *prima facie* vexatious to bring parallel proceedings with respect to the same matter in different countries: foreign proceedings are vexatious or oppressive only if there is a complete correspondence between the proceedings, or if 'complete relief' is available in the local proceedings and there is nothing which can be gained by the foreign proceedings over and above what may be gained in the local proceedings.

## C. Case-management Stays

There is a well-developed Australian jurisprudence in respect of so-called 'case management' or temporary stays on the basis of *lis alibi pendens*. The applicable principles were expounded by Lockhart J in *Sterling Pharmaceuticals Pty Ltd v Boots & Co (Aust) Pty Ltd*,[37] to which reference was made by the High Court in *Henry v Henry*, as follows:[38]

> Foreign proceedings usually fall for consideration in a context in which they involve the same or related factual issues as those involved in the local proceedings, but not the same legal issue and, perhaps, not the same parties. Even in cases of that kind it may sometimes be appropriate to grant a temporary stay of the local proceedings to allow the factual issues to be determined in the other jurisdiction [See, eg, *Sterling Pharmaceuticals Pty Ltd v Boots Co (Aust) Pty Ltd* (1992) 34 FCR 287]. There are more compelling considerations in favour of a stay of the local proceedings if, as can happen, there are proceedings in another country which has jurisdiction to entertain those proceedings and the proceedings are between the same parties and with respect to the same issue or controversy.

Lockhart J rejected a submission that the principles relating to the permanent stay of proceedings in Australia where there were other proceedings pending in a foreign country between the same parties for the same cause of action were applicable in the context of a temporary stay. His Honour said:[39]

> There is obviously a substantial difference between a motion for a permanent stay or dismissal of a proceeding and a motion for a temporary stay or lengthy adjournment of

[35] *Peruvian Guano Co* (n 22) 234; *CSR v Cigna* (n 26); *Bank of Tokyo Ltd* [1987] AC 45, 60.

[36] See, eg, *Peruvian Guano Co* (n 22) 232 (Jessel MR), 232–23 (Lindley LJ), 234 (Bowen LJ). The above discussion is based on what I wrote in *In the matter of Treadtel International Pty Ltd* [2014] NSWSC 1406.

[37] *Sterling Pharmaceuticals Pty Ltd v Boots & Co (Aust) Pty Ltd* (1992) 34 FCR 287.

[38] (1996) 185 CLR 571, 590.

[39] (1992) 34 FCR 287, 294.

> a case … The court remains in full control of the proceeding before it when it is stayed only temporarily or where, as I propose, the proceeding will be stood out of the list for a substantial time until later this year.

On an application for a temporary stay, the question is not whether the proceedings are vexatious and oppressive. The power of the court to grant a temporary stay of this kind is an aspect of its general power to control its own proceedings, and is exercisable where proceedings are pending in another court and it is desirable that those proceedings should proceed to their conclusion first. Its exercise is informed by the general principle that it is undesirable that two courts should determine the same dispute, and practical considerations based on common-sense and fairness guide which action should proceed first.[40] A non-exhaustive list of relevant considerations was provided by Lockhart J in *Sterling Pharmaceuticals*, as follows:[41]

- which proceeding was commenced first;
- whether the termination of one proceeding is likely to have a material effect on the other;
- the public interest;
- the undesirability of two courts competing to see which of them determines common facts first;
- consideration of circumstances relating to witnesses;
- whether work done on pleadings, particulars, discovery, interrogatories and preparation might be wasted;
- the undesirability of substantial waste of time and effort if it becomes a common practice to bring actions in two courts involving substantially the same issues;
- how far advanced the proceedings are in each court;
- the law should strive against permitting multiplicity of proceedings in relation to similar issues; and
- generally balancing the advantages and disadvantages to each party.

Thus, on an application for a temporary stay of proceedings in Australia where there are also proceedings pending in a foreign country between the same parties for the same cause of action, the question is not whether the Australian proceedings are vexatious and oppressive, but whether it is preferable in the interests of justice that the foreign proceedings should proceed to their conclusion first.

[40] *L Grollo Darwin Management Pty Ltd v Victor Plaster Products Pty Ltd* (1978) 33 FLR 170, 177; *Hughes Motor Service Pty Ltd v Wang Computer Pty Ltd* (1978) 35 FLR 346; *Muller v Fencott* (1981) 53 FLR 184, 189; *Bond Corporation Pty Ltd v Thiess Contractors Pty Ltd* (1987) 14 FCR 193; *Sterling Pharmaceuticals* (1992) 34 FCR 287, 291; *Bella Products Pty Ltd v Creative Designs International Ltd* (2009) 258 ALR 538, [22]–[24].

[41] (1992) 34 FCR 287, 291.

# IV. Evidence and Procedure

## A. Foreign Evidence Gathering

Traditional procedures such as letters of request are cumbersome and of limited utility. Audio-visual link evidence is a valuable aid, but – at least where there is a 10-hour time difference – poses difficulties for other than relatively short witnesses. Taking evidence on commission can be more useful, especially if the hearing can be video-recorded, or if the trial judge can sit as the commissioner, but this often requires the co-operation of the foreign country, which is usually forthcoming in nations with which there are established relationships, though not necessarily elsewhere.

While in domestic proceedings subpoenas are one of the most common means for gathering evidence, their utility for obtaining evidence from abroad has been very limited. The court will not usually issue a subpoena to a person (whether foreigner or Australian citizen) who is outside the jurisdiction. One reason for this is that the court lacks the ability to enforce compliance by a person outside the jurisdiction. Another is that there are other means by which the evidence or information sought may be sought – including taking evidence on commission in accordance with UCPR r 24.3.[42]

The harmonised rules (like their predecessors) have the effect that a subpoena may, with leave, be served outside the jurisdiction:

> **[r 11.8AB] Service of other documents outside Australia**
>
> **11.8AB** Any document other than an originating process may be served outside Australia with the leave of the court, which may be given with any directions that the court thinks fit.

However, while this rule applies to a subpoena for the production of documents and authorises the court to grant leave for service of a subpoena outside Australia, it does not authorise a grant of leave for such service in another country where to do so would be inconsistent with established criteria of international law with regard to comity.[43] It does not address the problems associated with enforcing compliance.

Those problems are addressed by pt 5 of the Trans-Tasman Proceedings Act 2010 (Cth), which makes provision for the reciprocal service and enforcement of subpoenas issued by certain Australian and New Zealand courts and tribunals. Division 2 allows for subpoenas issued by certain Australian courts and tribunals to be served on a person in New Zealand with leave of an Australian court, and

[42] *Arhill Pty Ltd v General Terminal Co Pty Ltd* (1990) 23 NSWLR 545, 551, 553–55; *Kuwait Asia Bank EC v National Mutual Life Nominees Ltd* [1991] 1 AC 187; *Mackinnon v Donaldson, Lufkin and Jenrette Securities Corp* [1986] Ch 482; *Southwell v Maladina* [2002] FCA 802, (2002) 194 ALR 51 (examination under s 81 of the Bankruptcy Act 1966 – order refused).

[43] *Arhill Pty Ltd v General Terminal Co Pty Ltd* (n 42) 550, 553; *Re Tucker (a bankrupt); Ex parte Tucker* [1988] 1 All ER 603.

provides for how the service is to be effected. It also allows the person named in the subpoena to apply for the subpoena to be set aside. Division 3 allows for subpoenas issued by New Zealand courts and tribunals to be served on a person in Australia in accordance with the New Zealand Evidence Act, and requires the person served with the subpoena in Australia to comply with it (by deeming non-compliance to be contempt of the Federal Court).

Perhaps this type of scheme could inform the development of an international convention on the service and enforcement of subpoenas.

## B. Proof of Foreign Law

Proof of foreign law is an issue because, when a court of the forum is considering a question which is governed by the law of a foreign country, it will ordinarily presume that, unless proven otherwise, the foreign law is the same as that of the forum.[44] Thus at least where a party contends that the foreign law differs from the law of the forum, that party will have to prove the relevant content of the foreign law.

The conventional position in Australia is, of course, that foreign law being a question of fact, it must be proved by the evidence of witnesses expert in the foreign law.[45] At common law, the content of foreign law could only be proved by expert evidence,[46] and not by simply placing foreign legislation or law reports before the court.[47] Given that it is a question of fact, courts were precluded from conducting their own research.[48] This left the court reliant on the testimony of experts and their supporting material,[49] and constrained by the evidence adduced by the parties and the quality of opinions of experts.

However, it has always been permissible for a court to look at the sources of foreign law adduced to ascertain its contents in the event of 'obviously false' expert evidence, expert opinion incompatible with the text of a foreign statute, or conflicting expert views.[50] This means that, in reality, where there is doubt or

[44] This presumption is not of universal application. It is more apt in relation to general legal principles and countries with similar legal systems, and may be disregarded in relation to complex technical or specialist issues, especially where a very different legal system is involved: *Damberg v Damberg* [2001] NSWCA 87, (2001) 52 NSWLR 492; *Boele v Norsemeter Holdings AS* [2002] NSWCA 363.

[45] *Neilson v Overseas Projects Corporation of Victoria Ltd* [2005] HCA 54, (2005) 223 CLR 331, [115]; *Tahiri v Minister for Immigration and Citizenship* [2012] HCA 61, (2012) 293 ALR 526.

[46] *Baron de Bode's Case* (1845) 8 QB 208, 246–47, 115 ER 854; *Nelson v Bridport* (1845) 8 Beav 527, 536; *Bumper Development Corp v Commissioner of Police of the Metropolis* [1991] 1 WLR 1362; *Optus Networks Pty Ltd v Gilsan (International) Pty Ltd* [2006] NSWCA 171.

[47] *Nelson v Bridport* (1845) 8 Beav 527, 542, 50 ER 215.

[48] See *Di Sora v Phillipps* (1863) 10 HLC 624, 640, 11 ER 1168; *Bumper Development Corp v Commissioner of Police of the Metropolis* [1991] 1 WLR 1362, 1369.

[49] See *Lazard Brothers and Co v Midland Bank* [1933] AC 289, 298 (Wright LJ); *Buerger v New York Life Assurance* (1927) 96 LKJB 930, 940 (Aitken LJ); *Subbotovsky v Wuang* [1968] 3 NSWR 261.

[50] *Dalrymple v Dalrymple* (1811) 2 Hagg Con 54, 161 ER 665; *Trimbey v Vignier* (1834) 1 Bing NC 151, 131 ER 1075; *Concha v Murietta* (1889) 40 Ch D 543; *Shiblaq v Sadikoglu* [2004] 2 All ER (Comm) 596; *Arros Invest Ltd v Nishanov* [2004] EWHC 576.

conflict, judges prefer to look at the foreign sources and draw conclusions based on them – informed by the expert evidence where appropriate – than merely to prefer one expert to the other. That approach has been facilitated by the internet, which has made much foreign statutory and case law readily accessible, and by statutory provisions which authorise the reception of foreign statutes and case law. Now, evidence of a statute (including of delegated legislation) of a foreign country may be adduced by producing a book or pamphlet containing the statute, that purports to have been printed by the government or official printer of the country or by the authority of the government or administration of the country, or that appears to the court to be a reliable source of information, or that is or would be used in the courts of the country to inform those courts about the statute, or an examined copy of the statute.[51] Moreover, evidence of the unwritten or common law of a foreign country may be adduced by producing a book containing reports of judgments of courts of the country, if the book is or would be used in the courts of the country to inform them about the unwritten or common law of the country,[52] and evidence of the interpretation of a statute of a foreign country may be adduced by producing a book containing reports of judgments of courts of the country if the book is or would be used in the courts of the country to inform the courts about the interpretation of the statute.[53] Courts increasingly resort to such material, not least because they are now often readily available, and the sources (if in intelligible form) are often of greater assistance than the opinions of foreign lawyers. Further, resort to the sources usually affords the best means of resolving conflicts between experts.

An illustration of this approach is provided by *Ace Insurance Ltd v Moose Enterprise Pty Ltd*,[54] in which a question arose as to whether a Californian court would give effect to a contractual choice of law clause and apply Australian law, or would apply Californian law. Each of the parties called a Californian lawyer, who gave contradictory opinions on the question. Their competing opinions provided a framework within which the Court analysed the Californian statutes and judicial decisions, to conclude what a Californian court would do. Another example is *Michael Wilson & Partners Ltd v Robert Colin Nicholls*,[55] where there was a question as to whether the law of Kazakhstan prohibited the defendants from producing documents of which the plaintiffs sought discovery. The Court was faced with competing evidence of two experts, neither of whom was cross-examined, nor descended to much detail in setting out the statutory or other authoritative basis for the opinions that they tendered, and was left in many respects with competing *ipse dixits*. The issue was resolved in large part by examination of the relevant

[51] Evidence Act 1995 (NSW) s 174(1).

[52] Evidence Act 1995 (NSW) s 175(1). This was not permissible at common law: *Homeward Bound Gold Mining Co NL v McPherson* (1896) 17 LR (NSW) Eq 281.

[53] Evidence Act 1995 (NSW) s 175(2).

[54] [2009] NSWSC 724, esp at [54]–[72].

[55] [2008] NSWSC 1230, (2008) 74 NSWLR 218, esp at [12]–[25].

Kazakhstan Codes, to form an opinion as to which of the opinions was more soundly founded in them.

Hence it is no longer essential that a party call an expert to prove the content of foreign law. However, the extent to which it may suffice to rely on tendering the foreign statute and case law may be influenced by the degree of connection and familiarity between the relevant systems of law. Although the law of England and Wales – and for that matter New Zealand and Canada – is, for relevant purposes, foreign law, its content and methodology is so familiar to us that recourse to expert evidence is rarely necessary, and we would usually embark with little concern on deciding its content. Similarly, to a lesser extent, with other common law countries – but decreasingly so the more they are influenced by other systems of law (such as Malaysia, Singapore and Hong Kong). Still less so is it the case with civil law countries, including those of the European Union and Azerbaijan and Kazakhstan.

## V. Conclusion

The evolution of private international law has always involved the reconciliation of the competing interests of internationalism, consistency and predictability on the one hand, with those of national sovereignty and comity on the other. Alongside the growth in international travel, the emergence of the internet, and with it e-commerce, has fostered an expansion in international commerce in a more closely connected global commercial environment. The rules of private international law are evolving to accommodate this environment.

The new harmonised rules reflect a national approach to service *ex juris,* in the light of the national jurisdiction now enjoyed by each State Supreme Court. The dichotomy between the 'more appropriate forum' test in the Cross-vesting Acts and SEPA (and the Trans-Tasman Proceedings Act), and the 'inappropriate forum' test applicable in the wider context, reflects a balancing of the general rule that courts should not refuse to exercise their jurisdiction if regularly invoked, with the considerations of comity appropriate in a federal or analogous system.

With the much-enhanced accessibility of information and communications (particularly from abroad) that information technology and the internet deliver, approaches to proof which were formerly influenced if not dictated by an environment in which access to sources of foreign law was much more difficult than now, can be relaxed. Courts increasingly access foreign statutes and case law for the purposes of ascertaining the content of the foreign law, and it is no longer essential to call an expert to prove the content of foreign law – although this may vary according to the difficulty of the question, and the degree of connection and familiarity between the relevant systems of law.

Foreign evidence gathering remains a challenge. In this respect there may be scope for an international convention on service and enforcement of subpoenas, for which the Trans-Tasman Proceedings Act could provide a model.

# INDEX

www.ingramcontent.com/pod-product-compliance
Ingram Content Group UK Ltd.
Pitfield, Milton Keynes, MK11 3LW, UK
UKHW021705230926
475560UK00015B/309

9 781509 922871